THE JUSTICE OF HUMANS

Justice for conflict-related sexual violence remains a critical problem for global society today. This groundbreaking book addresses pressing questions for 'international justice': what do existing approaches to international justice offer to victims of war and societies in conflict? And what possibilities do they provide for feminist social transformation? *The Justice of Humans* develops a new feminist approach to 'international justice'. Adopting a socio-legal perspective, it studies two major contemporary examples of legal and feminist approaches to justice, the International Criminal Tribunal for the former Yugoslavia and the Women's Court (former Yugoslavia), focusing on their treatment of sexual violence as a gender-based crime. Drawing on feminist social theory, legal analysis, and empirical research, the book offers an innovative feminist framework for understanding 'international justice' and offers new theoretical and practical strategies for building feminist justice.

KIRSTEN CAMPBELL is a professor in sociology at Goldsmiths College, University of London. She has been a visiting scholar at Sciences Po, Lund University, and University of California, Berkeley. Her research on gender, international criminal law, and transitional justice has been published in numerous journals and books. A leading expert on conflict-related sexual violence, Campbell has worked with non-governmental organisations, the United Nations, and the United Kingdom and European Union on policy and practice in this area.

THE JUSTICE OF HUMANS

Subject, Society and Sexual Violence in International Criminal Justice

KIRSTEN CAMPBELL
University of London

Shaftesbury Road, Cambridge CB2 8EA, United Kingdom

One Liberty Plaza, 20th Floor, New York, NY 10006, USA

477 Williamstown Road, Port Melbourne, VIC 3207, Australia

314–321, 3rd Floor, Plot 3, Splendor Forum, Jasola District Centre, New Delhi – 110025, India

103 Penang Road, #05–06/07, Visioncrest Commercial, Singapore 238467

Cambridge University Press is part of Cambridge University Press & Assessment, a department of the University of Cambridge.

We share the University's mission to contribute to society through the pursuit of education, learning and research at the highest international levels of excellence.

www.cambridge.org
Information on this title: www.cambridge.org/9781108497084

DOI: 10.1017/9781108683968

© Kirsten Campbell 2023

This publication is in copyright. Subject to statutory exception and to the provisions of relevant collective licensing agreements, no reproduction of any part may take place without the written permission of Cambridge University Press & Assessment.

First published 2023

A catalogue record for this publication is available from the British Library.

A Cataloging-in-Publication data record for this book is available from the Library of Congress

ISBN 978-1-108-49708-4 Hardback

Cambridge University Press & Assessment has no responsibility for the persistence or accuracy of URLs for external or third-party internet websites referred to in this publication and does not guarantee that any content on such websites is, or will remain, accurate or appropriate.

This book is dedicated to the survivors of sexual violence in the conflict in the former Yugoslavia. Their struggle for justice has been a constant source of hope and inspiration.

CONTENTS

List of Figures   *page* ix
Acknowledgements   x
List of Abbreviations   xii

1   The Justice of Humans? Outline of a Feminist Social Theory of International Criminal Justice   1

   PART I   Subjectivity and Sociality in Contemporary International Criminal Law

2   The International Crime   29

3   The International Legal Subject   65

4   The International Criminal Trial   96

5   International Criminal Justice   130

6   The Global Legal Form of International Criminal Law   164

   PART II   The Women's Court and Transformative Gender Justice

7   The Women's Court and the Feminist Approach to Justice   201

8   Building a Feminist Approach to Justice for International Criminal Law: Political Challenges and Conceptual Foundations   242

9   Building a Feminist Justice Approach to International Criminal Law in Practice: Strategies for Change   288

Bibliography 339
   References 339
   Cases 360
   Legislation 362
Index 364

FIGURES

5.1 The model of justice of the ICTY *page* 145
5.2 The phantasy of justice   158

ACKNOWLEDGEMENTS

Like all books, this book is the outcome of collective work. It began as my doctoral dissertation on the International Criminal Tribunal for the former Yugoslavia (ICTY) in the Law School at the London School of Economics and Politics. I would like to thank my supervisors, Stephen Humphreys, Nicola Lacey, and Gerry Simpson. I was very fortunate to have such supportive and intellectually challenging supervisors. Nicola Lacey, who oversaw the doctorate in its entirety, deserves special thanks for the care and acuity of her supervision. I would also like to thank my doctoral examiners, Costas Douzinas and Emilios Christodoulidis, whose engagement with the thesis was integral to the development of the arguments in the book.

The book has also benefitted immeasurably from the intellectual and personal generosity of many friends and colleagues at Goldsmiths, University of London, with special thanks to Dejan Đokić and Sari Wastell. My ongoing collaboration with the International Research Group, Sexual Violence in Armed Conflict has been particularly important. I would also like to acknowledge my discussions with two wonderful friends who have recently died, Chandra Lekha Sriram and Gabi Zipfel.

I am very grateful to the readers of my draft manuscript, including Suki Ali, Brian Alleyne, Alice Bloch, Svenja Bromberg, Beverley Brown, Kiran Grewal, Jasmina Husanović, Kate Nash, and Amal Treacher. I would especially like to thank my fantastic colleagues on the 'Gender of Justice' project, Jasenka Ferizović, Gorana Mlinarević, Elma Demir, Marina Veličković, Admir Yugo, and Maria O'Reilly, for reading the manuscript and for our many discussions of the question of international justice. I would like to thank Marina Veličković and Anousheh Haghdadi for their assistance with the preparation of the manuscript. I was also fortunate to have Marianne Nield and Finola O'Sullivan at Cambridge University Press as excellent and patient editors. Of course, all errors are my own.

I would like to thank the many feminist and human rights activists, and legal and policy practitioners, for the time that they gave, and the insights they shared, during my fieldwork and our collaborations.

Special thanks are due to my partner, David Bausor, who enabled me to write this book. His great insights and practical help were invaluable, and I would not have been able to complete the manuscript without his support. My profound love and gratitude as always. I am also very grateful for the love and support of my family during the long process of writing this book.

Finally, I would like to thank the organisers of the Women's Court for inviting me to participate in this important feminist initiative, and for the opportunity to work with my fellow Judicial Council members. I would also like to acknowledge the collective efforts of feminists and peace activists in the former Yugoslavia, whose struggle for justice made the Women's Court and the ICTY possible.

Chapters 3–5 are substantially revised versions of earlier publications:

'The Trauma of Justice: Sexual Violence, Crimes against Humanity, and the International Criminal Tribunal for the former Yugoslavia', (2004) 13(3) *Social & Legal Studies* 329–350.

'Victims and Perpetrators of International Crimes: The Problem of the Legal Person', (2012) 2(2) *Journal of International Humanitarian Legal Studies* 325–351.

'Testimonial Modes', in Jane Kilby and Antony Rowland (eds.), *The Future of Testimony* (London and New York: Routledge, 2014).

The research has received funding from the European Research Council under the European Union's Seventh Framework Programme (FP/2007–2013) / ERC Grant Agreement No. 313626, The Gender of Justice Project.

ABBREVIATIONS

Adel L Rev	*Adelaide Law Review*
AFLJ	*Australian Feminist Law Journal*
AJIL	*American Journal of International Law*
Alb L Rev	*Albany Law Review*
Am U J Gender Soc Pol'y & L	*American University Journal of Gender, Social Policy and the Law*
Cardozo L R	*Cardozo Law Review*
Case W Res J Int'l L	*Case Western Reserve Journal of International Law*
CEDAW Committee	Committee on the Elimination of Discrimination Against Women
CEDAW	Convention on the Elimination of All Forms of Discrimination Against Women 1979
Chinese JIL	*Chinese Journal of International Law*
CLP	*Current Legal Problems*
Colum Hum Rts L Rev	*Columbia Human Rights Review*
Colum J Transnat'l L	*Columbia Journal of Transnational Law*
Commission of Experts	UN Commission of Experts Established Pursuant to Security Council Resolution 780 UNSC, 1992
Council Control Law No. 10	Control Council Law No. 10, Punishment of Persons Guilty of War Crimes, Crimes against Peace and against Humanity, 1946
Crim L F	*Criminal Law Forum*
ECCC	Extraordinary Chambers in the Courts of Cambodia
EJIL	*European Journal of International Law*
EU	European Union
FLS	*Feminist Legal Studies*
Geneva Conventions	Geneva Convention I for the Amelioration of the Condition of the Wounded and Sick in Armed Forces in the Field 1949; Geneva Convention II for the Amelioration of the Conditions of Wounded, Sick and Shipwrecked Members of Armed Forces at Sea 1949; Geneva Convention III Relative to the Treatment of

	Prisoners of War 1949; Geneva Convention IV Relative to the Protection of Civilian Persons in Time of War 1949
Genocide Convention	Convention on the Prevention and Punishment of the Crime of Genocide 1949
GoJIL	*Goettingen Journal of International Law*
Harv Law & Pol'y Rev	*Harvard Law and Policy Review*
Hastings LJ	*Hastings Law Journal*
Hastings Women's LJ	*Hastings Women's Law Journal*
ICC	International Criminal Court
ICJ	International Court of Justice
ICRC	International Committee of the Red Cross
ICTR	International Criminal Tribunal for Rwanda
ICTY	International Criminal Tribunal for the former Yugoslavia
ICTY RPE	ICTY Rules of Procedure and Evidence
ICTY Statute	Statute of the ICTY 1993
IHRLR	*International Human Rights Law Review*
IHLS	*Journal of International Humanitarian Legal Studies*
IMT Charter	Charter of the International Military Tribunal, Annexed to the London Agreement for the Prosecution and Punishment of Major War Criminals of the European Axis 1945
Int CLR	*International Criminal Law Review*
Int'l J Soc L	*International Journal of the Sociology of Law*
Intl J Transitional Justice	*International Journal of Transitional Justice*
JICJ	*Journal of International Criminal Justice*
JL & Soc'y	*Journal of Law and Society*
Law and Crit	*Law and Critique*
LJIL	*Leiden Journal of International Law*
Mich J Int'l L	*Michigan Journal of International Law*
MICT	United Nations Mechanism for International Criminal Tribunals
MLR	*Modern Law Review*
NGO	Non-governmental organisation
Nuremberg Judgment	*France and ors* v. *Göring (Hermann) and ors*, Judgment and Sentence 1946
NWULR	*Northwestern University Law Review*
OSCE	Organization for Security and Co-operation in Europe
PTSD	Post-traumatic Stress Disorder
QLJ	*Queen's Law Journal*

Rev Soc L	*Review of Socialist Law*
Rome Statute	Rome Statute of the International Criminal Court 1998
S&LS	*Social and Legal Studies*
SCSL	Special Court for Sierra Leone
Seton Hall L Rev	*Seton Hall Law Review*
SFRY	[Former] Socialist Federal Republic of Yugoslavia
Tex Int'l LJ	*Texas International Law Journal*
Theo Inq L	*Theoretical Inquiries in Law*
UC Irvine L Rev	*UC Irvine Law Review*
UN	United Nations
UNCHR	United Nations Commission on Human Rights
UNSC	United Nations Security Council
Women's Court	Women's Court: Feminist Approach to Justice, 7–10 May 2015, Sarajevo, Bosnia and Herzegovina
Women's Court Preliminary Decision	'Women's Court: Feminist Justice: Preliminary Decisions and Recommendations', Judicial Council, 9 May 2015, Women's Court
Women's Court Proceedings	Published Proceedings of the Women's Court, in S. Zajović and M. Urošević (eds.), *Women's Court: About the Event in Sarajevo and about Continue the Process* (Belgrade: Women in Black, 2017), pp. 79–272
Women's Court Rules	Rules of the Women's Court, Women's Court, Sarajevo, 7 May 2015
Yale LJ	*Yale Law Journal*
Yale LJF	*Yale Law Journal Forum*

Note on Case Citation Abbreviations

The citation of cases is given in the form:

Accused Name, Case No., judicial body abbreviation (such as ICTY or ICTR); -T (Trial Chamber) or -A (Appeal Chamber).

Where sentencing judgements are cited and the case number includes the abbreviation (-S), then the citation is given with the suffix -T or -A.

1

The Justice of Humans?
Outline of a Feminist Social Theory of International Justice

In 2014, women peace activists from Syria and Bosnia met to discuss peace-building, gender-based violence, and justice. Their aim was 'the exchange of ideas and experiences between women who have gone through and are going through war'.[1] They met in Sarajevo in Bosnia and Herzegovina as part of the 'Women Organising for Change in Bosnia and Syria' initiative of the Women's International League of Peace and Freedom. The question of justice was central to these discussions. What did it mean to the women of Bosnia following the war in the former Yugoslavia? And what it might mean for the women of Syria whose war has yet to end?

The peace activists wanted justice for international crimes committed during the Yugoslavian and Syrian conflicts. These included wars of aggression (crimes against peace), attacks on civilians (crimes against humanity), the destruction of ethnic, racial, religious, or national groups (genocide), and war crimes (violations of humanitarian law). They also wanted justice for the sexual and gender-based crimes committed during these conflicts. Justice for these gendered crimes was seen an essential part of the wider cultural, economic, and social justice needed to build a sustainable peace in their war-affected societies. However, the peace activists also asked what forms that justice could, or should, take. How, then, to describe current forms of justice for international crimes? What ideas and practices of justice do they offer? What persons and societies do they envisage? And what prospects for social transformation do these forms of justice offer to victims of war and societies in conflict?

To answer these questions, this book develops a feminist social theory of justice for international crimes. It builds this social theory upon a case

---

[1] Barbro Svedberg, Laila Alodaat, et al., *Women Organising for Change in Bosnia and Syria* (Geneva: Women's International League for Peace and Freedom, 2014).

study of the International Criminal Tribunal for the former Yugoslavia (ICTY) and the Women's Court (Women's Court). The book undertakes the first study of the completed proceedings of the ICTY and of the Women's Court, focusing on their treatment of the international crime of sexual violence. The ICTY and the Women's Court are two leading and contrasting examples of justice for international crimes committed in the Yugoslavian conflicts of the 1990s. They exemplify existing forms of 'legal' and 'feminist' justice, which are characterised by distinctive practices, values, and aims. The book analyses the different models of justice of the ICTY and the Women's Court and examines what they offer to those seeking justice for international crimes.

The establishment in 1993 of the ICTY by the United Nations Security Council (UNSC) marked the emergence of international criminal law as the dominant form of international justice.[2] The ICTY was the first truly international criminal court established and mandated by the United Nations (UN).[3] It was established on an *ad hoc* basis for the limited purpose of prosecuting serious violations of customary international humanitarian law committed during the dissolution of the Socialist Federal Republic of Yugoslavia (SFRY) into its constituent states. The 'Yugoslavian' wars were fought from 1991 to 2001, and so began over a year before the ICTY was established. They can be described as a series of interlocking conflicts, beginning with secessionist conflict in Croatia in May 1991, the secession of Slovenia in June 1991, and the outbreak of hostilities in Bosnia and Herzegovina (BiH) in April 1992, in Kosovo in February 1998, and in Macedonia in January 2001. Bosnia is generally regarded as the most conflict-affected country. Under the ICTY's Statute, the violations criminalised under international law included war crimes (grave breaches of the Geneva Conventions and violations of the laws or customs of war), genocide, and crimes against humanity. These are considered the 'core crimes' prohibited by international law, together with the crime of aggression, which was not included in the ICTY's subject jurisdiction. With the establishment of the ICTY, sexual violence as an object of international criminalisation also emerged. Sexual violence was charged in operative indictments or judicially considered in

---

[2] U.N. Doc. S/RES/827 (1993).
[3] The International Military Tribunals at Nuremberg and Tokyo were established by the major Allied powers, and not the UN as an international organisation.

43 of 61 completed cases under all core crime categories.[4] By the time of the ICTY's closure on 31 December 2017, its jurisprudence had established the legal basis of sexual violence as an international crime. The ICTY had shown that sexual violence was an integral part of the illegal conduct of these conflicts and that it could be successfully prosecuted.

The Women's Court was the first women's court held in Europe to address international crimes committed in a specific conflict and the first transitional justice mechanism established in the region of the former Yugoslavia. Crucial to its establishment was the perception that the ICTY had not provided justice to women victims of war or created a just peace for all – including women.[5] In contrast, the Women's Court aimed to make women, and their experiences of war, central to building an alternative form of feminist justice. Ultimately, the aim of the Women's Court was to contribute to building a just peace in the region of the former Yugoslavia. The formal organisation of the Women's Court by non-governmental organisations across the former Yugoslavia began in 2010. The formal proceedings of the Court were held in May 2015 in Sarajevo and consisted of two days of testimonies, with oral and written preliminary decisions issued by the Judicial Council. The 'thematic crimes' considered by the Women's Court were: (1) 'War against the civilian population (militaristic/ethnic/gender-based violence)'; (2) 'Woman's body – a battlefield (sexual violence in war zones)'; (3) 'Militaristic violence and women's resistance'; (4) 'Persecution of those who are different, in war and in peace (ethnic violence)'; (5) 'An undeclared war (social and economic violence, women's resistance)'.[6] Thirty-eight victim witnesses and twelve expert witnesses from the

---

[4] *Banović* ICTY-02-65/1, *Blaškić* ICTY-95-14, *Blagojević & Jokić* ICTY-02-60, *Bralo* ICTY-95-17, *Brđanin* ICTY-99-36, *Češić* ICTY-95-10/1, *Delić* ICTY-04-83, *Đorđević* ICTY-05-87/1, *Furundžija* ICTY-95-17/1, *Gotovina* ICTY-06-90, *Hadžihasanović & Kubura* ICTY-01-47, *Halilović* ICTY-01-48, *Haradinaj et al.* ICTY-04-84, *Karadžić* ICTY-95-5/18, *Kordić & Čerkez* ICTY-95-14/2, *Krajišnik* ICTY-00-39, *Krnojelac* ICTY-97-25, *Krstić* ICTY-98-33, *Kunarac et al.* ICTY-96-23 & 23/1, *Kupreškić et al.* ICTY-95-16, *Kvočka et al.* ICTY-98-30/1, *Limaj et al.* ICTY-03-66, *Lukić & Lukić* ICTY-98-32/1, *Martić* ICTY-95-11, *Mladić* ICTY-09-92, *Mrkšić et al.* ICTY-95-13/1, *Mucić et al.* ICTY-96-21, *Naletilić & Martinović* ICTY-98-34, *Nikolić, D.* ICTY-94-2, *Plavšić* ICTY-00-39 & 40/1, *Prlić et al.* ICTY-04-74, *Rajić* ICTY-95-12, *Šainović et al.* ICTY-05-87, *Šešelj* ICTY-03-67, *Sikirica et al.* ICTY-95-8, *Simić, B.* ICTY-95-9, *Simić, M.* ICTY-95-9/2, *Stakić* ICTY-97-24, *Stanišić & Simatović* ICTY-03-69, *Stanišić & Župljanin* ICTY-08-91, *Tadić* ICTY-94-1, *Todorović* ICTY-95-9/1, *Zelenović* ICTY-96-23/2.
[5] See: https://www.zenskisud.org/.
[6] Women's Court, Program May 7–10, 2015, Bosnian Cultural Centre, Sarajevo, on file with the author.

former Yugoslavia testified before some five hundred people attending the Court.

The book focuses upon the rapidly developing international crime of sexual violence as the most condensed expression of developments in international justice, rather than treating it as an exceptional crime of war in conflict or law. During the Yugoslavian conflicts, it is estimated that 12,000–50,000 women were victims of rape.[7] Sexual violence against men was also a recognised feature of the conflict, although occurring at a significantly lower prevalence.[8] While precise figures are unknown, it is generally accepted that sexual violence was the most pervasive and visible gender-based violence against women in the Yugoslavian conflict. It should also be considered a gender-based crime insofar as the overwhelming majority of perpetrators were men.[9] Sexual violence is also the area in which international criminal law claimed the most significant advances in offering justice for gender-based crimes. Sexual violence offences are a crucial but contentious category of international crimes, and evidence of sexual violence was considered by both the ICTY and the Women's Court. The different approaches of the ICTY and the Women's Court to sexual violence crimes reveal the different models of the self and of society that underlie their models of justice. They also exemplify the differences between legal and feminist models of justice as social repair or as transformation, revealing what is at stake in these different models of justice for societies in or emerging from conflict.

This book develops a feminist social theory of the existing legal and feminist forms of international justice and a socio-legal methodology for empirically investigating them. It argues that we need to understand these forms of justice for international crimes as the 'justice of humans'. 'Justice' is a human activity, which expresses the relations and values of human society. Accordingly, we need to understand 'international

---

[7] The estimate of 20,000 victims is generally accepted. It was first provided by the European Community Investigative Mission into the Treatment of Muslim Women in the Former Yugoslavia, Warburton Report, (1993) E/CN.4/1993/92, para. 14, and is affirmed by Mahmoud Cherif Bassiouni in *Sexual Violence: An Invisible Weapon of War in the Former Yugoslavia* (International Human Rights Law Institute, De Paul University College of Law, 1996), p. 10

[8] This is not challenged by the figure of 4800 male victims commonly cited from Lara Stemple's work. The figure should have referred to women, and not men, and was a typographical error in Stemple's source, an earlier UN Population Fund study, 'Sexual and Gender-Based Violence in Post-Conflicts Regions', authored by Zeljka Mudrovcic. Personal communication, Zeljka Mudrovcic, 2015.

[9] For further discussion, see Chapter 4.

justice' as a form of human social life, rather than thinking it through abstract moral concepts or legal principles removed from social relations. Accordingly, the book focuses on understanding legal and feminist forms of international justice as *social phenomena*. It shows how 'international justice' is a human activity that expresses social relations and values and is an integral part of the constitution of modern global social relations. Accordingly, I use the analytic categories of social theory, the subject and the social, to capture the social dimensions of international justice.

The book examines two interrelated 'social' dimensions of international justice. The first 'social' dimension is its constitution of categories of persons and of society. These categories describe the specific construction of subjects (the characteristics attributed to personhood) and society (the organisation of social relations in collective social life) in legal and feminist forms of justice. The second 'social' dimension is that international justice is an integral part of transnational social processes and forces. International justice exists as a part of a global social system, which is 'a world-scale complex of relational networks or social structures'.[10] I take this important insight from world-system analysis, which uses the 'world' rather than nation-states as the appropriate unit of analysis for capturing interconnected social relations on a global scale.[11] However, I use the idea of 'global social system' to capture the totality of transnational social relations rather than 'world-system', because of the economic reductionism, neglect of 'cultural' politics, and missing gender analysis in this approach.[12] This idea of the *global* social system also emphasises that international justice is an integral part of wider shifts in transnational social relations. These transitional social relations are currently in transition in the social forces of globalisation, that is, the 'intensification of global interconnectedness'.[13]

The book is divided into two parts. This introductory chapter outlines the feminist social theory and socio-legal methodology. Part I, 'Subjectivity and Sociality in Contemporary International Criminal Law', examines the ideas of persons and society that inform the foundational legal concepts of the international crime, the international legal

---

[10] Immanuel Wallerstein, 'Structural Transformations of the World Economy', (2016) 39(1) Review 171–194, 171.
[11] Immanuel Wallerstein, *World-Systems Analysis* (Durham and London: Duke University Press, 2006), p. 16.
[12] Discussed in Chapter 6.
[13] Mary Kaldor, *New and Old Wars* (Cambridge: Polity, 2002), p. 3.

subject, the international trial, and international justice in international criminal law. Using the ICTY as a case study, this book shows how this legal form expresses the hierarchies of harm, person, and state in the contemporary international legal order and emerges in the broader context of globalisation. I argue that international criminal law's transformative potential cannot be found in its models of international justice as social repair. Part II, 'The Women's Court and Transformative Feminist Justice', examines alternative models of international justice. Using the Women's Court as a case study, the book sets out an alternative feminist approach to justice. I examine the concepts of harms, justice proceedings, subjects of justice and transformative justice in this alternative model and show how it also emerges in the broader context of globalisation. The book describes how legal and feminist forms of justice build social relations in different ways and argues that the transformative potential of the feminist approach to justice can be found in its model of building emancipatory social relations. I argue that this alternative model of justice offers the basis for developing a feminist approach to international criminal justice. The book concludes with strategies for building a feminist approach to international criminal law in practice. The strategies include developing an alternative legal framework, together with framework principles for conflict-related sexual violence prosecutions and for a draft international convention on sexual violence as an international crime.

1.1 Building a Feminist Social Theory of International Justice

How do different forms of international justice construct what is to be a person and the relations between members of a society? How do their justice institutions and practices shape the social life of individuals and collectives? And what do they imagine a just society to be? To answer these questions, it is necessary to build a feminist social theory that can describe the existing forms of legal and feminist justice and explain how these forms express or transform global social relations and forces. Such a theory needs to be able to describe these distinctive forms of justice, explain why they take these forms in particular historical and social conditions, and analyse whether they reproduce existing social orders or produce new social relations.

The first step in building this social theoretical framework is to develop a concept of international justice as a form of law. The fundamental premise of the dominant contemporary form of international justice is that it is *legal*. International criminal law is a body of formal legal rules, which prohibits certain categories of violence (but also permits others) at the international level. Its prohibitions are criminal, that is, they nominate certain acts as defined criminal offences with the juridical consequence of punishment, following determination of culpability at trial.[14]

There are clearly many forms of international justice, actual and possible, legal and non-legal. To explain why the dominant form of international justice takes the form of international criminal law requires answering what the Marxist international legal theorist China Miéville describes as the 'basic ontological question': '*why law?*'. It involves explaining 'how law can be a political process ... and yet how there is something in the structure of the modern social relations which maintains the integrity of the peculiarly legal form of conceptualising and articulating claims'.[15] The challenge, then, is how to address international criminal law 'in its specificity as a historical practice which operates through particular forms and mechanisms which are real, effective and differentiated, and which are related but irreducible to broader social relations'.[16]

To begin to answer this question, I draw on the legal form theory of the early Marxist legal theorist, Evgeny Pashukanis (as does Miéville). In his general theory of law, Pashukanis argues that it is not that law regulates social relations but that under certain conditions 'the *regulation* of social relationships assumes a *legal* character', that is, they assume a legal form.[17] For Pashukanis, law is a specific set of social relations. His general theory of law develops a method of analysing the legal form, that is, a set of principles for undertaking a materialist analysis of law as specific form of social relationships. First, the analysis of the legal form identifies 'the basic juridic abstractions' of legal norms, subjects, and relations.[18] Abstract legal categories, such as the legal person and contract, express the fundamental elements of the legal form, such as the autonomous individual able to enter into contractual relations of equal exchange. Second, the analysis examines the relationship between the

---

[14] *Kunarac et al.*, ICTY-96-23&23/1-T, Judgement, 22 February 2001, para. 470.
[15] China Miéville, *Between Equal Rights* (London: Pluto, 2005), p. 43. Emphasis in quoted texts throughout the book is as in the original, unless otherwise specifically stated as added.
[16] Alan Norrie, *Law and the Beautiful Soul* (London: Glasshouse, 2005), p. 30.
[17] Evgeny Pashukanis, *Law and Marxism* (London: Ink Links, 1978), p. 79.
[18] Pashukanis, *Selected Writings on Marxism and Law* (London: Academic Press, 1980), pp. 43–44.

system of legal concepts and the concrete historical social relations from which they emerge. Abstract legal categories, 'which are the closest definitions of the legal form, in general reflect specific and very complex social relations'.[19] In this context, 'abstract' does not imply that legal categories exist as an ideal but rather that they express concrete social relations in an abstract form. Pashukanis argues that 'the categories of law are objective forms of thought (objective for the historically given society) corresponding to the objective social relations'.[20] His aim was to understand law as a 'historical form of regulation' that emerged from the social relations of capitalism.[21] Accordingly, his analysis examines legal concepts as products of social orders and asks how their legal form expresses concrete social relations.

Legal form theory enables us to answer a fundamental question for a social theory of international justice: why does international justice take a legal form? Crucially, it provides the basis for an answer that avoids both idealist and economistic theories of law. This approach avoids an idealist conceptualisation of international criminal law, which presumes that it consists of moral values and legal norms, disconnected from their concrete existence in social institutions and practices and the social world that produces them. Instead, it asks under what specific historical conditions do global social relationships take the form of international criminal law. It also avoids an economist conceptualisation of international criminal law, which presumes that law simply reflects capitalist class interests. This is because, for Pashukanis, the legal form is an integral element of commodity exchange in capitalist social relations. The legal relation has actual concrete existence – in legal rules, institutions, and practices – which is an integral part of the production of capitalist social relations. The legal form is neither antecedent nor posterior to capitalist social relations. Rather, 'the juridical moment [...] is a constitutive part of it'.[22] For Pashukanis, the legal form is an integral part of the *production* of capitalist social relations.

The legal form theory, then, provides an analytic approach for describing the organising concepts of persons and social relations in legal and feminist forms of justice and for understanding why they take particular

---

[19] Ibid.
[20] Pashukanis, *Law and Marxism*, p. 74.
[21] Robert Fine, *Democracy and the Rule of Law* (London: Pluto, 1984), p. 155.
[22] Alan Norrie, 'Pashukanis and the "Commodity Form Theory"', (1982) 10 Int'l J Soc L 429–437, 423.

forms under specific historical conditions. In building on this analytic approach, I do not follow Miéville's influential development of Pashukanis' theory of modern international law as *'the legal form of the struggle of capitalist states among themselves for domination over the rest of the world'*.[23] While recognising the importance of Miéville's account of imperialism and international law, it does not develop a theory of international criminal law, other than briefly describing it as a form of hegemonic policing that enforces supposed international legal norms.[24] Pashukanis himself did not provide such a theory, as international criminal law as such did not exist at that time. However, he did examine the distinct expression of the legal form in both international law and criminal law, analysing them as different areas of law with distinctive juridical categories. Accordingly, I follow Pashukanis in engaging with the distinctive juridical categories of international criminal law, which arise from its concern with individuals, rather than states, and international crime, rather than the 'contractual' relations between states. Finally, unlike Miéville (and Pashukanis), my approach does not assume that the imperialist state monopoly capitalism that international law is thought to express remains unchanged in our new global orders.

Equally importantly, a *feminist* social theory of international justice must engage with what Rada Iveković describes as *'the social relations of sexes'*.[25] Iveković analyses violence against women in socialist and capitalist modernity, thereby situating it in the long-standing debate within socialist Yugoslavia concerning the priority of working-class or women's emancipation and highlighting the problem of Marxist theory that does not engage with gender relations. Because of the book's focus on sexual violence, addressing sexual social relations is crucial. Conflict-related sexual violence both makes visible gendered international violence and shows the 'hidden gender' of the supposedly gender-neutral international criminal law.[26] However, to address sexual violence requires more than simply adding women to theories of legal subjects or adding gender to accounts of legal institutions or practices. Rather, it involves developing

---

[23] Pashukanis, *Selected Writings*, p. 169.
[24] Miéville, *Between Equal Rights*, p. 309. For further discussion, see Kirsten Campbell, 'From Legitimacy to Legality', in Chris Thornhill and Samantha Ashenden (eds.), *Legality and Legitimacy* (Baden-Baden: Nomos, 2010).
[25] Rada Iveković, 'Violence and Healing', in Staša Zajović, (ed.) *Women's Court: About the Process* (Belgrade: Women in Black and Centre for Women's Studies, 2015), p. 120.
[26] Jenny Morgan and Regina Graycar, *The Hidden Gender of the Law* (Sydney: Federation Press, 2002).

an account of how not only capitalist social relations but also sexual social relations are part of systems of exploitation and commodification in the global order. As such, engaging with the social relations between the sexes must be an integral part of a feminist account of the legal form.

Accordingly, a feminist social theory of international justice needs to account for interlocking systems of exploitation in global social relations and to understand how these structures shape the global social system. Marxist theorists such as Wallerstein and Pashukanis emphasise capitalist economic relations (characterised by private ownership, exploitation and commodification of labour and resources, the exchange of commodities, and the accumulation of capital) and the political and economic domination and exploitation of states by other states (imperialism for Pashukanis or core-periphery state hierarchies for Wallerstein). However, feminist social reproduction theorists, such as Maria Mies, argue that such relations also involve patriarchal gender relations (the exploitation of women as a class by men).[27] As Mariana Valverde describes, Mies' important work 'considered the scale now called transnational or global to be crucial to [her] analyses of gendered subjectivity and patriarchal power' and is notable for her feminist reworking of Wallerstein's world-system analysis.[28] Mies proposes a triple system of intersecting structures of exploitation for understanding the globalising world system and offers a crucial reframing of global social relations for a feminist social theory of the legal form.

Building a feminist social theory of international justice requires explaining not only the legal form of justice of international criminal law but also the feminist form of justice of the Women's Court. Iveković argues that the question of the social relations of the sexes is integral to the political challenge *and* possibility of developing the feminist approach to justice of the Women's Court.[29] Accordingly, my social theory needs to move beyond the limits of the legal form theory to include three characteristics of the Women's Court. The first characteristic is that the Women's Court is a form of non-state justice. It is not a form of state law, nor does it derive from sovereign power. Moreover, it

---

[27] Marie Mies, *Patriarchy and Accumulation on a World Scale* (London: Zed Books, 1999), p. 36. This is known as the 'dual systems' debate, which concerns how to theorise patriarchy and capitalism as integrated rather than separate systems.

[28] Mariana Valverde, 'The Rescaling of Feminist Analyses of Law and State Power', (2014) 4 UC Irvine L Rev 325–352, 348.

[29] Iveković, 'Violence and Healing', p. 135.

offers a model of transnational justice, which is both regional, in that it attempts to build justice across the Yugoslav region rather than a given nation-state, and global, in that it derives from the international feminist movement and aims to contribute to building global feminist justice beyond the former Yugoslavia.

The second characteristic is that the feminist approach to justice is fundamentally concerned with the question of how to build feminist emancipatory social relations. However, the legal form theory cannot answer this question. Pashukanis argued if capitalist social relations produce the legal form, then the revolutionary transformation of those social relations should entail the withering away of law (and state) as such.[30] However, the feminist approach to justice does not assume that the withering away of the state and the legal form is an objective necessity of political action but instead takes emancipation as an objective to be pursued in struggle in our concrete historical conditions. How best to achieve this is the strategic question that the Women's Court poses.

Finally, it is necessary to explain the *feminist* form of the Women's Court. We need to ask why international justice can take a feminist form, just as we ask why international justice can take a legal form. Accordingly, it is necessary to explain under what specific historical conditions global social relationships can take the form of feminist justice. While legal form theory can explain how international criminal law expresses global social relations of domination, such as capitalist (and imperialist) social relations, it cannot offer an account of how other forms of justice, such as the Women's Court, might express social relations of feminist emancipation. It is crucial to keep hold of the Marxist insight that capitalist social relations will always produce contradictory social forces, both exploitative and emancipatory. As such, it is necessary to consider the dynamic and uneven nature of transnational social relations and to recognise contradictory forces that they produce. As Mies reminds us, these contradictions include not only class antagonisms but also antagonisms between nations and imperial power and man-woman relations (that is, the relations between the sexes).[31] Such antagonisms give rise to what Wallerstein and others describe as 'antisystemic movements', such as anti-colonial and women's movements,

---

[30] Pashukanis, *Law and Marxism*, p. 188.
[31] Mies, *Patriarchy and Accumulation on a World Scale*, p. 198.

which seek to build more democratic and egalitarian social relations.[32] As such, my social theoretical analysis looks to the production of forms of international justice in the contradictory social forces within global social relations and whether and how those forms express those contradictions.

Importantly, my analysis also recognises that accounts of international state monopoly capitalism do not capture ongoing shifts in global social relations from the 1970s onwards. Currently, the transnational social relations of the world system, and the inter-state system that developed with it, are in transition in globalisation. As Nancy Fraser describes, 'the ordering of social relations is undergoing a major shift in scale, equivalent to *denationalization* and *transnationalization*. No longer an exclusively national matter, if it ever was, social ordering now occurs simultaneously at several different levels.'[33] While Wallerstein emphasised that the world social system has always been global, nevertheless we have seen uneven but dynamic and qualitative shifts in this system since the 1970s. I use the term 'globalisation' to describe the intensification of 'flows of goods, capital, people, information, ideas, images, and risks across national borders, combined with the emergence of transnational and international networks'.[34] The nature of these changes and their impacts upon global social life are highly contentious. However, it is necessary to engage with globalisation to understand how forms of international justice are part of wider global social processes and forces and to identify where these transitions open new possibilities for political struggles for justice.

To build the legal form theory as a feminist social theory of international justice, then, first requires describing the legal and feminist forms of the ICTY and the Women's Court as distinctive systems of social relations. This involves examining the distinctive rules, institutions, and practices that give these forms concrete existence, analysing the categories of persons and social relations that characterise these forms, and identifying how these categories construct the subject and the social. It also requires explaining how legal and feminist forms of justice express or transform global social relations and forces. This involves situating the emergence of these forms of justice in wider global social processes and identifying whether they reproduce existing global

---

[32] See Giovanni Arrighi, Terence Hopkins et al., *Antisystemic Movements* (New York: Verso, 1989).
[33] Nancy Fraser, *Scales of Justice* (New York: Columbia University Press, 2009), p. 123.
[34] Kate Nash, *Contemporary Political Sociology* (Oxford: Wiley-Blackwell: 2010), p. 43.

social relations or can construct new *just* forms of social relations. I set out these analytic building blocks in the following section.

1.2 Building a Feminist Social Theory of International Criminal Law

This feminist social theory first describes the legal form of international criminal law in Chapters 2 to 6. Its first analytic element identifies the fundamental categories of the legal form of international criminal law. I build on Pashukanis' legal form theory of criminal law, which analyses how the basic juridical categories of criminal law express the legal form, and the legal relations and legal subjects that are its constituent elements. Given what distinguishes international criminal law from other areas of international law is that it regulates international crimes, my analysis begins with the creation of 'crime' as a legal category, as Pashukanis' analysis of criminal law does.[35] It then analyses the other fundamental legal concepts of international criminal law. Chapters 2 to 5 analyse each of these legal categories of the international crime, the international legal subject, the international criminal trial, and international justice. My analysis of these legal categories examines their construction of legal relations and legal subjects, as well as the legal form that they express.

The second element of my feminist social theory makes visible the gender relations shaping the ostensibly gender-neutral legal form. To do this, I examine how the legal form of international criminal law produces and reproduces hierarchical gender norms by analysing its treatment of sexual violence as an international crime in legal norms, practices, and institutions. My analysis builds on over two decades of feminist legal scholarship that has exposed how gender shapes international criminal law and draws on the work of feminist legal scholars and practitioners such as Fionnuala Ní Aoláin, Christine Chinkin, Rhonda Copelon, Michelle Jarvis, Catherine MacKinnon, Julie Mertus, Valerie Oosterveld, and Patricia Viseur Sellers.

The third element examines how the legal form constructs 'hegemonic ontologies', that is, hierarchical gendered and racialised categories of 'persons' and 'social orders', in international criminal law. My approach does not understand 'persons' and 'society' as given or fixed categories in international criminal law. Rather, it sees these categories as products of

---

[35] Pashukanis, *Law and Marxism*, p. 167.

social histories of power, which are hegemonic in the sense that they are shaped by the ideas and values of dominant groups in global social relations.[36] My analysis draws on the work of feminist critical theorists of international criminal law, notably Doris Buss, Karen Engle, Kiran Grewal, Chiseche Mibenge, and Dubravka Žarkov. These critical feminist theorists can be said to share a socio-legal approach to showing the problematic construction of 'gender', 'ethnicity', and 'nation' in this body of law, focusing not only on the repressive power of law to exercise power over subjects but also its productive power to create social identities and truths. As Doris Buss describes, 'criminal law can thus be read discursively for the ideas and legal subjects called into service in its operation, and it can be examined for its material effects, for example, on particular communities'.[37]

The fourth analytic element analyses how the legal form operates as a socio-cultural system, materialised in legal institutions and practices. It examines 'how social meanings are interpreted and communicated through the legal process'.[38] The narratives of international justice are performative, as Žarkov describes, in the sense that international criminal trials produce meaning, knowledge, norms, and categories about subjects and societies.[39] As such, international criminal law operates as a signifying system that has a constitutive role in the making of social relations. It operates as a socio-cultural system on two levels, which are representational and ideological. In Pashukanis, the form of law is expressed in the abstractions of legal categories and concepts. This level of operation of the form of law is symbolic, in the sense that it consists of a system of related legal concepts, which *express* or *represent* objective social relations in abstracted form. The legal form also operates on an ideological level in its hegemonic representation of persons and societies, in the Marxist sense of 'distorted, mystified mental images', which obscure or mystify the actual relations of domination from which they derive.[40] This level of operation is imaginary, in the sense that it consists of images and affect that give the legal form specific content.

---

[36] Dubravka Žarkov, 'Ontologies of International Humanitarian and Criminal Law', in Dubravka Žarkov and Marlies Glasius (eds.), *Narratives of Justice In and Out of the Courtroom* (New York: Springer, 2014), p. 18.
[37] Doris Buss, 'Performing Legal Order' (2011) 11(3) Int CLR 409–423, 411.
[38] Ibid.
[39] Žarkov, 'Ontologies of International Humanitarian and Criminal Law', p. 18.
[40] Pashukanis, *Law and Marxism*, p. 73.

I examine the legal form of international criminal law as a sociocultural system, which operates as a symbolic and imaginary structure that represents subjects and the relations between them. Building on my earlier feminist work on modern feminist and fraternal social discourses,[41] in this book I argue that international criminal justice is a modern discourse of legal subjects and legal relations. In Chapter 5, I show how the organising concepts of international criminal law, that is, the international crime, international legal subject, international trial, and international justice, form the basis of the discursive structure of the legal form of international criminal law. This discourse has symbolic and imaginary dimensions, and it operates as a signifying practice that produces subjects and social relations. However, the socio-symbolic structure of international criminal law is not 'closed' or 'fixed'. This is because international criminal law continually confronts the violation of its socio-symbolic order, namely, the traumatic collective violence of international crime. I argue that the modern legal form of international criminal law figures justice as an imaginary repair of the violation of its socio-symbolic order.

The fifth analytic element addresses the relationship between the legal form of international criminal law and the global social relations that produce it, and of which it is an integral part. In Chapter 6, I argue that international criminal law operates as a global legal form that orders categories of persons, crimes, and societies at the international level, drawing on Jasmina Husanović's feminist account of the 'state of exception' within modern political orders. Building on her important development of Giorgio Agamben's work, I show how the legal form structures 'international society' through the inclusion of certain categories of persons as social beings and excludes others as 'bare life' (the figure of exception to the international social order). This constitution of 'international society' universalises a modern fraternal and ethno-nationalist social order in global legal form and creates hegemonic legal relations between non-state subjects at international level. The global legal form emerges in the social processes of globalisation and expresses global relations of exchange. I show how international criminal law makes that exchange possible by creating global legal relations between universal legal subjects. In the 'universalisation' of the legal form, the global legal form operates as a juridical element of global social relations. It is a

---

[41] See Kirsten Campbell, *Jacques Lacan and Feminist Epistemology* (London and New York: Routledge, 2004), chapters 4 and 5.

constitutive part of globalisation because it functions as a new *legal* form of global association, making 'global society' in the form of endless chains of legal relations (following Pashukanis). The global legal form emerges from the dominating and emancipatory social relations that globalisation produces. These relations are expressed in the conceptual contradictions in the categories of the legal form.

The conceptual contradictions are apparent within legal conceptualisations of sexual violence in the legal form. On the one hand, global relations of exchange include sexual social relations as part of capitalist and patriarchal systems of exploitation and commodification in the global order, and the exchange of sexualised bodies between fraternal ethno-nationalist subjects at war. On the other hand, global relations also include feminist movements for women's emancipation, the increasing participation of women in 'global' social relations as economic and political actors, and the ascription of equal value to women and their human rights as formally equal subjects in the international legal order. The contradictory 'cultural value' of sexual bodies come to be articulated as legal values in the conceptualisation of sexual violence as an international crime.[42]

1.3 Building a Feminist Social Theory of the Women's Court

My feminist social theory next describes the feminist form of justice of the Women's Court and uses it as the basis for developing a feminist approach to international criminal law in Chapters 7 to 9. The fundamental premise of the Women's Court as a contemporary form of international justice is that it is *feminist*. I argue that the distinctive value informing this approach to justice is the idea of transformative feminist justice. To analyse this concept of feminist justice, I draw on feminist work on gender justice that links post-conflict justice for gender harms to social transformation and argues that forms of justice should not sustain the power relations that produce the violence of war but should instead seek to change them.[43] This work conceives 'gender justice' as involving 'societal transformation' that does not sustain social relations and structures of 'dependence and subordination' that exist prior to, and produce,

---

[42] See Patricia Viseur Sellers, 'The Legal and Cultural Value of Sexual Violence', in Kirsten Campbell, Regina Mühlhäuser et al. (eds.), *In Plain Sight* (New Delhi: Zubaan, 2019).

[43] See Nahla Valji, 'Gender Justice and Reconciliation', in Kai Ambos, Judith Large et al. (eds.), *Building a Future on Peace and Justice* (Berlin: Springer, 2009).

conflict.[44] Feminist scholars describe 'transformative gender justice' as 'the potential for justice mechanisms, in the broadest sense, to have transformative outcomes upon gender relations'.[45] I show how the idea of emancipatory social transformation is central to the concept of feminist justice developed in the Women's Court.

To build my account of feminist justice, I examine how the Women's Court develops a different form of justice to that of the global legal form of the ICTY. Chapter 7 analyses the Women's Court's critique of existing models of international justice, its development of a new paradigm of justice, and its building of an alternative justice mechanism. Like my analysis of the global legal form, my analysis of the Women's Court identifies the fundamental categories of the new feminist paradigm of justice, which are: (1) transformative feminist justice; (2) gender-based harms; (3) feminist justice proceedings; (4) feminist judgement; and (5) subjects of justice. Each of these categories builds new ideas and practices of justice.

Building on my earlier account of feminist discourse as the symbolisation of new forms of subjects and the relations between them, I argue that the Women's Court develops a new form of justice that can build social bonds based in emancipatory feminist relations between subjects. The feminist approach to justice necessarily confronts the limits of the hegemonic socio-symbolic order of international criminal law because of its orientation to concrete injustice. Accordingly, it builds a new feminist form of justice by developing new categories of harms, subjects, justice proceedings, and judgement, which construct persons and social relations through ideas of an emancipatory society. These categories create a new form of feminist justice, which expresses alternative forms of global exchange between women as subjects of justice. This form of justice is based in feminist social bonds, and an alternative model of collectivised justice, rather than the individualised ethno-fraternal contract of the global legal form. Drawing on the work of Husanović, I argue that the Women's Court reveals the *productive* capacities of collective action that can emerge in states of exception to law. I show how the feminist approach to justice is part of an alternative globalisation. It both articulates the structural injustices produced by the intensification of neoliberal globalisation in the former Yugoslavia, and also expresses the alternative

---

[44] See Susan Rimmer, 'Sexing the Subject of Transitional Justice', (2010) 32(1) AFLJ 123–147, 136.
[45] Jelke Boesten and Polly Wilding, 'Transformative Gender Justice', 51 (2015) Women's Studies International Forum 75–80, 75.

possibilities of social solidarity and emancipation that can emerge in the same global social processes.

In Chapter 8, I explore whether the feminist form of justice can provide the basis for developing a more emancipatory model of international justice. The feminist approach to justice reveals the double bind of the global legal form: that legal justice is necessary but the existing legal order does not provide it. This problem reflects wider feminist debates about whether it is possible to reform international criminal law so that can be used for transformative social change or whether to refuse to engage with international criminal law. It also mirrors the long-standing debate within Marxist theory concerning whether law can provide the basis for emancipatory social transformation. I argue that in the current concrete historical conjuncture the appropriate framing for a feminist approach to international criminal law is neither reform nor refusal. Rather, it is 'transitional' in the socialist sense of the struggle to create the conditions for the emergence of new emancipatory forms of social organisation at state, regional, and global levels, and it involves developing strategies that can build alternative feminist forms of legal social bonds.

I show how the Women's Court offers a feminist form of justice that provides the basis for developing new legal concepts, which can serve as the basis for developing a feminist approach to international criminal justice. In Chapter 8, I use the model of feminist justice to develop new feminist concepts of gender-based harms, legal proceedings, subjects, and justice, drawing on feminist theorists such as Nancy Fraser, Adrian Howe, and Iris Marion Young. These concepts, I argue, provide four key elements of an alternative conceptual framework for a feminist approach to international criminal law. First, the new concept of gender-based harms offers a consequentialist model of conflict-related sexual violence as the imposition of sexual subjectivity through collective violence. It conceptualises sexual violence as a form of social injury that harms groups of persons, where legal liability arises from participation in collective violence that sustains systemic domination. Second, it offers new feminist practices to build substantive justice proceedings and justice mechanisms. Third, it shifts the focus of models of accountability from the individual legal person to systems of coercive collective violence. Fourth, the feminist approach insists that justice is not reducible to the implementation of existing international criminal law but must be linked to wider social transformation.

So how can we build a feminist approach to international justice in practice, which does not simply enforce international criminal law in its existing form? Chapter 9 examines how the new legal categories outlined in Chapter 8 can be used to build a new feminist model of international criminal justice in practice. It argues that to build this new model involves developing new justice norms, practices, and institutions that can create new legal social bonds. I set out two key strategies for building the feminist approach to international criminal law in practice. These strategies include: (1) developing substantive, procedural, and institutional norms for an alternative feminist legal framework and (2) applying the legal framework to sexual violence as an international crime, which includes developing framework principles for sexual violence prosecutions, and for an international convention on sexual violence as an international crime.

1.4 The Case Study of International Justice

My feminist social theory of international justice is built upon an empirical mixed-method socio-legal case study of the ICTY and the Women's Court and their treatment of sexual violence as a gender-based international crime.

1.4.1 The Case Study

1.4.1.1 Why Use a Case Study?

The case study methodology provides a means of turning the large and complex field of 'international justice' into an investigable object of research. It treats the object of investigation as a 'bounded system' comprised of related social practices.[46] Crucially, case-study research enables the use of a 'mixed-method' approach, which uses a range of methods appropriate for the different kinds of practices under investigation. As such, it enables the socio-legal analysis of the complex and dynamic practices of this area and to move beyond the limitations of engaging with international justice in purely doctrinal or normative terms.

The rich empirical description of 'the cases' of international justice are used for the theory-building that is the purpose of the research.[47] The feminist social theory of international justice is created through an ongoing comparison of current literature, case data, and the emergent descriptive and explanatory theory. The aim is not to generalise the

---

[46] Robert Stake, 'Case Studies,' in Norman Denzin and Yvonna Lincoln (eds.), *Strategies of Qualitative Inquiry* (Thousand Oaks: Sage, 2003), p. 136.
[47] David de Vaus, *Research Design in Social Research* (London: Sage, 2001), p. 223.

empirical conclusions from the case study to other instances of international justice 'but to engender patterns and linkages of theoretical importance'.[48] These theoretical insights can then be used to inform how we describe, explain, and transform international justice.

1.4.1.2 Why Study the ICTY and the Women's Court?

The ICTY and the Women's Court exemplify two different types of justice mechanisms addressing international crimes. Both were established to provide justice for the crimes committed in the war in the former Yugoslavia in the 1990, but each uses different forms of justice, respectively, formal criminal justice and transformative feminist justice.

The ICTY is chosen as a 'case' of international justice for three key reasons. First, the establishment of the ICTY in 1993 marked a new concern of the international community about sexual violence in conflict. Second, the ICTY is widely regarded as leading substantive and procedural developments in the prosecution of sexual violence as an international crime. Third, the ICTY's formal justice typifies the now established model of international criminal law, which uses criminal courts to prosecute and punish international crimes. The Women's Court is chosen as a contrasting case of 'transformative feminist justice' for international crimes for three key reasons. First, it provides an important counterpoint to the ICTY, since it sought to develop an alternative feminist approach to justice for crimes committed in the Yugoslavian conflict, including sexual violence. Second, and more broadly, the Women's Court sought to develop a model and practice of transformative justice that aimed to change post-conflict societies. Third, the Women's Court is the only successfully established regional transitional justice mechanism and is the first to be held in Europe. It is now considered a leading example of alternative accountability mechanisms.[49]

1.4.1.3 Why Study Sexual Violence as an International Crime?

The case study examines international justice through the lens of how it has dealt with sexual violence as an international crime. It focuses on sexual violence characterised as a so-called 'core crime' of international criminal

---

[48] Alan Bryman, *Research Methods and Organisation Studies* (London: Routledge, 1989), p. 144.
[49] Radhika Coomaraswamy, *Preventing Conflict, Transforming Justice, Securing the Peace* (New York: UN Women, 2015), p. 112.

law, namely, as a war crime, crime against humanity, and genocide. While the accepted terminology for this criminalised conduct is now 'conflict-related sexual violence', customary international law does not require a nexus to armed conflict for prosecutions of sexual violence as genocide or crimes against humanity. However, because the term is 'generally understood short-hand for sexual violence prosecuted under the provision of international criminal law', I use this terminology throughout the book.[50]

The book follows the standard international definition of sexual violence as a form of gender-based violence where it is 'directed against a woman because she is a woman or that affects women disproportionately'.[51] I use the concept of gender-based violence to capture the gendered patterns of perpetration and victimisation in the Yugoslavian conflicts for my analysis of international justice. However, my analysis also shows the under-theorisation of 'gender' in this definition, and Chapters 7 to 9 develop a fuller conceptualisation of sexual violence as a gender-based crime.

The case study focuses upon the rapidly developing international crime of sexual violence, which reveals the models of persons and social relations in forms of international justice. By examining the development of this crucial and contentious category of the crimes of war, we can see the models of selfhood, society, and social transformation underlying contemporary international justice. Conversely, understanding these ideas of subjects and society helps unravel the current contentious and unresolved debates concerning sexual violence as an international crime and points to new directions for understanding, and providing justice for, conflict-related sexual violence.

1.4.2 The Feminist Legal Form Methodology

I develop the 'feminist legal form methodology' by building on legal form theory. This methodology first identifies the basic categories of the forms of justice in the ICTY and the Women's Court, focusing on their

---

[50] Michelle Jarvis, 'Overview: The Challenge of Accountability for Conflict-Related Sexual Violence Crimes', in Serge Brammertz and Michelle Jarvis (eds.), *Prosecuting Conflict-Related Sexual Violence at the ICTY* (Oxford: Oxford University Press, 2016), p. 17.

[51] Committee on the Elimination of Discrimination against Women (CEDAW Committee), General Recommendation No. 19: Violence against Women, UN Doc A/47/38 (1992). I follow General Recommendation No. 35 in describing sexual violence as a form of gender-based violence against women: CEDAW Committee, General Recommendation No. 35: Gender-based violence against women, updating general recommendation No. 19, CEDAW/C/GC/35 (2017).

treatment of sexual violence, and then examines how these categories construct concepts of the person, society, and social values.

1.4.2.1 The ICTY

I describe the legal form of the ICTY by examining the models of persons and society in the categories of the international crime, the international legal subject, the international criminal trial, and international justice. This description draws on my analysis of statutes and rules, judgements, written transcripts, and live proceedings, as well as my fieldwork in the ICTY from 2005 to 2017.

I undertake a 'legal' analysis of ICTY positive law and doctrine (the legal rules and principles), jurisprudence (the body of case law), and practice (the law in action) across all completed cases. My approach builds on Patricia Viseur Sellers' 'gender jurisprudence' methodology: '(f)irst, case observations should be aggregated and their [jurisprudential] holdings probed jointly and comparatively. Second, rather than being studied only for their immediate judicial pronouncements, gender holdings should be viewed through the doctrinal prism of specific international crimes.'[52] Following this approach, I reviewed the jurisprudence as a whole, rather than focusing only on definitions of sexual violence as an international crime or on descriptions of gender-based harms. Taking such an approach avoids focusing only on early 'direct perpetrator' or lower level cases, which first establish the elements of offences (as is typical of studies of sexual violence as an international crime). The problem of doing so is that the doctrinal development of these offences is contested and uneven in subsequent cases. Moreover, the jurisprudential development of sexual violence offences as international crimes under all core categories is found in later cases, and particularly in 'higher level' leadership cases. Considering only lower level or higher level cases gives a misleading picture not only of the positive law but also of the body of jurisprudence, and hence of international criminal law as a whole.

Having reviewed the complete body of jurisprudence as a whole, I identified exemplary and contentious areas of doctrinal development to focus my legal analysis. Accordingly, my doctrinal analysis examines

---

[52] Patricia Viseur Sellers, '(Re)Considering Gender Jurisprudence', in Fionnuala Ní Aoláin, Naomi Cahn et al. (eds), *The Oxford Handbook of Gender and Armed Conflict* (Oxford: Oxford University Press, 2018), p. 220.

the development of substantive offences (Chapter 2), international criminal responsibility and liability (Chapter 3), evidence and procedure (Chapter 4), and jurisdiction, sentencing, and fair trial principles (Chapter 5). This analysis focuses on the jurisprudence of sexual violence cases, defined as completed cases in which sexual violence is expressly charged or is the factual basis underlying charges in the operative indictment, or where sexual violence is subject to judicial consideration.[53] The jurisprudence 'crystallises' the legal practices of the institution, in the sense that it is the outcome of a set of practices concerning investigation, charging, prosecution, and adjudication.

To fully capture legal practices in the courtroom and wider legal institution, I use two complementary methods. First, I undertake in-depth case analysis, which examines specific legal decisions and trial practices in particular cases. The case selection is informed by the gender jurisprudence methodology, in that the cases selected develop doctrine or practice or set out legal principles. Second, I draw on my extensive field research in the ICTY from 2005 to 2017. This field research consisted of 'rolling ethnographic field visits' in the ICTY.[54] It included two months of courtroom observation, 27 formal qualitative semi-structured interviews as well as ethnographic interviews with staff from all sections of the ICTY in the Hague, Zagreb, and Sarajevo offices (Defence, Chambers, Office of the Prosecution, and Registry, including Victims and Witnesses Section and Outreach), and participation in ICTY workshops and conferences. My interviews and participation in ICTY expert closed events were generally undertaken on a 'not for attribution' or confidential basis.[55] Accordingly, I primarily use publicly available sources on the ICTY as a legal institution, but my use of these sources is informed by my field research.

I use this field research to complement my legal analysis. The interviews and court room observation provided a 'snapshot' of the practices of the legal institution at particular moments over its 'life course' from establishment to closure. As Hagan and Levi show, external political

---

[53] These include cases completed to trial before the UN International Residual Mechanism for the International Criminal Tribunals (MICT) but excludes cases where the trial was not completed to final verdict due to withdrawal of indictments or death of the accused.
[54] John Hagan, Ron Levi et al., 'Swaying the Hand of Justice', (2006) 31(3) Law and Social Inquiry, 585–616, 596. These visits were undertaken in 2006, 2007, 2010, 2014, and 2016.
[55] Due to the non-attribution basis and sensitive nature of my field research, where I draw on interview material, I refer to pseudonymous interview number, interviewee role, and interview year.

forces shape the working of the legal institution but are refracted through internal organisational culture.[56] My focus is not on the internal organisational culture of the ICTY, nor on the legal actors within it. However, I share their methodological concern with how 'the coercive apparatus of criminalization is actualized through prosecutorial and court practices'.[57] My analysis aims to capture the norms, practices, and values of the institution that construct the legal form of international criminal law. As such, I draw on my fieldwork across the 'life course' of the ICTY to understand how the jurisprudence is the outcome of legal practices and institutional cultures that are an integral part of making the legal form of international criminal law.

1.4.2.2 The Women's Court

In the case of the Women's Court, I analyse the models and practices of crime, subject, trial, and justice in the feminist approach to justice in Chapters 8 through 10. In each category, I examine how the rules, judgements, written testimonies, and live proceedings construct concepts and practices of international justice, and the ideas of persons, society, and values that inform them. My analysis draws on rolling field ethnographic research visits of three months annually during the period 2015–2017 to Bosnia and Herzegovina, as well as field visits to the former Yugoslavia during 2005–2015.[58] This field research included 35 qualitative interviews, as well as ethnographic interviews, with transitional justice, victims' associations, and feminist non-governmental organisations, staff from all sections of the War Crimes Chamber, State Court of Bosnia and Herzegovina (Chambers, Defence, Prosecutor's Office, and Registry, including Victim Support), and staff in the UN (BiH) Organisation for Security and Co-operation in Europe (OSCE BiH) working on sexual violence and war crimes programmes in Bosnia, as well as participation in events, workshops, and training on conflict-related sexual violence in Bosnia and Herzegovina during this period.

I study the Women's Court as an existing alternative justice mechanism. Like the ICTY, it is a concrete institution and can be studied as such. My analysis draws on my experience of sitting as a Judicial Council

---

[56] Hagan and Levi, 'Swaying the Hand of Justice', 585–616.
[57] John Hagan and Ron Levi, 'Crimes of War and the Force of Law', (2005) 83(4) Social Forces 1499–1534, 1499.
[58] These visits took place in 2005–2007, 2011–2012, and 2014.

member of the Women's Court. The role of the Judicial Council was to 'give a public verdict on the political and civic responsibility of the perpetrators, appealing to judicial institutions with its requests and proposals, and monitoring the response of said institutions'.[59] As part of this role, I co-authored with the seven other Council members the preliminary public verdict 'Women's Court: Feminist Justice: Preliminary Decisions and Recommendations'.[60] My analysis of the Court as an alternative model of justice draws on my observation of the live proceedings of the Court, which I attended as a Judicial Council member. Because of my role on the Court, I primarily use publicly available sources on the operation of the Court as an alternative justice institution. These include the information materials and rules issued by the Organising Committee of the Court; the Preliminary Decisions and Recommendations of the Women's Court; 'The Women's Court: A Feminist Approach to Justice' video recording of the proceedings by the organisers;[61] and the testimonies and materials from the Court edited by the organisers, *Women's Court: About the Process*[62] and *Women's Court: About the Event*.[63] Where I use these materials, I do so on the basis of my experience of the Court and my contemporaneous notes. I also draw on my fieldwork in Bosnia and Herzegovina during this period. My analysis of the Women's Court reflects my personal views and does not necessarily reflect the views of the Judicial Council or the participants in the Women's Court.

My participation in the Court could be characterised as feminist participatory action research, in the sense that I am not 'directing' research but participating in a political process.[64] Moreover, feminist

---

[59] Rules of the Women's Court, Organising Committee, Sarajevo, May 2015, on file with the author.

[60] 'Women's Court: Feminist Justice: Preliminary Decisions and Recommendations', Judicial Council, 9 May 2015, Women's Court, Sarajevo, https://www.zenskisud.org/en/pdf/2015/Womens_Court_Preliminary_Decision_Judicial_Council_2015.pdf

[61] 'Women's Court: A Feminist Approach to Justice: Sarajevo, 7th–10th May 2015', directed by Filip Marković and produced by Women in Black, video, https://www.zenskisud.org/en/filmovi.html

[62] Staša Zajović (ed.) *Women's Court: About the Process*; https://zenskisud.org/en/stampane-publikacije.html.

[63] Staša Zajović and Miloš Urošević, (eds.), *Women's Court: About the Event in Sarajevo and About Continue the Process* (Belgrade: Women in Black, 2017).

[64] Colleen Reid, Allison Tom et al., 'Finding the "Action" in Feminist Participatory Action Research', (2006) 4(3) Action Research, 315–331, 316. My thanks to Maria O'Reilly for her formulation of feminist participatory action research.

participatory research is committed to transformative social change and to identifying strategies to enable that change.[65] My analysis of the Women's Court also draws together action and reflection to 'facilitate building knowledge to change the conditions of women's lives, both individually and collectively'.[66] However, I did not participate in the Women's Court to to undertake 'research', and nor were the participants in the Women's Court passive 'objects 'of research. The Women's Court participants were active political subjects who led the justice process, and my participation in this process should be seen as part of my commitment to feminist practice. During the last 15 years, I have participated in a number of national and international formal and informal justice initiatives. These experiences were invaluable sources of insight into the workings of international justice. However, they were much more than this. They reflect my ongoing commitment to feminist justice in all its forms, which grounds the research in the book. Ultimately, this book aims to contribute to that collective struggle.

---

[65] Vesna Nikolić-Ristanović and Ivana Stevanović, 'The Method and the Sample', in Vesna Nikolić-Ristanović (ed.), *Women, Violence and War* (Budapest: Central European University Press, 2000), pp. 35–39.

[66] Reid and Tom, 'Finding the "Action"', 316.

PART I

Subjectivity and Sociality in Contemporary
International Criminal Law

2

The International Crime

No definition of rape can be found in international law.[1]

The Prosecutor v. *Furundžija*, 1998

After three years of trial proceedings, the ICTY confronted the problem that there was no definition of the offence of rape under international law and set out the elements of the offence in *The Prosecutor* v. *Furundžija*.[2] Despite the extensive doctrinal development of sexual violence offences since *Furundžija*, the definition of sexual violence as an international crime remains unsettled. These definitional issues are no mere technical matter. Rather, they reveal the ideas of harms to persons and society that inform the criminalisation of conflict-related sexual violence. How, then, do we understand the criminalisation of sexual violence as an international crime? And what does it reveal about the ideas of persons and of social relations in the legal category of the international crime?

2.1 The Legal Category of International Crimes

In formal terms, the legal category of international crimes 'names and defines the particular offences'.[3] It consists of the substantive offences that define conduct as criminal under international law and give rise to criminal liability. Other legal concepts of responsibility (the attribution of culpability for crimes), proof (determination of responsibility by the trial process), and punishment (appropriate sanction for crimes) rest upon this category of crime. As such, this legal category distinguishes

---

[1] *Furundžija*, ICTY-95-17/1-T, Judgement, 10 December 1998 (*Furundžija* Trial Judgement), para. 175.
[2] Sexual violence conduct had been considered in previous proceedings but had not been charged as such.
[3] George Fletcher, *The Grammar of Criminal Law* (Oxford: Oxford University Press, 2007), p. 18.

international criminal law from other branches of international law and is typically understood as the building block of modern international criminal law.[4]

As the building block of international criminal law, the category of international crimes is the foundation of the legal form of international criminal law. Criminalisation under international law constructs relations between persons as *legal*, because it constructs these relations as legal duties and rights. As such, all legal relationships in international criminal law are contingent on this fundamental category. The category of international crime creates not only the legal relations between individuals as legal subjects but also the legal relations of individuals to 'society' at the international level. This is because 'modern criminal law starts out ... from the violation of the norm', where the norm is an abstract and formal expression of the injured public interest of 'society', as Pashukanis describes.[5] The legal norms of international criminal law can be seen as an abstract and formal expression of the injured public interest of 'society as a whole' at the international level.

These legal norms determine what is characterised as 'social injury', that is, legally defined socially injurious conduct.[6] The concept of social injury captures how international criminal law articulates the protected interests of 'society' at the international level. As Maureen Cain and Adrian Howe argue, 'harm language is used in the law to identify what has taken place and to describe the fact that it is contrary to "the common welfare of society"'.[7] The concept of social harm expresses the idea of the 'irreversibly negative impact on the protected interests of another, typically another person', but also the interests of the state or society.[8] My analysis focuses on how the international criminalisation of sexual violence as a gender-based harm expresses 'injured public interests'. By focusing on the concept of 'harm' in sexual violence offences, it becomes possible to see the connected ideas of who is harmed (ideas of persons) and how it is harmful (ideas of society) in the legal category of international crimes. My analysis of the legal category of international

---

[4] Roger O'Keefe, *International Criminal Law* (Oxford: Oxford University Press, 2015), p. 47.
[5] Evgeny Pashukanis, *Law and Marxism* (London: Ink Links, 1978), p. 177.
[6] Adrian Howe, 'The Problem of Privatised Injuries', in Martha Fineman (ed.), *At the Boundaries of Law* (London: Routledge, 1990), p. 149.
[7] Maureen Cain and Adrian Howe, 'Introduction', in Maureen Cain and Adrian Howe (eds.), *Women, Crime and Social Harm* (Oxford: Hart, 2008), p. 3.
[8] Fletcher, *The Grammar of Criminal Law*, pp. 39–40.

crimes follows Howe in privileging gender-specific injuries to 'locate and politicise the "hidden injuries" not only of class society, but also gender-ordered societies'.[9] By identifying how the international criminalisation of conflict-related sexual violence expresses 'injured public interests' at the international level, it becomes possible to identify the construction of the subject and society in international criminal law. Examining how international criminal law emerges 'as a distinct body of rules with a defined area of application', and sexual violence as an 'object to be regulated',[10] brings into view 'the relative and fundamentally historically limited nature of the fundamental juridical concepts' of international criminal law and the ideas of persons and society that they express.[11]

2.2 The International Criminalisation of Sexual Violence

[I]t is extremely important [...] that rape has been listed for the first time in the history of humanitarian law as a crime.

Judge Odio Benito, *The Prosecutor* v. *Tadić*, 1994[12]

When the ICTY was established in 1993, neither a specified and distinct criminal offence of sexual violence nor a definition of sexual violence existed under international law. Rape was prohibited under various customary international humanitarian law provisions but was not expressly legally characterised as an international crime.[13] So how did sexual violence come to be constructed as *legally defined* socially injurious conduct under public international law, such that it would be prosecuted as such before the ICTY, and considered in the majority of its cases?

---

[9] Adrian Howe, '"Social Injury" Revisited', (1987) 15 Int'l J Soc L 423–428, 433.
[10] Lindsay Farmer, *Making the Modern Criminal Law* (Oxford: Oxford University Press, 2016), p. 5.
[11] Pashukanis, *Law and Marxism*, p. 34.
[12] Application for a Formal Request for Deferral to the Competence of the International Tribunal in the Matter of Dusko Tadić, ICTY-94-1-D-T, Trial Transcript, 8 November 1994, p. 33.
[13] Council Control Law No. 10 of the Allied forces occupying Germany after World War Two expressly specifies rape as a crime against humanity, but it was not prosecuted as such before the International Military Tribunals of Nuremberg or Tokyo or subsequent prosecutions under Council Control Law No. 10. Rape and other forms of sexual violence were prosecuted as conventional war crimes or as the underlying factual basis of other international crimes. This is not to say that rape was not criminalised under international law, but that it was not expressly legally characterised as an international crime.

The express criminalisation of sexual violence under public international law occurs at the intersection of a series of social shifts at national and international levels from the 1970s onwards. The shifts can be described as transnational, in the sense that they extend and operate beyond states. They all contribute to the conceptualisation of sexual violence as an injury to the individual and to 'society' at the international level and hence to its construction as an international crime at the ICTY. The dominant explanations of the international criminalisation of sexual violence are liberal stories of the progressive diffusion of human rights norms or critical stories of the rise of 'governance' feminism, told most often from the perspective of US feminist politics or foreign policy.[14] By focusing on the *transnational* context of the *legal* construction of sexual violence, a different explanation emerges.

2.2.1 The Characterisation of Sexual Violence as a Harm to Persons

From the 1970s onwards, sexual violence was increasingly seen as a serious crime of violence against the person. National and international feminist movements made the prevalence and harmfulness of sexual violence a political and public issue and campaigned for legal reform in many national jurisdictions, including the former Yugoslavia.[15] During this period, there was an increasing, if uneven and incomplete, recognition that sexual violence was harmful to women as individuals and as a class of persons, with a resulting 'global wave' of criminal law reform in national jurisdictions.[16] During the establishment of the ICTY, the proposals of states and organisations called for the adoption of international norms taking these national legal reforms into account.[17] This national criminal law reform also informed the 'evolution of international humanitarian law', the legal basis of the substantive jurisdiction of the

---

[14] See, for example, Tuba Inal, *Looting and Rape in Wartime* (Philadelphia: University of Pennsylvania Press, 2013) and Janet Halley, 'Rape at Rome', (2008) 30(1) Mich J Int'l L 1–123.
[15] See Zsófia Lóránd, *The Feminist Challenge to the Socialist State in Yugoslavia* (Cham: Palgrave Macmillan, 2018), pp. 192–209.
[16] David Frank, Bayliss Camp, et al., 'Worldwide Trends in the Criminal Regulation of Sex, 1945 to 2005', (2010) 75(6) American Sociological Review 867–893.
[17] See Virginia Morris and Michael Scharf, *An Insider's Guide to the International Criminal Tribunal for the Former Yugoslavia* (New York: Transnational, 1995), volume 2, sections VII and VIII.

ICTY,[18] as well as its jurisprudence, such as *Furundžija*, which drew on the greater stigmatisation and widening of concepts of rape in national criminal codes to identify the elements of the international offence of rape.[19]

During this same period, sexual violence against women came to be characterised as a discriminatory violation of human rights at the international level, and the equal protection of women by humanitarian law was explicitly established as an international legal norm. In the UN system, the Commission on the Status of Women led efforts to address the specific issue of women in armed conflict, culminating in the General Assembly Declaration on the Protection of Women and Children in Emergency and Armed Conflict in 1974.[20] The issue of the effects of armed conflict upon women, including conflict-related sexual violence in specific conflicts such as Bangladesh, was raised throughout the UN Conferences on Women held in 1975 (Mexico City), 1980 (Copenhagen), and 1985 (Nairobi).[21] Moreover, the international women's movement pushed for recognition of 'violence against women' in the UN system from the mid-1970s onwards.[22] While 'women and armed conflict' as a specific topic was less visible in the formal UN agenda between 1974 and 1990, it re-emerged in the context of 'violence against women' in the 1990s.[23] At a formal level, the Convention on the Elimination of All Forms of Discrimination against Women (1979) (CEDAW) did not address violence against women or women's rights in armed conflict in its formal provisions. However, in February 1992, General Recommendation No. 19 addressing violence against women was adopted by the CEDAW Committee.

---

[18] Christine Cleiren and Melania Tijssen, 'Rape and Other Forms of Sexual Assault in the Armed Conflict in the Former Yugoslavia', in Roger Clark and Madeleine Sann (eds.), *The Prosecution of International Crimes* (Brunswick: Transaction, 1996), p. 265.

[19] *Furundžija* Trial Judgement, paras. 174–186.

[20] G.A. Res. 3318.

[21] These issues were raised in the context of critiques of imperialist and colonial conflicts by 'Second World' and 'Third World' women and are echoed in the CEDAW Preamble, if not its formal provisions. See the respective UN reports of the conferences, Mexico City, E/Conf. 66/34; Copenhagen, A/Conf. 94/35; and Nairobi, A/Conf. 116/281 ReYI.

[22] Rashida Manjoo, 'Normative Developments on Violence against Women in the United Nations System', in Rashida Manjoo and Jackie Jones (eds.), *The Legal Protection of Women from Violence* (London and New York: Routledge, 2018), p. 75.

[23] Judith Gardam and Michelle Jarvis, *Women, Armed Conflict, and International Law* (The Hague: Kluwer Law International, 2001), p. 146.

General Recommendation No. 19 did not address conflict-related sexual violence as such. However, it clarified that discrimination under CEDAW included gender-based violence against women, and it included 'sexual harm' in its list of acts constituting such violence. The Recommendation also clarified that gender-based violence violated the right not to be subject to torture (19(7)(b)) and the 'right to equal protection according to humanitarian norms in time of international or internal armed conflict' (19(7)(c)). This definition of gender-based violence was adopted by the Declaration on the Elimination of Violence against Women by the UN General Assembly in 1994.[24]

While this 'soft' international law was not legally binding upon states, it was nevertheless legally significant in the development of sexual violence as an international crime for two reasons. First, it established that sexual harm was a breach of international human rights norms. Second, it established that 'sexual harm' is a violation of the principle of equal protection of women by humanitarian legal norms. The legal characterisations of sexual violence as a breach of fundamental international legal norms would become important for the recognition, and jurisprudential development, of crimes of sexual violence at the ICTY.

2.2.2 The Characterisation of Sexual Violence as a Harm to International Society

2.2.2.1 Sexual Violence as a Matter of Public Concern to International Society

By 1992, sexual violence in the conflict in the former Yugoslavia had become recognised as a matter of public concern to 'international society'. It came to be seen as an injury, which was given value (recognised as socially harmful), politicised (seen as a public matter), and actionable (giving rise to legal accountability).[25] This recognition was built on four key factors. The first factor was the increasing participation of women in 'international society', such as the UN World Conferences on Women discussed in Section 2.2.1. Though women remained under-represented in the UN system, there was increased participation of women's rights

---

[24] G.A. Res. 48/104. Both the UN General Assembly Declaration and General Recommendation No. 19 were drafted in 1991, that is, prior to the war in the former Yugoslavia.

[25] Howe, '"Social Injury" Revisited', 434.

advocates in the international system.²⁶ For example, as a member of the UN Commission on the Status of Women, Judge Florence Mumba participated in drafting a resolution to the General Assembly in early 1992 to have rape included as a war crime in the jurisdiction of war crimes tribunals. The first woman to be appointed to the Zambian High Court, Judge Mumba became one of the three female permanent judges sitting at the ICTY in 1997.²⁷

The second factor was the rise of the international women's movement and transnational feminist non-governmental organisations (NGOs) and women's coalitions in global civil society, together with more visible women's rights advocacy around conflict-related sexual violence from the late 1980s onwards. Two important examples are the campaign for redress for the 'comfort women' of World War Two that began in the 1990s, led by Korean feminists and culminating in the Tokyo Women's Tribunal in 2000, and the Global Tribunal on Violations of Women's Human Rights, held as part of the World Conference on Women's Rights in 1993.²⁸ Yugoslavian feminists participated in both tribunals, including on the issue of sexual violence. The Global Tribunal on Violations of Women's Human Rights included a session on war crimes against women, with testimony by Yugoslavian feminists about crimes committed against women in the conflict, including rape.²⁹ Judge Elizabeth Odio Benito, former minister of justice in Costa Rica, was a presiding judge of the Global Tribunal. She was appointed as a permanent judge to the ICTY in 1993.³⁰

The international media reporting of the Yugoslavian conflicts was the third factor. Widely regarded as the first war covered by a global media, the UN and governments from Europe to the Middle East faced widespread media and public pressure to respond to the war crimes appearing in the daily newspapers or nightly news from 1991 onwards.³¹

---

[26] UN Joint Inspection Unit, *Advancement of the Status of Women in the UN Secretariat in an Era of Human Resources Management and Accountability: A New Beginning*? JIU/REP/94 3 1994.

[27] The other 14 permanent judges sitting that year were male.

[28] Gardam and Jarvis, *Women, Armed Conflict, and International Law*, pp. 144–147.

[29] Niamh Reilly (ed.), *Testimonies from the Global Tribunal on Violations of Women's Human Rights* (New York: Rutgers University Center for Women's Global Leadership, 1994).

[30] Both Mumba and Benito were challenged at the ICTY on impartiality grounds for their involvement in human rights and women's rights.

[31] On North America and Europe, see Richard Sobel and Eric Shiraev (eds.), *International Public Opinion and the Bosnian Crisis* (Maryland: Lexington Books, 2003). Non-Western

The international media reported war-time rape of women in the Croatian conflict in late 1991, but it was not until the war moved to Bosnia that it was widely reported 'as a war on civilians', from July 1992 onwards.[32] The rape of women in the context of 'ethnic cleansing' and detention camps in Bosnia became the subject of extensive reporting by August 1992. Sexual violence against men was also reported.[33] The media coverage of war-time rape reflected in part the unprecedented number of women journalists covering the war.[34]

The fourth and crucial factor was women's groups in the former Yugoslavia. These groups undertook media, legal, and humanitarian activism and advocacy projects and built global networks that made visible the impact of the war on women, including sexual violence.[35] The groups were responsible for disseminating the first reports of widespread sexual violence in 1992.[36] They did not agree on how to characterise war-time rape, nor did the 'international community' adequately respond to their demands for support, protection, and refugee status for survivors.[37] Nevertheless, these campaigns played a critical role in the international recognition of war-time sexual violence. Both Yugoslavian and international feminist organisations (often working together) called for accountability for war-time rape, including prosecutions before an international court.[38]

---

governments, such as Turkey and Saudi Arabia, also faced similar pressures: for example, Alan Cowell, 'Turkey Faces Moral Crisis over Bosnia', 11 July 1992, and Chris Hedges, 'Muslims from Afar Joining "Holy War" in Bosnia', *The New York Times*, 5 December 1992.

[32] For example, Ed Vulliamy, 'Eyewitness: Shots in the Dark on the Ethnic Front Line', *The Guardian*, 14 September 1991 (Croatia); Michael Kaufman, 'A War on Civilians', *The New York Times*, 18 July 1992 (Bosnia).

[33] For example, *The Guardian*, *The Independent*, and *The New York Times* published 21 news reports on the conflict, including rape, in August 1992. Source: Lexis.

[34] Margaret Gallagher, *An Unfinished Story* (Paris: UNESCO, 1995), p. 59.

[35] Gardam and Jarvis, *Women, Armed Conflict, and International Law*, p. 157.

[36] Maja Korać, 'Feminists against Sexual Violence in War', (2018) 7(10) Social Sciences 182–195.

[37] Dubravka Žarkov, 'Feminism and the Disintegration of Yugoslavia', (2003) 24(3) Social Development Issues 59–68.

[38] See, for example, Lepa Mladjenović, Vesna Kesić, et al., 'Voices from a War', (1993) 23(5) Off Our Backs 6–9, 12–15; Diana Kapidžić and Aida Daidžić, 'BISER: A Conversation with Bosnian Women Living in Exile', (1994) 5(1) Hastings Women's L.J. 53–67; Maja Korać, 'Women's Groups in the Former Yugoslavia', (1995) 14(8) Refuge 16–18, 19; and Vesna Nikolić-Ristanović, 'Sexual Violence, International Law and Restorative Justice', in Doris Buss and Ambreena Manji (eds.), *International Law: Modern Feminist Approaches* (Oxford: Hart, 2005), p. 280.

2.2.2.2 Sexual Violence as Legally Actionable under Public International Law

In the context of the war in the former Yugoslavia, '[f]or the first time, sexual violence against women in armed conflict emerged as a distinct issue within the U.N. system'.[39] Sexual violence was first characterised as a violation of human rights (as was all other conduct) by the UN Commission on Human Rights (UNHCR) and as a violation of women's human rights (on the basis of General Recommendation No. 19) by the CEDAW Committee, in keeping with their mandates.[40] It subsequently became characterised as an international crime, which gave rise to individual criminal accountability as a serious violation of international humanitarian law or to state responsibility for breaches of obligations to prevent and punish the international crime of genocide. Following Nicola Lacey, we can describe this process as involving both formal criminalisation, which characterised sexual violence as a crime under the 'formal' rules of international law creating criminal offences, and substantive criminalisation, which enforced those rules in legal institutions and practices.[41]

However, the process of criminalisation was contingent on the prior characterisation of the conduct of the conflict as being contrary to public international law and the conflict itself as being injurious to international society. As can be seen in the UN Security Council (UNSC) Resolutions from September 1991 onwards, the conflict in Yugoslavia, and most particularly in Bosnia, was characterised as such because it (1) involved widespread and serious violations of international human rights and humanitarian law and (2) was a threat to international peace and security under Chapter VII of the UN Charter.[42]

Within this framing, sexual violence came to be 'formally' criminalised at the international level. It was first legally characterised as a serious violation of international humanitarian law in the reports of the UN

---

[39] Gardam and Jarvis, *Women, Armed Conflict, and International Law*, p. 148.

[40] The UNHCR Special Rapporteur undertook the first investigation of violations of international law in the conflict in August 1992. The CEDAW Committee played a key role in raising the situation of women in the former Yugoslavia with the UNHCR: Twelfth Session, Summary Record of the 214th Meeting, CEDAW Committee, 21 January 1993, CEDAW/C/SR.214.

[41] Nicola Lacey, 'Historicising Criminalisation', (2009) 72(6) MLR 936–960, 943.

[42] U.N. Doc. S/RES/713 (1991) establishing an arms embargo and peacekeeping force. This was followed by a number of other resolutions concerning peace and humanitarian issues and actions.

Commission of Experts, established by the UNSC in October 1992 and reporting in February 1993 (Commission of Experts).[43] It was also accepted as the factual basis for an application to establish state responsibility for genocide by the International Court of Justice (ICJ) on March 1993.[44] The first UNSC Resolution to characterise sexual violence as a criminal violation of humanitarian law was in April 1993, where 'the massive, organized and systematic detention and rape of women' was expressly listed in a general condemnation of humanitarian law violations in the conflict.[45] This same formulation was used in the Resolution establishing the ICTY in May 1993.[46]

The formal criminalisation of sexual violence was therefore contingent on its characterisation as a serious violation of international humanitarian law. Given this, it is unsurprising that sexual violence first became visible at the international level where it could be recognised as an illegal means and method of warfare and as an illegitimate political objective of war, namely, as the torture of men in detention settings and as the systematic and widespread rape of women.[47] The construction of sexual violence as an international crime rested upon it being *legally articulable* as a military and political crime of conflict and, as such, a crime of concern to the international community as a whole. Sexual violence then became legally articulable as an international crime within the legal framework of international humanitarian law.

Enforcement of these international legal norms required establishing an international court before which these offences could be prosecuted, as no such court existed. Establishing such a court was conditional upon the characterisation of the conflict as a threat to international peace and security (rather than sexual violence as is sometimes claimed). The threat to international peace and security is the protected public interest of 'international society', which provides the legal basis for the establishment of the ICTY under the UN Charter.[48] Accordingly, the

---

[43] UN, Interim Report of the Commission of Experts Established Pursuant to SC Resolution 780, (1992), (S/25274), 10 February 1993, paras. 66(c), 58–60.

[44] *Application of the Convention on the Prevention and Punishment of the Crime of Genocide (Bosnia and Herzegovina v. Serbia and Montenegro)*, ICJ, 20 March 1993 (ICJ Genocide Case).

[45] U.N. Doc. S/RES/820 (1993).

[46] U.N. Doc. S/RES/827 (1993).

[47] See, for example, the Special Rapporteur and Expert Commission reports and ICJ Genocide Case.

[48] U.N. Docs. S/RES/808 (1993).

criminalisation of sexual violence in the Yugoslavian conflicts was contingent on its formal characterisation as a serious violation of humanitarian law and the serious violations of humanitarian law committed in the conflict as being a threat to the international legal and social order. It is in this context that sexual violence emerges as a crime under public international law.

The establishment of the ICTY gave concrete existence to international criminal law, giving it a 'material reality ... in practices and social institutions'.[49] For the first time, an international criminal court was established to prosecute international crimes under international law, and sexual violence was included in those crimes that it was tasked to prosecute. The agreement to establish a tribunal was widely agreed to be 'an act of tokenism by the world community' and should be seen in the wider context of the evident unwillingness and then failure of the 'international community' to enforce international law or peace under the UN Charter.[50] As such, the establishment of the ICTY should be described the outcome of a highly contested political struggle, rather than as an inevitable victory of moral ideals or international law (much less feminist politics).

Current feminist scholarship often describes this process as a shift in conflict-related sexual violence from being seen as a private national matter for states to becoming a public matter for international society.[51] However, sexual violence in international conflict has long been regarded as a 'public' matter for international law insofar as it affects the protected public interests of states (in military law or the laws of war) or the values of the international society of states (in crimes against humanity).[52] If we follow Doris Buss in seeing 'private' and 'public' spheres as interdependent rather than separate, then seemingly 'private' matters for states should not be seen as *unregulated* or free from interference, but as subject to different types of regulation'.[53] Understood in these terms,

---

[49] Sonja Buckel, *Subjectivation and Cohesion* (Leiden and Boston: Brill, 2021), p. 137.

[50] Gary Bass, *Stay the Hand of Vengeance* (Princeton: Princeton University Press, 2000), p. 207.

[51] See, for example, Aisling Swaine, *Conflict-Related Violence against Women* (Cambridge: Cambridge University Press, 2018).

[52] That is, as contrary to the values set out in the so-called Marten Clause of the Hague Convention (1899), which served as the legal basis for establishing crimes against humanity at Nuremberg.

[53] Doris Buss, 'Going Global', in Susan Boyd (ed.), *Challenging the Public/Private Divide* (Toronto and Buffalo: University of Toronto Press, 1997), p. 373.

sexual violence in the Yugoslavian conflict becomes subject to a different type of regulation under public international law, that of international criminalisation.

The emergence of sexual violence as an international crime shows how international criminal law comes to be a distinct body of international rules with a defined area of application, and 'international crime' as the object to be regulated, with criminalisation prohibiting conduct injurious to *international society*. In 1950, George Schwarzenberger argued that there was no international criminal law in the 'material sense of the word', because a true 'international society' had not yet developed that can be considered to be comparable to the 'social group [whose] highest values and interests are protected by criminal law' at the municipal level.[54] However, international criminal law presumes this idea of an 'international society', and the establishment of the ICTY marks its emergence at the international level.

The establishment of the ICTY marks the shift from international humanitarian law, the body of law governing armed conflict, to international criminal law, the body of law governing international crimes, and from the protected interests of the international society of states to the protected interests of international society. In this process, we see the creation of the first fundamental category of the legal form, the legal category of international crime. The category of international crime creates legal relations between individuals, and the legal relations of individuals to this 'society', expressed in the form of the protected interests of the person and of 'international society'. With the construction of the legal category of international crime, sexual violence emerges as a crime under international law. What, then, is the international crime of sexual violence and what are the individual and social interests that it seeks to protect?

2.3 The International Crime of Sexual Violence

In order to evade the legal and political difficulties that had prevented the establishment of an international criminal court since the end of World War Two, the territorial and temporal jurisdiction of the ICTY was limited to crimes committed in the former Yugoslavia from 1991 onwards. Its subject-matter jurisdiction (*ratione materiae*) was limited

---

[54] George Schwarzenberger, 'The Problem of an International Criminal Law', (1950) 3 CLP, 263–296, 272–273.

to serious violations of customary international humanitarian law, that is, the rules that are established by the general practice accepted as law by states.[55] These rules bind all states, regardless of whether they are signatories to specific conventions or treaties.[56]

The ICTY Statute set out the following categories of violations criminalised under customary humanitarian law: war crimes, that is, grave breaches of the Geneva Conventions (Art. 2) or violations of the laws or customs of war (Art. 3); genocide, that is, the intent to destroy, in whole or in part, a national, ethnical, racial, or religious group (Art. 4); and crimes against humanity, that is, a widespread and systematic attack directed against any civilian population (Art. 5).[57] Following the position under international customary law, the Statute expressly specified only one crime of sexual violence, namely rape, as a crime against humanity (Art. 5(g)).[58] While waging an aggressive war is also a crime under customary law, it was not included within the subject-matter jurisdiction of the ICTY Statute. It is now widely accepted that the categories of international crimes consist of the so-called 'core crimes' of aggression, war crimes, genocide, and crimes against humanity.

Sexual violence was prosecuted before the ICTY as numerated charges or as the underlying factual basis of charges in all core crime categories of war crimes, genocide, and crimes against humanity. The ICTY jurisprudence established that under international customary law, 'rape and other serious sexual assaults in armed conflict entail the criminal liability of the perpetrators'.[59] It also established that sexual violence can constitute crimes against humanity and genocide, which can occur in times of war or peace and so do not require a connection to armed conflict.[60]

---

[55] Article 38(1), Statute of the International Court of Justice, 18 April 1946.
[56] Report of the Secretary-General Pursuant to Paragraph 2 of SC Resolution 808 (1993), UN Doc. S/25704.
[57] *Kunarac et al.*, ICTY-96–23&23/1-T, Judgement, 22 February 2001, (*Kunarac* Trial Judgement), paras. 427–429.
[58] It is arguable that the act of 'imposing measures to prevent births within the group' specified under the offence of genocide can be considered a sexual violence crime. However, this provision refers not only to reproductive violence, such as forced sterilisation or abortion, but also marriage laws and sex segregation, which would not necessarily be characterised as sexual violence under current legal approaches. My thanks to Jasenka Ferizović for this point.
[59] *Furundžija* Trial Judgement, para. 169.
[60] *Tadić*, ICTY-94–1-A, Judgement, 15 July 1999, (*Tadić* Appeals Judgement), para. 251.

The jurisprudence also confirmed that sexual violence could constitute a grave breach of the Geneva Conventions,[61] and an act of genocide,[62] giving rise to state obligations of prevention and enforcement under the grave breaches regime of the Geneva Conventions and under the Genocide Convention.

However, it did not establish a distinct offence of sexual violence under international law, and nor has such an offence been subsequently established. Neither international criminal tribunal jurisprudence nor the International Criminal Court (ICC) establish rape or sexual violence as a distinct offence under conventional or customary norms.[63] Rather, sexual violence as a crime under international law consists of a category of prohibited acts within the general crime categories of war crimes, crimes against humanity, and genocide. As such, sexual violence is criminalised where it is a constituent component of these 'core' international crimes. Sexual violence remains characterised as a subsidiary act, which is recognised as an international crime only when framed by the contextual element of international crimes, that is, by other forms of international illegality. The crime of sexual violence under international law therefore consists of two distinct parts. The first part is the so-called international element, which consists of war crimes, genocide, and crimes against humanity. The second concerns sexual violence as it is defined under international criminal law.

2.3.1 The International Component of the Crime under Customary International Law

The 'international' element of sexual violence offences consists of war crimes, genocide, or crimes against humanity. This context is understood to establish a sexual offence as an international crime and to distinguish it from a breach of human rights under international law or an offence

---

[61] *Tadić*, ICTY-94-1-T, Judgement, 7 May 1997, para 243.
[62] *Application of the Convention on the Prevention and Punishment of the Crime of Genocide (Bosnia and Herzegovina v. Serbia and Montenegro)*, Judgement, ICJ, 26 February 2007, para. 300. For the relevant case law, see Laurel Baig, Michelle Jarvis et al., 'Contextualising Sexual Violence', in Serge Brammertz and Michelle Jarvis (eds.), *Prosecuting Conflict-Related Sexual Violence at the ICTY* (Oxford: Oxford University Press, 2016), p. 201.
[63] It should be noted that the Rome Statute of the ICC (Rome Statute) sets out numerated offences of rape and sexual violence as war crimes and crimes against humanity but not genocide.

under national criminal codes. The context of armed conflict (war crimes), an attack on a civilian population (crimes against humanity), or an intent to destroy a protected group (genocide) shifts sexual violence from being 'a simple sexual assault' subject to national jurisdiction to an international crime, a category of conduct prohibited under international law.[64] This international element reveals the shift from international humanitarian law, a body of law that regulates the conduct of armed conflict, to international criminal law, which does not require international crimes to have a nexus to conflict.

Within the general crime categories of war crimes, crimes against humanity, and genocide, sexual violence consists of a category of prohibited acts. Because sexual violence offences are not expressly set out under international law, these offences were developed as customary norms in the jurisprudence. Sexual violence as a category of acts prohibited under international criminal law falls into three categories: first, where it is characterised as a prohibited act under the general crime category, such as causing serious bodily or mental harm to members of a protected group as genocide;[65] second, where specified acts of sexual violence are prohibited under the general crime category, such as rape as a crime against humanity; third, where it is considered to constitute a specified sexual offence, such as forced marriage or forced abortion as a war crime.[66] It should be noted that sexual violence has not been established for all prohibited acts under general crime categories, such as wilful killing as a grave breach of the Geneva Convention.[67] Neither have the elements of sexual violence as a prohibited act been established under all general crime categories, such as genocide. Finally, the specified sexual offences are not prohibited acts under all general crime categories. It remains the case that 'there are significant gaps in protection from sexual violence, in the normative scheme for its prohibition and in the punishment of offenders'.[68]

---

[64] *Furundžija* Trial Judgement, para. 184. See also *Tadić*, ICTY-94–1, Decision on the Defence Motion on Jurisdiction, 10 August 1995 (*Tadić* Jurisdiction Decision Trial Judgement).
[65] *Karadžić*, ICTY-95–5/18-T, Judgement 24 March 2016 (*Karadžić* Trial Judgement), para. 545.
[66] *Kvočka et al.*, ICTY-98–30/1-T, Judgement, 2001, (*Kvočka* Trial Judgement), para. 180.
[67] See *Kordić and Čerkez*, ICTY-95–14/2-T, Judgement, 26 February 2001.
[68] Mahmoud Cherif Bassiouni, *The Law of the International Criminal Tribunal for the Former Yugoslavia* (New York: Transnational, 1996), p. 560.

2.3.2 The Sexual Violence Component under Customary International Law

As there was no established definition of sexual violence as a distinct offence under international law, the jurisprudence first develops 'sexual violence' as an 'umbrella' category of prohibited sexual acts. The leading case, *Akayesu* (decided before the International Criminal Tribunal for Rwanda), (ICTR)), defines 'sexual violence, which includes rape, as any act of a sexual nature which is committed on a person under circumstances which are coercive. Sexual violence is not limited to physical invasion of the human body and may include acts which do not involve penetration or even physical contact', such as forced nudity.[69] This category of sexual violence crimes includes 'sexual mutilation, forced marriage, and forced abortion as well as the gender related crimes explicitly listed in the Rome Statute as war crimes and crimes against humanity, namely "rape, sexual slavery, enforced prostitution, forced pregnancy, enforced sterilization" and other similar forms of violence'.[70] Although the ICC Elements of Crimes are commonly assumed to provide the definitive definition of sexual violence as an international crime, they should not be regarded as declarative of the current position under customary law.[71]

Sexual penetration marks the distinction between rape and other sexual violence offences within this category of prohibited acts, with later cases developing the elements of rape and of sexual assault as distinct crimes.[72] The first definition of rape was given in *Akayesu*, where the ICTR held that 'the central elements of the crime of rape cannot be captured in a mechanical description of objects or body parts' and used a holistic definition of the offence as 'a physical invasion of a sexual nature, committed on a person under circumstances which are coercive'.[73] This conceptual approach to the definition of rape, 'which recognizes that the essence of rape is ... the aggression that is expressed in a sexual manner

---

[69] *Akayesu*, ICTR-96-4-T, Judgement, 2 September 1998, (*Akayesu* Trial Judgement), para. 688.
[70] *Kvočka* Trial Judgement, para. 180.
[71] See Article 10, Rome Statute, and William Schabas, *The International Criminal Court* (Oxford, New York: Oxford University Press, 2010), p. 269.
[72] *Milutinović et al.* characterises 'sexual assault' as a genus crime that includes rape: *Milutinović et al.*, ICTY-05-87-T, Judgement, 26 February 2009 (*Milutinović* Trial Judgement). This was not followed in later jurisprudence.
[73] *Akayesu* Trial Judgement, paras. 597–598.

under conditions of coercion', was subsequently followed in a number of ICTY and ICTR cases.

However, the ICTY's later *Furundžija* decision adopted a more traditional 'mechanical' approach and considered it necessary 'to arrive at an accurate definition of rape based on the criminal law principle of specificity' by drawing upon 'principles of criminal law common to the major legal systems of the world'.[74] The *Kunarac* case followed this 'mechanical' approach but held that the *Furundžija* definition of the objective elements of rape was more narrowly stated than required under international law.[75] In *Kunarac*, the ICTY defined the elements of the offence as:

> The *actus reus* of the crime of rape in international law is constituted by: the sexual penetration, however slight: (a) of the vagina or anus of the victim by the penis of the perpetrator or any other object used by the perpetrator; or (b) of the mouth of the victim by the penis of the perpetrator; where such sexual penetration occurs without the consent of the victim. Consent for this purpose must be consent given voluntarily, as a result of the victim's free will, assessed in the context of the surrounding circumstances. The *mens rea* is the intention to effect this sexual penetration, and the knowledge that it occurs without the consent of the victim.[76]

Later ICTR decisions followed this distinction between conceptual and mechanical definitions and affirmed the mechanical approach of *Kunarac*. In *Muhimana*, the ICTR held that these definitions are 'not incompatible or substantially different', as *Kunarac* provides 'additional details on the constituent elements of acts considered to be rape' under *Akayesu*.[77] Nevertheless, the *Kunarac* definition has been followed in the subsequent decisions of the ICTR, ICTY, Special Court for Sierra Leone (SCSL), and the Extraordinary Chambers in the Courts of Cambodia (ECCC).[78] As such, the *Kunarac* definition should be regarded as the leading case setting out the current elements of the offence under customary law.

---

[74] *Furundžija* Trial Judgement, para. 177.
[75] *Kunarac* Trial Judgement, para. 438.
[76] *Kunarac* Trial Judgement, para. 460, affirmed on appeal.
[77] *Muhimana*, ICTR-95-1B-T, Judgement, 28 April 2005, paras. 549–551.
[78] Most recently, ICTR: *Ngirabatware*, ICTR-99-54-T, Judgment, 20 December 2012, para. 1381; and ICTY: *Karadžić* Trial Judgement, paras. 511–512; SCSL: *Charles Ghankay Taylor*, SCSL-03-1-T, Judgement, 18 May 2012, para. 415; ECCC: *Nuon Chea and Khieu Samphan* ECCC-002/02-T, Judgement, 16 November 2018, para. 731.

That the elements of the offence are not settled is particularly evident in relation to the issue of consent. The ICTY first described rape as a 'forced or coerced [act] of sexual penetration'.[79] However, in *Kunarac*, the ICTY Appeals Chamber rearticulated the element of coercion or force in terms of absence of consent and held that the circumstances of conflict are 'almost universally coercive'.[80] The ICTR Appeals Chamber provided an extensive consideration of consent in *Gacumbitsi*,[81] and it affirmed non-consent and knowledge thereof as elements of rape. *Kunarac* remains the leading decision in the area, with later jurisprudence emphasising the coercive circumstances of armed conflict, genocide, or crimes against humanity as evidence of the absence of consent.[82]

The elements of the offence of sexual assault were set out later in the case of *Milutinović et al.* in 2009:

(a) The physical perpetrator commits an act of a sexual nature on another; this includes requiring that other person to perform such an act.
(b) That act infringes the victim's physical integrity or amounts to an outrage to the victim's personal dignity.
(c) The victim does not consent to the act.
(d) The physical perpetrator intentionally commits the act.
(e) The physical perpetrator is aware that the act occurred without the consent of the victim.[83]

This definition has been followed in later jurisprudence.[84]

The category of sexual violence under international law is generally understood to be gender-neutral, in the sense that 'the prohibition of sexual violence is recognised to encompass violence not only against women and girls, but any person, including men and boys'.[85] The definitions of rape and sexual violence in the *ad hoc* tribunals are

---

[79] *Kvočka* Trial Judgement, para 182.
[80] *Kunarac et al.*, ICTY-96–23&23/A, Judgement 12 June 2002 (*Kunarac* Appeals Judgement), para. 130.
[81] *Gacumbitsi*, ICTR-01–64-A, Judgement, 7 July 2006, para. 153.
[82] See: *Kvočka* Trial Judgement, para. 178; *Milutinović* Trial Judgement, para. 200; *Karemera & Ngirumpatse* ICTR-98–44-T, Judgement, 2 February 2012, paras. 1676–1677; *Karadžić* Trial Judgement, paras. 511–512.
[83] *Milutinović* Trial Judgement, para. 201.
[84] See, for example, *Karadžić* Trial Judgement, paras. 512–513, and cited jurisprudence.
[85] International Committee of the Red Cross (ICRC), *Customary International Humanitarian Law* (Cambridge: Cambridge University Press, 2009), p. 327.

gender-neutral, and charges of sexual violence against male and female victims were laid from the first trial of the ICTY onwards and were brought against both male and female perpetrators. However, certain sexual violence offences, such as forced pregnancy or abortion, and other forms of sexual violence, such as vaginal penetration, are sex specific.

2.4 The International Crime of Sexual Violence and the Protected Interest of Persons and of International Society

2.4.1 Sexual Violence and the Protected Interest of the Person

The description of the protected interests of the person in sexual violence offences builds upon these categories of international crimes. The jurisprudence develops its characterisations of sexual violence in terms of the protected interests of the person described in core crime categories, such as the war crime of 'outrages on personal dignity' or persecution as a crime against humanity. The criminalisation of sexual violence in these different legal characterisations constitutes the category of sexual offences under international law and so constructs the models of harm to the person of sexual violence.

In sexual violence as a so-called 'umbrella' category, sexual violence is characterised as a crime of violence, expressed in sexual form, which causes harm to the person. Sexual violence requires that 'an act of a sexual nature takes place' to be characterised as such, and it 'should not be treated differently from other violent acts because of its sexual component'.[86] Because this violence is recognised as giving rise to serious harm to the person, it rises to sufficient gravity to be considered the 'severe pain or suffering' required to constitute torture as a war crime,[87] the 'serious bodily and mental harm' to members of a group required to establish genocide,[88] or a violation of fundamental rights defining persecution as a crime against humanity.[89] The harm need not be permanent or irreversible.[90]

The nature of these harms is not clearly conceptualised in the jurisprudence. However, it is possible to identify two models. The first model

---

[86] *Đorđević*, ICTY-05-87-A, Judgement, 27 January 2014 (*Đorđević* Appeals Judgement), para. 852, 887.
[87] *Kunarac* Appeals Judgement, para. 150.
[88] *Karadžić* Trial Judgement, para. 545.
[89] *Đorđević*, ICTY-05-87-T, Judgement, 23 February 2011, para. 1767.
[90] *Kunarac* Trial Judgement, para. 501.

is that sexual violence injures the integrity of the person, and the second is that it constitutes discrimination. The first model characterises sexual violence as a harm to bodily, personal, and sexual integrity. At the formal level of the elements of crimes, this model builds on the concepts of criminalised harm in international humanitarian law and genocide. In relation to humanitarian law, the jurisprudence develops the older model of rape as a war crime as forced or coerced penetration, as well as articulating the harm through the criminalised prohibitions upon inhuman treatment, wilfully causing great suffering or serious injury to body or health, violence to life and persons, and outrages on personal dignity. Such harms are considered inconsistent with 'the human dignity of every person, whatever his or her gender'.[91] In relation to genocide, sexual violence is characterised as serious bodily or mental harm, which is sufficient to contribute to the destruction of the group of which that person is a member.[92]

In the case of rape, these injuries are characterised as harms to the bodily, personal, and sexual integrity of the victim. This harm is physical, in that by definition rape involves 'physical invasion of a sexual nature', which is described in the elements of the offence as the sexual penetration of the body by another's body part or an object. The harm is also mental, in that rape injures the physical integrity, human dignity, and sexual autonomy of the person.[93] These are injuries to the 'self', not only because rape gives rise to psychological suffering but also because it violates the personhood of the victim, which is attributed with the inherent qualities and rights of integrity, dignity, and autonomy. The harms of rape include 'intimidation, degradation, humiliation, discrimination, punishment, control or destruction of a person'.[94] In this formulation, rape is harmful because it is a form of indignity, which harms the intrinsic worth of the person as a human and, for this reason, 'strikes at the very core of human dignity and physical integrity'.[95] The most recent characterisation of rape is the injury to sexual integrity, understood as a violation of sexual autonomy.[96] As Nicola Lacey argues, this is a modern

---

[91] *Furundžija* Trial Judgement, para. 183.
[92] *Karadžić* Trial Judgement, para. 545. Sexual violence charged as other genocidal acts has not been fully considered in the ICTY jurisprudence.
[93] See *Delalić et al.*, ICTY-96-21-T, Judgement, 16 November 1998, (*Delalić* Trial Judgement), para. 495, and *Kunarac* Trial Judgement, para. 457.
[94] *Furundžija* Trial Judgement, para. 176.
[95] *Delalić* Trial Judgement, para. 495.
[96] *Kunarac* Trial Judgement, para. 457.

conception of rape as the violation of the 'liberal ideal' of 'sexual autonomy' because it negates the exercise of the free will of the person over her physical body.[97] Ngaire Naffine points out that 'this is generally how law interprets our physical natures: it posits us as whole, integrated and individuated being'.[98] These characterisations of rape link the integrity of the body and the self, such that the violation of bodily integrity is understood to injure the integrity of the individual as a human being.

The same models of harms to bodily, personal, and sexual integrity can be seen in the elements of sexual assault. In the case of sexual assault, the harm does not arise from sexual penetration of the body but from the attack upon the 'integrity of the person', defined by the physical integrity and personal dignity of the victim.[99] The recognition of victims other than the person subjected to sexual assault, such as victims forced to observe or forced to perform sexual assaults on others, underscores the characterisation of the harm as being to the integrity of the individual as a human being.

The second model characterises the harm of sexual violence as the discriminatory treatment of persons. This model can be seen as drawing on CEDAW soft law norms, namely, that 'sexual harm' is a violation of the fundamental right to not to be subject to torture or to cruel, inhuman, or degrading treatment or punishment and of the right to equal protection of women under humanitarian law. At the formal level of the elements of crimes, the jurisprudence has recognised sexual violence as sex- or gender-based discrimination and, as such, a prohibited purpose of torture as a war crime or a crime against humanity,[100] and a prohibited ground of persecution as a crime against humanity.[101] Laurel Baig and Michelle Jarvis point out that sexual violence has been most frequently charged as persecution as a crime against humanity before the ICTY and that physical integrity is the fundamental human right most often considered to be violated.[102] This characterises sexual violence against both men and women as a denial of this fundamental right, which occurs on

---

[97] Nicola Lacey, *Unspeakable Subjects* (Oxford: Hart, 1998), pp. 104–105.
[98] 'Who are Law's Persons? From Cheshire Cats to Responsible Subjects', (2003) 66(3) MLR 346–367, 360.
[99] *Karadžić* Trial Judgement, paras. 512–513.
[100] *Delalić* Trial Judgement, para. 493; *Kvočka* Trial Judgment, para. 560; *Brđanin*, ICTY-99-36-T, Judgment, para. 523.
[101] *Kvočka* Trial Judgement, para. 323.
[102] 'Contextualising Sexual Violence', pp. 200, 202.

prohibited grounds of racial, political, or religious discrimination.[103] These discriminatory grounds do not include gender, because the ICTY and ICTR statutes reflected the customary law position. However, the leading cases on persecution also conceptualise sexual violence as 'ethnic and gender discrimination',[104] because it is 'directed only against women of non-Serb origin'.[105] They describe sexual violence 'directed against a woman because she is a woman [as] a form of discrimination that seriously inhibits the ability of women to enjoy human rights and freedoms'.[106]

The protected interest of the person in international criminal law therefore consists of their individual bodily, personal, and sexual integrity and the intrinsic equality of each human person. In international criminal law, as Patricia Viseur Sellers describes, 'protection against sex-based crimes has become quite individualised, that is, committed against persons ... with moral and physical integrity ... women ... have become persons and thus human with rights'.[107] However, that injury is criminalised at the international level not only because it harms the individual or violates their human rights but also because it injures the public interest of 'international society'. The individual harm becomes an international crime only when it is committed in the context of armed conflict (war crimes), is part of the intended destruction of a protected group (genocide), or is a systematic attack on a civilian population (crimes against humanity). What, then, is the model of the injury to the protected interest of the state or of society in sexual violence as an international crime?

2.4.2 Sexual Violence and the Protected Interest of International Society

At a formal level, the legal category of the international crime prohibits particular forms of violence. International criminal law is often described

---

[103] See, for example, *Karadžić* Trial Judgement, para. 2505.
[104] *Kunarac* Trial Judgement, para. 867.
[105] *Kvočka et al.*, ICTY-98-30/1-A, Judgement, 28 February 2005, para. 370.
[106] *Delalić* Trial Judgement, para. 493. The jurisprudence also draws on ideas of gender-related crimes, but these are not consistently developed as conceptual or legal elements of offences.
[107] Patricia Viseur Sellers, 'The Legal and Cultural Value of Sexual Violence', in Kirsten Campbell, Regina Mühlhäuser et al. (eds.), *In Plain Sight* (New Delhi: Zubaan, 2019), p. 296.

as protecting human rights and international peace, as it was in the UN resolutions establishing the ICTY. Ruti Teitel describes this as the emergence of a new paradigm of 'humanity's law'.[108] However, human rights and peace are neither the objects of legal regulation nor of protection in international criminal law.[109] Instead, it presumes the pacification of illegal violence through law and permits lawful killing. As such, it rests upon a classical liberal model of the relationship between law and violence, in which, as Hans Kelsen describes: '[t]he law makes the use of force a monopoly of the community. And precisely by doing so, law ensures peace.'[110]

International criminal law does not presume peace, with violence functioning as its illegal exception. Instead, it permits lawful violence, with unlawful violence as its criminal counterpart. The central issue for this body of law concerns which forms of violence fall into the category of unlawful conduct. So, for example, deaths of civilians that are proportional and necessary to military objectives may be lawful, while a systematic attack upon civilians may not be. As China Miéville describes, 'the most extraordinary forms of violence can thus be viewed as legal'.[111] Criminalisation at the international level functions as a regime of inculpation and exculpation of violence.[112] Because international crimes demarcate between permissible and culpable violence, international criminal law presumes legal violence and demarcates illegal violence that lies 'outside' the boundaries of international legality. International criminal law thereby defines legitimate (legal) and illegitimate (illegal) violence within the international legal order. Accordingly, international criminal law presumes lawful violence rather than peace as the state of sociality at the international level.

The illegal violence prohibited by the category of international crimes has three characteristics. First, it consists of physical and symbolic violence, ranging from the physical violence of murder to the symbolic violence of incitement to genocide. Second, the category of international crimes prohibits particular forms, objects, and aims of violence. For

---

[108] Ruti Teitel, *Humanity's Law* (Oxford: Oxford University Press, 2011).
[109] Costas Douzinas, *Human Rights and Empire* (London: Routledge, 2007), pp. 186–187.
[110] Hans Kelsen, *Law and Peace in International Relations* (Cambridge MA: Harvard University Press, 1942), pp. 11–12.
[111] China Miéville, *Between Equal Rights* (London: Pluto, 2005), p. 288.
[112] Christopher Kutz, 'The Difference Uniforms Make', (2005) 33(2) Philosophy and Public Affairs 148–180, 148.

example, it criminalises specific forms of violence, such as chemical or biological weapons; violence with certain aims, such as the destruction of protected groups; and particular objects of violence, such as civilians. Third, the category of crimes prohibits physical and symbolic violence that is collective. These crimes involve a collective means, subject, or object of violence, rather than individuals as such. This threshold of collective violence is evident in the contextual elements of war crimes, which require the existence of an armed conflict, and crimes against humanity, which require a systematic or widespread attack. While the customary definition of genocide does not have an equivalent contextual element, such as a requirement for a policy or a plan, the crime of genocide nevertheless prohibits symbolic or physical violence that destroys the protected collective group.[113] This 'collective' violence is presumed in the 'international' element of each offence but is not conceptually or doctrinally elaborated.

The category of international crime establishes which particular forms of collective violence injure the public interest of 'international society'. It conceives the injured public interest as the violation of positive international law and of universal values. These two ideas of international legality and universal value typically ground the criminalisation of conduct in the ICTY jurisprudence.[114] In this concept of criminalisation, customary international crimes violate both positive international law *and* important universal values.[115]

The first ground of criminalisation contends that positive international law defines the category of international crimes. Antonio Cassese offers a now classical, if tautological, definition of international crimes as 'breaches of international rules entailing the personal criminal liability of the individuals concerned'.[116] The principle of *nullum crimen, nulla poena sine lege* – that there is no crime without law – entails that without a law prohibiting an act, there can be no crime and thus no legally recognised wrong that can be brought before the law. In this model of

---

[113] See Gerhard Werle, *Principles of International Criminal Law* (The Hague: TM Asser Press, 2005), p. 29.
[114] *Furundžija* Trial Judgement, paras. 258–259.
[115] See Mahmoud Cherif Bassiouni, 'The Sources and Content of International Criminal Law', in Kalliopi Koufa (ed.), *The New International Criminal Law* (Athens: Sakkoulas, 2003), p. 71.
[116] *International Criminal Law* (Oxford: Oxford University Press, 2003), p. 23.

criminalisation, the rules of international law determine criminal conduct, ultimately resting on customary norms where there are no relevant statutory or conventional provisions. This was the case for sexual violence, where, for example, the *Furundžija* judgement reviewed customary international humanitarian law to establish that there are 'universally accepted norms of international law prohibiting rape as well as serious sexual assault [that] are applicable in any armed conflict [and] entail the criminal liability of the perpetrators'.[117] Where there are no international rules, the ICTY looks to national legal systems to establish the relevant elements of the offences. This is a classical positivist approach, which uses formal criteria to determine criminalisation irrespective of normative claims. In this strand of judicial reasoning, the rules of international law produce the international crime. International legal rules provide the ground of criminalisation, constructing some forms of violence as criminal and other forms as permissible.

As a violation of positive international legal rules, sexual violence offences are characterised as injuring the protected interests of the international community of states that is understood to constitute 'international society'. States agree as sovereign powers to be bound by positive law, which expresses their mutually shared or collective interests. These protected public interests include a rule-based international order and the international peace and security that this legal order is understood to guarantee. International criminal law is seen as protecting international 'peace and security' by distinguishing between permissible and impermissible violence in the international society of states. By criminalising sexual violence as a war crime, crime against humanity, or genocide, it becomes characterised as impermissible violence contrary to international society. This injury to international society, characterised as the international community of states, harms their collective interests as agreed and expressed through positive international legal rules.

The second ground of criminalisation is the violation of universal values, characterised as the breach of 'values considered important by the whole of the international community'.[118] In this model, criminalisation derives from violations of the shared values of international society, such as 'elementary considerations of humanity'.[119] For example, the

---

[117] *Furundžija* Trial Judgement, paras. 168–169.
[118] Cassese, *International Criminal Law*, p. 23.
[119] See, for example, *Tadić*, Trial Judgment Jurisdiction Decision.

Trial Chamber in the *Furundžija* case decided that 'forced oral penetration' should be classified as rape under international criminal law because 'the essence of the whole corpus of international humanitarian law as well as human rights law lies in the protection of the human dignity of every person'.[120] This model of international crimes suggests that 'this body of law is not grounded on formalistic postulates'.[121] Rather, conduct is criminalised because it violates the 'basic human values' of the international community.[122]

As a violation of universal values, sexual violence as an international crime is characterised as injuring the protected values of international society. In this model, international criminal law protects these universally held values, which are shared by all humankind, by prohibiting and punishing international crimes. These protected values include the intrinsic qualities of the human person, the principles of humanity, and the value of collective humanity. Accordingly, sexual violence as an international crime injures the human person, the values of humanity, and humanity as a universal group of persons. By criminalising sexual violence, international criminal law claims to value the intrinsic equal worth of victims as human persons, as well as their equal value to collective humanity. In this model, international society consists of the 'world community' or the 'whole of mankind', and sexual violence as an international crime injures all human society, understood as the universal society of all persons.

The legal category of international crimes characterises war crimes, crimes against humanity, and genocide as particular forms of collective violence that injure international society. These forms of violence injure the rule- and value-based order of international society, in that they breach its foundation in international rules and universal value. As such, the protected interest of the legal category of the international crime is 'international society'. The legal category of the international crime reframes the protected interests of humanitarian law, namely, the mutual interests of the society of states regulating by agreement legitimate forms of force, through the broader conception of the public interest of international society, a social order based in universal rules and values, and composed of all humankind.

---

[120] *Furundžija* Trial Judgement, para. 183.
[121] *Tadić* Appeals Judgement, para. 96.
[122] *Kupreškić, et al.*, ICTY-95-16-T, Judgement, 14 January 2000, para. 547.

2.5 Conceptual Problems in the Criminalisation of Sexual Violence as an International Crime

The criminalisation of sexual violence under international law shows the emergence of the legal category of international crimes. However, the surfacing of sexual violence as a gender-based crime (as Rhonda Copelon describes it) also reveals the doctrinal and conceptual fault-lines concerning harms to the person and the protected interests of international society in that legal category.[123] These fault-lines continue to be seen in ongoing doctrinal and conceptual debates concerning the criminalisation of sexual violence, which have been predominantly led by feminist scholars and practitioners.

2.5.1 The Problem of Criminalisation

The development of sexual violence as an international crime shows the problematic legal grounds of criminalisation at the international level. While this problem is typically cast as a contradiction between state interests and universal values, the criminalisation of sexual violence reveals that the concepts of positive law and universal value themselves rest on problematic foundations.

If national criminal justice systems conventionally seek to found criminalisation upon either the recognised legal rules of a polity or the shared values of a community, this is not the case at the international level. International criminal law does not derive from laws authorised by the sovereign power of a nation-state. Unlike municipal systems, there is no sovereign body that can determine criminalisation in the international system similar to that of a state legislature or sovereign authority.[124] As the *Delalić* case explains:

> Whereas the criminalisation process in a national criminal justice system depends upon legislation which dictates the time when conduct is prohibited and the content of such prohibition, the international criminal justice system attains the same objective through treaties or conventions, or after a customary practice of the unilateral enforcement of a prohibition by States.[125]

---

[123] Rhonda Copelon, 'Surfacing Gender', (1994) 5(2) Hastings Women's LJ, 243–266.
[124] Bassiouni, 'The Sources and Content of International Criminal Law', p. 40.
[125] *Delalić* Trial Judgement, para. 404.

International criminalisation thereby becomes dependent upon international customary law 'as a decentred source of right', in which that source of right is founded upon positive international law or the universal values of human society.[126] From this foundation, two key problems follow.

The first problem is the idea of international criminalisation resting upon a body of positive law, which expresses mutual interests of the society of states. As the example of conflict-related sexual violence shows, such positive rules may not exist. This returns international criminalisation to developing criminal offences from international customary or conventional law or the principles of national legal systems. The difficulty of establishing the former is indicated by the piecemeal and fragmented development of sexual violence offences at the international level. The problem of the latter is indicated by the *Kunarac* survey of national legal systems, which revealed that there is no 'universal' positive law as to whether forced oral sex is classified as rape. Positive law alone cannot provide the foundation of international criminal norms.

The second problem is the idea that international criminalisation of conduct expresses the shared values of 'international society'. However, as the example of the international criminalisation of sexual violence shows, this 'international society' does not exist *a priori*. If criminalisation is understood to express universal values of the international society of states, then such an approach confronts the problem that a pluralist order of nation-state communities does not necessarily share values. So, for example, states have sought to protect different 'values' in their criminalisation of sexual violence, as can be seen in the negotiations during the establishment of the ICTY. Conversely, if criminalisation is understood to express the values of all 'human' society, then it is contingent upon the existence of a global society of all persons. However, such a global society cannot be said to exist, other than as it is 'made' in transnational social relations beyond the state. Accordingly, 'universal values' as such also cannot provide the foundation of international criminal norms.

The criminalisation of sexual violence is not founded upon positive law or universal values in themselves but emerges in the 'decentred source of right'. That is, 'the procedural character of the production [of customary law], and the consequent passage from the negotiation of

---

[126] Michael Hardt and Antonio Negri, *Labor of Dionysus*, (Minneapolis: University of Minnesota Press, 1994), p. 100.

agreements to a procedural institutionalisation of agreements' in transnational social relations produce criminalisation of this conduct.[127] As such, it is the outcome of transnational struggles at each stage of this process. Given these contested foundations of international criminalisation, it is unsurprising, then, that the definition of sexual violence as an international crime remains unsettled. It is also unsurprising that there is a lack of clarity at a doctrinal level concerning the legal concept of sexual violence, given that it does not exist as a criminal offence. These unsettled substantive legal issues reflect the struggles in transnational social relations to characterise the protected interests and values of this international crime.

2.5.2 Gender-Based or Gender-Neutral Crime?

In formal terms, sexual violence is ostensibly a gender-neutral harm that refers to violence of a sexual nature against either women or men. Commentators have long argued that gender-neutral provisions are important because they capture both male and female sexual violence.[128] Moreover, this gender-neutrality reflects the predominant liberal framework of formal legal equality in public international law.

However, the gender-neutral model still relies on notions of gendered bodies and actions to identify the sexual nature of sexual violence. The gender-neutral model of sexual violence focuses on the 'sexual aspect of the violence', as Karen Engle describes.[129] These sexual acts belong to the same category of criminal conduct because their sexual nature harms the 'self', whether characterised as physical integrity, human dignity, or sexual autonomy. The harm is prohibited because of its sexual nature. The *sexual* distinguishes violence (such as assault, an unlawful application of force to another) from sexual violence (such as sexual assault, a non-consensual sexual act). For example, there is no intrinsic reason to understand either a person's mouth or an object such as a bottle as

---

[127] Ibid.
[128] Patricia Viseur Sellers, 'Individual('s) Liability for Collective Sexual Violence', in Karen Knop (ed.), *Gender and Human Rights* (Oxford: Oxford University Press, 2004). There has been considerable debate concerning the shift from gender-specific to gender-neutral definitions of sexual assault in national common law jurisdictions, but less discussion of this issue at an international level.
[129] Karen Engle, 'The Grip of Sexual Violence', in Gina Heathcote and Dianne Otto (eds.), *Rethinking Peacekeeping, Gender Equality and Collective Security* (London: Palgrave Macmillan, 2014), p. 28.

sexual, whereas a bottle that is used to simulate fellatio can involve a sexual crime and not simply an assault. As Ann Cahill points out, 'those objects or orifices not always perceived as sexual *become sexualised* in the context of the assault'.[130] This model of sexual violence defines the criminality of the act in terms of its sexual nature, and its *sexual* nature derives from the sexual meaning given to the interaction of particular acts and bodies. For example, the *Kunarac* definition of the criminal conduct or *actus reus* of 'sexual penetration' identifies parts of the body that carry sexual meaning, such as the penis, vagina, anus, or mouth. However, particular gendered understandings of bodies and sexuality give content to these acts of sexual violence. Sexual violence may refer to violence against men or women, but the 'sexual' nature of the offence relies upon ideas of sexual difference and sexuality, namely, norms of masculinity and femininity that signify bodies and acts as sexual in specific ways.

Far from being gender-neutral, the legal harm of sexual violence is always already gendered. As in many national jurisdictions, international criminal law defines rape in terms of two elements: the act of penetration and the intent of the perpetrator. Penetration becomes the paradigmatic sexual harm, and the perpetrator's intent defines the illegality of the sexual harm. This model has been criticised for its mirroring of masculine models of sexuality,[131] as it defines the harm by the sexual intent of the perpetrator rather than the experience of the victim and understands the sexual act in terms of an active masculine body that penetrates a passive feminine body. It has also been criticised for reiterating heteronormative ideas of female sexuality, which characterise 'rape more as a sexual matter involving damage to a woman's honour than a violent crime' (as is the case under the humanitarian law 'protective framework').[132] That the harm of rape is tied to heteronormative ideas of female sexuality is seen as reinforcing the idea that *victims* 'are forever destroyed by rape, in part due to the shame and stigmatization'.[133]

---

[130] Ann Cahill, *Rethinking Rape* (Ithaca and London: Cornell University Press, 2001), p. 139.
[131] See Anne-Marie Brouwer, *Supranational Criminal Prosecution of Sexual Violence*, (Antwerp, Oxford: Intersentia, 2005), pp. 107 –108, for an overview of these arguments.
[132] Michelle Jarvis and Kate Vigneswaran, 'Challenges to Successful Outcomes in Sexual Violence Cases', in Brammertz and Jarvis (eds.), *Prosecuting Conflict-Related Sexual Violence*, p. 34.
[133] Karen Engle, 'Feminist Legacies', (2016) 110 AJIL Unbound, 220–226, 225.

Moreover, in the Yugoslavian conflict, sexual violence was not gender-neutral but occurred in different forms and prevalence for men and women. Sexual violence that targeted or disproportionately affected women was a feature of this conflict. Nevertheless, the jurisprudence does not legally characterise this sexual violence as gender-based harm. Instead, the legal conceptualisation of sexual violence slips between ideas of biological sex (bodies identified as biologically female and male), gender identity (social norms of femininity and masculinity), and gendered social groups (the organisation of society into groups according to gender). It does not sustain the distinction between harms to sexed bodies, such as the targeting of specific reproductive capacities of women; the gendered shaping of harms, such as the social meaning given to those reproductive capacities; and harms to social groups, such as the targeting of women as civilians. Where the jurisprudence does engage with sexual violence as a gender-based harm, it does so through the gender-neutral model of formal equality. This characterises sexual violence as a form of discrimination, understood as the unequal treatment of persons, rather than violence that reproduces gender hierarchies. This position is clearly stated in *Kvočka*, which held that the rape of women was discriminatory because 'Radic did not rape any of the male non-Serb detainees'.[134] On this logic, such sexual violence would not be discriminatory if the accused raped both 'non-Serb' men and women. Ultimately, sexual violence is not legally characterised as a gender-based crime in terms of the concept of the harm of sexual violence or the definition of these offences. Whether and how sexual violence is a gender-based or gender-neutral crime remains unclear at a conceptual and legal level.

2.5.3 Sexual or Violent Crime?

Connected to the problem of the 'gender' of sexual violence is the question of whether it is a sexual or violent crime. Because rape is seen as the archetypal crime of *sex* against women, this gives rise to 'misconceptions about sexual violence that can impede accountability' for gender-based sexual violence against women, such as:

---

[134] *Kvočka et al.*, Trial Judgement, para. 560. For a fuller discussion of this problem, see Kirsten Campbell and Gorana Mlinarević, 'A Feminist Critique of Approaches to International Criminal Justice in the Age of Identity Politics', in Valerie Oosterveld, Indira Rosenthal et al. (eds.) *Gender and International Criminal Law* (Oxford: Oxford University Press, 2022).

discounting the seriousness of sexual violence, assuming that it is necessarily an 'opportunistic' and 'personally motivated crime', rather than something connected to a broader pattern of violent conduct, and disregarding sexual violence unless it is perceived to be part of large scale, systematic and/or committed pursuant to orders.[135]

This is because these crimes against women are seen as sexual rather than violent crimes. In contrast, sexual violence against men was characterised as a serious physical assault (typically legally characterised as torture), rather than being characterised as a sexual crime (such as rape).[136] Moreover, in the ICTY cases, male sexual violence did not typically involve physical perpetrators themselves sexually penetrating male victims but involved the use of objects or forcing others to commit sexual acts upon each other.[137] As such, male sexual violence was more readily seen as a violent crime connected to the conflict, and not as a 'sexual' crime as such. It thereby becomes visible as form of political and military violence, clearly connected to the forms of organised violence prohibited under international law.

Jarvis refers to the 'sexual' and 'violence' components of these offences in her important discussion of the legal characterisation of the harm of sexual violence.[138] This dual model reflects the long-standing debate in feminist literature concerning whether rape is a crime of violence or of sex and, accordingly, whether the harm arises from its coercive or sexual nature.[139] On the one hand, conflict-related sexual violence is argued to be a sexual crime because it attacks sexual identity and sexuality, in terms of both the harm that the perpetrator intends to inflict and the experience of the harm by the victim.[140] On the other hand, conflict-related sexual violence is argued to be a violent crime because it involves aggression and

---

[135] Jarvis and Vigneswaran, 'Challenges to Successful Outcomes in Sexual Violence Cases', p. 34.
[136] Ibid., pp. 41–42.
[137] See Kirsten Campbell, 'The Gender of Transitional Justice', (2007) 1(3) Int J Transitional Justice 413–432, 428, and Patricia Viseur Sellers, and Leo Nwoye, 'Conflict-Related Male Sexual Violence and the International Criminal Jurisprudence', in Marysia Zalewski, Paula Drumond, et al. (eds) *Sexual Violence against Men in Global Politics* (New York: Routledge, 2018).
[138] Michelle Jarvis, 'Overview: The Challenge of Accountability for Conflict-Related Sexual Violence Crimes', in Brammertz and Jarvis (eds.), *Prosecuting Conflict-Related Sexual Violence*, p. 13.
[139] For an overview of these debates, see Cahill, *Rethinking Rape*.
[140] For example, Fionnuala Ni Aoláin 'Rethinking the Concept of Harm and Legal Categorizations of Sexual Violence during War', (2000) 1(2) Theo Inq L, 307–340.

force.[141] A third approach brings the sexual and violent components of the crime together in the idea that sexual violence is a 'crime of inequality, whether of physical or other force, status, or relation'.[142] The characterisation of sexual violence as a sexual or violent crime remains unresolved in the jurisprudence and theory.

2.5.4 Connection to Illegal International Violence?

The question of the violent nature of sexual violence raises the further challenge of how to characterise this harm in relation to the international element of the offence, that is, the violence that is prohibited under international law. If it is argued that the prohibited harm is the *violence* of sexual violence, there is nevertheless a further component to the 'violence' that informs the concept of the international crime. This is the 'international' violence of armed conflict, an attack on a civilian population, or the intent to destroy a protected group that characterises this 'harm' at the international level.

If the object of criminal proscription is internationally illegal violence, then this raises the question of how sexual violence is conceptualised as a form of that violence. From the very first 'surfacing of gender' in the criminalisation of sexual violence, feminists have pointed to the problem that the 'line between war and "peace" is not so sharp'.[143] As Copelon argued, if we recognise the atrocity of rape in war, then we must also recognise the atrocity of rape in peace, in terms of its injury to both individuals and women as a group. Moreover, if international criminal law is understood to pacify violence within and between states, then the 'unregulated male violence' of sexual violence in all states also challenges this idea of 'regulated state violence'.[144] Finally, feminists have long drawn attention to where the line between war and peace is drawn in the substantive criminalisation of sexual violence. They point to how geopolitical orders shape what comes to be seen as the 'protected interest' of international society and how it expresses the hegemonic interests of

---

[141] For example, Susan Brownmiller, *Against Our Will: Men, Women and Rape*, (New York: Fawcett Columbine, 1975).
[142] Catherine MacKinnon, 'Defining Rape Internationally', (2005) 44(3) Colum J Transnat'l L, 940–958, 941.
[143] Copelon, 'Surfacing Gender'.
[144] Marie Mies, *Patriarchy and Accumulation on a World Scale* (London: Zed Books, 1999), p. 27.

the great powers.¹⁴⁵ Sexual violence as a gender-based harm clearly reveals what Stephen Ratner calls a 'schizophrenia' of international criminal law, namely, that it rests on 'a broad distinction between criminality for atrocities in wartime and those in peacetime'.¹⁴⁶

The recent emergence of the term 'conflict-related sexual violence' in international policy and soft law instruments is indicative of this problem of conceptualising sexual violence as a form of internationally illegal violence. It is not technically accurate to describe 'conflict-related sexual violence' as an international crime, because legally the conduct does not require a connection to conflict to be criminalised. We might more precisely say that sexual violence is criminalised where it is connected to the collective violence of armed conflict, attacks on civilian populations, or intent to destroy protected groups. However, this characterisation raises two key conceptual and practical issues. The first issue is the conceptualisation of sexual violence itself as an internationally illegal violence. On the one hand, the context of collective violence can be considered to give individual acts of sexual violence their 'harmful' quality as an international crime. On the other hand, sexual violence as an international crime itself can be considered to consist of coercive collective acts and to be harmful because of its coercive and collective nature. A practical example of this problem can be seen in whether sexual violence is 'charged under the umbrella of more general provisions, such as persecution as a crime against humanity, or whether it should be the subject of stand-alone charges, such as rape as a crime against humanity'.¹⁴⁷ These 'umbrella' charges were used in the ICTY to link sexual violence crimes to senior leaders, by presenting it as part of a 'campaign of crimes, such as genocidal or persecutory strategy'. However, as Jarvis and Vigneswaran note, the specific intent requirements of these crimes (that is, genocidal or persecutory intent) are more onerous than sexual violence crimes and 'could also reduce the prominence afforded to the crimes and obscure their gendered nature'.¹⁴⁸ This issue arises because the relationship between the criminalisation of individual acts of sexual

---

[145] See, for example, Vasuki Nesiah, 'Gender and Forms of Conflict', in Fionnuala Ní Aoláin, Naomi Cahn et al. (eds.), *The Oxford Handbook on Gender and Conflict* (Oxford University Press, 2018).
[146] Steven Ratner, 'The Schizophrenias of International Criminal Law', (1988) 33(2) Tex Int'l LJ, 237–256, 238.
[147] Jarvis and Vigneswaran, 'Challenges to Successful Outcomes in Sexual Violence Cases', p. 50.
[148] Ibid., p. 59.

violence and the criminalisation of their 'international' elements is unclear.

The second problem is the difficulty of legally characterising the connection between the sexual and violent components of the individual act of sexual violence and the collective violence in which they occur. This difficulty is due to the integral conceptual connection between the violence against the person and the violence against international society in the models of harm in international crimes, which conflates these components. If the legal category of international crimes 'names and defines the particular offences', it does not do so in the case of sexual violence. As Hilmi Zawati argues, the 'abstractedness and lack of accurate description of gender-based crimes ... lead to inconsistent verdicts and punishments, and constitute a barrier to justice'.[149] It gives rise to the practical problem of 'fair labelling', namely, that the nature and gravity of the crime need to be presented to society in order to capture the wrongfulness of the conduct and culpability for it.[150] The problem of fair labelling arises because of these conceptual issues, which result in the distinct grounds of the wrongfulness and culpability of each sexual offence remaining unsettled and contentious.

2.6 The Conceptual Contradictions of the Legal Concept of the International Crime

The development of sexual violence as a crime under public international law shows how this crime expresses the conceptions of the injured person and the 'injured public interest' of 'international society' that develop in the new legal category of the international crime. The 'surfacing' of sexual violence has been crucial in establishing that it is an international crime that injures persons and international society. However, it also reveals a set of unresolved doctrinal and conceptual tensions in these grounds of criminalisation. The first is the tension between the idea of the 'international society' as a society of states, in which the protected interest is the mutual interests of states, and as human society, in which the protected interest is the universal community of all humanity. The second is the tension between universal value, held by all human persons, and culturally specific value, held by particular societies. The third is the

---

[149] *Fair Labelling and the Dilemma of Prosecuting Gender-Based Crimes at the International Criminal Tribunals* (Oxford University Press, 2015), p. 3.
[150] Ibid., pp. 12–13.

tension between the formal equality models of gender-neutral harms, in which all persons are equal, and the substantive inequality models of gender-based harms, in which gendered social relations are unequal. Finally, there remains the problem of whether international criminal law criminalises harm to the person or to international society, as well as whether it is an individual or collective violence. Ultimately, these problems reveal the profound contradictions in the concept of the international crime itself.

3

The International Legal Subject

[C]riminal prosecution is targeting exactly the human dimension of each criminal offence – the perpetrators and the victims.[1]

Carla del Ponte, Prosecutor, ICTY

In the legal form of international criminal law, individuals appear as legal subjects in the international legal order. However, from the ICTY's establishment, the category of legal person has been a matter of considerable doctrinal and scholarly dispute. How, then, should we understand the legal subject as a fundamental category of the legal form of international criminal law? What are the types of legal persons that international criminal law constructs, and what duties and rights does it attribute to them? And how does this category of the legal person construct individuals as subjects with particular characteristics and relations to others?

3.1 The Legal Subject of International Criminal Law

3.1.1 *The Category of the Legal Person in International Criminal Law*

The concept of legal personhood in international law defines individuals and entities as possessors of international rights and duties. It remains a principle of international law that the state is the primary subject of the international legal order, insofar as it possesses full legal personality.[2] However, as Marco Sassoli points out, 'international criminal law, a branch piercing the corporate veil of the state, is directly addressed to individuals'.[3] International law 'thereby replaces its traditional subject,

---

[1] Chief Prosecutor Carla Del Ponte, Address, Conference, 'Establishing the Truth about War Crimes and Conflicts', Zagreb, Croatia, 8 and 9 February 2007.
[2] Ian Brownlie, *Principles of Public International Law* (Oxford: Oxford University Press, 2003), p. 58.
[3] 'Taking Armed Groups Seriously' (2010) 1(1) IHLS, 5-51, 9.

the State, with a non-traditional subject, the individual'.[4] In the legal form of international criminal law, the individual functions as the legal subject, rather than the state. That international criminal law attributes rights and duties to the individual, and not the state, distinguishes it from other branches of international law.

The legal subject can therefore be described as the second fundamental category of international criminal law, which constructs individuals as legal subjects who possess rights and duties. As Pashukanis describes, the individual appears in criminal law as a formal legal subject, abstracted from their concrete social relations.[5] Accordingly, this formal legal subject of rights and duties should not be 'mistaken for the real natural being'.[6] Rather, it is 'an artificial entity which serves as the logical support of legal relations ... a constructed *subjectus*, a legal creation or fiction'.[7] However, as Naffine describes, 'all branches of law have their version of a person ... and this person is given quite a particular character'. If the legal person is the formal bearer of rights and duties, nevertheless those rights and duties construct a particular kind of subject 'who is deemed to act in certain ways, to wield certain rights, and to assume certain responsibilities'.[8] Accordingly, international law represents the individual as a legal subject by attributing to them particular rights and duties, and particular characteristics and qualities. The construction of the legal subject is not therefore merely 'ideological' but is made in the concrete legal rules, institutions, and practices of international criminal law.

The legal subject should not be understood as a single isolated individual but is always constituted in relation to other legal subjects in international criminal law. As Pashukanis describes it: 'every legal relation is a relation between subjects'.[9] Duties and rights represent relations between persons as *legal*. The rights and duties of the subject are legal relationships, which constitute the relationship between persons in juridical terms. In this way, the legal form constructs the individual as a legal person on the international plane by recognising certain persons as legal subjects and attributing to them specific legal relationships of rights and duties to other legal subjects. These relationships of rights and

---

[4] Mark Drumbl, 'Collective Violence and Individual Punishment', (2005) 99(2) NWULR, 539–610, 570.
[5] Evgeny Pashukanis, *Law and Marxism* (London: Ink Links, 1978), p. 167.
[6] Ngaire Naffine, *Law's Meaning of Life* (Oxford: Hart Publishing, 2009), p. 1.
[7] Costas Douzinas, *The End of Human Rights* (Oxford: Hart Publishing, 2000), pp. 233–234.
[8] Ngaire Naffine and Rosemary Owens, 'Sexing Law', in Ngaire Naffine and Rosemary Owens (eds.), *Sexing the Subject of Law* (Sydney: Sweet and Maxwell, 1997), p. 7.
[9] Pashukanis, *Law and Marxism*, p. 109.

duties are the 'juridical relation' of the legal form, which constructs legal subjects and the legal relationship between them.

The individual thereby appears in international criminal law as a legal subject existing in legal relations. These legal relations consist of 'a bundle of rights, obligations, and competences'.[10] This bundle constitutes individuals as legal subjects of different kinds on the international plane. When natural persons come to appear as legal persons attributed with rights and duties on the international plane, they do so as victims attributed with protective entitlements or perpetrators attributed with criminal responsibility.[11] For example, the doctrine of individual criminal responsibility constructs relationships of legal obligation and rights between perpetrator and victim, in which the victim possesses legal entitlements (such as the right not to be subject to torture) while the perpetrator bears legal duties (such as compliance with international rules prohibiting torture). International criminal law thereby constitutes bundles of legal relationships between victims and perpetrators as they appear on the international plane.

If we take gender 'as a relevant category of victimisation' and perpetration,[12] then sexual violence jurisprudence reveals the construction of the legal subject and relations in international criminal law. Reinscribing sexual violence as a gender-based crime makes visible how international criminal law constructs persons as legal subjects and attributes to them specific legal relationships of rights and duties to other persons. By analysing how international criminal law attributes actions, rights, and responsibilities to individuals as victims and perpetrators of international crimes of sexual violence, it becomes possible to see how its legal form constitutes the person and society in the international legal order.

3.2 The Legal Subject of Criminal Responsibility: Perpetrators as Legal Subjects

3.2.1 Individual and Collective Criminal Responsibility

The doctrine of individual criminal responsibility defines the category of the legal person of international criminal law and structures the individual perpetrator as a legal subject. While international law recognises state

---

[10] Jan Klabbers, 'The Concept of Legal Personality', (2005) 11 Ius Gentium 35–66, 47.
[11] The term 'rights' describes the bundles of entitlements, obligations, and substantive rights owed to victims (which are not only natural persons but may also be 'things', such as protected cultural monuments). It does not imply that these 'rights' give rise to legally enforceable rights of victims under international criminal law (even if they may do so under other legal regimes).
[12] Rhonda Copelon, 'Surfacing Gender', (1994) 5(2) Hastings Women's LJ, 243–266, 262.

responsibility for internationally wrongful acts, it does not characterise this as criminal responsibility.[13] It does not characterise the state as a 'perpetrator' of conflict-related sexual violence. Rather, state responsibility for internationally wrongful acts is similar to corporate civil liability, in which a legal entity is held liable for wrongful acts.[14] International criminal responsibility attaches to individuals, not states.

The principle of individual criminal responsibility was established by the Charter of the International Military Tribunal at Nuremberg following World War Two and is considered a key step in the development of international criminal law.[15] It marked a move away from both older notions of collective responsibility involving the punishment of peoples or nations and the then contemporary idea that only the state could be considered responsible for violations of international law.[16] However, the Nuremberg Tribunal did establish individual criminal liability for collective criminality, in terms of both command responsibility and the 'system criminality' of the organisation of the Nazi State.[17] It characterised this collective criminality as 'cooperation for criminal purposes', namely, a common plan or conspiracy in the case of the major war criminals, or as a group or organisation, such as the SS or the Leadership Corps of the Nazi Party, constituting a criminal organisation.[18] The subsequent trials of 'second rank' major war criminals prosecuted individuals as members of groups connected to the political and economic order of the state, such as industrialists or the judiciary, as well as criminal organisations.[19] Sexual

---

[13] See *Blaškić*, ICTY-95-14-AR108bis-A, Judgment on the Request of the Republic of Croatia for Review of the Decision of Trial Chamber II of 18 July 1997, 29 October 1997, and *Application of the Convention on the Prevention and Punishment of the Crime of Genocide (Bosnia and Herzegovina v. Serbia and Montenegro)*, Judgement, ICJ, 27 February 2007.

[14] Frédéric Mégret, 'The Subjects of International Criminal Law', in Philipp Kastner (ed.), *International Criminal Law in Context* (London and New York: Routledge, 2017).

[15] Charter of the International Military Tribunal, Annexed to the London Agreement for the Prosecution and Punishment of Major War Criminals of the European Axis, and Establishing the Charter of the International Military Tribunal, August 8, 1945, 82 U.N.T.S. 27 (IMT Charter).

[16] Nuremberg Judgment, *France and ors v Göring (Hermann) and ors*, Judgment and Sentence, (1947) 41(1) AJIL 172, 220–221 (Nuremberg Judgment).

[17] Bert Röling, 'The Significance of the Laws of War', in Antonio Cassese (ed.), *Current Problems of International Law* (Milan: Dott A. Giuffre, 1975), p. 138.

[18] Nuremberg Judgment.

[19] *Trials of the War Criminals before the Nuremberg Military Tribunals under Council Control Law No 10*, Volume I–XIV, (Washington, D.C.: U.S. G.P.O. 1949-1953). Subsequent trials of 'second rank' war criminals were not undertaken in Japan.

violence was prosecuted as an integral evidential element of these collective criminal activities but not charged or judicially considered as such.

Drawing upon the Nuremberg Tribunal, the ICTY clearly established individual criminal responsibility as the foundation of the legal subject in international criminal law. The ICTY Statute establishes that persons are individually responsible for international crimes (Art. 7) and specifies that only 'natural persons' are within the Tribunal's competence *ratione personae* (personal jurisdiction) (Art. 6). The legal basis for the establishment of the Tribunal explicitly excluded 'juridical persons', such as associations or organisations from the Tribunal's *ratione personae*, and rejected the Nuremberg notion of collective criminal responsibility based on group membership.[20] The ICTY did follow the Nuremberg rejection of collective responsibility in the broader sense of explicitly refusing ideas of the collective guilt and punishment of persons and nations.[21] In the contemporary category of the legal subject, criminal responsibility is individual, and there is a clear doctrinal and normative rejection of collective criminal responsibility.

The model of international criminal responsibility assumes that the legal subject is an individual to whom international criminal law attributes both obligations to obey international legal norms and criminal responsibility for their breach. In this model, the 'foundation of criminal responsibility is the principle of personal culpability'.[22] The concept of personal culpability draws upon two related notions: that a person cannot be held criminally liable for acts (1) for which they did not have the requisite state of intention or (2) that are perpetrated by other persons.[23] It requires that the perpetrator intends to commit the international crime and is only liable for their participation in that crime.

This model of personal culpability can be clearly seen in the first case to consider charges of rape, *The Prosecutor* v. *Furundžija*. Anto Furundžija was charged with torture and outrages upon personal dignity, including rape, as war crimes. The charges arose from the rape of Witness A, by another soldier, Accused B, during her interrogation by

---

[20] Report of the Secretary-General pursuant to paragraph 2 of resolution 808 of the Security Council, 3 May 1993, S/25704.
[21] Report of the ICTY, UN Doc. S/1994/1007, para. 16.
[22] *Tadić*, ICTY-94-1-A, Judgement, 15 July 1999, para. 186 (*Tadić* Appeals Judgement).
[23] Antonio Cassese, *International Criminal Law* (Oxford: Oxford University Press, 2003), p. 136.

Furundžija.[24] Furundžija was Accused B's commanding officer. His responsibility was characterised as being a co-perpetrator of torture, but he was not considered to be a co-perpetrator of rape.[25] Commentators have noted this apparently confusing characterisation of personal culpability.[26] However, principal liability for rape is based upon direct participation in the offence, such that the perpetrator physically penetrates the victim (that is, commits the criminal act), knowing the victim did not consent (that is, possesses the requisite state of intention). Furundžija was not considered to have participated in the rape but to have aided and abetted it (a form of secondary liability). Following the model of personal culpability, the Trial Chamber held Furundžija only responsible for actions for which he had the requisite intent and in which he participated, namely, torture and the aiding and abetting of rape.

While the individual legal subject is the foundation of international criminal responsibility, modes of collective liability also give rise to personal culpability under international criminal law. These forms of liability do not impose responsibility on the basis of the direct and physical perpetration of the crime by the individual. Instead, individual criminal responsibility arises from the liability for collective criminality. This 'collective liability' may arise from participation of the perpetrator in the collective commission of the crime (co-perpetration) or culpable omission in relation to the criminal acts of others (command responsibility). Following the approach at Nuremberg, the ICTY Statute recognised these different forms of collective liability (Art. 7). In subsequent jurisprudence, the ICTY also developed the doctrine of 'joint criminal enterprise' (JCE), which built upon the Nuremberg concept of a common criminal purpose.[27] JCE consists of different forms of collective participation in a common criminal purpose and was explicitly developed to address the collective nature of international criminality.[28] Typically of

---

[24] See *Furundžija*, ICTY-95-17/1-T, Judgement, 10 December 1998. Furundžija was tried for his individual responsibility for these crimes rather than under the principle of 'command responsibility'.

[25] Ibid., paras. 257, 273.

[26] See, for example, Gideon Boas, James Bischoff, et al., *International Criminal Law Practitioner Library* (Cambridge: Cambridge University Press, 2007), Volume 1, p. 13.

[27] *Tadić* Appeals Judgement, para. 195.

[28] Ibid., para. 190–193. While there is considerable debate concerning JCE, the following discussion is equally pertinent to all forms of collective liability: See Susana SàCouto, Leila Nadya Sadat et al., 'Collective Criminality and Sexual Violence', (2020) 33(1) LJIL, 207–241.

international criminal law, ICTY cases involved multiple crimes committed by a plurality of perpetrators in complex military and civilian organisations, and who did not necessarily directly perpetrate the crime. So, for example, all these 'collective' modes of liability, with the exception of instigation, have been charged in ICTY sexual violence cases, with JCE operating as a 'pivotal mode' of liability.[29]

International criminal law thereby imposes duties and liabilities upon individuals as members of collectives, in the sense of groups of persons acting collectively. These duties and liabilities construct the perpetrator not only as an individual but also as a member of a collectivity. The legal subject does not only consist of the individual 'atomistic' physical perpetrator of the crime. Rather, it also consists of groups, in that international criminal law imputes liability for the actions of the perpetrator within that group. The perpetrator as legal subject is therefore also a collective entity, insofar as its duties and liabilities are collective and arise from collective criminality. As the ICTY noted in the *Tadić* Appeal Judgement: 'most of the time these crimes do not result from the criminal propensity of single individuals but constitute manifestations of collective criminality'.[30]

The model of collective criminality is integral to international criminal law, as can be seen in the sexual violence cases before the ICTY. This model attributes individual criminal responsibility for sexual violence not only to the direct physical perpetrator but also to the accused participating in the collective criminality of which sexual violence is an integral part. These 'collective' modes of liability have been crucial for contextualising sexual violence within the broader 'international elements' of war crimes, genocide, or crimes against humanity and linking its commission to senior officials in ICTY cases.[31] For example, the leading case of *Prosecutor* v. *Stakić* established that sexual violence could be characterised as an integral element of a common criminal purpose. Stakić was not a physical perpetrator of rape but was found to be responsible for rape committed by direct perpetrators. This was due to

---

[29] Barbara Goy, Michelle Jarvis et al., 'Contextualising Sexual Violence and Linking It to Senior Officials', in Serge Brammertz and Michelle Jarvis (eds.), *Prosecuting Conflict-Related Sexual Violence at the ICTY* (Oxford: Oxford University Press, 2016), p. 221 ff.
[30] *Tadić* Appeals Judgement, para. 191.
[31] Goy, Jarvis et al., 'Contextualising Sexual Violence and Linking It to Senior Officials', p. 221 ff.

his participation in the common criminal purpose of persecution as a crime against humanity, which included the underlying persecutory acts of rape.[32] Accordingly, he was found to have primary liability as a direct participant in the JCE.

This characterisation of criminal responsibility rests on three concepts of 'collectivity'. The first concept is collective action, insofar as these crimes are forms of collective violence that involve collective acts, organisation, or co-ordination. The second concept is collective entities, which involve groups, organisations, or economic, military, or political systems. The third concept concerns collective criminality, insofar as war crimes, genocide, and crimes against humanity involve the existence of an armed conflict, genocidal intent, or an attack on a civilian population. The collective duties and liabilities of international criminal law construct a collective legal subject, which attributes collective action to the legal subject and characterises it as a collective entity undertaking collective criminality.

3.2.2 The Perpetrator as Legal Subject and Sexual Violence

The model of the perpetrator as legal person draws upon the longstanding Western legal tradition of the '"abstract, juridical individual"... an autonomous, moral agent whose abstract will provides the basis for individual responsibility'.[33] In this modern model of the legal subject, the individual appears as a formal legal subject without social or sexual differentiation, thereby removing 'natural persons' from their concrete social conditions and corporeal existence. It assumes an individual whose criminal intent derives from their capacity to exercise control over a bounded body and self.[34] In the case of sexual violence, this responsibility derives from the capacity of persons to exercise will, that is, control, over the sexual body and self. As Alan Norrie explains, the idea of the free moral agent ties together the legal and moral liability of the individual perpetrator.[35]

---

[32] *Stakić*, ICTY-97-24-T, Judgement, 31 July 2003, para. 882.
[33] Alan Norrie, *Punishment, Responsibility, and Justice* (Oxford: Oxford University Press, 2000), p. 45.
[34] Ngaire Naffine, 'The Body Bag', in Ngaire Naffine and Rosemary Owens (eds.), *Sexing the Subject of Law*, p. 85.
[35] Norrie, *Punishment, Responsibility, and Justice*, p. 3.

The legal form of international criminal law thereby constructs perpetrators as legal subjects by postulating an abstract concept of the individual that attributes certain capacities to them, namely, that they are free subjects. As Pashukanis describes, '[i]n modern criminal law, the concept of strict personal liability corresponds to the radical individualism of bourgeois society'.[36] It constructs legal persons as 'isolated egoistic subjects, the bearers of autonomous private interests'.[37] Perpetrators exist as atomistic responsible agents, who have the freedom to choose to 'pay the price' of their punishment. In this transactional logic, 'the offender answers for his offence with a portion of his freedom corresponding to the gravity of his action', such that there is the equivalent exchange between retribution and deprivation of the freedom that the responsible agent possesses.[38] Their punishment takes 'the form of equivalent exchange, [that is] exchange according to values'.[39] These values (of exchange) emerge with modern European capitalist economic relations and bourgeois state political forms.[40]

However, at the international level, the legal subject is not only individual but is also collective. International criminal law constructs perpetrators as legal subjects in terms of their relations to other perpetrators. It is on this basis that individual criminal responsibility for sexual violence is attributed to those participating in the collective criminality of which sexual violence is an integral part, and not only to the direct physical perpetrator. The individual legal subject is in fact contingent upon the construction of collective legal subjects. This is because the collective violence of international crime also requires a collective to commit it. International criminal law constructs collective legal subjects, attributed with the capacity for the collective commission of physical and symbolic violence. The legal form constructs the collective nature of these groups through abstract legal duties and obligations, and members of these groups as legal subjects where they engage in the collective violence that 'international society' prohibits.

Moreover, international criminal law constructs the perpetrator as a legal subject existing in legal relations to all humanity, and, accordingly,

---

[36] Pashukanis, *Law and Marxism*, p. 178.
[37] Ibid., p. 188.
[38] Ibid., p. 179.
[39] Ibid., p. 170.
[40] Ibid., pp. 180–181.

as a member of global human society. Jacques Lacan reminds us that 'responsibility – that is, punishment – is an essential characteristic of the idea of the Human that prevails in a given society'.[41] This is because the punishment that is given to the perpetrator depends upon a notion of responsibility, which, in turn, attributes that person with particular 'human' qualities. In international criminal law, the punishment of the perpetrator is based upon the idea of 'Humanity' prevailing in 'global human society' rather than the idea of the 'Human' prevailing in any given 'national' society. It constructs the perpetrator as breaching the fundamental obligations owed to the global society of all humanity, in that the actions for which they are responsible repudiate protected interests of all humans (expressed as the universal laws and values of international criminal law). In doing so, it assumes the individualised 'universal human personhood' that transcends place and time, which Nicola Lacey describes as the foundation of modern European ideas of criminal responsibility.[42] As such, it reflects an 'essentially [Western] modern understanding of human being'.[43] At the same time, it also recognises perpetrators as particular collective subjects, which exist in historically and culturally specific groups and societies. International criminal responsibility holds these ideas together by condemning the individual *actions* of the perpetrator as 'inhuman', rather than characterising the perpetrator as outside global 'humanity' or their society as being outside the global social order.

By focusing upon the punishment of criminal actions (rather than persons or societies), the legal form constructs the perpetrator as human and their particular society as within global human society. It understands the legal subject through a 'post-Westphalian frame' rather than the 'state-territorial principle'.[44] In effect, individual and collective subjects displace the state in the legal form of international criminal law. However, their frame is no longer the international relations of states but of global social relations.

---

[41] Jacques Lacan, 'A Theoretical Introduction to the Functions of Psychoanalysis in Criminology', (1996) 1(2) Journal for the Psychoanalysis of Culture and Society, 13–26, 19.
[42] Nicola Lacey, *In Search of Criminal Responsibility* (Oxford: Oxford University Press, 2016), p. 5.
[43] Ibid, p. 6.
[44] Nancy Fraser, *Fortunes of Feminism* (Verso, London, 2013), pp. 201–202.

3.2.3 Conceptual Problems in Individual and Collective Criminality of Sexual Violence

3.2.3.1 The Problem of Individual and Collective Liability

As Gerry Simpson describes, a fundamental debate in international criminal law concerns 'the tension between individual guilt and collective responsibility'.[45] This debate counterposes individual and collective criminality and assumes that the problem of assigning individual and collective liability derives from the tension between them. However, sexual violence cases, which have been central to the doctrinal development of forms of collective criminal liability,[46] reveal that the problem lies in concepts of individual and collective legal relations that construct the legal subject itself.

In these cases, conflict-related sexual violence is conceptualised as an individual criminal act committed by an individual perpetrator, with principal liability arising from the physical perpetration of the criminal act. This model of liability can be seen in the earlier discussion of the *Furundžija* case, which is typical of such early ICTY cases. As Laurel Baig and Michelle Jarvis et al. describe, these sexual violence cases 'proved to be the least complicated and the most successful'. However, as the focus of prosecutions moved to leadership cases, 'the difficulty of proving the cases increased'.[47] In the leadership cases, the challenges of connecting sexual violence to the international 'contextual' elements of crimes, such as the attack on a civilian population or an armed conflict, and of linking it to senior officials became more apparent.[48] These challenges emerge because these cases require understanding sexual violence as a collective crime, that is, a crime of many perpetrators and victims occurring in the context of collective violence.

Where sexual violence is successfully characterised as a collective rather than individual crime in leadership cases, it is seen as the 'natural and foreseeable consequence' of collective violence rather than as the

---

[45] Gerry Simpson, *Law, War, and Crime* (Cambridge and Malden: Polity, 2007), p. 71. For an important sociological discussion of this issue, see David Hirsh, *Law against Genocide* (London: Glasshouse Press, 2003).
[46] See SàCouto, Sadat et al., 'Collective Criminality and Sexual Violence', 212–218.
[47] Baig, Jarvis et al., 'Contextualising Sexual Violence: Selection of Crimes', in Brammertz and Jarvis (eds.), *Prosecuting Conflict-Related Sexual Violence*, p. 174.
[48] See, for example, *Đorđević*, ICTY-05-87; *Šainović et al.* ICTY-05-87; *Prlić et al.* ICTY-04-74.

object or aim of that violence.⁴⁹ So, for example the criminal object of the JCE is characterised as persecution, rather than as rape, as it was in *Stakić*. This characterisation understands sexual violence as individual acts committed with other crimes in the collective criminal conduct rather than as a form of collective violence itself. Unless sexual violence is seen as the explicit aim or object of that violence, namely, that it is planned or ordered, the collective nature of sexual violence itself becomes invisible. Given this, it is unsurprising that cases of planning, ordering, and instigating sexual violence were not brought before the ICTY, and 'the notion of "systematic" sexual violence being perpetuated pursuant to a "formal" policy, as suggested by the Commission of Experts, has not emerged as consistently through the judgements as might have been expected'.⁵⁰

These prosecutorial challenges in leadership cases are attributable to what Michelle Jarvis and Kate Vigneswaran call the 'misconceptions' of sexual violence as an 'individualised' crime. The first misconception is that sexual violence is a personal or opportunistic crime and hence is an isolated event not connected to the conflict. The second misconception is that sexual violence can only be prosecuted if it is 'systematic/widespread or committed pursuant to orders', as it is then connected to conflict.⁵¹ This understanding of sexual violence as an individual crime leads to jurisprudential debates in this area concerning whether such crimes are 'opportunistic' or 'systematic', reflect sexual motive or criminal intent, and whether the higher level perpetrator has 'participated' in sexual violence committed by others.

These jurisprudential debates reveal the problem of conceptualising sexual violence as a crime of collective participation. For example, the so-called individual 'opportunistic' rape occurs in the context of collective violence against targeted ethnic groups and with the expectation of impunity for this reason.⁵² However, 'opportunistic' rape is not simply the act of an individual. Rather, it has collective features, since it is

---

⁴⁹ *Stakić*, ICTY-97-24-A, Judgement, 22 March 2006, para. 65.
⁵⁰ Saeeda Verrall, 'The Picture of Sexual Violence in the Former Yugoslavia Conflicts as Reflected in ICTY Judgements', in Brammertz and Jarvis (eds.), *Prosecuting Conflict-Related Sexual Violence*, pp. 329–331.
⁵¹ Michelle Jarvis and Kate Vigneswaran, 'Challenges to Successful Outcomes in Sexual Violence Cases', in Brammertz and Jarvis (eds.), *Prosecuting Conflict-Related Sexual Violence*, pp. 37–40.
⁵² See Gabi Mischkowski and Gorana Mlinarević, *And That It Does Not Happen to Anyone Anywhere in the World* (Cologne: Medica Mondiale, 2009).

framed within the collective meaning given to communal group belonging and to the social meaning given to sexed bodies. It also has collective dynamics; in that it mobilises collective symbolic and physical resources and involves multiple social actors. Finally, it expresses collective social relations, as it draws on and amplifies unequal gender social orders.

The challenges of successfully prosecuting sexual violence reflect not only the misconception of sexual violence as an individualised crime but also the wider legal problem of how international criminal law constructs legal relations between collective perpetrators. This problem is most evident in those ICTY cases that fail to establish links between non-state actors and individual accused, and between individual accused and states, namely, Serbia and Croatia.[53] Conflict-related sexual violence, then, reveals fundamental conceptual problems underlying these collective legal relations. These problems derive from the inherently social and collective features of international criminality, as both Mark Osiel and Mark Drumbl have powerfully argued.[54] I build on their social model of collective criminality to develop a feminist analysis of the problematic concept of collective legal relations.

The first problem concerns the role of the state in collective criminality. Legally addressing state systems as a form of the social organisation of violence is crucial for capturing the most effective form of collectivised violence, namely, the modern state. From a sociological perspective, organised violence is crucial to both the emergence and functioning of the modern state as a 'power container' in the international order.[55] Given this, it is unsurprising that the concept of system criminality, which identifies state structures and systems as integral to the collectivisation of violence, emerges from the prosecution of the Nazi state waging total war.

However, the ICTY sexual violence cases also challenge the idea that the state is a sexually neutral entity. Instead, they show that the organisation of power within the state is gendered. In these cases, the state is highly patriarchal, with men dominating its political and military power

---

[53] See, for example, *Šešelj* ICTY-03-67; *Gotovina* ICTY-06-90, *Perišić* ICTY-84-01; *Stanišić & Simatović* ICTY-03-69.

[54] See Mark Osiel, *Making Sense of Mass Atrocity* (Cambridge: Cambridge University Press, 2009) and Mark Drumbl, *Atrocity, Punishment, and the Law* (Cambridge: Cambridge University Press, 2007).

[55] Anthony Giddens, *The Nation-State and Violence* (Cambridge, Polity Press: 1985), p. 13.

structures. There is only one ICTY case involving charges of sexual violence against a female accused, Biljana Plavšić. Plavšić was not alleged to have been a direct perpetrator but as responsible for these crimes because of her leadership role in the Presidency of Republika Srpska.[56] It has been suggested that the failure to indict other women reflects an assumption that women are only victims rather than agents of conflict.[57] Instead, it reflects the gendered patterns of conflict and power within the Yugoslavian state and war, where (like many other states) women were significantly under-represented in the military and political institutions involved in the conflict and further under-represented in leadership roles such as those held by Plavšić.[58] Accordingly, any account of system criminality must also account for the patriarchal nature of state structures and systems in conflict.

The ICTY sexual violence cases also challenge the idea of *state* system criminality, because conflict-related sexual violence need not involve a state plan or policy. State system criminality understands the state as the single source of sovereign authority exercising the legitimate monopoly of violence in a given territory and assumes that criminal liability is attributable where an order or policy emanates from the state. However, the ICTY cases reveal the interconnected systems that collectivise sexual violence, but which do not necessarily have a single source of unitary coercion and control (that is, a single state apparatus within a state), nor do they exercise force only within state borders (that is, they exercise extra-territorial violence). A similar problem can be seen in the model of superior responsibility as the exercise of centralised authority over subordinate. This model characterises liability for collective sexual violence as arising from an order of that superior (and hence as a public act of warfare) or the reasonable foreseeability of that conduct (and thus as exceptional violence rather than an integral and intended part of warfare). However, as Regina Mühlhäuser points out, permitting sexual violence in war enables commanders to utilise this conduct in their

---

[56] *Plavšić*, ICTY-00-39-T, Sentencing Judgement, 27 February 2003.
[57] Karen Engle, *The Grip of Sexual Violence in Conflict* (Stanford: Stanford University Press, 2020), p. 99.
[58] Olivera Pavlović, 'The Participation of Women in Politics – Analysis of the 2000 Local and General Elections in Bosnia and Herzegovina', 4(3) (2001) South-East Europe Review 125–140. On women's participation in war crimes in the conflict, see Jasenka Ferizović, 'The Case of Female Perpetrators of War Crimes', (2020) 31(2) EJIL, 455–488.

tactical and strategic thinking, even if that permission is not communicated or ordered.[59] This utility can be seen throughout the ICTY cases.

To describe the system criminality of sexual violence requires a model of system violence understood not as Leviathan but as Behemoth – as Franz Neumann describes. In Neumann's model, the state consists of distinctive groups operating together to directly rule through violence (the system of criminality).[60] This alternative model informed the prosecutions of the component organisations and systems of the Nazi regime in the subsequent Nuremberg trials of doctors, industrialists, scientists, and generals under Council Control Law No. 10. The problem remains how to conceptualise collective criminality as interconnected systems enabling the commission of collective violence across and within state territories.

The second, and more fundamental problem, is the conceptualisation of collective criminality as social institutions, systems, or structures. The existing concepts of collective liability do not adequately address how sexual violence is a form of collective violence (that is, a form of collective action, organisation, or co-ordination of violence), how it constitutes collective criminality (as an integral element of an armed conflict, destruction of a protected group, or an attack on a civilian population), or how collective entities commit it (as groups, organisations, or systems). In particular, the concept of the collective legal subject does not address how collective violence is a form of gendered social organisation or how gender shapes these groups, institutions, and state apparatuses. Without including how gender shapes the groups, states, and societies that commit collective violence, it is not possible to describe collective criminality or to accurately characterise legal culpability. To provide an adequate legal account of the collective perpetration of sexual violence requires a description of the gendered organisation of collective violence and the patriarchal societies from which it emerges.

Part of the difficulty of developing such an account lies in the framing of collective criminality through ideas of 'political violence', which refers to 'the commission of violent acts motivated by a desire, conscious or otherwise, to obtain or maintain political power'.[61] *Political* violence is

---

[59] Regina Mühlhäuser, 'You Have to Anticipate What Eludes Calculation', in Kirsten Campbell, Regina Mühlhäuser et al. (eds.), *In Plain Sight* (New Delhi: Zubaan, 2019), p. 25.
[60] Franz Neumann, *Behemoth* (London: Victor Gollancz, 1942).
[61] Caroline Moser, 'The Gendered Continuum of Violence and Conflict', in Caroline Moser and Fiona Clark (eds.), *Victims, Perpetrators or Actors? Gender, Armed Conflict and Political Violence* (New York: Palgrave Macmillan, 2001), pp. 36–37.

seen as collective (not individual), public (not private), and organised (not disorganised). This idea shapes the category of collective criminality through a statist model of 'public' 'mass' armed force, with a central source of (sovereign) power, because political power in the international state system is predicated upon the monopoly of violence in a territory. In effect, it rearticulates the model of the legal subject as the sovereign willing individual at the level of the collective. This understanding of political violence underwrites the 'misconceptions' concerning conflict-related sexual violence. It frames sexual violence against women as an 'individual' sexual act (and not public collective violence) and sexual violence against men as a political (rather than sexual) act, and hence as connected to public collective criminality, as the ICTY sexual violence cases clearly show. One feminist approach to this problem has been to expand the category of public political violence to include the violence against women that is normally regarded as 'private', such as sexual violence. While this shift is important, it still leaves the state framing of the category intact and reproduces the individual-collective conceptual structure of the legal form. Another approach is needed to legally capture the concrete social reality of the international crime of sexual violence, with its inherently collective features, organisational dynamics, and power relations.

3.3 The Subject of Rights: Victims as Legal Persons

3.3.1 Individual and Collective Victims

Unlike the perpetrator, international criminal law does not formally recognise the individual victim of international crimes as a legal person. That is, the victim does not have a formal status as a legal person with enforceable duties and rights. At the ICTR and ICTY, 'proceedings were adversarial in nature, and victims' only function was to give evidence. Their right to obtain protection and support from the Tribunal was only related to that function.'[62] Later developments in international criminal law, such as the ICC, emphasise procedural rights of victims, such as participatory and reparatory rights. However, this does not alter the functional role of victims in international crime law or their incapacity to enforce their substantive rights. In formal terms, prosecutions are not

---

[62] Robert Cryer, Darryl Robinson et al., *An Introduction to International Criminal Law and Procedure* (Cambridge: Cambridge University Press, 2019), p. 445.

brought on behalf of individual victims. Rather, the 'public' prosecutor brings prosecutions to the court on behalf of 'society'.[63] Given this structure, victims need not appear as witnesses before the court, be living persons, or persons at all. In international criminal trials, many victims fall into these categories. Nevertheless, the victim of international crime is clearly central to international criminal law. This importance in part derives from their evidential function (as discussed in the next chapter). However, it also arises because, the 'abstraction of injured public interest rests on the fully real figure of the victim, who participates in the process – personally or through representatives – and who gives this process a living significance', as Pashukanis describes.[64]

That victims have substantive duties owed to them, and possess rights on this basis, has long been recognised in humanitarian law, such as the criminalisation of serious violations of duties owed to protected persons that are *hors de combat* or civilians. With the emergence of post-war human rights regimes protecting the individual, and the development of humanitarian norms that individualise harms against the person, the victim comes to be conceived as a rights-bearing person. As commentators suggest, '[t]he question of the status in international law of individuals is closely bound up with rise in the international protection of human rights'.[65] In this conception of the victim as legal subject, international criminal law seeks to protect the individual and to prohibit violations of their fundamental rights. The procedural rights granted to victims before the ICC can be seen as the most recent development of this model of victims as rights-holders.

This concept of the victim as an individual rights-holder is evident in the leading jurisprudence on sexual violence offences. As described in Chapter 2, the jurisprudence describes these offences as a violation of the victim's right to physical integrity or sexual autonomy and so on. Sexual violence 'undermines the integrity of the personhood of the victim by denying their right of consent over that property which is most personally held: the body'.[66] Where consent to the sexual act is freely given, there is no violation of this right to exercise free will over the use of the body. The model conceives the victim as a legal person possessing the

---

[63] Ibid.
[64] Pashukanis, *Law and Marxism*, p. 177.
[65] Malcolm Shaw, *International Law* (Cambridge: Cambridge University Press, 2003), p. 232.
[66] Anne Cahill, *Rethinking Rape* (Ithaca: Cornell University Press, 2001), p. 170.

right to bodily integrity and sexual autonomy and thereby constructs the victim as an individual subject that possesses rights (whether in positive or negative form).

In this model, individuals hold rights in their own person, and it is these rights that international criminal law seeks to protect. In this respect, the construction of victims as legal subjects appearing on the international plane mirrors the legal individualism typical of liberal national legal systems. The individual victim is bearer of 'autonomous private interests', namely, their right of their ownership of their body, which they can choose to exchange with others through consent (the bodily equivalent of the alienation of property). This model of the victim as legal person draws on the long Western tradition of possessive individualism, which posits the legal person as an individual possessing rights 'over' their bodies and selves.[67]

However, if we examine the construction of the victim as legal subject closely, then a more complex picture of the nature of these rights emerges. While these rights take both a positive and negative form, what characterises these 'rights' is that they are conditional upon the status of the victim. International criminal law does not seek to protect all individuals on the basis of their human rights, in contrast to international human rights regimes. Rather, it identifies particular categories of persons that it seeks to protect. This crucial difference between the protection of certain categories of victims by international criminal law and the protection of the human rights of all persons by international human rights law becomes apparent in the core international crimes of war crimes, genocide, and crimes against humanity.

The rules governing war crimes do not protect the human rights of all persons in all circumstances. Rather, they contingently protect specific classes of persons (civilians, prisoners of war, sick and wounded combatants) in particular circumstances (international or non-international armed conflict) from certain harms (wilful killing, torture or inhumane treatment, and so on), or grant defined entitlements (such as the rights of prisoners of war). Furthermore, the categories of persons that humanitarian law seeks to protect differ according to the combatant or civilian status of the victim and whether the conflict itself is international (between states) or internal (within the state).

In contrast, crimes against humanity aim to protect civilians from being the object of attack. These rules protect civilians as a group of

---

[67] See Ngaire Naffine, 'The Legal Structure of Self-Ownership', (1998) 25(2) JL & Soc'y 193–212.

persons, and protection is given to individuals as members of that civilian population. As the ICTY jurisprudence describes, 'the emphasis is not on the individual victim but rather on the collective, the individual being victimised not because of his individual attributes but rather because of his membership of a targeted civilian population'.[68] That is, the group is protected because of its civilian nature. Crimes against humanity are 'intended to safeguard basic human values by banning atrocities directed against human dignity', and the victims that are protected are civilians.[69] While ICTY jurisprudence draws upon international human rights law to define particular harms to that population (such as persecution), it does not do so for the remaining underlying offences. The criminal nature of the act does not derive from the breach of the rights of the individual. Rather, it derives from the wrongful act against the person *qua* human being, because it violates the principle of humanity that bars attacks upon civilians.

Similarly, the criminalisation of genocide seeks to prevent the physical destruction of national, racial, ethnic, and religious groups. As the ICJ describes, genocide involves 'a denial of the right to existence of entire human groups'.[70] While there is considerable debate concerning the nature – and definition – of the groups that the Genocide Convention seeks to protect, there is little question that 'whereas it is the individuals that constitute the victims of most crimes, the ultimate victim of genocide is the group', which constitutes 'a separate and distinct entity'.[71] The victim of genocide is the group, which is always legally defined.

International criminal law constructs victims as legal subjects in terms of their relations to other persons. The victim as legal subject is not individual but collective. Mahmoud Cherif Bassiouni describes these legal subjects as 'collective victims', 'that category in which the individual victims are targeted because they belong to a certain group or collectivity'.[72] In the case of war crimes, the victim is protected as a member of particular classes of persons, whether combatant, civilian, or *hors de combat*. In the case of crimes against humanity, the victim is protected

---

[68] *Tadić*, ICTY-94-1-T, Judgement, 7 May 1997, para. 644.
[69] *Kupreškić et al.*, ICTY-95-16-T, Judgement, 14 January 2000, para. 547.
[70] Advisory Opinion, Reservations to the Convention on the Prevention and Punishment of the Crime of Genocide, ICJ, 28 May 1951, p. 15.
[71] *Blagojević*, ICTY-02-60-T, Judgement, 17 January 2005, para. 665, 670.
[72] Mahmoud Cherif Bassiouni, 'The Protection of "Collective Victims" in International Law', in Mahmoud Cherif Bassiouni (ed.), *International Protection of Victims* (Siracusa: Association internationale de droit penal, 1988), p. 183.

as a member of a group of persons, the civilian population. In genocide, the group itself is the 'ultimate victim'. International crimes thereby constitute the victim as legal subject not as an individual but as a member of a group, whether that collective is the armed forces, the civilian population, or the national, racial, ethnical, or religious group. The model of the victim as legal subject is collective in nature, and the entitlements of the individual are conditional upon membership of that group of persons.

If international criminal law protects victims as members of collectivities, it nevertheless only protects particular social groups in certain circumstances. It does not seek to protect all persons at all times, or even all victims of collective violence. Rather, it only seeks to prohibit specific harms against specific groups, such as the combatant from war crimes, the civilian population from crimes against humanity, or the national group from genocide. In this way, international crimes constitute particular forms of legal relations. They seek to protect only particular groups, prohibit only certain types of harms, and preserve particular values and interests. These bundles of rights of, and duties to, victims construct the victim as legal subject. In the legal form, the victim as legal subject has three characteristics. The first characteristic is that the victim is the individual subject of rights. The second is those rights and duties are attributed to the victim by virtue of group membership. The third is these rights and duties protect particular groups of victims, such as combatants, civilians, or the groups recognised by the Genocide Convention.

However, the particularity of these rights and duties is not apparent because the victim is attributed with universal 'human' characteristics as a legal subject. If, as Nijman claims, the international legal person 'forms the *cords* between the individual human being and the universal human society', then in international criminal law the legal entitlement and rights of the individual derives from their status as a member of the global class of human beings, 'humanity'.[73] The victim as legal subject is attributed with the qualities of all human persons and as belonging to 'global human society', the collective community of global humanity. Because international criminal law seeks to protect the individual member of 'humanity' in the name of all of humanity, the abstraction

---

[73] Janne Nijman, *The Concept of International Legal Personality* (The Hague: TMC Asser, 2004), p. 473.

of the 'injured public interest' of international society rests on the fully real figure of the individual victim as a member of 'global human society'.

3.3.2 Sexual Violence and the Conceptual Problem of Individual and Collective Victims

Sexual violence as a gender-based harm brings clearly into view the tensions in the concepts of individual and collective victimisation. The tensions in ideas of individual harm, which presume the individual subject of rights, and of collective harm, which presume collective victimisation based upon gender, can be seen most sharply in the doctrinal and conceptual debates concerning 'consent' and 'genocidal rape'.

3.3.2.1 The Problem of the Victim as Individual Legal Subject: Consent or Coercion?

The first set of doctrinal and conceptual debates concern 'consent' as an element of sexual violence offences and turn on the idea of the victim of sexual violence as an individual rights-holder. The doctrinal debates concern the legal concept of the 'consent' of the victim to sexual acts (as discussed in Chapter 2). In terms of the substantive elements of the offence, the doctrinal issue is whether consent should be characterised in terms of coercion (vitiation of consent through force or the coercive circumstances of conflict) or autonomy (non-consent as the violation of physical integrity or sexual autonomy and so on). This doctrinal issue arises from three problems in the concept of the victim as individual rights-holder. The first problem is that international criminal law does not in fact construct the victim as a legal subject possessing individual rights. While international criminal law attributes the victim as legal subject with particular (limited) fundamental rights, it does not thereby recognise the individual victim as a legal person with enforceable positive human rights against the perpetrator, states, or 'international society'. The second problem is that while human rights standards and values inform the development of international criminal norms, these norms establish criminal offences giving rise to criminal sanction for their violation (and not human rights).[74] The third problem is that the nature of right itself remains unsettled, such as whether it protects the right to physical dignity or sexual autonomy.

---

[74] *Kunarac et al.*, ICTY-96-23&23/1-T, Judgement, 22 February 2001, (*Kunarac* Trial Judgement), para. 470.

Feminist scholars opened these legal debates and led conceptual discussions on how to characterise 'consent' in international criminal law. The feminist debates have now solidified around so-called 'coercion' or 'consent' models of sexual violence. As Catherine MacKinnon describes, the non-consent model 'views the crime fundamentally as a deprivation of sexual freedom, a denial of individual self-acting', and the coercion models 'see rape fundamentally as a crime of inequality, whether of physical or other force, status, or relation'.[75] While the jurisprudence draws on both models, they have come to represent two distinct feminist positions.

The first position is exemplified by MacKinnon's work. It contends that consent should not be an element of the international crime of sexual violence, on the grounds that the coercive circumstances of conflict create such conditions of inequality as to vitiate consent.[76] Kiran Grewal critiques this approach for its collective concept of the victim, which reduces 'individual consent to a sexual encounter with a broader question of collective consent to armed attack'. She also highlights how this approach creates the problematic figures of the 'always raped/rapeable woman' or the subjugated 'Third World Woman'.[77]

The second position on consent is exemplified by the work of Karen Engle. It focuses upon the agency of individual women and contends that the coercive model removes their agency by making them 'legally incapable of consenting to sex'.[78] However, this approach rests upon an individualistic model of the legal subject, in that it presumes an individual asserting sexual agency through consent to sex with another individual. So, for example, Engle inaccurately ascribes freedom of movement to sexual violence witnesses in *Kunarac* and argues that it indicates their capacity to consent to sexual relationships with the accused.[79] The approach problematically abstracts the claimed 'consent' of the individual victim from the material conditions of conflict established in the case, which involved multiple rapes of multiple victim-witnesses by multiple

---

[75] Catharine MacKinnon, 'Defining Rape Internationally', (2006) 44(3) Colum J Transnat'l L, 940–958, 941.
[76] Catharine MacKinnon, 'Rape Redefined', (2016) 10(2) Harv Law & Pol'y Rev, 431–478.
[77] Kiran Grewal, 'International Criminal Law as a Site for Enhancing Women's Rights?', (2015) 23(2) Fem LS, 149–165, 157–159.
[78] Engle, *The Grip of Sexual Violence in Conflict*, p. 96. In fact, there is no such legal incapacity, and the prosecution was required to establish that the victim did not consent as a matter of proof of elements of the offence.
[79] Ibid., p. 95. This claim was put forward by the Defence and rejected on factual grounds by the Trial Chamber.

armed perpetrators in the context of the military 'ethnic cleansing' of over 20,000 Bosniak inhabitants of the Foča municipality.[80] The problem of this individualised approach is equally evident in those cases where the victims are men, such as male sexual violence committed in detention camps in *Tadić*. While not addressed by Engle, such cases highlight the importance of addressing the collective context of conflict, without which such critiques reproduce naturalised assumptions about women's sexuality, agency, and consent.

However, retaining consent as an element of international sexual violence offences remains problematic. This problem derives from the adoption of municipal models of rape as non-consent, which presume that women as a group have always already consented to sex, unless it is established otherwise through proof of non-consent. To remove consent as an element of the offence withdraws the presumption of consent that underlies this model of rape, rather than making women legally incapable of consent. Moreover, other international crimes concerning harms against the person, such as murder or torture, do not include consent as an element of the offence, and so sexual violence would be the only crime against the person requiring the additional element of consent.

To avoid the problems with these two dominant positions, a third argument has emerged. This argument builds on *Kunarac* and argues that sexual violence should be understood as a violation of the right to sexual autonomy.[81] In her important intervention in this debate, Grewal argues that sexual violence needs to be rethought in terms of sexual rights, which 'focuses less on the identity of the victim, and more on the nature and the circumstances of the act'.[82] However, the potential of this powerful suggestion is blunted if based upon a model of the individual right-holder. In current legal terms, the right to sexual autonomy *per se* does not exist in international criminal law, and such rights would only be legally relevant to crimes against humanity and torture, as discussed in Chapter 2.[83] Moreover, even if the victim were understood to be a holder

---

[80] *Kunarac* Trial Judgement, paras. 570–592. See also *Karadžić* ICTY-95-5/18-T, Judgement, 24 March 2016, (*Karadžić* Trial Judgement), paras. 834–934.
[81] Kristen Boon, 'Rape and Forced Pregnancy under the ICC Statute', (2001) 32(3) Colum Hum Rts L Rev, 625–675. See also Kiran Grewal, 'The Protection of Sexual Autonomy under International Criminal Law', (2012) 10(2) JICJ, 373–396.
[82] Grewal, 'International Criminal Law as a Site for Enhancing Women's Rights?', 162.
[83] The ICTY did not create a 'human right to sexual self-determination', as is sometimes claimed. The phrase appears in the judgement summary of the Trial Chamber in *Kunarac* but not the official full written judgement nor in any other judgements.

of positive human rights, violence against women remains a 'normative gap' in the legal framework of international human rights, as it does in international humanitarian law.[84] In conceptual terms, this approach returns us to the problem of the individual right-holder, as it understands the harm as a violation of that right to sexual autonomy discussed earlier in this chapter.

Ultimately, both positions rely on the same model of the victim as an individual holder of rights. For this reason, lack of consent – whether characterised as non-consent or coercive circumstances vitiating consent – becomes central to the concept of sexual violence, because it is the indicator of the denial of the right to 'exercise the right of consent over that property which is most personally held: the body'.[85] The notion of consent thereby necessarily becomes the marker of sexual autonomy in either model. Accordingly, it captures the victim in the problematic logic of the model of the rights-bearing individual of the legal form.

3.3.2.2 The Problem of the Victim as Collective Subject: Genocidal Rape

The second set of debates concern the conceptualisation of the victim of sexual violence as a collective legal subject. These debates concern whether the collective victim of sexual violence is women as a group, the civilian population (crimes against humanity), or the national, ethnic, racial, or religious group (genocide) of which they are a member. The issues concerning how to characterise rape committed in the context of collective violence are most sharply seen in the legal and conceptual debates concerning so-called 'genocidal rape'.

At the doctrinal level, a series of issues arise as to how to characterise sexual violence as a gender-based harm, insofar as it raises the problem of how to characterise women as a victimised group. The Genocide Convention does not specify sexual violence as an underlying act of genocide, and 'women' or 'gender' are not included in the groups protected under the Convention. Under customary law, and the ICTY Statute, rape is specified as a crime against humanity, that is, as an international crime when committed in the context of a widespread or systematic attack on a civilian population. However, the crime of persecution is a separate offence, which has the additional element of

---

[84] See Rashida Manjoo, and Jackie Jones, (eds.), *The Legal Protection of Women from Violence* (London and New York: Routledge, 2018).
[85] Cahill, *Rethinking Rape*, p. 170.

discriminatory intent on political, religious, or racial grounds. As a result, sexual violence as a crime against humanity can be characterised as rape (without gender discrimination) or persecution (with political, religious, or racial discrimination). These doctrinal issues were clearly set out by Rhonda Copelon in 1994, and they continue to be live issues, as can be seen in the ICC jurisprudence.[86]

From 1996 onwards, the ICTY recognised that rape could constitute genocidal acts (that is, the *actus reus* of the offence).[87] In subsequent cases, sexual violence was charged as (1) causing serious bodily or mental harm to members of the group and/or (2) deliberately inflicting on the group conditions of life calculated to bring about its physical destruction in whole or in part, as in the leading 'high-level' leadership cases of *Karadžić* and *Mladić*.[88] While there have been no convictions for sexual violence charged as genocide, as Baig and Jarvis et al. point out, this must be understood in the broader context of the failure to obtain convictions for charges other than crimes committed at Srebrenica, primarily because of the failure to establish the *mens rea*, or specific intent to destroy the protected group.[89]

The 'Srebrenica' cases, in which genocide has been successfully prosecuted, read as a whole 'surface' gendered harms within genocide. These cases characterise the genocide as having specific gender dimensions for male and female victims, as Patricia Viseur Sellers describes. However, she also observes that they reveal the 'limits of international criminal law's protection'.[90] The limits in surfacing gender-based crimes in general, and sexual violence in particular, can be clearly seen in *Karadžić* and *Mladić*. Karadžić and Mladić were charged with genocide, crimes against humanity, and war crimes committed across municipalities in Bosnia (BiH municipalities) and Srebrenica, together with crimes against humanity and war crimes committed in Sarajevo. In both cases, genocide was established for Srebrenica, which did not involve sexual violence charges. However, it was not established for the BiH municipalities, due

---

[86] See Copelon, 'Surfacing Gender'.
[87] *Karadžić and Mladić*, Review of the Indictment Pursuant to Rule 61, ICTY-95-5-R61/ IT-95-18-R61-T, July 11 1996, para. 93.
[88] *Karadžić* ICTY-95-5/18; *Mladić* ICTY-09-92.
[89] Baig, Jarvis et al., 'Contextualising Sexual Violence', p. 210.
[90] Patricia Viseur Sellers, '(Re)Considering Gender Jurisprudence', in Fionnuala Ní Aoláin, Naomi Cahn et al. (eds.), *The Oxford Handbook of Gender and Armed Conflict* (Oxford: Oxford University Press, 2018), p. 222.

to failure to establish genocidal intent. These crimes were instead held to constitute persecution, a crime against humanity.[91]

Despite the failure to establish genocidal intent in the BiH municipalities, these important cases confirm that sexual violence constitutes the genocidal acts of causing serious bodily or mental harm to members of a group.[92] However, while recognising sexual violence as underlying genocidal acts of causing serious bodily or mental harm, these acts are described in gender-neutral terms. For example, the *Karadžić* Trial Chamber describes sexual violence thus: 'Bosnian Muslim women, men, girls, and boys were subjected to rape and other acts of sexual violence ... these acts were of such a serious nature as to contribute or tend to contribute to the destruction of the Bosnian Muslims and Bosnian Croats.'[93] Although the evidence presented in the Judgement clearly indicates different patterns of male and female victimisation, this gender-neutral characterisation of genocide does not capture the gendered nature of this collective victimisation. The *Mladić* Judgement similarly characterises the underlying genocidal acts in gender-neutral terms while drawing on evidence referring to female victimisation.[94] Accordingly, the jurisprudence does not identify whether these are gender-based acts of genocide, which involve gender-specific targeting as part of a genocidal campaign. Given this, it does not identify how sexual violence is a gender-based crime.

This approach can be contrasted to the genocide charges in relation to Srebrenica in both the *Karadžić* and *Mladić* judgements. *Karadžić* and *Mladić* both describe the different gendered patterns of underlying genocidal acts, that is, the killing of men and the forced displacement of women, and held that the specific impact of the killing of male members of the community and the forced removal of women and children constitute serious mental or bodily harm to the surviving women. *Karadžić* and *Mladić* also accept the murder of men and the forced displacement of women as evidencing the intent to destroy the

---

[91] Confirmed on appeal in both cases: *Karadžić* MICT-13-55-A, 20 March 2019, and *Mladić* MICT-13-56-A, 8 June 2021.
[92] *Karadžić* Trial Judgement, paras. 2581 – 2582. The Trial Chamber did not consider whether sexual violence constituted the genocidal acts of 'deliberately inflicting on the group conditions calculated to bring about its physical destruction in whole or in part' (para. 2583).
[93] Ibid., paras. 2581–2582.
[94] *Mladić* ICTY-09-92-T, Judgement, 22 November 2017, (*Mladić* Trial Judgement), para. 3451.

group.⁹⁵ *Karadžić* followed the reasoning in *Krstić* in finding that the murder of 'all able bodied men while forcibly removing the remainder of the population would have severe procreative implications for the Bosnian Muslims in Srebrenica and thus result in their physical extinction', and therefore was evidence of genocidal intent.⁹⁶ *Karadžić* relied in part on the *Krstić* finding that the surviving women of Srebrenica would suffer particular harms because of the 'patriarchal society' of Bosnian Muslims.⁹⁷ It should be noted that although *Mladić* accepted that incidences of rape occurred during the forced displacement of women, these were not discussed in *Karadžić*.

In doctrinal terms, in contrast to the prohibited genocidal acts of murder and forced displacement, it remains unclear whether sexual violence is characterised as a gender-based crime and how it is a component of the attack on the protected group. It remains uncertain whether international criminal law prohibits sexual violence because it is a gender-based harm (women are targeted because they are women), a group-based harm (women are targeted because they are female members of the protected group), or because it harms the group as such (women are targeted as members of the protected group). Feminist scholars such as Doris Buss have argued that 'the tribunals see rape only as an added layer to ethnic conflict, and that an overdetermination of ethnicity constrains the types of sexual violence – and victims – that tribunals are able to see'.⁹⁸ As Chiseche Mibenge argues, this approach focuses on a 'single axis construction of discrimination', which is ethnicity.⁹⁹ However, the 'narrative of ethnic genocide, by privileging ethnicity as the requisite condition of sexual victimisation, denies gender-based discrimination [and] suggests that sexual violence ... is a type of ethnic violence rather than gender-based violence'.¹⁰⁰ Accordingly, it does not provide an adequate conceptualisation of sexual violence in genocide, nor of the structuring of ethnic based harms through other axes of

---

⁹⁵ *Mladić* Trial Judgement, para. 3553; *Karadžić* Trial Judgement, paras. 5664 – 5665.
⁹⁶ *Karadžić* Trial Judgement, paras. 5671.
⁹⁷ Ibid., paras. 5664–5665.
⁹⁸ Doris Buss, 'Sexual Violence, Ethnicity, and Intersectionality in International Criminal Law,' in Emily Grabham, Davina Cooper et al. (eds.), *Intersectionality and Beyond* (London and New York: Routledge-Cavendish, 2008), p. 118.
⁹⁹ Chiseche Mibenge, *Sex and International Tribunals* (Pennsylvania: University of Pennsylvania Press, 2013), p. 86.
¹⁰⁰ Ibid., p. 62.

discrimination beside ethnicity, such as gender, age, or class.[101] Given these issues, we can say that international criminal law does not provide a legal conceptualisation of sexual violence as a form of collective victimisation.

At a conceptual and political level, feminists have long debated how to characterise the victim of conflict-related sexual violence as a collective subject. Yugoslavian feminist scholars and activists were active interlocutors in the international feminist legal debates concerning the nature of so-called 'genocidal rape' that quickly emerged in the 1990s. The debates first emerged amongst Yugoslavian feminists in 1992, as they confronted the problem of how to engage politically and legally with the collective victimisation of women in the war first in Croatia and then in Bosnia (as discussed in Chapter 2). Particularly acute was the question of whether war-time rape should be seen as the victimisation of women of all ethnic backgrounds by men of all ethnic or national backgrounds or as the victimisation of women as members of (Croatian or Bosnian) ethnic or national groups by men of (Serbian) ethnic or national groups.[102] This debate became (and remains) a significant political issue within feminist circles but also in the wider society in the Yugoslavian successor states.

Four key debates concerning 'genocidal rape' emerged in these discussions, all of which turn on the problem of conceptualising sexual violence as collective victimisation. The first debate concerns 'genocide against Bosnian Muslims versus rape on all sides', that is, whether rape in the conflict was genocidal (was intended to destroy Bosnian Muslims as a group) or whether it was perpetrated by all parties against women generally.[103] In legal terms, this debate concerns whether the collective victim is the ethnic, national, or religious group or whether it is all women as a gender group. The second debate centres on 'rape as genocide', which concerns whether it is possible to identify the distinctive characteristics of rape as a component of genocide.[104] In legal terms, the debate focuses upon how particular forms of sexual violence are genocidal (such as forced impregnation) and whether these acts are intended to destroy women as a group (that is, a form of gender-based violence) or the ethnic/religious/national group (that is, a form of ethnic-based

---

[101] Ibid., pp. 75–76.
[102] For an overview of these debates, see Dubravka Žarkov, *The Body of War* (Durham: Duke University Press, 2007), chapter 11.
[103] Karen Engle, 'Feminism and Its (Dis)Contents', (2005) 99(4) AJIL, 778–816, 785.
[104] Ibid., 788.

violence).¹⁰⁵ The third debate concerns the 'connections between the recognition of rape in war and rape in the time called peace'.¹⁰⁶ This debate concerns the continuity between peace-time rape and war-time rape of women and whether there is a distinction between sexual violence against women in war and peace. In legal terms, the debate concerns whether sexual violence is characterised as a municipal or international crime. The fourth debate is how to develop an intersectional analysis of conflict-related sexual violence that can capture how 'rape together with genocide inflicts multiple, intersectional harms'.¹⁰⁷ In legal terms, the issue is how to develop intersectional discriminatory grounds for relevant international crimes.

These debates continue in current feminist discussions, which have yet to resolve three key underlying problems in the existing legal concepts of victims of collective crimes. The first problem is the tension within the conceptualisations of the individual and collective victim. On the one hand, there is a concept of individual women as rights-holders, such as sexual autonomy. On the other hand, those rights are contingent upon the victim's membership of the group that international criminal law seeks to protect (such as non-combatants, civilians, or an ethnic group). Sexual violence is therefore understood both as a crime against the individual (the possessor of individual autonomy) *and* as a crime against the collective group (the classes of persons protected by humanitarian law, the civilian population in crimes against humanity, or the protected group in genocide). As a result, the legal concept of collective victimisation does not adequately clarify the relationship between individual and collective victims.

The second problem concerns the concept of collective victims. If, as Bassiouni describes, '[t]he criminal conduct, goals, and outcomes are in this predicated on the fact that the victim belongs to an identifiable group or collectivity',¹⁰⁸ then conflict-related sexual violence raises the question as to which identifiable group or collectivity the victim belongs. It can be understood as a gender-based harm, which targets or disproportionately affects women and in which women are the identifiable collectivity. Alternatively, sexual violence can also be understood as an ethnic, religious, or nationality-based harm if those women belong to such a

---

[105] Copelon, 'Surfacing Gender', 248.
[106] Ibid.
[107] Ibid., 247.
[108] Cherif Bassiouni, 'The Protection of "Collective Victims" in International Law', p. 183.

targeted group, and in which the ethnic, religious, or national group is the identifiable collectivity. Accordingly, the legal concept of collective victimisation does not clearly describe the group grounds of victimisation.

The third problem concerns the collectivities that are recognised as victims in international criminal law. Because sexual violence *per se* is not accorded the status of an international crime, it becomes criminalised when committed against those groups that are recognised under international criminal law (unless prosecuted as a stand-alone offence). Given this, sexual violence becomes criminalised when directed towards groups protected by humanitarian norms in the case of war crimes (such as prisoners of war or civilians, but protected differently according to whether they are members of state parties to the conflict); the civilian population in the case of crimes against humanity (and in persecution, the racial, ethnic, religious, or national group); or the racial, ethnic, religious, or national group in the case of genocide. As Doris Buss describes, sexual violence becomes an international crime 'by targeting a community of people'.[109] However, understood in this way the crime surfaces particular forms of sexual violence, since it privileges conduct recognisable as a crime against a victim's group belonging, whether that group is characterised as a communal group, nation, or state. The communal group, nation, or state stands in as the collective victim. Accordingly, it solidifies those very boundaries of community, nation, and state that are so often themselves at stake in collective violence, and as if those boundaries are not themselves constituted in global power relations and histories. As a result, the notion of the collective or group to which the victim belongs, and the imagined communities upon which it is conditional, remains problematic.

3.4 The Conceptual Contradictions of the Legal Concept of the International Legal Subject

The concept of the international legal subject attributes rights and obligations to individuals as victims and perpetrators while also making those rights and obligations contingent upon collective participation or group membership. The surfacing of sexual violence as a gender-based harm shows how these models of legal subjects continually oscillate

---

[109] Doris Buss, 'Rethinking "Rape as a Weapon of War"', (2009) 17(2) FLS 145-163, 150.

between person and group, and individual and collective legal subjects. This oscillation repeats the ontological categories that serve as the problematic foundation of the legal subject of international criminal law. However, the sexual violence cases also demonstrate that this repetition also 'repeats and reinforces the dominant ideologies of gender and violence' that sustain these ideas of subject and society in international criminal law.[110]

---

[110] Doris Buss, 'Women at the Borders', (1998) 6(2) FLS, 171–203, 203.

4

The International Criminal Trial

> Every criminal trial involves two issues: first, that the crimes charged have been committed and, second, that an accused is responsible for those crimes. The object of evidence is to ascertain the truth of the facts with respect to these two issues.[1]
>
> *The Prosecutor v. Brđanin*

In international criminal law, international criminal trials are the foundation of findings on the commission of crimes and on the criminal responsibility of the accused for those crimes. If every international criminal trial aims to make findings on fact and responsibility, then these determinations rest on a set of international evidential and procedural norms and practices. With the development of international criminal law also came the development of these norms and practices as an international procedural and evidential system. What then are the characteristics of the third category of the legal form, the international criminal trial? And what ideas of persons and social relations does this model of international criminal trials assume?

4.1 The Legal Category of the International Criminal Trial

The first function of the international criminal trial is to determine the facts that establish the criminal responsibility of the accused. It arises from the primary objective of international criminal proceedings: 'to convict – and punish – those individually responsible for their crimes'.[2] This fact-finding on individual culpability can be said to be the 'purpose

---

[1] *Brđanin*, ICTY-99-36-T, Judgement, 1 September 2004, (*Brđanin* Trial Judgement), para. 21.
[2] *Momir Nikolić*, ICTY- 02-60/1-T, Sentencing Judgement, 2 December 2003, para. 59.

of any criminal trial', whether at national or international level.³ However, international criminal trials also have a second 'truth-finding function'.⁴ This is the factual determination on the nature of the conflict itself, because of the so-called 'international element' of these offences. This 'truth'-finding function establishes public historical truths, whether understood narrowly as the specific criminal conduct of the accused or more broadly as a historical record of the wider conflict.⁵ This is a collective truth-finding function, because it involves both a determination on collective (and not only individual) action and the establishment of a social (and not only individual) truth.

With the establishment of the ICTY, the international criminal trial came to be the third category of the legal form of international criminal law. In using the international criminal trial as the primary mechanism for fact-finding and determining criminal responsibility, the ICTY followed the precedent of the Nuremberg trials, the fair trial requirements set out under the 1949 Geneva Conventions, and post-war development of human rights norms governing fair trial rights.⁶ However, no code of international criminal procedure and evidence existed at the time of the establishment of the ICTY (as remains the case). Accordingly, the ICTY Statute provided general principles for trial proceedings, together with provisions for judges to draft and adopt rules of evidence and procedures (Art. 15). The ICTY developed a *sui generis* international procedural and evidential system, which reflected 'the specificity of international criminal proceedings [and] the unique traits of such proceedings'.⁷ As the ICTY Trial Chamber describes, 'the legal system that applies before this Tribunal is not common law or civil law. It is a hybrid, and it is a system that applies and develops on its own premises and its own terms.'⁸

In this hybrid international legal system, trial proceedings are similar to adversarial domestic criminal jurisdictions. The prosecution and

---

³ *Milošević*, ICTY-02-54-T, Decision on Prosecution Motion for Reconsideration Regarding Evidence of Defence Witnesses, 17 May 2005, para. 16.
⁴ *Sikirica*, ICTY-95-8-T, Sentencing Judgment, 13 November 2001, para. 149.
⁵ See, for example, *Kristić*, ICTY-98-33-T, Judgement, 2 August 2001, para. 2.
⁶ Virginia Morris and Michael Sharf, *An Insider's Guide to the International Criminal Tribunal for the Former Yugoslavia*, Volume 1 (New York: Transnational Publishers, 1995), pp. 175–176.
⁷ *Furundžija*, ICTY-95-17/1-T, Judgement, 10 December 1998, (*Furundžija* Trial Judgement), para. 178.
⁸ *Stanišić and Župljanin*, ICTY-08-91, 15 October 2009, Trial Transcript, p. 1508.

defence present and test evidence, and the prosecution has the burden of proving the case against the accused (Rule 85, ICTY Rules of Procedure and Evidence) (ICTY RPE). The role of the judge is also similar, in that they act as an 'impartial referee' adjudicating between defence and prosecution and do not have an active role in case investigation or presentation.[9] Trial proceedings also have inquisitorial elements, as judges can put questions to witnesses (Rule 85B ICTY RPE) and call additional evidence at trial (Rule 98 ICTY RPE). The ICTY also developed a permissive evidential regime, which it describes as similar to inquisitorial criminal procedure, because of the evaluation of evidence by judges rather than juries.[10] Accordingly, the Chamber could 'admit any relevant evidence which it considers to have probative value' (Rule 89 ICTY RPE).

The Trial Chamber is required 'to ensure that a trial is fair and expeditious and that proceedings are conducted in accordance with the rules of procedure and evidence, with full respect for the rights of the accused and due regard for the protection of victims and witnesses' (ICTY Statute, Art. 20(1)). This liberal legal model rests on notions of the fair trial and procedural fairness, which emphasise the impartial application of legal rules to all parties.[11] It defines fair judicial process in terms of typical liberal ideas of the rule of law (to prevent the arbitrary exercise of power) and of formal legal equality (to ensure the equal treatment of the accused before the law). Because individuals appear before it as formally equal legal subjects, Pashukanis describes the 'law court and the judicial process [as] the most consummate manifestation of the legal form'. He argues that 'the transformation of the actions of a concrete person into the proceedings of a legal party, i.e. into a legal subject, is particularly apparent in the court case'.[12] In the criminal trial, legal subjects exist in juridic relations of equal exchange (giving rise to the principle of equality of arms). This legal form of the criminal trial emerges with modern European bourgeois state.[13]

---

[9] Gideon Boas, 'A Code of Evidence and Procedure for International Criminal Law?', in William Schabas and Gideon Boas (eds.), *International Criminal Law Developments in the Case Law of the ICTY* (Leiden and Boston: Martinus Nijhoff Publishers, 2003), p. 24.

[10] *Tadić*, Case No. IT-94-1-T, Decision on Defence Motion on Hearsay, 7 August 1996, paras. 17-19.

[11] Frédéric Mégret, 'Beyond Fairness', (2009) 14(1) UCLA Journal of International Foreign Affairs, 37–76, 48ff.

[12] Evgeny Pashukanis, *Law and Marxism* (London: Ink Links, 1978), p. 167.

[13] See Pashukanis, chapter seven, ibid.

The modern 'culture of fact', with its emphasis upon procedural fairness and objective proof, founds the international criminal trial.[14] It relies on fact-finding practices considered to be appropriate procedures and methods of enquiry and grounds for the justification of its findings.[15] The practices function as epistemic norms, which serve as the foundation of legal determination of 'fact' in the international criminal trial, and warrant factual findings on individual guilt and the conflict itself. As Carol Smart describes, law 'claims to have the method to establish the truth of events. The main vehicle for this claim is the legal method ... A more "public" version of this claim, however, is the criminal trial, which ... is thought to be a secure basis for findings of guilt and innocence.'[16] The 'general principles' of the international criminal trial, and its rules and practices of evidence and procedure, are the epistemic norms and practices that found the legal method of objective fact-finding.

To identify the epistemic norms and practices that construct the legal category of the international criminal trial, I examine the procedural and evidential norms and practices in two leading cases on evidence, *The Prosecutor* v. *Furundžija*, and *The Prosecutor* v. *Brđanin*. Both are sexual violence cases that establish fair trial and evidential evaluation principles. They also typify modes of evidence and evaluation in so-called 'lower level' direct perpetration and 'higher level' leadership cases. I examine the presentation and evaluation of sexual violence evidence in these cases to identify the epistemic norms and practices that govern fact-finding in international criminal trials, as well as the concepts of persons and society upon which they rely.

4.2 Victim-Witness Testimony as a Mode of Evidence in International Criminal Trials

Some 4,650 witnesses have appeared before the ICTY. The majority of witnesses appear as 'fact witnesses' and are called to give evidence to their experience of the crimes they lived through. Of these witnesses, 87 per cent were male and 13 per cent were female.[17] The majority of female

---

[14] Barbara Shapiro, *A Culture of Fact* (Ithaca: Cornell University Press, 2003), p. 12.
[15] William Twining, *Globalisation and Legal Theory* (London: Butterworths, 2000), p. 204.
[16] Carol Smart, *Feminism and the Power of the Law* (London and New York: Routledge, 1989), p. 10.
[17] http://www.icty.org/en/about/registry/witnesses/statistics, as of 30 June 2015.

witnesses appear in sexual violence cases, but the exact number is unknown.[18] Of the male witnesses, an unknown but significant proportion also testify to sexual violence.[19]

A victim is defined as a 'person against whom a crime over which the Tribunal has jurisdiction has allegedly been committed' (Rule 2A ICTY RPE). Under the Statute, the ICTY has a duty to provide for the protection of victims and witnesses in its rules of evidence and procedure (Art. 22). The rules include general provisions for the protection of victims and witnesses under Rule 69 and 75, which include non-disclosure of identity and other protective measures, such as closed sessions, pseudonyms, or visual and audio distortion of the witness. They were intended to protect all victims and witnesses 'in the light of the particular nature of the crimes committed in the former Yugoslavia ... especially in cases of rape and sexual assault'.[20] These measures recognise the importance of providing procedural safeguards for all witnesses giving evidence, including sexual violence victim-witnesses.

Two rules directly address victims of sexual violence. Rule 34 makes provision for a Victim and Witness Section, with specialist support for rape and sexual assault and the appointment of qualified women. Rule 96 governs evidence in cases of sexual assault. It removes the requirement of corroboration; bars consent as a defence where the victim (or another) is subjected to, or threatened with, 'violence, duress, detention, or psychological oppression'; requires that the Trial Chamber determine that evidence of consent is reasonable and credible before being admitted; and bars admission of the victim's prior sexual conduct. Rule 96 was an 'explicit rejection of standards of evidence which have traditionally discriminated against women in court and impeded their access to criminal justice systems domestically'.[21] These traditional standards were based on discriminatory notions of the inherent unreliability of the evidence of rape victims. In effect, Rules 34 and 96 were intended to

---

[18] Kimi King and James Meernik, *The Witness Experience* (Cambridge: Cambridge University Press, 2017), p. 179.

[19] See Kirsten Campbell, 'The Gender of Transitional Justice', (2007) 1(3) Int J Transitional Justice 413–432, 428; Gabi Mischkowski and Gorana Mlinarević, *And That It Does Not Happen to Anyone Anywhere in the World* (Cologne: Medica Mondiale, 2009), pp. 30–32.

[20] Report of the Secretary-General pursuant to paragraph 2 of resolution 808 of the Security Council, 3 May 1993, S/25704, para. 108.

[21] Kate Fitzgerald, 'Problems of Prosecution and Adjudication of Rape and Other Sexual Assaults under International Law', (1997) 8(4) EJIL 638–663, 639.

apply the principle of non-discrimination to the evidence of rape victims.[22]

The procedural safeguards generally aim to protect the ICTY's 'ability to obtain witness testimony ... [and] the administration of justice'.[23] 'Testimony' is 'the statement of a witness in court offered as evidence of the truth of that which is stated'.[24] Witness testimony is important because it may be the only available evidence. It is also seen as the most reliable form of evidence, as reflected in the express preference for live witness testimony under the first ICTY RPE (1994, Rule 90A). As Priya Gopalan et al. note, 'the modern international tribunals have made extensive use of victim and witness testimonies to establish the facts.' As they describe, '[v]ictims have played a prominent role in establishing crimes of sexual violence' at the ICTY.[25]

4.2.1 Victim-Witness Testimony as a Mode of Evidence: The Prosecutor v. Furundžija

The first mode of evidence is victim-witness testimony, which reflects the centrality of victim-witness evidence to international criminal trials. This mode of evidence is most visible in the earlier ICTY cases involving lower level direct perpetrators and victim-witnesses. *The Prosecutor v. Furundžija*, the first case to consider charges of rape as such, typifies victim-witness testimony as a mode of evidence in such 'direct perpetrator' cases. As described in Chapter 3, the charges arose from the rape of Witness A, by another soldier, during her interrogation by the Accused, Furundžija. It was a short trial of 10 days and limited evidence, with the Prosecution calling 8 witnesses and submitting 15 exhibits and the Defence calling 6 witnesses and submitting 22 exhibits. Such cases 'present the evidence relating to crimes of sexual violence at a focused and detailed level with a significant amount of victim witness

---

[22] Morris and Scharf, *An Insider's Guide to the ICTY*, pp. 263–264.
[23] *Šešelj*, ICTY-03-67-R77.2-A, First Contempt Proceedings, Judgement, Contempt Chamber, 9 May 2010, para. 39.
[24] Colin Tapper, *Cross and Tapper on Evidence* (Oxford: Oxford University Press, 2010), p. 53.
[25] Priya Gopalan, Daniela Kravetz, et al., 'Proving Crimes of Sexual Violence', in Serge Brammertz and Michelle Jarvis (eds.), *Prosecuting Conflict-Related Sexual Violence at the ICTY* (Oxford: Oxford University Press, 2016), p. 112.

testimony'.[26] *Furundžija* established key principles concerning the evidential evaluation of victim-witness testimony and fair trial requirements. The evidential issues concerned the reliability and credibility of Witness A's evidence and arose from the Defence claims that she had post-traumatic stress disorder (PTSD), for which she had received treatment or counselling.

The court of law is often characterised as utilising a realist model of testimony as the mirror of 'reality' in memory.[27] However, as *Furundžija* shows, participants in the international court of law do not utilise 'literalist' evidential models, in that they do not understand testimony as an identical reproduction of an event. Rather, they share a concern with the evidential value of victim-witness testimony, with the nature of the re-presentation of an event in testimony and its value as evidence of that event. However, the criminal trial structures this 'evidential' model according to the role of the participants in the proceedings, namely, their roles as complainant witness, prosecution, defence, and judge. Each role understands the testimony of the victim-witness in a different way and so gives it different evidential meaning.

4.2.1.1 The Prosecution: Testimony as Truth

The role of the prosecution is to submit evidence to establish the criminal conduct in issue according to the burden of proof. In meeting that burden, the majority of prosecution witnesses are victims of crimes or witnesses to crimes. For the prosecution, victim-witness testimony provides evidence of material facts of the guilt of the accused. For this reason, the Prosecution presents to the Trial Chamber a model of testimony that assumes that there is a truthful relationship between the recollection of the victim-witness and the event. It does not characterise that relationship as a reproduction of 'reality' but rather as an accurate account of the relevant facts of the event. For example, the Prosecution argued that 'intense experiences such as the events in this case are often remembered accurately despite some inconsistencies' and that Witness A recalled the 'core' events of this experience.[28]

---

[26] Saeeda Verrall, 'The Picture of Sexual Violence in the Former Yugoslavia as Reflected in ICTY Judgments', in Brammertz and Jarvis (eds.), *Prosecuting Conflict-Related Sexual Violence*, p. 319.

[27] Michael Lambek, 'The Past Imperfect', in Paul Antze and Michael Lambek (eds.), *Tense Past* (London and New York: Routledge, 1996), p. 242.

[28] *Furundžija* Trial Judgement, para. 105.

Giorgio Agamben argues that in Latin 'there are two words for "witness"'. The first, *testis*, from which our word testimony derives, etymologically signifies the person who, in a trial or lawsuit between two rival parties, is in the position of a third party'.[29] For the Prosecution, the complainant is a *testis*, a third-party witness to the occurrence of the event. The veracity of the complainant derives from her position as a witness to the event. Her testimony evidences the criminal act, attesting to the fact of its commission. This model of testimony assumes that the witness re-presents the criminal act in her evidence. The fallibility and incompleteness of the witness's memory do not call into question 'the validity of her whole testimony'. Rather, that testimony re-presents the 'meaningful truth' of the event.[30] Accordingly, in this model testimony does not function as a photographic image or reproduction of reality. Rather, it captures the experience of the event, which the Prosecutor listens to, and for. The Prosecutor listens for the truthful account of the crime as factual event.

4.2.1.2 The Victim-Witness: Testimony as Experience

In formal terms, the role of the victim-witness is to offer evidence to the court of the criminal guilt of the accused. The witness offers 'testimony', an act of attesting to the truth of an event that offers 'one's own speech as material evidence for the truth'.[31] Her evidence is a testimonial to the injurious event since 'the evidence she gave was the way she, as the person who endured these events, saw them happen'.[32] However, for the victim-witness, testimony evidences both the injurious act, that is, the harm to her, *and* the wrong committed against her, that is, the injustice of this harm. Her testimony expresses both the truth of the event and the injustice of the crime, and so it has a necessary relation not only to the harmful act but also to its unjust or wrongful nature.

The victim-witness embodies the second position of witnessing identified by Giorgio Agamben, which he names by the second Latin word for witness, *superstes*. *Superstes* 'designates a person who has lived through an event from beginning to end and can therefore bear witness to it'.[33]

---

[29] Giorgio Agamben, *Remnants of Auschwitz* (New York: Zone, 1999), p. 17.
[30] Shoshana Felman and Dori Laub, *Testimony* (New York and London: Routledge, 1992), pp. 60–63.
[31] Ibid., p. 5.
[32] *Furundžija* Trial Judgement, para. 116.
[33] Agamben, *Remnants of Auschwitz*, p. 17.

The complexity of the position of the victim-witness arises from the fact that she testifies to the wrong committed against her – she is both a complainant to an injustice and a witness to an event. Because she is a complainant, she is not a 'neutral' third-party witness in a trial. Her testimony is a description not just of an event but also of a wrongful event – that of the injustice to her. For this reason, in her testimony, 'a non-juridical element of truth exists, such that the *quaestio facto* can never be reduced to the *quaestio iuris*'.[34] This is because the testimony of the victim-witness evidences the truth of the event that is not reducible to its legal determination. The non-juridical element of truth in this model is that the complainant testifies about not simply a wrongful act but a wrong to her person. Unlike the *testis*, she is not simply a witness to an event.

In sexual violence testimony, that wrong is an injury to the victim as a subject. The wrong concerns a violation of the integrity of the body, as well as the assault on the integrity of the 'self' of the victim.[35] It arises from the harm to not only her body but also her selfhood. As such, her testimony materialises the injustice to her social subjectivity, that is, what it is to be a person. She is living proof of this injustice, which her testimony evidences, and embodies the wrong brought before the court. For the victim-witness, the fact of the event and the claim of injustice are inseparable, for her testimony to the event is also testimony to the injustice done to her. As such, her testimony is given 'in order to *address* another, to impress upon a listener, to *appeal* to a community'.[36] That appeal is an address to justice.

4.2.1.3 The Defence: Testimony as Fallible

The role of the defence is to raise reasonable doubt as to the prosecution's case. In principle, it is not necessary for the defence to present evidence for the prosecution to fail to establish its case. This is because the accused is entitled to the benefit of the doubt as to whether the offence has been empirically established.[37] However, in practice the defence seeks to test the prosecution's case: to refute its arguments and to impugn its proofs.

---

[34] Ibid.
[35] Drucilla Cornell, *At the Heart of Freedom* (Princeton: Princeton University Press, 1998), pp. 36–37.
[36] Felman and Laub, Testimony, p. 204.
[37] Delalić et al., ICTY-96-21-T, Judgement, 16 November 1998, para. 601.

Accordingly, the model of evidence for the Defence is 'fallibilistic' in epistemological terms.

For this reason, the model of testimony that circulates throughout the Defence case severs it from any necessary relation to the event and hence to the crime. Rather, it understands testimony as a labile mental representation, which is a fallible re-presentation of an image of the event. The Defence argued that victim-witnesses' testimonial narrative of events 'is actually an opinion or belief as to what occurred'.[38] This model can be called testimony as mentality, in the sense that the model posits a causal relation between the claimed psychological or neurological 'state of mind' of victim-witness and the content of her or his memory of events re-presented in their testimony. As the Prosecutor described, the essence of the Defence case was that Witness A's memory of her assault is flawed because of her 'mental health or psychological state'.[39] The Defence argued that her memories were unreliable as they claimed that she suffered PTSD and were influenced by her medical treatment by an organisation campaigning for prosecutions of war crimes.[40]

The model of testimony put forward by the Defence contends that the testimony of Witness A is unreliable because she suffers from a psychopathology because of her traumatic experience of rape. In this model, the rupture of bodily integrity results in a rupture of psychic integrity, and consequently a rupture of the integrity of memory. That understanding of trauma implies both that she is suggestible, and therefore susceptible to a reworking of her memory by others, and that she is psychologically unstable, and therefore inherently unreliable in her recollections. In this way, the Defence's model of testimony seeks to establish a nexus between the experience of rape, psychopathology, and the unreliability of memory.

The Defence uses this nexus to argue that the Court cannot rely on this evidence to establish the guilt of the Accused. As such, it relies on 'fair trial' arguments, which concern a right of 'the accused to procedural safeguards to prevent an unjust conviction'.[41] Drawing on these fair trial arguments, the Defence successfully contended that the trial proceedings

---

[38] *Furundžija*, ICTY-95-17, Trial Transcript, 8 June 1998, p. 86.
[39] *Furundžija*, ICTY-95-17/1-A, Judgment, 21 July 2000 (*Furundžija* Appeals Judgement), para. 56.
[40] *Furundžija* Trial Judgement, para. 103.
[41] Hilary Charlesworth and Christine Chinkin, *The Boundaries of International Law* (Manchester: Manchester University Press, 2000), p. 328.

should be re-opened to consider the impact of the claimed PTSD and medical treatment of the victim-witness upon the reliability and credibility of her evidence.

4.2.1.4 The Court: Testimony as Evidence

The role of the judges is to determine the facts of the case on the basis of the evidence presented in the proceedings before the court. Accordingly, the Trial Chamber regards victims as 'witnesses of justice', rather than of the Defence or Prosecution, and evaluates their testimony as evidence of those facts.[42] The Trial Chamber utilises all three ideas of experience, mental state, and meaningfulness to evaluate the re-presentation of the event in testimony. The Trial Chamber establishes itself as the arbiter of testimony (and so uses the evidence of an expert witness to establish that science cannot offer the law definitive answers on the nature of memory).[43] It looks to its own judgement of witnesses and other evidence submitted in the case to assess the evidential weight of testimony. In effect, the Chamber assesses the accuracy of the testimonial re-presentation of the event.

To evaluate the testimony of the witness, the Trial Chamber deploys notions of reliability, or the accuracy of the testimony, and credibility, or truthfulness of the witness. It also looks to the material internal consistency of the testimony of the complainant. While there is no legal requirement of corroboration, the Trial Chamber also looks to other testimony and evidence to confirm the veracity of the testimony. For example, the Trial Chamber accepted the testimony of Witness A because of her 'honest and confident' presentation and her coherent account of the events, confirmed by corroborative evidence.[44] It also accepted her testimony that while her experience was traumatic, her memory was not psychopathological.[45] In effect, the Trial Chamber undertakes an evidential assessment of the re-presentation of the event in testimony.

The Trial Chamber therefore utilises an evidential model of testimony, where testimony is understood as the re-presentation of an event that is proved or disproved. In this sense, it is a 'cognitivist, empirical epistemology', in which true statements are thought to correspond with the

---

[42] *Furundžija* Trial Judgement, para. 108.
[43] Ibid., para. 110.
[44] Ibid., para. 116.
[45] Ibid., para. 108.

occurrence of events.⁴⁶ In this model, proving testimony involves assessing issues of the probability and fallibility of the truthfulness of statements. Following this model, the Trial Chamber assesses the re-presentation of the event in victim-witness testimony in terms of the 'reliability and credibility' of those statements. The assessment of those statements fundamentally turns on the assessment of the complainant as victim-witness and, in particular, her reliability and credibility. For this reason, the Trial Chamber accepts that the psychological state of the witness is relevant to the issue of reliability as a matter of 'fair trial' rights of the Accused. The complainant's testimony is also assessed in relation to other witnesses and evidential material, namely, corroboration. The Trial Chamber uses these models of evidence to judge whether the event that testimony attests to a legal fact. The Trial Chamber thereby constructs legal facts through these epistemic notions of credibility, reliability, consistency, and corroboration. The ICTY itself recognises this constitutive dimension of judgement on testimony, both in terms of the legal principles and rules that govern evidence (Section 3 RPE) and in terms of the right to appeal on errors of fact or law under the Statute (Art. 25).

4.2.2 *Conceptual Problems in Modes of Fact-Finding in Victim-Witness Testimony to Sexual Violence*

The so-called 'direct perpetration' early ICTY sexual violence cases can be considered most analogous to domestic sexual offence trials, in that the charges allege the direct participation of the accused in the criminal conduct (whether the 'active' participation in torture or the 'passive' participation of aiding and abetting rape). The prosecution must establish that the victim was penetrated, that they did not consent, and that the accused participated in the acts charged. Accordingly, the testimony of the victim-witness evidences the harm to the person that legally characterises sexual violence crimes, namely, penetration, lack of consent, and participation of the accused (as discussed in Chapter 2). Her testimony *materialises* the crime, because it both articulates the harm and evidences it. As such, her testimony will be most stringently judged on its reliability, credibility, consistency, and corroboration, and most subjected to an 'evidential' assessment of its re-presentation of the event.

---

[46] John Jackson and Sean Doran, 'Evidence', in Dennis Patterson (ed.), *A Companion to Philosophy of Law and Legal Theory* (Oxford: Blackwell, 1996), p. 173.

In such cases, the evidential model requires proof of the complainant's testimony to the harm. Given the burden of proof, the complainant's testimony of itself does not adequately evidence the wrong for the Chamber. Rather, other grounds of adjudication establish the evidential value of testimony. One ground is corroboration. As a matter of law, the testimony of the complainant does not require corroboration.[47] As a matter of evidence, its proof entails the corroborative confirmation of further evidence. Accordingly, the issue of evidential corroboration returns.[48] Another ground is the credibility and reliability of the victim-witness. To challenge this ground, the Defence sought to discredit the victim-witness by claiming that she had PTSD, arguing that it made her identification of the Accused, and her evidence of his conduct, unreliable. The Chamber accepted that this challenge was reasonable, despite it being put forward to discredit only Witness A. It was not put forward to discredit other Prosecution witnesses, including a witness who had received psychiatric treatment, nor the Accused, who like other combatants could reasonably have been expected to suffer from PTSD.[49] Moreover, it had not been put forward in previous trials, despite the reasonable assumption that other witnesses in previous trials had PTSD. Accordingly, the testimony of Witness A was thereby subject to unequal testing because of these additional requirements of corroboration and witness evaluation.

The presumption of a relationship between the evidential value of testimony and the person of the sexual violence victim-witness amplifies this unequal testing. As we know from the work of Beverley Brown and Michelle Burman on sexual assault cases in domestic jurisdictions, issues of reliability and credibility 'are focused on very strongly'.[50] In such cases, the court subjects the reliability and credibility of the complainant to greater scrutiny and does not maintain the distinction between these two

---

[47] *Aleksovski*, ICTY-95-14/1-A, Judgment, 24 March 2000, paras. 62–63.
[48] *Furundžija* Trial Judgement, para. 116. See also Gopalan, Kravetz et al., 'Proving Crimes of Sexual Violence', p. 137.
[49] *Furundžija*, ICTY-95-17/1, Amicus Curiae Brief Respecting the Decision and Order of the Tribunal of 16 July 1998 Requesting That the Tribunal Reconsider Its Decision Having Regard to the Rights of Witness 'A' to Equality, Privacy and Security of the Person, and to Representation by Counsel, 6 November 1998 (*Furundžija Amicus Curiae Brief*), para. 23. In subsequent cases, the Chambers rely on *Furundžija* to establish that PTSD raised no inherent assumption as to the reliability of evidence.
[50] Beverly Brown, Michelle Burman et al., *Sex Crimes on Trial* (Edinburgh: Edinburgh University Press, 1993), p. 21.

criteria of evidential evaluation. These same issues reappear in international trials of sexual violence. For example, in *Furundžija*, the accuracy of the testimony, characterised as its reliability, becomes predicated on the credibility of the complainant. For this reason, it becomes legitimate to challenge the reliability of the complainant's testimony by calling her credibility into question. Issues of reliability – the 'accuracy' of the testimony – thus devolve into issues of credibility – the 'trustworthiness' of the witness. The credibility of the complainant thus becomes an essential part of the assessment of the evidential value of her testimony. Credibility is figured as the ground of testimony, and so the truth of the testimony becomes linked to the truth of the person of the witness.

In conceptual terms, the sexual violence trial turns, like no other, on the perceived capacity of the female complainant *to be* a trustworthy witness.[51] This myth of the inherently uncreditworthy complainant whose testimony cannot be trusted reappears in *Furundžija*. Untrustworthy because she is a 'feminine' witness, she must demonstrate that she is not subjective, irrational, passive, and emotional.[52] That the Trial Chamber accepts arguments concerning the relationship between the psychological or neurological state of the witness and the reliability of her testimony reproduces this problem. By allowing a nexus between the psychological state of the witness and her credibility to be made, the Trial Chamber relied upon an ontological concept of the victim-witness to assess the reliability of victim-witness testimony.

This ontological conception of the victim-witness assumes that there is a relationship between bodily and psychic integrity and the integrity of memory. However, a conception of the witness as a heteronormative 'masculine' subject underpins this idea of bodily and psychic integrity. Kaja Silverman describes the normative masculine subject as projecting an 'unimpaired masculinity' of coherent identity and bodily integrity.[53] For the masculine subject, the 'coherence and ideality of the corporeal ego' rests on 'an unimpaired bodily "envelope"'.[54] Coherence of the

---

[51] *Furundžija Amicus Curiae* Brief, para. 31.
[52] Fiona Raitt and Suzanne Zeedyk, *The Implicit Relation of Psychology and the Law* (London and New York: Routledge, 2000), p. 43. See also *Furundžija Amicus Curiae* Brief.
[53] Kaja Silverman, *Male Subjectivity at the Margins* (London and New York: Routledge, 1992), p. 42.
[54] Kaja Silverman, *The Threshold of the Visible World* (London and New York: Routledge, 1996), p. 25.

masculine self thereby rests on the integrity of its body. Accordingly, the model of the witness that possesses coherent identity and bodily integrity rests on a model of masculine subjectivity. However, if the masculine subject supposes its corporeal and subjective coherence, the 'feminine' subject is imagined to suffer the lack or loss he does not, and explicitly so in the case of penetrative rape. 'The feminine' thus 'represents the site at which the male subject deposits his lack'.[55] For this reason, the position of the 'feminine' witness is that of a subject that lacks bodily integrity and therefore the stable identity of a 'bounded self'.[56]

In victim-witness testimony, the sexual violence victim testifies to the rupture of psychic and bodily integrity. In articulating the wrong of sexual assault, the witness must testify to a trauma to bodily and subjective unity, because proving sexual violence requires evidencing the violation of sexual and bodily integrity. In evidencing this crime, the victim becomes a 'feminine' witness. Moreover, they become an inherently untrustworthy witness. The model of the masculine witness assumes that there is a relationship between bodily integrity, psychic integrity, and integrity of memory. In this model, a breach of bodily integrity ruptures psychic integrity of the self, and with it, the coherent and integrated memory of the event itself. Accordingly, the witness who testifies to sexual violence also becomes subject to challenge as to the unreliability of memory, as is the case in *Furundžija*. To testify to a breach of self and corporeal integrity places the witness in a 'feminine' position of subjective and bodily lack, and so in the position of the 'feminine' witness whose credibility and reliability are in doubt.

The Trial Chamber accepted the testimony of Witness A because she was able to demonstrate that the trauma to her body and her person did not entail a trauma to her memory. Paradoxically, she was able to meet the higher standard of credibility because her trauma did not appear to have a material effect on the coherence and integrity of her memory. The paradoxical position of victim-witness derives from the fact that she must demonstrate the breach to her bodily integrity while also demonstrating that her 'self' and hence her memory remain 'intact'. Her testimony must attest to the harm of the assault on the integrity of her 'self' while also establishing that her 'self' is coherent and stable. Because of the sexed conception of the witness, the credibility of the complainant is not presumed; instead, she must establish that credibility. The fact-finding

---

[55] Silverman, *Male Subjectivity at the Margins*, p. 46.
[56] See Jennifer Nedelsky, *Law's Relations* (Oxford: Oxford University Press, 2011), p. 215.

process thereby imposes a higher standard of proof of reliable testimony upon the sexual violence victim-witness, as we see in the process of evidential adjudication in *Furundžija*.[57] These adjudicative processes produce both the subjective 'integrity' of the witness and the harm to this integrity as the ground of evidential evaluation of victim-witness testimony.

Because of heteronormative ideas of sexuality, either male or female victims of sexual violence may occupy the position of feminine witness if they testify to the violation of bodily integrity.[58] However, the ICTY cases of male sexual violence were not seen as analogous to female rape, as they did not involve perpetrators directly engaging in sexual acts or penetrative anal rape and were legally characterised as violent rather than sexual crimes (as discussed in Chapters 2 and 3).[59] Moreover, there is no equivalent case to *Furundžija* for male sexual violence, in which sexual violence against male victims forms the sole basis of the charges. As a result, male victim-witnesses did not generally become seen as 'feminine' victim-witnesses.

The so-called direct perpetration cases show how gendered social relations structure victim-witness testimony as a mode of evidence. This is because of the structure of the trial process, the evidential model of testimony, the sexed subjectivity, and the position of the witness testifying to sexual violence. However, it is also because in the Yugoslavian conflict women were more likely to suffer rape than men, and often in settings without other corroborating witnesses.[60] Gopalan et al. identify certain challenges to victim evidence as unique to sexual violence crimes, such as corroboration or prior sexual conduct. They also point out that other challenges that are not unique (corroboration, inconsistent statements, trauma impact, and inducements to testify) 'may take on a greater dimension due to misconceptions, assumptions, and stereotypes about sexual violence crimes and victims'.[61] While they focus on inappropriate defence challenges, they also acknowledge that these discriminatory ideas permeate trial proceedings.

---

[57] *Furundžija Amicus Curiae* Brief, para. 21.
[58] Sue Lees, *Ruling Passions* (Buckingham: Open University Press, 1997), p. 106.
[59] The two cases in which male sexual violence was charged as rape, *Todorović* ICTY-95-9/1 and *Češić* ICTY-95-10/1, were completed by plea agreement and did not proceed to trial.
[60] Gopalan, Kravetz, 'Proving Crimes of Sexual Violence', p. 136.
[61] Ibid., pp. 130–131.

Evidencing sexual violence has been more in issue for defence, prosecution, and judges because of the gendered shaping of victim-witness testimony as a mode of evidence. The gendered shaping of trial processes can be seen from the earliest revisions of Rule 96, which reduced the strength of these protections,[62] and the subsequent re-emergence of corroboration in practice, if not in principle (*Furundžija*); the refusal of full protective measures on 'fair trial' grounds (*Tadić*); the consideration of evidence concerning consent and prior sexual conduct of the victim-witness (*Kunarac*); and the removal of protective measures on the grounds that the victim-witness spoke publicly of her experiences (*Karadžić*).

The global legal culture of the international criminal trial constructs formally equal subjects before the law. However, it does so through hegemonic ideas of masculine identity and of just process as narrow (masculine) fair trial rights. In contrast, the victim-witness does not have equivalent trial rights and, moreover, is subject to unequal treatment where providing evidence of gender-based crimes. From the establishment of the ICTY onwards feminist scholars were concerned by the problem of discriminatory gender bias,[63] the limits of the adversarial process for enabling women to witness their experiences of sexual violence,[64] and the 'prevailing beliefs and conceptual frameworks that shape how and when a gender lens is used by both lawyers and judges'.[65] The early ICTY cases, such as *Furundžija*, show the 'phallogocentric trial' in municipal criminal law re-emerges at the international level. The phallogocentric trial not only treats women unequally but also 'reflects cultural values about female sexuality', such that it 'distils' 'the problem of legal method, the problems of the "maleness" of law, the disqualification and disempowering of women'.[66] It creates a form of 'testimonial injustice' that occurs when 'prejudice causes a hearer to give a deflated level of credibility to a speaker's word'.[67] In the context of the international criminal trial, such testimonial injustice is better described not as

---

[62] Fitzgerald, 'Problems of Prosecution and Adjudication of Rape', 639.
[63] Fionnuala Ní Aoláin, 'Radical Rules', (1996-1997) 60(3) Alb L Rev 883-905.
[64] Julie Mertus, 'Shouting from the Bottom of the Well', (2004) 6(1) International Feminist Journal of Politics, 110–128.
[65] Doris Buss, 'International Criminal Courts', in Jill Steans and Daniela Tepe-Belfrage (eds.), *Handbook on Gender in World Politics* (Cheltenham and Northampton MA: Elgar, (2016), p. 166.
[66] Smart, *Feminism and the Power of the Law*, p. 26.
[67] Miranda Fricker, *Epistemic Injustice* (Oxford: Oxford University Press, 2007), p. 1.

prejudice but as bias. Such bias includes the contextual values that unfairly reduce credibility, namely, the prevailing beliefs and conceptual frameworks that shape the operation of 'gender' in the international criminal trial.

If, however, we move from the lower level cases, which most closely resemble municipal trials of sexual violence, to the so-called leadership cases, then the distinctive 'international' dimension of international criminal trials becomes visible, and another mode of evidence comes into view.

4.3 Collective Witnessing and Modes of Evidence in International Criminal Trials

Leadership trials typically try 'high-level' accused who did not physically perpetrate criminal acts, which were carried out by their subordinates. In these cases, the prosecution has to establish the link between sexual violence committed by direct perpetrators (the 'crime base') and the senior officials responsible for those crimes (the 'acts and conduct of the accused'). The shift to senior leadership cases occurs with the increasing focus upon the completion of ICTY trials from 2001 onwards, culminating in the so-called Completion Strategy in 2003. The Strategy concentrated prosecutions on 'the most senior leaders suspected of being most responsible for crimes' and aimed to increase the efficiency of trial proceedings.[68]

With the increasing complexity of leadership trials and the need to reduce trial time, there is a shift from the preference for live testimony to the wider admissibility of written evidence, as well as greater powers being given to judges to manage evidence at trial (ICTY RPE, as amended on 19 January 2001).[69] This shift includes the admission of written statements and transcripts in lieu of oral testimony, where the evidence does not go to the acts or conduct of the accused (Rule 92*bis*).[70]

---

[68] Theodor Meron, ICTY Completion Strategy Report, May 21, 2004, S/2004/420.
[69] The characterisation of live witness testimony as more reliable than other forms of evidence remains: *Lukić and Lukić*, IT-98-32/1-A, Judgement, 4 December 2012, para. 614.
[70] Such evidence going to the acts or conduct of the accused was admissible under restricted circumstances under Rule 92*ter*, *quater*, and *quinquies*.

4.3.1   Collective Witnessing and Modes of Evidence: The Prosecutor v. Brđanin

With this shift to the leadership cases, another mode of evidence becomes visible. This is collective witnessing as a mode of evidence, which involves multiple witnesses and forms of evidence. *The Prosecutor v. Brđanin* was one of the first leadership trials and is typical of these modes of evidence in later 'higher level' ICTY cases. In contrast to the *Furundžija* case, the Accused in the case of *Brđanin* was a senior political and military leader who was not a physical participant in the crimes. Brđanin was charged with multiple counts of genocide, war crimes, and crimes against humanity on the basis of individual and superior criminal responsibility (that is, command responsibility). The charges included multiple allegations of sexual violence during 'ethnic cleansing', as well as in camps and other detention centres, in the Banja Luka region.[71]

Reflecting the legal and evidentiary complexity of the case, the *Brđanin* proceedings ran from January 2002 to April 2004. The trial ran for over two years, with 202 witnesses called by the Prosecution and 19 witnesses called by the Defence. There were 2736 Prosecution exhibits and 350 submitted by the Defence. Both the Trial Chamber and counsel characterised *Brđanin* as the first major documentary trial,[72] and the decisions in the case laid down important principles regarding the admission and evaluation of evidence in international criminal trials.

4.3.1.1   Modes of Evidence

In the leadership trials, evidencing sexual violence came to take different forms: 'greater use [was] made of written evidence, such as witness statements and transcripts of prior witness testimony, as well as adjudicated facts from earlier ICTY cases'.[73] While documentary evidence was particularly important in *Brđanin*,[74] sexual violence evidence was not submitted in this form. Rather, it was submitted in all three forms of testimony, namely, live testimony, written witness statements, and transcripts of evidence given in prior proceedings.[75]

---

[71] *Brđanin*, ICTY-99-36, Sixth Amended Indictment, 9 December 2003.
[72] *Brđanin*, ICTY-99-36, Trial Transcript, (*Brđanin* Trial Transcript), 10 December 2001, p. 386.
[73] Gopalan, Kravetz et al., 'Proving Crimes of Sexual Violence', p. 112.
[74] *Brđanin* Trial Judgement, paras. 29–34.
[75] *Brđanin* Trial Transcript, 20 April 2004, p. 25262.

While the Trial Chamber judgement reiterates the traditional distinction between testimonial and non-testimonial evidence, this distinction is not clearly sustained in the use and evaluation of evidence in the case. The Judgement instead focuses upon the different evidential functions of information. In this approach, '[e]verything depends upon the *purpose or purposes* for which the evidence is adduced or employed in the trial'.[76] In *Brđanin* there is an emphasis upon the function of evidence rather than its form, which is shared by all parties. For example, the Trial Chamber accepted two witness statements by sexual violence victims submitted by the Prosecution under Rule 92*bis*, despite the fact that these witnesses were unavailable to testify before the court.[77] This was because the statements went to proof of crime base conduct, rather than the acts and conduct of the Accused, and was not challenged by the Defence.[78]

In the context of crime base conduct, then, all parties appear to share a model of victim-witness testimony as evidence. Victim-witness testimony – whether in written or oral form – was regarded as sufficient in itself to establish the occurrence of sexual violence in the conflict. It provided sufficient epistemic justification for the belief that the event occurred and consequently for its existence as legal fact. However, where testimony is used to establish the criminal responsibility of the accused, there is no longer a shared acceptance of the evidential value of testimony, and different models of evidence emerge.

4.3.1.2 The Prosecution: Testimony as Truth

As in *Furundžija*, the Prosecutor in *Brđanin* utilises an evidential model of testimony as truth. In this model, witness testimony provides evidence of the facts that the Prosecution seeks to establish and so functions as the proof of those facts.[79] It is on this basis that the Rule 92*bis* witness statements were submitted 'to have some evidence on rapes' in the Kotor Varoš municipality.[80] This veridical model of testimony presents testimony as a truthful description of the event. However, as in *Furundžija*, in *Brđanin* too, the Prosecution does not understand testimony as a straightforward reflection of reality. Rather, it utilises a model

---

[76] Paul Roberts and Adrian Zuckerman, *Criminal Evidence* (Oxford: Oxford University Press, 2010), p. 113.
[77] *Brđanin* Trial Judgement, para. 835.
[78] *Brđanin* Trial Transcript, 25 June 2003, pp. 18175–18179.
[79] *Brđanin* Trial Transcript, 19 April 2004, p. 25131.
[80] *Brđanin* Trial Transcript, 25 June 2003, pp. 18175–18179.

of testimony as a reliable re-presentation of the event to the court. In the case of witnesses, that re-representation is a 'honest, truthful, and accurate' account of those events.[81] In the case of documents, eyewitnesses or expert witnesses re-present the content or meaning of the text.[82] Testimony does not reproduce reality. Rather, it re-presents a truthful description of an event.

However, *Brđanin* also reveals the complexity of the Prosecution's evidential reconstruction of an event for the ICTY. First, the event is in the past and can only be recreated for the court in the present. This epistemological problem marks ICTY trials such as *Brđanin*, in which the trial takes place some ten years after the alleged crimes. Second, testimony is not a single mirror of a single act. Rather, the Prosecution uses many testimonies to establish the multiple facts of multiple events. In cases of collective criminality, multiple events generally require multiple testimonies to establish them as facts, or to 'build' the case. For example, the Prosecution submitted five witness statements to evidence rapes in the Kotor Varoš municipality,[83] and these multiple testimonies were used to establish that (1) these acts of sexual violence occurred as part of a wider 'event' of persecution in the municipality and (2) similar events occurred across 13 municipalities.[84]

4.3.1.3 The Witness: Testimony as Experience

As in *Furundžija*, in formal terms, all witnesses are witnesses of truth for the Tribunal rather than for the parties. As such, these witnesses occupy the position of the neutral third party, the *testis*. However, the majority of these are victims of, or witnesses to, crimes, called by the Prosecution as fact witnesses to meet the evidential burden of proof (reflected in the significantly larger number of witnesses called by the Prosecution than the Defence in the case). The fact witnesses found the veracity of their testimony upon their epistemological status as 'a person who has lived through an event from beginning to end and can therefore bear witness to it', that is, their position as *superstes*.[85] As one witness says to the Trial Chamber, 'thank you for giving me this opportunity to speak about the

---

[81] *Brđanin* Trial Transcript, 19 April 2004, p. 25136.
[82] *Brđanin* Trial Transcript, 2 July 2003, p. 18688.
[83] *Brđanin*, ICTY-99-36-T, Decision on Prosecution's Motions for Admission of Statements Pursuant to Rule 92*bis* – Kotor Varoš Municipality, 7 July 2003 (*Brđanin* Kotor Varoš Decision).
[84] *Brđanin* Trial Transcript, 20 April 2004, p. 25262.
[85] Agamben, *Remnants of Auschwitz*, p. 17.

truth that I personally experienced'.[86] In this classical empiricist model, the witness's sense experience of the event provides them with their knowledge of it. The witness gives such direct evidence, namely evidence directly perceived by the senses of the witness, in the form of their 'eyewitness testimony'.

However, in *Brđanin* multiple witnesses testify to multiple harms against multiple victims, whereas in *Furundžija*, witnesses testify to the crime against the victim-witness. The witnesses attest to many wrongs to many persons, rather than solely to the harm to the victim-witness. Leadership cases make visible this 'international' context of collective violence, which makes international criminal trials distinct from municipal trials. The nature of collective criminality entails that witnesses do not only testify to their experience of a single event but also testify to their experience of the multiple events that constitute the collective criminality of war, such as the multiple sexual assaults upon others during the 'ethnic cleansing' of a village. For example, Witness BT-71 gives evidence not only of her experience of rape but also of multiple crimes against others she witnessed during the 'ethnic cleansing' of her village in the Kotor Varoš municipality.[87] The experiential position of the witness is refracted through multiple experiences and relations to others. If the word 'evidence' derives from the Latin *videre* – 'to see' – then these multiple acts of seeing testify to a multiplicity of acts. This mode of testimony is not individual but is collective. It is collective in that it consists of collective witnesses and attests to collective violence.

4.3.1.4 The Defence: Testimony as Fallible

The fallibilistic defence model of evidence becomes fully evident in *Brđanin*. If the prosecution adduces testimony as the demonstration of an event, then the defence seeks to challenge that evidence. So, for example, the Defence sought to have the right to properly test the evidence of victim-witnesses providing crime base evidence in affidavit form, including sexual violence witnesses who had previously testified before the ICTY.[88] That the Defence did not exercise that right to

---

[86] *Brđanin* Trial Transcript, 7 June 2002, p. 6843.
[87] *Brđanin* Trial Transcript, 16 June 2003, p. 17613 ff.
[88] *Brđanin*, ICTY-99-36-T, Decision on Prosecution's Eleventh Motion for Protective Measures for Victims and Witnesses, 10 October 2002.

challenge evidence through live cross-examination was regarded as a mitigating factor in sentencing.[89]

In this fallibilistic model, the Defence tests testimony by seeking to falsify it. This is done by raising questions of whether testimony is internally consistent, empirically justified, and, most commonly, provided by a reliable observer. Like all good sceptics, the Defence begins from a position of doubt, rather than belief, in the evidential value of testimony. They present their own evidence with the function of raising doubt as to the guilt of the accused. The Defence's scepticism is sharpest where evidence goes to establishing the criminal responsibility of the Accused. In *Brđanin*, for example, the Defence accepts sexual violence evidence given by victim-witness BT-71 submitted as part of 'crime base' evidence but contests its submission to establish the acts or conduct of the Accused. This is because in leadership cases, 'by not contesting that a victim was raped or sexually assaulted, an accused does not admit their liability', which instead requires linking sexual violence to the acts and conduct of the accused.[90] In leadership cases, the defence may accept testimony to sexual violence as truthful but not as establishing the legal 'fact' of the accused's responsibility for those crimes.

4.3.1.5 The Court: Testimony as Evidence

If the role of the Trial Chamber is to adjudicate upon evidence, as we saw in *Furundžija*, *Brđanin* shows the criteria for that adjudication. *Brđanin* is a leading case on principles for the evaluation of evidence.[91] According to these principles, the evidential value of live testimony should be assessed on the basis of the credibility of the witness (such as their 'demeanour, conduct and character') and the objective reliability of their evidence (such as consistency, knowledge of facts).[92] These criteria determine the probative value of testimony, that is, the weight it should be given in legally establishing a fact. The testimony of the witness is not evaluated in isolation but is assessed in relation to other corroborative, documentary, and circumstantial evidence.[93] So, for example, Prosecution witness Rašim Čirkić testified to sexual violence against two murdered men that he had witnessed, but the Trial Chamber did

---

[89] *Brđanin* Trial Chamber Judgement, para. 1137.
[90] Gopalan, Kravetz et al., 'Proving Crimes of Sexual Violence', p. 126.
[91] *Brđanin* Trial Judgement, paras. 22–24.
[92] Ibid., para. 25.
[93] Ibid., para. 35.

not consider it safe to rely on this testimony because the Defence was unable to cross-examine him and there was 'absolutely no other evidence on them'.[94]

Evidence is thus assessed as part of a set of all evidence, that is, as part of the totality of evidence against the Accused.[95] The Trial Chamber assesses the case against the Accused 'upon the evidence before it' as a whole, such that testimony becomes part of an evidential totality.[96] So, where sexual violence has been successfully established, the ICTY has taken a 'predominately contextual approach' to their evaluation of the evidence.[97] For example, in *Brđanin*, the Defence appealed the guilty verdict on sexual violence charged as a crime against humanity on the grounds these were 'individual domestic crimes' not connected to the conflict. However, the appeal was dismissed on the grounds that the Trial Chamber had reasonably relied on evidence of the context of the sexual violence to establish the 'international elements' of the crime, namely, that it occurred in the context of military forces undertaking weapons searches or attacks on Muslim civilians within a broader campaign targeting businesses and mosques.[98]

The determination of legal facts is an adjudication upon whether or not a fact has been established by the evidence presented and rests upon epistemic evaluation of that evidence. At an epistemological level, the 'culture of fact' in the international criminal trial utilises both correspondence and coherence models of truth-seeking. The evaluation of evidence uses correspondence model of truth, namely, a model in which true statements are statements that correspond with real events, and these events exist independently of human observation.[99] In this model, judges use rational modes of decision-making, including inductive reasoning, to come to warranted beliefs about the external world. These warranted beliefs serve as the basis for the court to claim that it makes determinations of fact that correspond to the real event.

However, evaluating the 'evidential totality' to establish facts also involves assessing evidence in terms of relational epistemic criteria, such

---

[94] Ibid., para. 742, footnote 1796.
[95] *Brđanin* Trial Judgement, paras. 20–22; *Brđanin*, ICTY-99-36-A, Judgement, 3 April 2007 (*Brđanin* Appeals Judgement), para. 12.
[96] *Brđanin* Trial Judgement, para. 21.
[97] Laurel Baig, Michelle Jarvis et al., 'Contextualising Sexual Violence', in Brammertz and Jarvis (eds.), *Prosecuting Conflict-Related Sexual Violence*, p. 183.
[98] *Brđanin* Appeals Judgement, paras. 256–257.
[99] Jackson and Doran, 'Evidence', p. 178.

as 'corroboration with other evidence', the 'circumstances of the case', and the 'overall context of the evidence received'. There is an evaluation of testimony not simply in its own terms but also in relation to other evidence and the context of the case. Accordingly, this approach assesses testimony in terms of its place within the whole body of evidence, and understands the body of evidence as a whole as a differential system composed of elements or units of evidence. It assigns meaning or value to each piece of evidence according to its place within this differential system. This is a coherence model of truth, in which beliefs are justified by their coherence with a set of believed propositions.[100] Nevertheless, this 'coherence' understanding of the meaning of evidence retains a referential emphasis upon the existence of an external world of real events. The Trial Chamber assumes that its determination of the facts captures an event, such that its fact-finding will conform to an external reality of events that have taken place. Its decisions, therefore, require a link to the world of facts. They require more than justified belief, since that justified belief cannot be severed simply from the empirical world of events that it is asked to judge.

The Trial Chamber uses testimony as evidence to link its judgement and the empirical event in its adjudicative fact-finding. Testimony functions as the '*epistemic link* between a subject, the hearer, and the state of affairs whose obtaining he comes to believe in as a result of the exercising of this link'.[101] For example, victim-witness testimony re-presents the experiences of the victim to the court. As a form of social knowledge, testimony permits us to have knowledge of experiences that are not our own. In the courtroom, witness testimony is a re-presentation by a witness of a world of facts not known to the judicial fact-finder. Testimony thereby plays a crucial role as an epistemic link between the knowledge of the hearer – those sitting on the bench – and the external world – the fact of the event. For this reason, the witness becomes crucial to the 'culture of fact'. Their testimony reveals the world of persons (victims and perpetrators) and social relations (collective violence) that create that 'event'.

The collective nature of the violence produces many witnesses to multiple harms done by numerous perpetrators. The 'evidential totality'

[100] Ken Kress, 'Coherence', in Patterson (ed.), *A Companion to Philosophy of Law and Legal Theory*, p. 533.
[101] Elizabeth Fricker, 'The Epistemology of Testimony', (1987) 61 Proceedings of the Aristotelian Society *(Supplementary Volumes)* 57–83, 58.

of collective witnessing thereby functions as a primary epistemic link between the judgement of the court and the events of collective violence. Collective witnessing thus re-presents these events as an 'evidential totality' to the finder of fact. As a mode of evidence, it re-presents the actors, actions, and organisation of collective violence. Collective witnessing, then, not only describes a visible world of facts seen by the witness but also reveals an invisible world of social relations. The 'evidential totality' describes the *collective violence* that produces this event. Collective witnessing 'evidences' the social dimensions of collective violence. As a mode of witnessing, this 'collective evidence' demonstrates not only the legally relevant 'event' but also the social world of collective violence.

If the legal culture of fact relies upon testimony as evidence to tie together the legal determination of facts and the occurrence of an event, then it also relies upon a community of witnessing and judging. If testimony is the address of one social subject to another, then that address presumes a shared social world.[102] The assumption that witnesses share a social world gives testimony its epistemic value as a source of knowledge. This is because testimony presumes that members of that social world share 'collective interpretative resources', a collective understanding that enables them to describe and explain their individual experience to others.[103] In domestic criminal trials, the membership of that shared social world (a society, community, or group) warrants the truth (or otherwise) of testimony. The evidential value of testimony thereby presumes a community of witnesses, with shared social understanding.

To legally adjudicate upon testimony also implies a community of judgement. If testimony is a social practice that involves the communication of knowledge from one speaking subject to another, then that model implies that both witness and judge must belong to a shared epistemic community for that testimony to be understood and judged. Jennifer Nedelsky points out that '[w]hat enables one to judge is membership in a community of other judging subjects who share a common sense that makes their judgements, and their inherent claims of validity for the community, possible'.[104] This model of testimony implies that

---

[102] Alvin Goldman, *Knowledge in a Social World* (Oxford: Clarendon, 1999), pp. 103–104.
[103] Fricker, *Epistemic Injustice*, p. 1.
[104] Jennifer Nedelsky, 'Communities of Judgment and Human Rights', (2000) 1(2) Theo Inq Law 245–282, 262.

there is a community to address, whose members are able to interpret, understand, and evaluate the evidence it offers. It also implies that the community shares a normative horizon of judgement and can recognise and respond to the evidence of injustice.

4.3.2 Conceptual Problems in Collective Modes of Evidencing Sexual Violence

The legal form of the international criminal trial relies on ideas of a global legal culture as the warrant of juridical truth at the international level. The epistemic norms and practices of this legal culture warrant the juridical fact-finding of the trial and form the juridical category of the international criminal trial. These epistemic norms rely on the presentation and testing of evidence, witnesses as neutral observers who provide evidence, trial processes as objective methods of fact-finding, and judges as unbiased arbiters of fact. Accordingly, the global legal culture comes to be the foundational warrant of legal truths in international criminal trial, rather than the 'national' society or community of municipal criminal law. In this global legal culture, the subjective 'integrity' of the witness and the epistemological 'integrity' of the community of judgement come to found juridical 'truth'. The legal category of the international criminal trial thereby relies on two assumptions. The first is that there is a universal witnessing subject able to testify to collective violence, and the second is that there is a universal community of judgement able to adjudicate it.

4.3.2.1 The Problem of Communities of Witnessing and Judging

The global legal culture confronts the fundamental problem of the destruction of social communities of witnessing and judging in war. In destroying the social world of persons living together, collective violence also devastates the society that would judge that destruction. It ruptures the social – but not ethical – community of judgement. The damage to society in war is both literal, in that it devastates physical and functional municipal criminal justice systems, and metaphorical, since it fractures the social relations constituting that society as such. In the context of collective violence, the devastation of societies commonly instigates international criminal trials. However, it also leads to the paradoxical position that testimony in such international trials describes and relies upon shared communities of meaning while also demonstrating the broken social relations of conflict. The international criminal trial relies upon shared social worlds to warrant its truth while also revealing the destruction of that social world.

In this context, three epistemic problems of legitimating legal fact-finding emerge. Following Miranda Fricker, we can describe these problems as forms of 'hermeneutic injustice', that is, 'when a gap in collective interpretive resources puts someone at an unfair disadvantage when it comes to making sense of their social experiences'. Hermeneutical or interpretative injustice 'is caused by structural prejudice in the economy of collective hermeneutical resources'.[105] As discussed above, it is preferable in the legal context to describe hermeneutical injustice as being caused by structural bias and discriminatory contextual values (rather than prejudice) in the economy of collective hermeneutical resources. With this reframing, we can say that hermeneutic injustice points to a structural gap in collective interpretative resources, and it is this hermeneutic gap that international trials reveal.

The first epistemic problem is the apparent destruction of a shared social world. At the ICTY, the conflict in the former Yugoslavia is understood as destroying the idea of a society in common, replacing it with membership in ethnic communities and 'different' languages. This framing figures witnesses as testifying from within (and against) separate communities, with each considered to have its attendant perspective and experience, rather than as testifying from within a shared society. As a consequence, it becomes structurally difficult for witnesses from the former Yugoslavia to take up the position of the *testis*, that is, of the impartial or neutral witness.[106] A typical example of this problem can be found in *Brđanin*, where a witness was challenged by the Defence and the Bench for ethnic bias because of his experiences of the conflict, particularly his experiences as a Croat of 'ethnic cleansing'.[107] It frames the witness as the representative of a given community, even as they describe themselves as members of the destroyed society of Yugoslavia.

The second problem is that modes of collective evidence rely upon a testimonial community, which collective violence may damage. This is a common evidential problem in cases before the ICTY, where there may not be witnesses to appear before the court to testify to the crime. In *Brđanin*, this evidential problem appears in the form of absent witnesses

---

[105] Fricker, *Epistemic Injustice*, p. 1.
[106] This issue was first discussed in *Tadić*, ICTY-94-1-T, Judgement, 7 May 1997, para. 541.
[107] *Brđanin* Trial Transcript, 23 June 2003, p. 17981.

and is exemplified by the evidence concerning two murdered male victims of sexual violence discussed previously. In circumstances where there are no survivors of crimes, then there are no witnesses to testify. Missing persons, families, and villages continually appear like ghosts throughout the case transcripts.[108]

The third problem is that witnessing and judging subjects do not necessarily share collective interpretative resources or a common social world in the international criminal trial. Persons, objects, and texts can only 'speak for themselves' in a shared social world. As a witness described of his testimony on Serbian propaganda: 'if you had been there you would have understood what the words meant to people'.[109] There are a number of specific difficulties for the evaluation of testimony posed by the lack of a shared social world between judge and witness in international criminal trials. These include language interpretation and translation, conflict-particular language, and the 'role of culture in witness evaluation'.[110] However, as the Trial Chamber acknowledges, there is also the broader hermeneutic problem of the interpretation of evidence in its relevant historical and social context by judges who do not share that context.[111] In essence, this is the problem of how the community of judgement 'sees' the evidential totality presented to it.

Of course, the problem of 'seeing' the evidential totality includes the values and 'world view' of judges. The argument of 'unintentional bias against the Serb' raised by the Defence in *Brđanin* was correctly rejected by the Chamber as being unsubstantiated, which held that '[i]t is the duty of the Trial Chamber to decide what, if any, is the individual criminal responsibility to be ascribed to an accused, irrespective of nationality, religion, ethnicity or other grounds'.[112] However, the ICTY judgements are replete with references to archaic ethnic hatreds and conservative Muslim cultures to explain the conflict and crimes, reflecting orientalist assumptions about the 'Balkans' generally and Yugoslavian ('Bosnian Muslim') society in particular.[113] As Dubravka Žarkov reminds us, such narratives also reflect hegemonic state relations within the international

---

[108] See, for example, *Brđanin* Trial Transcript, 6 December 2002, p. 12512, and 11 December 2002, p. 12609.
[109] *Brđanin* Trial Transcript, 24 June 2003, p. 18086.
[110] Robert Cryer, 'Witness Evidence before International Criminal Tribunals', (2003) 2(3) The Law and Practice of International Courts and Tribunals, 411–439, 428.
[111] *Brđanin* Trial Judgement, para. 45.
[112] Ibid., para. 42.
[113] See Doris Buss, 'Knowing Women', (2014) 23(1) S&LS, 73–92.

order, which counterpose 'civilised' Western nations (whose own war crimes are seen as aberrations) to the 'brutality of men and sexual vulnerability of women in the Balkans and Africa', which are seen as 'symbolic continents of violence'.[114] These evaluative frames may also include 'gender bias' and patriarchal understandings of sex and sexuality, such as assuming that 'for a woman, rape is by far the ultimate offence', as the *Brđanin* Trial Chamber describes.[115] The patriarchal reasoning linking rape and women's sexual dishonour becomes visible in the earlier *Stakić* decision that *Brđanin* approvingly cites.[116]

However, these epistemic problems are also political and ethical problems. The construction of collective evidence is crucial to the 'international' dimension of fact-finding in international criminal trials, and the capacity to produce juridical truths about collective violence gives the international criminal trial its discursive power. Because international criminal trials 'legitimate' facts and narratives about what happened and who is responsible for it, they warrant the juridical truth about what happened not only to individuals but also to societies. As Doris Buss describes, because they are 'authoritative institutions that produce "official knowledge" about conflict and its effects, international criminal courts are an important site to secure recognition of women and men's experience of conflict'.[117]

4.3.2.2 The Problem of Evidencing Sexual Violence

Given that these findings are warranted by the epistemic norms and practices of the international criminal trial, legal methods of fact-finding are crucial to understanding how and when a gender lens is used in international criminal trials. In international criminal trials, fact-finding methods involve the construction and evaluation of evidence not only in individual modes of witnessing and judging, as in *Furundžija*, but also in collective witnessing and judging, as *Brđanin* shows. Like other leadership cases, *Brđanin* can be said to make the collective evidence of sexual violence visible but not to 'see' it as evidence of gender-based collective violence. This is because the legal form of collective modes of witnessing

---

[114] Dubravka Žarkov, 'Ontologies of International Humanitarian and Criminal Law', in Dubravka Žarkov and Marlies Glasius (eds.), *Narratives of Justice in and out of the Courtroom* (New York: Springer, 2014), p. 18.
[115] *Brđanin* Trial Judgement, para. 1009.
[116] *Stakić*, ICTY-97-24-T, Judgement, 31 July 2003, para. 803.
[117] Buss, 'International Criminal Courts', p. 167.

and judging raise three conceptual problems for fact-finding on conflict-related sexual violence.

The first problem is the contextualisation of sexual violence evidence within the social world of collective violence in which it takes place. To understand the value of the evidence of sexual violence, it must be understood in terms of the values it expresses and the values about sex and sexuality in the society in which it takes place. For example, in *Brđanin*, the evidential totality shows different forms of sexual violence against men and women, such as the rape of women by men in private settings and men forcing male victims to engage in forced sexual acts with other each or female victims in public settings, as is typical across the ICTY cases. To appropriately identify, interpret, and legally characterise this evidence requires a contextual understanding of the values about sex and sexuality that this violence expresses (such as 'public'/'private', 'homosexualisation'/'heterosexualisation') and how this shapes patterns of perpetration and victimisation. However, neither the charging nor judgement in *Brđanin* provide this 'gender lens' on the evidence presented, and so they do not reveal the gendered shaping of sexual violence in the Yugoslav conflict that produces these gendered patterns of victimisation and perpetration.

The second problem is the 'value' that is given to the evidence of sexual violence. If the legal form of criminal trials expresses contextual values about sex, sexuality, and sexual subjectivity, then these ideas will shape how evidence is valued. On the one hand, it is possible to see that women are 'valued' as victim-witnesses to sexual violence, with female victim-witnesses predominantly giving sexual violence evidence in both *Furundžija* and *Brđanin*. On the other, they are 'devalued' as credible victim-witnesses, as in *Furundžija*, or as witnesses to other crimes besides sexual violence, as in *Brđanin*. Of the sexual violence witnesses in *Brđanin*, only one gave public evidence of her experience of 'ethnic cleansing' in her municipality. Moreover, the highly disproportionate ratio of male to female witnesses in *Brđanin* approximates that of the ICTY more generally.[118]

In this same heterosexual framing, we see that high value is given to the rape of women, the archetypal war crime against women, with a devaluation of other 'feminised' sexual harms against women and of 'feminised' sexual violence against men. So, for example, Michelle Jarvis

---

[118] Insofar as it is possible to determine, evidence was provided by approximately 35 women of 202 Prosecution fact witnesses.

and Kate Vigneswaran note that possible forced pregnancy charges were not laid in *Brđanin*.[119] Similarly, incidences of male sexual assault are not described as such in the legal findings on rape and sexual assault in the *Brđanin* Trial Chamber judgement.[120] Finally, no male sexual violence case equivalent to *Furundžija* was brought before the ICTY, in which 'rape and sexual assault was the single charge'.[121]

The values given to sexual violence evidence in *Brđanin* and *Furundžija* are typical of the ICTY cases.[122] In this gendered evidencing of the crimes of war, women become visible victims of sexual violence while men remain invisible victims. If primarily men narrate war, then they appear to function as actors (political party members, soldiers, village defenders, and so on) within the conflict. If women only narrate rape, then they appear as passive victims of sexual violence. Such a narrative framing reproduces traditional models of active masculinity and passive femininity and so (re)produces the problem of the legal representation of women as actors and agents in factual findings on the conflict.

The third problem is establishing evidence of sexual violence through collective witnessing. Because of the gendered nature of this crime, and the model of legal fact-finding, sexual violence may not become evidence of collective violence if it is not collectively witnessed. For example, as Gopalan et al describe, in *Brđanin* the Prosecution was able to establish multiple incidents of rape in the Trnopolje camp on the basis of the evidence of single victim-witness and corroborating non-victim witnesses. However, they also note that because generally sexual assault against men was committed in public, whereas the rape of women was not, 'there may be more direct eyewitness evidence available of sexual violence against males'.[123] Accordingly, the model of collective witnessing as evidence raises two further questions. The first concerns how sexual violence becomes part of the evidential totality of collective violence. If the victim-witness becomes the evidential personification of the sexual violence crime against her (as described earlier), then this raises

---

[119] Michelle Jarvis and Kate Vigneswaran, 'Challenges to Successful Outcomes in Sexual Violence Cases', in Brammertz and Jarvis (eds.), *Prosecuting Conflict-Related Sexual Violence*, p. 58.
[120] *Brđanin* Trial Judgement, para. 1010.
[121] Charlesworth and Chinkin, *The Boundaries of International Law*, p. 322.
[122] See Campbell, 'The Gender of Transitional Justice', and Mischkowski and Mlinarević, *And That It Does Not Happen to Anyone Anywhere in the World*.
[123] Gopalan, Kravetz, 'Proving Crimes of Sexual Violence', p. 151.

the problem of evidencing the crime without the victim-witness, which arises repeatedly through the *Brđanin* proceedings. For example, Ivo Atlija testified that a number of women were raped in Briševo on the basis of contemporaneous family member reports and his observation of their injuries. However, the Trial Chamber made no factual finding on these rapes in its determination on crimes committed in this village.[124] The second concerns how sexual violence becomes part of the public narratives of the conflict, when victim witness evidence does not appear in the public record of the trial proceedings. For example, three victim-witnesses refused to give evidence at trial, and so their evidence was submitted in the form of 92*bis* statements.[125] This is also the case with other sexual violence witnesses whose testimony is redacted.

Because of the gendered shaping of evidence and fact-finding, women's experiences of war and its forms of collective violence do not become visible in the judicial determination of fact and responsibility. For example, when describing the pattern of conduct by Serb forces across 16 municipalities, the Trial Chamber identifies that rape occurred in 2 municipalities (with women specified as victims in only one).[126] However, in its findings on rape as a crime against humanity, the Trial Chamber also found that rape of women occurred in an additional 4 municipalities.[127] While the apparent gender-neutrality of the judgement hides the gendered shaping of fact-finding, in fact it produces gendered narratives of war that reflect the experience of men, rather than women. Because of the power of the international criminal trial to produce knowledge about women's and men's experiences of war, the stakes of addressing the problem of collective fact-finding on sexual violence for survivors and their societies is very high indeed.

4.4 The Conceptual Contradictions of the Legal Concept of the International Criminal Trial

The international criminal trial has been crucial for making visible the evidence of conflict-related sexual violence, for establishing the truth of these events, and for including sexual violence in its public narratives of conflict. The international criminal trial warrants the production of these

---

[124] *Brđanin* Trial Transcript, 21 November 2002, p. 11948.
[125] *Brđanin*, Trial Transcript, 25 June 2003, p. 18175.
[126] *Brđanin* Trial Judgement, paras. 104, 110.
[127] Ibid., para. 1010.

juridical truths through the fact-finding process of the criminal trial and the epistemic norms and practices of that process. However, that process presumes shared communities of witnessing and judging, which rely on particular social values in warranting truthful witnessing and objective judgement. In the case of the individual victim-witness, it presumes a model of bodily and psychic integrity. In the case of collective witnessing, it presumes shared communities of witnessing and judging. In both cases, international crimes disrupt these presumptions and create the legal problem of how to warrant these juridical truths. The international criminal trial resolves these conceptual contradictions by founding its determinations upon a global legal culture of legal fact-finding. However, the sexual violence cases also show that while this global legal culture claims to produce epistemic justice, it also creates testimonial, hermeneutic, and social injustice through the gendered shaping of legal narratives of fact, victimisation, and perpetration of conflict-related sexual violence.

5

International Criminal Justice

> Determined to put an end to such crimes and to take effective measures to bring to justice the persons who are responsible for them,
>
> Convinced that in the particular circumstances of the former Yugoslavia the establishment of an international tribunal would enable this aim to be achieved and would contribute to the restoration and maintenance of peace.
>
> UNSC Resolution 808[1]

Ideas of 'justice' have always served as the foundational value of the existence and purpose of international criminal law. As such, the idea of 'international criminal justice' operates as the fourth fundamental category of international criminal law. However, 'justice' is also the most contentious concept in this legal form. How, then, does international criminal law construct the 'justice' it seeks to render? What are the principles of justice that function as the axiological bases for its decisions? And what ideas of persons, society, and values does the category of 'international criminal justice' produce?

5.1 The Category of Justice of International Criminal Law

International criminal law scholarship has largely treated the category of 'international justice' as synonymous with the objectives of international criminal law. It has identified these functions, such as fact-finding or reconciliation, by analysing institutional, policy, or scholarly discourses about international criminal justice. This 'functionalist' framing treats the goals of international criminal law as an 'abstract concept of justice', which functions as 'an absolute and eternal criterion upon which one can erect an ideal' of (universal) just social relations.[2] This approach treats

---

[1] 22 February 1993, S/RES/808 (1993).
[2] Evgeny Pashukanis, *Law and Marxism* (London: Ink Links, 1978), p. 161.

'international justice' as a concept of an 'extra-juridical nature',[3] that is, as an ideal that is external to international criminal law, which it then assesses on normative or empirical grounds (such as: Should reconciliation be a goal of international justice? Does international criminal law provide reconciliation?). From the emergence of international criminal law onwards, there has been a series of debates regarding what the ideal of international justice should be and whether international criminal law provides it. However, such debates now focus on an apparent crisis in 'international criminal justice' as the justificatory foundation of international criminal law.[4] Recently, this justificatory crisis has become visible in the increasing rejection of international criminal justice *per se* for conflict-related sexual violence.[5] Too often, these discussions devolve into circular and unproductive discussions of this crisis, which reproduce their framing assumptions concerning the 'external' normative or social objectives of international justice.

My analysis instead begins with the prior question of how to describe 'international justice' as a legal category. It examines how international criminal law itself constructs 'international justice' as a category of values, that is, a set of values concerning what is good, right, and just. These values serve as the grounds of the 'justice' of international criminal law, which legitimate its operation as a legal institution and provide the axiological foundations of its decisions. These ideas of 'value' express specific social values, in that they represent particular ideas of the subject and the social order.

To trace the construction of 'international justice' as a legal category, I examine how ideas of justice come to have 'juridical specificity' in the positive law and jurisprudence of the ICTY and identify the values that serve as their legitimating principles and justifications.[6] My jurisprudential analysis focuses on decisions in sexual violence cases in which considerations concerning 'justice' are brought most sharply into focus, namely, jurisdictional challenges, 'fair trial' issues, and sentencing principles. By using this approach, it becomes possible to identify four

---

[3] Evgeny Pashukanis, *Selected Writings on Marxism and Law* (London: Academic Press, 1980), p. 41.
[4] Serge Vasiliev, 'The Crises and Critiques of International Criminal Justice', in Kevin Heller, Frédéric Mégret et al. (eds.), *The Oxford Handbook of International Criminal Law* (Oxford: Oxford University Press, 2020).
[5] Anette Houge and Kjersti Lohne, 'End Impunity!', (2017) 51(4) Law and Society Review, 755–789.
[6] Alan Norrie, *Law and the Beautiful Soul* (London: Glasshouse, 2005), p. 29.

distinctive models of justice. These models are more or less visible at different times, are given different prominence over the 'life course' of the judicial institution, and are regarded as more or less appropriate by different judicial actors, as I saw across the course of my fieldwork at the ICTY. However, the models themselves remain consistent. These are two classical juridical models of 'international justice' as *punishment* and *procedure* and two more recent models of justice as *recognition* and *reconciliation*.

5.1.1 The International Justice of Punishment

The first model is international justice as *punishment*. As the ICTY describes, 'one of the fundamental aims of international criminal courts and tribunals is to end impunity and ensure that serious violations of international humanitarian law are prosecuted and punished'.[7] UNSC Resolutions 808 and 837 set out the purpose of establishing the ICTY as ending the commission of international crimes and prosecuting and punishing their perpetrators. From its establishment, punitive justice was seen as the primary function of the ICTY as a judicial institution.[8] As discussed in Chapter 2, the model of punitive justice involves the prosecution of criminal offences that attract the juridical consequence of penal sanction. The ICTY Statute specified imprisonment as the form of sanction (Art. 24), while the Rules set out sentencing factors and maximum term of imprisonment (Rule 101 RPE). While the ICTY's public narratives of its objectives may have shifted over time, the ICTY jurisprudence consistently identifies deterrence and retribution as the two key aims of punitive justice.[9]

The first aim of criminal deterrence was evident from the UNSC resolutions onwards, which described establishing the ICTY as contributing to the aim of ending the crimes committed in the then ongoing conflict. While active conflicts in the former Yugoslavia formally ended

---

[7] *Karadžić*, ICTY-95-5/18-AR73.4-A, Decision on *Karadžić*'s Appeal of Trial Chamber's Decision on Alleged Holbrooke Agreement, 12 October 2009, (*Karadžić* Alleged Holbrooke Agreement Decision), para. 52.

[8] Antonio Cassese, Report of the International Criminal ICTY for the Prosecution of Persons Responsible for Serious Violations of Humanitarian Law Committed in the Territory of the Former Yugoslavia Since 1991, A/49/324, S/1994/1007, 1994 (Cassese Report), para. 190.

[9] *Karadžić*, ICTY-95-5/18-T, Judgement, 24 March 2016, (*Karadžić* Trial Judgement), para. 6025.

in 2001 with the Macedonian peace agreement, ideas of deterrence remained central to the model of punitive justice. The jurisprudence characterises deterrence as being both individual and general. As *Karadžić* describes: 'the penalty imposed by a Chamber should be adequate to dissuade a convicted person from re-offending (individual deterrence) and should also ensure that other potential perpetrators are dissuaded from committing the same or similar crimes (general deterrence)'.[10] The jurisprudence draws on classical utilitarian ideas of the role of punishment in preventing both the accused and others from committing crimes. It emphasises the importance of general deterrence, describing the purpose of punishment as warning 'persons who believe themselves to be beyond the reach of international criminal law ... that they have to abide by the norms underpinned by substantive criminal law or face prosecutions and, if convicted, sanctions'.[11] Deterrence is seen as an essential element of enforcing international criminal norms, since it protects international society through the repression of international crime.[12] This liberal utilitarian model of deterrence conceives international criminal law as a global social contract and punishing breaches of this contract as a necessary condition of the international social order.

The second aim of punitive justice is retribution. The ICTY characterises the call to bring perpetrators to justice in its founding resolutions as judicial retribution, which brings perpetrators to justice for breaking the law.[13] In the jurisprudence, retribution 'expresses society's condemnation of the criminal act and of the person who committed it and imposes a punishment for what he or she has done'.[14] This modern concept of punishment draws on classical liberal Enlightenment ideas of retribution as the 'just deserts' of the perpetrator for their criminal conduct, which 'unlike vengeance, requires the imposition of a just and appropriate punishment, and nothing more'.[15] As such, retribution is necessary because '*punitur quia peccatur* (the individual must be punished because

---

[10] Ibid., para. 6026.
[11] *Mladić*, ICTY-09-92-T, Judgement, 22 November 2017, para. 5183.
[12] *Dragan Nikolić*, ICTY-94-2-T, Sentencing Judgement, 18 December 2003, (*D. Nikolić* Sentencing Judgement), para. 139.
[13] *Furundžija*, ICTY-95-17/1-A, Judgement, 21 July 2000, para. 201.
[14] *Češić*, ICTY-95-10/1-S-T, Sentencing Judgement, 11 March 2004, (*Češić* Sentencing Judgement), para. 23.
[15] *Karadžić* Trial Judgement, para. 6026.

he broke the law)'.[16] However, it also draws on more modern expressive conception of retribution, as declaring 'the attitudes of the community ... to affirm its rejection and revulsion at certain types of conduct. In doing so, it affirms the values of the community as a whole.'[17] Reflecting this idea, the jurisprudence describes retribution as 'an expression of the outrage of the international community at the crimes committed',[18] which affirms 'public reprobation and stigmatisation [of these crimes] by the international community'.[19] The aim of retribution is to reinstitute the legal order of the international community by punishing and condemning the breach of its laws. As such, it understands punitive justice as restoring the legal norms and moral values of the international society as a whole. It is seen as restoring these norms and values not only within international society but also within those societies that have not observed them in the conduct of war.[20]

Freud reminds us that what prevails in law 'is no longer the violence of the individual, but that of the community'.[21] In the model of punitive justice, punishment 'conveys the indignation of humanity for the serious violations of international criminal law'.[22] These are crimes 'which are universally recognized and condemned as such ("Universally Condemned Offences")'.[23] 'Universally Condemned Offences are a matter of concern to the international community as a whole', which has 'essential interests in their prosecution'.[24] As such, like the domestic prosecutor who acts on behalf of the society that they represent, 'the Prosecutor acts on behalf and in the interests of the international

---

[16] *Tadić*, ICTY-94-1-Tbis-R117-T, Sentencing Judgement, 11 November 1999, para. 7. In later cases, this classical formulation of the 'infallibility' of punishment is rendered as 'ending impunity' for these crimes. See, for example, *Karadžić* Alleged Holbrooke Agreement Decision, para. 52.

[17] Alan Norrie, *Crime, Reason, and History* (2nd edn.) (Cambridge: Cambridge University Press, 2000), p. 205.

[18] *Karadžić* Trial Judgement, para. 6026.

[19] *Furundžija*, ICTY-95-17/1-T, Judgement, 10 December 1998, para. 289.

[20] *Kordić & Čerkez*, ICTY-95-14/2-A, Judgement, 17 December 2004, (*Kordić* Appeals Judgement), para. 1073.

[21] Sigmund Freud, 'Why War?', in Albert Dickson (ed.), *Civilization, Society and Religion* (Harmondsworth: Penguin, 1985), p. 351.

[22] *Češić* Sentencing Judgement, para. 23.

[23] *Dragan Nikolić*, ICTY-94-2-AR73-A, Decision on Interlocutory Appeal Concerning Legality of Arrest, 5 June 2003, para. 24.

[24] Ibid., paras. 25 and 30. This approach was affirmed in *Karadžić* Alleged Holbrooke Agreement Decision, para. 46.

community'.²⁵ Following Freud, in models of punitive justice, the coercive force of the international community replaces the violence of the individual perpetrator.

According to this model, 'one of the most important purposes of a sentence imposed by the International Tribunal is to make it abundantly clear that the international legal system is implemented and enforced'.²⁶ In Hegelian terms, at the objective level of international society, punishment 'is the reconciliation of the law with itself; by the annulment of the crime, the law is restored and its authority is thereby actualised'.²⁷ In punitive justice, the global social contract of international society (the rule of law) replaces the war of all (lawless violence), and the universal legal norms and moral values of that society replace illegal violence.²⁸ In this post-Westphalian model of justice, punishment instantiates the universal values of global humanity. It conceives international crimes as breaching the collective norms of all human society, which punitive justice then reinstitutes in the form of international criminal law. In this model, justice replaces the particularism of collective violence with international legal norms that express universal values of all humanity. It understands punitive justice as enforcing the laws and values of the international society of all humanity.

5.1.2 The International Justice of Procedure

While the primary function of the ICTY is to render justice through the punishment of those found guilty, punitive justice must be determined by the conduct of a 'fair trial by a truly independent and impartial tribunal'.²⁹ As discussed in Chapter 3, these ideas of the 'fair trial' are set out in the ICTY Statute (Arts. 20–22), the ICTY RPE, and developed in the jurisprudence.

This model of international justice is *procedural*, in that it represents the institution of the 'formal justice' of the rule of law. It understands justice as the 'regular and impartial administration of public rules'

---

²⁵ *Halilović*, ICTY-01-48-A, Decision on Motion for Prosecution Access to Defence Documents Used in Cross-Examination of Prosecution Witnesses, 9 May 2005, para. 8.
²⁶ *Kordić* Appeals Judgement, para. 1080.
²⁷ G.W.F. Hegel, *The Philosophy of Right* (London: Oxford University. Press, 1967), p. 141.
²⁸ *Šešelj*, ICTY-03-67-T, Judgment, 31 March 2016, Partially Dissenting Opinion of Judge Flavia Lattanzi, para. 150.
²⁹ Cassese Report, para. 15.

136 SUBJECTIVITY AND SOCIALITY IN INTERNATIONAL CRIMINAL LAW

through a judicial process.[30] This idea is a founding precept of the jurisdiction of the ICTY. For example, the leading *Tadić* Jurisdiction Decision held that the ICTY was established 'in accordance with the rule of law, [that is] the guarantees of fairness, justice and even-handedness, in full conformity with internationally recognised human rights instruments', and hence was duly constituted in accordance with the rule of law.[31] This liberal legal model defines procedural justice as the impartial, consistent, and equitable application of rules in judicial process. While the jurisprudence is typically concerned with defendant fair trial rights, it also presents a broader notion of procedural justice, which includes the principle of the 'interests of justice'. This principle posits 'due process and fundamental fairness [as] the cornerstone of international justice'.[32] These wider 'interests of justice' include the proper administration of justice (such as the integrity of trial proceedings and determination of facts to the appropriate standard of 'reasonableness'),[33] as well as the protection of public interests (such as the public interest of the international community in the prosecution of 'Universally Condemned Offences').[34]

In this model, justice consists of the procedural rule of law, in the 'thin' sense of having formal rules govern the adjudication of social conflict, according to the underlying values of 'openness, impartiality, certainty, and prospectivity'.[35] The judicial process is seen as a 'civilised' model of social conflict that is governed by rules and 'standards of procedure and evidence that commend themselves to all civilised nations'.[36] According to this model, these 'rules (of evidence, procedure, and professional ethics) serve as "enabling constraints"' of the legal regulation of social conflict.[37] This is a liberal conception of international criminal justice, in which the rule of law replaces the rule of power and legal disputation

---

[30] John Rawls, *A Theory of Justice* (Oxford: Oxford University Press, 1999), p. 206.
[31] *Tadić*, ICTY-94-1-A, Decision on the Defence Motion for Interlocutory Appeal on Jurisdiction, 2 October 1995 (*Tadić Jurisdiction Decision Appeals Judgement*), para. 45.
[32] *Karadžić*, MICT-13-55-A, Judgement, para. 13. See footnote 30 for leading jurisprudence on this point.
[33] The concept of interests of justice is used throughout the ICTY RPE in framing judicial discretion in evidential and procedural matters.
[34] See *Karadžić* Alleged Holbrooke Agreement Decision, para. 49.
[35] Fionnuala Ní Aoláin, Dina Francesca Haynes et al., *On the Frontlines* (Oxford: Oxford University Press, 2011), p. 223.
[36] *Kupreškić et al.*, ICTY-95-16, Trial Transcript, 23 October 2001, par. 944-946.
[37] Mark Osiel, *Mass Atrocity, Collective Memory, and the Law* (Brunswick: Transaction, 2000), pp. 45-46.

replaces armed conflict. As Cassese describes, '[t]he only civilized alternative to this desire for revenge is to render justice'.[38] This model understands the procedural rule of law as transforming collective responsibility into individual liability and vengeance into lawful sanction. It contends that procedural justice displaces violent conflict by ordering social relations through just rules of adjudication. Procedural justice seeks to substitute individualised legal conflict conducted according to formal rules for that of collective social conflict without them. These procedural norms are seen as having universal legitimacy and their observance as reflecting values of all 'civilised' societies. In this model of international criminal justice, rational legal rules replace irrational conflict and the procedural rule of law displaces social violence.

5.1.3   International Justice as Recognition

The third model is international justice as *recognition* of the wrong to the victim. In *The Prosecutor* v. *Nikolić*, a leading decision on plea agreements, the ICTY describes its mandate as 'to bring justice to both victims and their relatives and to perpetrators'.[39] The model of justice as recognition is described as 'giving a "voice" to the suffering of the victims',[40] and in which judicial proceedings give 'victims the opportunity to have their voices heard'.[41] Such recognition should not be misunderstood as giving individual victims legal standing before the court or rights in proceedings *per se* (as discussed in Chapter 4). Rather, it is the legal recognition of the harm to victims and their relatives, whether in trial proceedings or sentencing. It involves the legal recognition of all victims of these crimes, in which the individual victim appearing before the court stands in for the collective victims of these crimes, who do not appear before the court. For example, in assessing the gravity of crimes, the Tribunal takes into account 'the scale and brutality of the crimes, the vulnerability of the victims, the consequences and the effect or impact of the crime upon the victims and their relatives', including the 'long-term physical, psychological, and emotional suffering of the immediate

---

[38] Cassese Report, para 16.
[39] D. *Nikolić* Sentencing Judgement, para. 120.
[40] *Krstić*, ICTY-98-33-T, Judgement, 2 August 2001, para. 703; *Kvočka et al.*, ICTY-98-30/1-T, Judgement, 2 November 2001 (*Kvočka* Trial Judgement), para. 702.
[41] *Martić*, ICTY-95-11-T, Decision, 8 March 1996, para. 3.

victims'.⁴² For the ICTY, bringing justice to victims is 'an acknowledgement of the harm done to the victims'.⁴³ For this reason, the harms to individual and groups of victims are regarded as directly relevant to sentencing.⁴⁴ In this model of justice, law recognises the harms that victims suffered and the wrongful nature of those harms. There is a legal recognition of the injustice to victims (their harm) and that the harm is a crime punishable by law (their harm is criminal).

In the recognition model, international justice is the legal recognition of the harms to individual and collective victims. It understands the prosecution of the harms before an international tribunal as recognition by the international community that they are both unjust and unlawful. That legal acknowledgement aims to restore victims to the status of legal subjects (as discussed in Chapter 3). It recognises victims as international legal subjects by virtue of being human, a quality and status that the international crime is understood to deny. In this model, the recognition of victims as entitled to protection *qua* human beings repudiates the injustice of the perpetrator's denial of their humanity. This acknowledgement of the harm to victims by international criminal law 'would restore the equilibrium so severely disturbed by atrocious crimes'.⁴⁵

5.1.4 International Justice as Reconciliation

The fourth model of international justice is that of *reconciliation*. The idea of the ICTY as 'a tool for promoting reconciliation and restoring true peace' was present from its establishment onwards.⁴⁶ The jurisprudence of the ICTY accepts that the justice of 'peace-building and reconciliation among the affected communities is an integral part of the mission of the ICTY',⁴⁷ and it describes 'justice [as] being of paramount importance for the restoration and maintenance of peace'.⁴⁸ This idea of

---

[42] *Karadžić* Trial Judgement, para. 6031.
[43] *M. Simić*, ICTY-95-9/2-T, Sentencing Judgement, 17 October 2002 (*M. Simić* Sentencing Judgement), para. 33.
[44] *Krnojelac*, ICTY-97-25-T, Judgement, 15 March 2002, para. 512.
[45] Aryeh Neier, 'Rethinking Truth, Justice and Guilt after Bosnia and Rwanda', in Carla Hesse and Robert Post (eds.), *Human Rights in Political Transitions* (New York: Zone, 1999), p. 49.
[46] Cassese Report, para. 16.
[47] *Banović*, ICTY-02-65/1-S-T, Sentencing Judgement, 28 October 2003, para. 66. See also *M. Simić* Sentencing Judgement, para. 33.
[48] *D. Nikolić* Sentencing Judgement, para. 4.

justice as reconciliation is used as a broad policy consideration in a wide range of issues from procedure to sentencing. In the jurisprudence, the contribution of the judicial functions of the ICTY to reconciliation is seen as an integral part of international justice. For example, in *The Prosecutor v. Karadžić*, the Trial Chamber described how 'an important function of the trial process, as originally envisaged by the Security Council of the United Nations in the very creation of the Tribunal, was to seek to further peace and reconciliation amongst and between the various factions involved in the conflict in the former Yugoslavia'.[49] In the reconciliation model, criminal prosecutions have this social function because of judicial fact-finding by a trial process and legal determination of individual accountability and criminal sanction.

The 'judicial function' of fact-finding by the trial process described in Chapter 4 is seen as a crucial part of social reconciliation in the model. The jurisprudence links the 'truth-finding function' of the ICTY to the task of 'furthering reconciliation in the former Yugoslavia'.[50] The role of the ICTY in 'establishing the facts' is seen as crucial because 'the search for the truth is an inalienable pre-requisite for peace'.[51] In this task, the ICTY is seen as working analogously to truth and reconciliation commissions, since establishing an accurate record of the conflict is seen as an essential part of the process of reconciliation.

The 'judicial functions' of determining criminal accountability and sanction are also seen as a crucial element of the task of reconstructing a society in conflict.[52] As described in Chapter 3, the ICTY jurisprudence determines individual accountability, rather than collective guilt. In the sentencing jurisprudence, the attribution of individual rather than collective responsibility is seen as an important element of reconciliation. So, for example, the perpetrator's subsequent contribution to reconciliation is recognised as a sentencing factor in mitigation.[53] The guilty plea is also recognised as mitigation, because 'acknowledgement of wrongdoing is extremely important for the entire community in its continuing

---

[49] *Karadžič*, ICTY-95-5/18-T, Decision on Appointment of Counsel and Order on Further Trial Proceedings, 5 November 2009, para. 20.
[50] *Sikirica et al.*, ICTY-95-8-T, Sentencing Judgement, 13 November 2001, para. 149.
[51] *Stakić*, ICTY-97-24-T, Judgement, 31 July 2003, para. 901.
[52] *Plavšić*, ICTY-00-39&40/1-T, Sentencing Judgement, 27 February 2003, (*Plavšić* Sentencing Judgement), paras. 66–80.
[53] *Karadžić* Trial Judgement, para. 6057, confirmed on appeal.

process of recovery and reconciliation'.[54] Rehabilitation is considered a secondary purpose to retribution and deterrence in sentencing.[55] However, where it is considered, the idea of personal and 'community' rehabilitation are typically linked.[56]

In this model, criminal justice functions as a therapeutic process. It understands that process as involving the telling of the horrors of war in a cathartic and normative narrative and, by that telling, the judgement and punishment of the perpetrator. It sees the judgement and punishment of individuals as preventing the emergence of 'the primitive and archaic concept' of 'collective responsibility', which leads to further violence.[57] The inscription of both blame and condemnation in law is seen as crucial to 'breaking the cycle of hatred' and as an integral part of the transitional process of substituting individual for communal responsibility.[58] This is a paradigm of international criminal justice as reconciliation.[59] In this paradigm, international criminal justice enables a confrontation with the violence of the past and allows the 'working through' of these memories of harm. The function of criminal justice is seen as providing a cathartic resolution of traumatic violence so that the reconstruction of 'social connection' is possible.[60] This resolution works through the affect of the victim, perpetrator, and communities that have been traumatised by collective violence. The model figures justice as a collective act of memory that can represent collective trauma, recreate social solidarity, and reconstitute a traumatised society. This is a model of international justice as therapy.

The reconciliation model of justice sees the criminal process not only as changing individual victims and perpetrators but also as changing the traumatised society itself. It posits a process of 'collective reconciliation', that is, a process of reconciliation by the entire community, not only as individuals but as a collective. It gives the universalised and general aim

---

[54] *Bralo*, ICTY-95-17-T, Sentencing Judgement, 7 December 2005, (*Bralo* Sentencing Judgement), para. 71.
[55] *Karadžić* Trial Judgement, para. 6025.
[56] *Bralo* Sentencing Judgement, para. 69. See also Marina Maier, 'Offender Rehabilitation in International Criminal Justice', (2021) 53(1–2) Case W Res J Int'l L 269–328.
[57] Cassese Report, para. 16.
[58] Martha Minow, *Breaking the Cycles of Hatred* (Princeton: Princeton University Press, 2002), pp. 21–22.
[59] See, for example, Ruti Teitel, *Transitional Justice* (Oxford: Oxford University Press, 2000).
[60] Osiel, *Mass Atrocity*, p. 291.

of rendering justice a specific social context, namely, the former Yugoslavia and its successor states.[61] The model characterises international criminal law as a form of transitional justice, in that it provides justice that enables the society in conflict to become a society in peace. The transition from conflict to peace also enables the reconstruction of the peace and security of 'international society'.

The two classical juridical models of international justice as procedure and punishment emphasise the injustice of the violation of universal law and values. They seek to redress those injustices by reinstituting and enforcing of the laws of the international community. The punitive model enforces global legal norms, while in the procedural model, the rule of law replaces social conflict. The more recent models of international justice as recognition and reconciliation emphasise the violation of the person and of the society. These models seek to redress the injustices of war by the legal recognition of victims and the legal reconciliation of violent social conflict. In the recognition model, international criminal law recognises victims as human beings, while in the reconciliation model it reconstructs warring groups as peaceful communities. The different models of justice all share the same structure, in which the axiological category of justice ties together the legal categories of harm, subject, and trial in the legal form. All four models posit justice as the legal resolution of unjust lawless violence, breaches of the collective values of humanity, violations of the human subject, and the social rupture of war. They assume that international criminal law institutes international justice and that the institution of this legal justice can resolve the injustices of the destruction of societies and their constituent social bonds. In this structure, 'justice' operates as the *legal* resolution of injustice.

5.2 The Justice of Law

All these models of justice presume that international criminal law can redress the injustice of international crimes. In these forms of international justice, 'the prosecution would speak on behalf of the victims, and the judges would do justice for them'.[62] International criminal law will punish the perpetrator, prove the perpetrator's guilt, recognise their suffering, and reconcile their society. However, international criminal

---

[61] *Plavšić* Sentencing Judgement, para. 79.
[62] Neier, 'Rethinking Truth', p. 49.

law does not always offer justice to victims, as the ICTY jurisprudence acknowledges. The *Kvočka* case offers a typical but distressing example of this failure, in which the Trial Chamber held that it had 'no difficulty believing that this witness has suffered a terrible and traumatizing ordeal. However, her testimony was so confused as to the details of the rape that it cannot be relied upon to establish guilt.'[63] In this case, the ICTY found that the victim had suffered a grave injustice but concluded that it could not offer her the possibility of redress. As discussed in Chapter 4, victims may be missing or dead, and the crime against them may be unknown or without witnesses. This is particularly the case for sexual violence offences.[64]

The possibility that the ICTY may not offer justice to the victim is also an integral part of any judicial process of judgement. The international criminal trial must offer justice to the accused as well as the victim. Justice for the accused requires that an innocent person should not be convicted of crimes they did not commit and that all convictions should be decided according to given legal standards. For this reason, the ICTY may refuse to take an indictment to trial, to accept the evidence of a victim, or to find the accused guilty beyond reasonable doubt at trial. The procedural justice of the fair trial requires that the ICTY recognise the accused as a subject of rights. It does so by claiming to impartially weigh the evidence for indictment, assess the persuasiveness of the witness, and, ultimately, judge the guilt of the accused.

For these reasons, it is necessary to distinguish between the application of particular law and the institution of universal justice, as sexual violence prosecutions show. Universal justice as an absolute value may function as the axiological foundation for the judgements of the ICTY. However, those judgements institute the particular justices of law in a specific social and historical context according to specific contextual values. For example, evidential issues have been particularly contentious in sexual violence cases before the ICTY, as discussed in Chapter 4. Typically, such issues concern the conflict between the rights of the accused to a fair trial and the rights of witnesses to equality before the law. However, these decisions are not a neutral determination upon the just balance of each claim, since contextual values inform the judgement upon 'justice' of the ICTY. Rather, as Christine Chinkin points out, conventional 'fair trial'

---

[63] *Kvočka* Trial Judgement, para. 557.
[64] Other typical examples are *Kunarac* (ICTY-96-23&23/1), where evidence of a missing girl sold to traffickers was given but no charges regarding offences against her were brought, or *Mrkšić* (ICTY-95-13/1), where it was alleged by witnesses that a woman was sexually assaulted before her murder but the Court found the allegation was not established.

requirements rest upon 'human rights standards [that] have been defined by men in accordance with male assertions of what constitutes the most fundamental guarantees required by individuals', as can be seen in Chapter 4.[65] For these reasons, it is not possible to assume that international criminal law can, or will, necessarily institute justice for these particular victims of sexual violence.

Even if, as Neier claims, that the 'judges would do justice' for the victims, it does not necessarily follow that it is possible for them to do so. The ICTY can offer only finite justice. As the ICTY acknowledges, it 'cannot realistically be expected to prosecute every offender which may fall within the strict terms of its jurisdiction. It must of necessity make decisions as to the nature of the crimes and the offenders to be prosecuted.'[66] Case selection is an integral part of international criminal justice, because of the nature of collective crimes. Sometimes that selection is strategic, such as considerations of gaps in jurisprudence or appropriate representation of particular regions of the conflict.[67] Sometimes it reflects gendered legal practices, which do not prioritise victims of sexual violence or sexual violence crimes.[68] Regardless of the reasons, the selection reflects a fundamental structural problem confronting all international prosecutions: there are many victims, perpetrators, and crimes in the destruction of societies by collective violence.

Even if the ICTY were able to hear all cases of criminal conduct, its remedies are limited. The ICTY is a criminal, not a civil, court and its focus 'has been on punishing the wrongdoers, not on providing compensation and support to those who have suffered'.[69] It offered neither individual compensation nor restitution, which were left to be pursued in national courts, nor 'collective' reparations arising from state responsibility, which had to be pursued before the ICJ.[70] Accordingly,

---

[65] Christine Chinkin, 'Due Process and Witness Anonymity', (1997) 91(1) AJIL 75–79, 78.
[66] Mucić et al. ICTY-96-21-A, Judgement, 20 February 2001, para. 602.
[67] Interview 1, Senior prosecutor, Office of the Prosecutor, ICTY, 2007. See also Saeeda Verrall, 'The Picture of Sexual Violence in the Former Yugoslavia Conflicts as Reflected in ICTY Judgments', in Serge Brammertz and Michelle Jarvis (eds.), *Prosecuting Conflict-Related Sexual Violence at the ICTY* (Oxford: Oxford University Press, 2016), pp. 320–334.
[68] Michelle Jarvis and Kate Vigneswaran, 'Challenges to Successful Outcomes in Sexual Violence Cases', in Brammertz and Jarvis (eds.), *Prosecuting Conflict-Related Sexual Violence*, p. 46 ff.
[69] Hilary Charlesworth and Christine Chinkin, *The Boundaries of International Law* (Manchester: Manchester University Press, 2000), p. 334.
[70] The ICTY Statute provides that it may order restitution of property, which has not been done to date (Art. 24, see also Rule 105 ICTY RPE). There are no similar provisions

the ICTY does not offer reparative justice, which seeks to 'repair' the harm done to the victim or their society. Even if such reparative justice was provided, it is necessary to ask, what form of redress or remedy could render justice for sexual violence committed as part of 'ethnic cleansing'? After the destruction of identity, family, and community, what could constitute justice? What could constitute justice in the face of the destruction of people and their social bonds in international crimes?

This formulation of *injustice* reveals the fundamental paradox in conceiving justice as the institution of the existing form of law, namely, that international criminal law institutes justice and yet injustice remains. International criminal law cannot provide redress for the overwhelming injustice of international crimes, which rupture social bonds as such. In municipal jurisdictions, crimes under domestic law are not seen to destroy that society. In contrast, by their very nature international crimes destroy national and transnational social relations as such. That international criminal law fails to enact justice is not simply an empirical problem, in the sense that it could be possible that certain actions could remedy this failure. Rather, it reflects a logical paradox in models of justice in international criminal law. Derrida describes this logical knot in terms of the relationship between calculable law and incalculable justice: '[l]aw is the element of calculation, and it is just that there should be law, but justice is incalculable, it requires us to calculate with the incalculable'. In Derridean terms, the incalculability of justice founds its logical impossibility, since 'justice would be the experience we are not able to experience ... Justice is an experience of the impossible.'[71]

Justice is impossible because it is beyond the limits of determinate international criminal law. The 'determinate law' is the specific legal form of crimes, subjects, and trials of international criminal law that determine what international criminal justice is and in which justice takes the form of punishment, procedure, recognition, and reconciliation. International criminal law can only institute legal justice, that is, it can only institute justice as determined by its particular legal calculation of injustice. Accordingly, justice as such will always exceed the determinate legal calculation of the just. For this reason, the models of justice that serve as the axiological foundation of the ICTY – the ideas of justice as punishment, procedure, recognition, and recognition – figure 'justice'

concerning compensation. Rule 106 ICTY RPE provides that compensation is to be claimed in national courts.

[71] Jacques Derrida, 'Force of Law', in Drucilla Cornell, Michel Rosenfeld et al. (eds.), *Deconstruction and the Possibility of Justice* (New York: Routledge, 1992), p. 16.

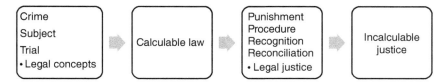

Figure 5.1 The model of justice of the ICTY

as that which must exist 'outside' the calculability of the determinate legal order of international criminal law (see Figure 5.1):

In this figuration of justice, incalculable justice is 'outside' the determinate legal form of calculable international criminal law. Justice is a logical impossibility for all law. However, the legal form of international criminal justice is always and profoundly structured by justice's incalculability. This is because it is not possible to legally calculate the just redress for the incalculable injustice of the destruction of persons and social relations.[72]

This Derridean frame helps to identify the structure of the relationship between determinate law and incalculable justice in the legal form of international criminal law. However, this understanding of the legal form remains at a metaphysical level, rather than understanding the relationship between law and justice in its concrete existence.[73] The next step, then, is to develop an account of determinate law and incalculable justice in the existing social order of international criminal law. This account examines how the legal form of international criminal law operates as a socio-symbolic order, understood as a constitutive structure that represents the individual as legal subject, and the legal relations between those subjects, as a social order.

5.3 The Legal Form of International Criminal Law as a Socio-symbolic Order

5.3.1 *The Legal Form of International Criminal Law*

The legal form consists of the fundamental categories of the international crime, international legal subject, international criminal trial, and international justice. The first and foundational category of the international crime criminalises particular forms of collective violence in positive international law (as described in Chapter 2). It criminalises those forms

---

[72] However, this is not to say that justice may not be experienced on an individual or collective level, as discussed in the next chapter.
[73] Emilios Christodoulidis, 'Strategies of Rupture', (2009) 20(1) Law and Crit 3–26, 19.

of violence characterised as injurious to persons and to international society, namely, violations of positive law or the universal values of global human society. The category of the international crime creates the international legal subject, the second fundamental legal category of international criminal law. The positive rules of international criminal law create the legal duties and rights of subjects, which represent relations between subjects as legal. These duties and rights construct the individual as an international legal subject owing obligations and possessing rights (as described in Chapter 3). This model of the legal subject is predicated upon ideas of the human and their membership of 'human' society. Whether an international crime has been committed, and who are perpetrators or victims of those crimes, is determined by the international criminal trial, the third fundamental category. The international criminal trial is a form of adjudication that assumes particular ideas of persons and communities who witness and judge (as described in Chapter 4). The international criminal trial is predicated upon ideas of the universal witnessing subject and a universal community of judgement. The fourth fundamental category of the legal form is justice, conceived as punishment, procedure, recognition, and reconciliation. As a legal concept, international justice is predicated upon ideas of the resolution of injustice through the application of the existing legal rules and values of international criminal law.

International criminal law thereby constructs subjects and their relations in the legal form. The legal form expresses those relations as juridical obligations or entitlements. As such, it posits an abstract and formal conception of the individual, which attributes certain legal capacities and obligations to them. These rights and duties are legal relationships, which constitute the relationship between persons in juridical terms. International criminal law thereby represents legal subjects and their relations as fundamental categories of 'international society'. These legal categories structure the subject, their relations to other subjects, and 'society' at the international level.

5.3.2 *The Discourse of International Criminal Law*

If in international criminal law, 'the *regulation* of social relationships assumes a *legal* character',[74] the legal character of this regulation has a

---

[74] Pashukanis, *Law and Marxism*, p. 79.

symbolic dimension. It is symbolic in the sense that it consists of a system of related legal concepts, which *express* or *represent* objective social relations in abstracted form. This system of legal concepts consists of abstract symbolic legal categories – such as the crime, the subject, the trial – that represent the subject and social order at the international level. The legal categories of crime, juridical subject, and trial constitute harms as crimes, social subjects as legal subjects, and their social relations as legal entitlements and obligations. These categories structure which social relations of violence will be legal (and which will be illegal), which persons will be legal subjects (and which will not), and which social relationships will be legal relationships (and which will not).

Accordingly, the legal form consists of a system of symbolic elements that give meaning to subjects and social relations. Drawing on Lacanian psychoanalytic theory, the legal form can be described as chains of symbolic elements, connected together 'in the symbolic order which founds interhuman relations, and which is called the law'.[75] These symbolic elements represent (or signify) particular forms of subjectivity and social order at the international level. Because it functions as a signifying system of persons and social relations, international criminal law operates as a socio-symbolic order. That is, international criminal law is a symbolic system that orders social relations in particular ways. This approach emphasises what Drucilla Cornell describes as the 'active' role of law in constituting persons through its symbolic ordering of subjects and their relations, understanding this 'legal system as a symbolic Other; a system that does not merely recognize, but constitutes and confirms who is to be valued, who is to *matter*'.[76]

To describe the socio-symbolic order of the legal form, I draw on my earlier feminist psychoanalytic model of discourse.[77] While Cornell's account is important for understanding the symbolic 'constitutive' dimension of the legal form, it nevertheless focuses upon the constitution of the (sexed) subject in the 'classical' Lacanian model of the Symbolic order, the foundational order of language and culture. This focus returns us to the long-standing feminist problem of Lacan's structuralist determinism that naturalises women's oppression because of its conception of the Symbolic order as a 'fixed, monolithic symbolic system' that founds a

---

[75] Jacques Lacan, *Freud's Papers on Technique* (New York: Norton, 1991), p. 197.
[76] Drucilla Cornell, *The Imaginary Domain* (London: Routledge, 1995), p. 42.
[77] Kirsten Campbell, *Jacques Lacan and Feminist Epistemology* (London and New York: 2004).

phallic (patriarchal) social order.⁷⁸ Instead, my 'feminist discourse' approach builds on the later Lacanian theory of discourse to develop a feminist account of modern fraternal and feminist social relations.

While 'discourse' in the Foucauldian sense emphasises the organisation of concrete speech acts as epistemological and political systems, my feminist discourse approach follows Lacan in emphasising the underlying socio-symbolic system that produces those speech acts.⁷⁹ For Lacan, '[d]iscourse is a fundamental apparatus which is prior to and which determines the whole relation of subjects to subjects and subjects to objects'.⁸⁰ In the Lacanian sense, discourse operates as 'a social link (*lien social*)', which is founded on the ordering of symbolic elements.⁸¹ The later Lacanian theory shifts away from his 'classical' conception of the Symbolic as a monolithic and closed structure, and instead emphasises the open and incomplete nature of symbolic systems. It also shifts from his 'classical' account of 'phallic' femininity fully defined by patriarchal norms to the later conception of the failure of the phallic socio-symbolic to determine female subjectivity. Finally, this model ties different forms of discourse to historically specific social relations, and enables my feminist approach to situate the emergence of fraternal and feminist discourses in modern capitalist social relations.

The feminist discourse approach offers three important theoretical strategies for building a social theoretical account of the legal form of international criminal law. First, it offers a model of discourse as constituting subjects and the relation between subjects.⁸² This model enables the analysis of the legal form as a socio-symbolic order that produces subjects and their relations. Second, the model provides a methodology for identifying how the legal form operates as a structure of signifiers, which produces the position of the legal subject and their legal relation to other subjects. It builds on the Lacanian schemas of discourse, which aim to 'formalise' the structure of discourse and to identify the symbolic elements of the social bond it produces. Third, this approach understands the form of discourse as being contingent upon the practices that produce it. It does not see discourse as a fixed and frozen structure but emphasises how new practices create new social bonds.

---

[78] Nancy Fraser, *Fortunes of Feminism* (London: Verso, 2013), p. 149.
[79] Paul Verhaeghe, *Does the Woman Exist?* (London: Rebus, 1997), p. 100.
[80] Parveen Adams, *The Emptiness of the Image* (London: Routledge, 1996), p. 72.
[81] Jacques Lacan, *Encore* (New York and London: Norton, 1998), p. 17.
[82] For further discussion of this model, see Campbell, *Jacques Lacan and Feminist Epistemology*, p. 48ff.

My approach does not propose an analogy between law and psychoanalysis. Lacan offers a theory of psychoanalytic practice, rather than legal practice, and it is clearly problematic to transpose this theory from the psychoanalytic to the legal field. Accordingly, my use of Lacanian theory does not follow other legal theorists in applying the Lacanian discourses of the master or the analyst and so on to law.[83] Rather, it reconfigures the Lacanian model in the legal and feminist fields in order to develop an account of legal and feminist practice.

5.3.3 The Discursive Structure and Operation of International Criminal Law

My analysis of the discourse of the legal form begins by identifying its structure, understood as the elements of the discourse, and its operation, namely, how that structure works. To develop this analysis, I use two leading sexual violence cases involving female and male sexual violence victims, *Kunarac* and *Tadić*. These early cases make the discursive structure and operation of the legal form more visible than the later leadership cases because of their case presentation and jurisprudential development.

The legal discourse of international criminal law begins with an injustice that demands international justice. This is a demand not only of the living but also of the dead. The demand arises from the injustice itself, in that it calls upon others to provide justice. As such, it is a social relation, insofar as it requires others to respond to it, and so is not contingent on the individual victim. In the case of the former Yugoslavia, affected persons and communities, and those acting in solidarity with them, collectively articulated the demand for international justice (as discussed in Chapter 2.) The particularised articulation of this demand begins what would become *The Prosecutor* v. *Tadić* and *The Prosecutor* v. *Kunarac* cases.[84] In *Tadić*, the particular demand for justice begins with Omarska survivors reporting Tadić to the German police, while in *Kunarac* it begins with Foča survivors reporting their experiences to the Commission of Experts.[85]

---

[83] See, for example, the important work of Dragan Milovanovic and Jeanne Schroder.
[84] *Tadić* ICTY-94-1 and *Kunarac et al.* ICTY-96-23 & 23/1.
[85] Melinda Crane Engel, 'Germany vs. Genocide', *New York Times*, 30 October 1994. See also Grace Harbour, 'International Concern regarding Conflict-Related Sexual Violence in the Lead-up to the ICTY's Establishment', in Brammertz and Jarvis (eds.), *Prosecuting Conflict-Related Sexual Violence*, p. 26.

The naming of these injustices as international crimes, that is, as legally defined socially injurious conduct, inaugurates the discourse of international criminal law. The process of symbolising the harms as international crimes introduces the first signifying element of the legal discourse of international criminal law. This is the master signifier (S_1), so called because this signifier is the first or key element of the discourse, which shapes its structure and starts its operation. The master signifier symbolises the harm as an international crime. For example, the recognition of conflict-related sexual violence as a legally defined socially injury begins the process of symbolising the harm of sexual violence as an international crime, as described in Chapter 2. The importance of criminalisation is that it marks the determinate category of legally cognisable harms, demarcating the boundary of determinate legal category of crime and the wider social category of harm. The signification of the harm as an international crime thereby includes it in the legal order of international criminal law.

The naming of harms as international crimes generally involves applying the existing legal category of international crimes to them. So, for example in *Tadić*, sexual violence against men was charged as torture or inhuman treatment, wilfully causing suffering or injury, and cruel treatment as war crimes, and inhumane acts as a crime against humanity. This is because it was seen as a political and military, rather than sexual, crime. Similarly, the sole charge of rape arose where Tadić was the direct perpetrator of penetrative sexual violence against a female civilian victim, the archetype of prohibited war-time rape. As such, sexual violence was charged as rape as a crime against humanity, the only numerated rape offence, and inhuman or cruel treatment as a war crime, because rape was not a numerated offence under the war crimes provisions of the ICTY Statute.[86] Within these gendered framings, these forms of sexual violence were able to be symbolised as already existing offences under international criminal law (but not rape as a war crime). In these charges of sexual violence, the discourse of international criminal law operated as in any other crime. What is distinctive about the *Tadić* case is that it is the first international prosecution in which rape appears as a numerated charge, that is, an international crime in its own right. It recognises the victim as an international legal subject, having express legal rights and entitlements under international criminal law. For the first time, the

---

[86] *Tadić*, ICTY-94-1, Second Amended Indictment, 14 December 1995, para. 5.

discourse of international criminal law expressly incudes women victims of war-time rape.

The *Tadić* case shows how the signifier (S_1) naming harms as international crimes thereby operates as the first term, or element, of legal discourse. The function of the master signifier in legal discourse can be seen in similar terms to Hart's arguments concerning the rules of recognition of 'the legal' and the 'non-legal'.[87] It brings into existence 'the legal' as a distinctive form of social relations, and hence shapes the discourse within it. It names a domain of social action as legal, and the act of naming introduces a system of regulatory norms that are recognised as international criminal law. It names harms as crimes, persons as legal subjects, and their relations as legal rights and obligations. In this regard, the crucial function of the master signifier is to name harms as international crimes and so to symbolise them in terms of the foundational legal category of the international crime.

By symbolising harms as international crimes, the master signifier constitutes particular social values and actions as legal, and orders social relations in juridical terms. It connects the signifier of the international crime (S_1) to the symbolic system of legal rules, practices, and institutions of international criminal law (S_2). This symbolic system can be thought of as a stable structure of meaning materialised in legal rules, practices, and institutions, constituting a formal network of symbolic relations. The process of linking the master signifier to the symbolic network (S_2) gives acts and persons their legal meanings and the 'abstract' categories of international criminal law their material existence.

The act of naming 'the legal' not only is symbolic but also has material effect. In the act of legal naming, we find what Bourdieu describes as the *force* of law, 'a form *par excellence* of symbolic power – and of symbolic violence – given the possibilities possessed by its practitioners to create institutions and with them historical and political realities through a simple exercise of naming'.[88] Creating institutions, and with them historical and political realities, gives the naming of harms as crimes, persons as legal subjects, and their legal relations the force of law, that

---

[87] See Jeanne Schroeder, *The Four Lacanian Discourses* (Abingdon and New York: Birkbeck Law Press, 2008), p. 30 ff.
[88] Mauricio Garcia Villegas, 'On Pierre Bourdieu's Legal Thought', (2004) 56–57 Droit et Société, 57–71, 60. See also Pierre Bourdieu, 'The Force of Law', (1986-7) 38(3) Hastings LJ, 814–853.

is, their concrete existence.[89] However, unlike 'domestic' criminal law that already exists in national legal systems, the rules, practices, and institutions of international criminal law must be continually built and given concrete existence.

The master signifier may name this or that social phenomena as legal. However, the idea of legality can only be given content in relation to a system of regulatory norms, institutions, and practices, which allow it to function as a socio-symbolic order with material, concrete existence. So, for example, the *Kunarac* case becomes part of a socio-symbolic order given concrete existence in the ICTY. The case involved naming new harms as criminal, as it provided the first decision establishing that rape can constitute enslavement as an international crime. This symbolisation was given concrete existence as a new legal norm that became part of the legal rules of international criminal law. The case also established that sexual enslavement occurred in the Foča region, which would then be included in crime base evidence in the later leadership cases of *Mladić* and *Karadžić*. The signifier of the harm – sexual enslavement – thereby becomes part of a stable network of meaning, materialised in legal rules, practices, and institutions.

The next element in the discourse of international criminal law is the legal subject, S. The operation of the legal form produces the legal subject, S, with its symbolic support, the positive legal order. However, '[t]he legal subject only functions as such in so far as she has rights and duties, and the very concept of rights and duties requires that these must be enforceable against or by the legal subject by or against other legal subjects', as Jeanne Schroeder describes.[90] That is, the legal subject always exists in relation to other legal subjects. In the discourse of international criminal law, the positive legal order (S_2) produces the legal subject (S), linked to the other legal subjects through juridical relations. The relations consist of the rights and responsibilities that this positive legal order articulates and materialises in its judicial institutions and processes. For example, the ICTY's decision that it had jurisdiction to hear the case against Tadić established that he was a legal subject under international criminal law (rather than a subject under domestic German law). As such, he came to exist as an international legal subject with legal duties to the victims of his crimes. Conversely, his victims also became international legal subjects, having legal rights and entitlements under international criminal law.

---

[89] Sonja Buckel, *Subjectivation and Cohesion* (Leiden and Boston: Brill, 2021), p. 137.
[90] Schroeder, *The Four Lacanian Discourses*, p. 14.

Where sexual violence surfaces as a gender-based crime, it disrupts the operation of the legal discourse of international criminal law. For example, the *Kunarac* case begins with the call for justice by the women survivors of crimes in Foča. As Witness 75 testifies, she has come before the ICTY to see that 'justice is done'.[91] However, the existing legal discourse did not adequately symbolise the harm experienced by the victims. The signifier that would otherwise represent this harm was missing in international criminal law, which can be described as a fault in the existing socio-symbolic order. Accordingly, it was necessary to create a new symbolic element to name the harm, namely, the concept of sexual enslavement.[92] This act of naming invents a new symbolic element. In Lacanian terms, the act of nomination involves the creation of a *sinthome*, involving the construction of a new signifier that enables a new way of knotting together the real, symbolic, and imaginary dimensions of discourse.[93] The invented signifier operates as a supplementary term to the existing legal discourse, which repairs the fault in the discursive structure.[94] The new signifier thereby functions as symbolic supplement for the lack in legal discourse. The nominative act repairs the 'fault' of the missing discursive element by attaching the new signifier (S_1) to the existing legal discourse.[95]

The *Kunarac* case makes visible how the production of new signifiers for sexual violence as a gender-based harm can shift the operation of international criminal law. It creates a *new* signifier in the discourse of international criminal law, which ties together its existing elements in a different way. In this process, the new signifier (S_1) attaches to the existing legal order, that is, the legal rules, practices, and institution that 'materialise' that order (S_2). Establishing this link between the act of nomination (S_1) and legal rules, practices, and legal institution (S_2) produces a shift in the operation of legal discourse. If the new signifier successfully attaches to the structure of the existing legal discourse, it can

---

[91] *Kunarac et al.*, ICTY-96-23 &23/1, Trial Transcript (*Kunarac* Trial Transcript), 3 April 2000, p. 1581.
[92] Peggy Kuo, 'Prosecuting Crimes of Sexual Violence', (2002) 34 Case W Res J Int'l L, 305-321.
[93] See Jacques Lacan, *The Sinthome* (Cambridge: Polity, 2016).
[94] Paul Verhaeghe, 'Lacan's Analytic Goal', in Luke Thurston (ed.), *Re-Inventing the Symptom* (New York: Other Press, 2002), pp. 59–82, p. 74. See also Campbell, *Jacques Lacan and Feminist Epistemology*, pp. 164–165.
[95] Ron Harari, 'The *Sinthome*', in Luke Thurston (ed.), *Re-Inventing the Symptom*, pp. 45–55, p. 48.

create a new signifying chain $(S_1\text{-}S_2)$. The linking of the new signifier to the existing elements of the discourse of international criminal law thereby 'knots' them together in a different way. The inclusion of the new signifier thereby shifts the stable network of meaning in the existing discursive structure, changing the concept of the legal subject (S) and its relationship to other legal subjects articulated in the existing legal rules and practices of the legal institution (S_2).

However, this shift in the operation of legal discourse is contingent upon attaching the new signifier to the existing legal rules and practices of the legal institution. The process of attaching the new signifier of international crime to the existing legal discourse involves building rules, practices, and institutions that support it. Where these practices do not exist, fail, or are unable to support this attachment, that harm does not enter the legal field, and the existing legal discourse fails to operate for it. So, for example, *Tadić* was the first case in which a charge of rape was brought before the ICTY. However, the sole charge of rape was withdrawn following the victim's decision not to appear due to public disclosure of her identity in breach of protective measures.[96] Conversely, the legal rules, practices, and institution can enable this attachment to take place. For example, in the later case of *Kunarac*, this attachment did take place. This was because of the focus upon prosecuting sexual violence, investigative and case preparation practices, support for witnesses, and the Trial Chamber accepting the new signifier of the harm and evidence of it.[97]

The surfacing of sexual violence in *Kunarac* also reveals that the legal discourse of international criminal law has a structural, and not only contingent, fault. In the *Kunarac* trial, the Prosecutor acknowledged that 'it can be said that no sentence this Court can possibly devise will adequately deal with the injustices that the victims suffered at the hands of these men. Yet the International Community will expect that not only will justice be done, but that it will also be seen to be done.'[98] Justice must be done in the form of calculable international criminal law. However, it

---

[96] Gabi Mischkowski and Gorana Mlinarević, *And That It Does Not Happen to Anyone Anywhere in the World* (Cologne: Medica Mondiale, 2009), p. 35.

[97] The importance of these factors was noted in four interviews with ICTY witness support staff and prosecutors in 2006 and 2007. See also Michelle Jarvis and Najwa Nabti, 'Policies and Institutional Strategies for Successful Sexual Violence Prosecutions', in Brammertz and Jarvis (eds.), *Prosecuting Conflict-Related Sexual Violence*, p. 77; and Kuo, 'Prosecuting Crimes of Sexual Violence'.

[98] *Kunarac* Trial Transcript, 20 November 2000, para. 6330.

is necessarily incomplete and lacking, in that it cannot provide justice for the injustices the victims experience. The *Kunarac* case thereby also makes visible the fourth term of this legal discourse. The fourth term is the *a*, the term that stands in for that which cannot be represented in the discourse. In the symbolic register, the *a* marks the excluded term of discourse, the gap in (or void of) its symbolic structure. It stands in for what cannot be signified in the discourse, the absent term that is barred or struck-through to show it cannot be symbolised (*a̶*). The *a* is the constitutive 'outside' of the limits of a given discourse, which indicates the foundational gap within that discourse. With this description of the structure and operation of international criminal law as a legal discourse, it becomes possible to see the relationship between law and justice in the socio-symbolic order of international criminal law.

5.4 The Trauma of International Criminal Law and the Phantasy of International Justice

The *Kunarac* case reveals the traumatic relationship between determinate law and incalculable justice in international criminal law. In Lacanian theory, an event becomes traumatic if it is not possible to represent or symbolise that event with the existing symbolic order.[99] It understands trauma as the interruption of the 'automatic self-reiteration of the symbolic order's regular functioning, the moment when it *happens to fail*, where some purely contingent irruption derails its normative operations with something *stricto sensu* impossible'.[100] The event becomes an experience of the impossible when it is not possible to represent that experience within the existing socio-symbolic order.[101] For this reason, the traumatic event appears as a gap or a lack in the socio-symbolic order. The traumatic event is not symbolised, because there is no signifier that can represent it. In these terms, the discursive operation of international criminal law figures justice as an event that is impossible to represent. The determinate socio-symbolic order of international criminal law cannot represent incalculable justice.

This traumatic structure emerges because the legal form of international criminal law both constitutes the legal socio-symbolic order that

---

[99] Jacques Lacan, *The Other Side of Psychoanalysis* (New York and London: Norton, 2007), p. 123.
[100] Kenneth Reinhard, 'Lacan and Monotheism', (1999) 3(2) Jouvert, 1–28, 15.
[101] Lacan, *Freud's Papers on Technique*, pp. 190-191.

founds 'interhuman relations' at the international level and at the same time constitutes the injustice as an international crime that violates that order. In the legal form, the injustice symbolised by the international crime breaches the foundation of international society and with it the legal subject of rights and its global legal relations, which international criminal law then repairs This formulation of international crimes is well illustrated by Justice Abi-Saab's argument in the *Tadić* Jurisdiction Decision:

> [t]he crimes constituting the serious violations of international humanitarian law for the prosecution of which, according to Article 1 of the Statute, the ICTY was established ... are all of relatively recent origin going back to the immediate aftermath of the Second World War. They were part of the cathartic reaction of the international community to the traumas of the untold horrors committed during that war.[102]

However, 'international society' and its subjects are themselves created by the socio-symbolic order of international criminal law. This creates the paradox that international criminal law cannot symbolise injustice, because that injustice violates its socio-symbolic order. The socio-symbolic order of international criminal law cannot assimilate the injustice within its existing symbolic structures other than as a violation of its legal order. This injustice is impossible to integrate within the socio-symbolic order, because international criminal law cannot symbolise it as such.

Shoshana Felman claims that "[e]very trial is related to an injury, a trauma for which it compensates and that it attempts to remedy and overcome".[103] However, international criminal justice has a traumatic structure because it cannot provide justice – in the sense that it is not possible to compensate, remedy, or overcome the injury to the idea of the person – the 'human being' – or the idea of society – 'global human society' - in the legal form of international criminal law. The injustice is 'outside' the socio-symbolic order of international criminal law because it violates the conceptions of persons and of society that found the existing legal order. Given this structure, this prohibited violence ruptures the legal social bonds that serve as the foundation of 'international society'. The legal form of international criminal law constitutes the injury to

---

[102] *Tadić* Jurisdiction Decision Appeals Chamber Judgement, Separate Opinion of Judge Abi-Saab, I.
[103] 'Forms of Judicial Blindness', in Austin Sarat and Thomas Kearns (eds.), *History, Memory, and the Law* (Ann Arbor: University of Michigan Press, 1999), p. 36.

international society as a crime because it breaches the socio-symbolic order of the international legal order but at the same time that very breach structures the injury as that which is 'outside or beyond' the legal order. The injustice of collective violence thereby appears as a traumatic breach of the legal order that threatens to undo it. Accordingly, it is distinct from the ordinary crime of municipal law, which transgresses the law but does not threaten the legal order – or the society – itself.[104] International criminal law prohibits collective violence that destroys the very categories of persons and society that this legal order creates but for which it cannot provide justice.

The ICTY's models of justice figure 'justice' as that which is both a predicate of the socio-symbolic order of international criminal law *and* that which it cannot enact. Because international criminal law cannot institute justice, justice appears as a gap or a lack in the socio-symbolic order of international criminal law. In structural terms, international criminal law will always be incomplete and lacking because it cannot provide incalculable justice for these crimes. 'Justice' thereby becomes an impossible event. If justice appears to be an experience of the impossible (as Derrida suggests), it is because international criminal law cannot symbolise justice as such within its determinate socio-symbolic order. For this reason, justice becomes the trauma of international criminal law, and hence the ICTY's notion of the justice of law has the symbolic structure of trauma. The trauma of international criminal justice is its juridical impossibility.

The paradox of these models of justice is that the traumatic violation of international criminal law requires the institution of the existing determinate legal form. They understand injustice as the violation of international criminal law and that violation as requiring legal justice in the extant forms of procedure, punishment, recognition, and reconciliation. For this reason, the models of justice assume that international criminal law in its current form institutes justice and that the institution of these specific forms of legal justice can suture the violation of international society and its legal subjects. Accordingly, it figures justice as the *legal* resolution of the injustice that breaches the existing legal order of international criminal law.

---

[104] In Felman's terms, international criminal justice would be a 'trauma trial' that deals with 'collective trauma': *The Juridical Unconscious* (Cambridge, MA, and London: Cambridge University Press, 2002), p. 6. However, I argue that 'trauma' is not 'outside' international criminal law but is a constitutive gap within its socio-symbolic order.

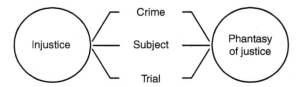

Figure 5.2   The phantasy of justice

The conception of justice as the legal suture of the trauma of international crimes functions as a 'phantasy' in the psychoanalytic sense of an '[i]maginary scene in which the subject is a protagonist, representing the fulfilment of a wish ... in a manner which is distorted ... by defensive processes'.[105] It is not a fantasy in the common sense meaning of an unrealistic and delusionary daydream of justice or a misrecognition of the reality of injustice. Rather, Lacan reminds us that 'phantasy is never anything more than the screen that conceals something quite primary', the lack or gap in the socio-symbolic order.[106]

The four models of justice conceal the traumatic structure of international criminal law with a fundamental phantasy of their legal resolution of the subjective and social trauma of the international crime. In the legal form, 'justice' functions as a phantasmatic suture because it covers over the fundamental and constitutive breach of the legal social bonds of international criminal law. This fundamental phantasy of justice functions as a defence against the impossibility of the existing form of international criminal law instituting justice. The phantasy of justice represents the fulfilment of a wish, that wish being that law *could* institute justice. In this imaginary scene, international criminal law can suture the trauma of injustice (Figure 5.2).

Because the socio-symbolic order of international criminal law is necessarily an incomplete structure, it is always missing a symbolic element that would complete it as a system of signification and fix meaning. As a signifying order, the legal form is always incomplete. For this reason, unsymbolised injustices appear as a lack in the socio-symbolic order of international criminal law. In Lacanian terms, this 'gap' or 'lack' in the legal form is the real (the missing symbolic *a*). This

---

[105] Jean Laplanche and Jean-Bertrand Pontalis, *The Language of Psychoanalysis* (New York and London: Norton, 1973), p. 314.
[106] Jacques Lacan, *The Four Fundamental Concepts of Psycho-Analysis* (London: Peregrine, 1986), p. 60.

gap is filled with the imaginary content of phantasy (the imaginary *a*). Phantasy veils the gap, giving it consistency and filling it with content. In the legal form, the 'fantasy' of justice covers over this gap, filling it with phantasmic content and attaching the subject to international criminal law. This operation is imaginary, in the sense that it consists of images and affect that give the socio-symbolic order of the legal form content.

'Justice' functions as a phantasmatic suture because it covers over the fundamental gap in the socio-symbolic order of international criminal law, namely, the injustice of the crime. In this discursive operation of international criminal law, the category of 'justice' is given content through its supporting phantasy that legal procedure, punishment, recognition, and reconciliation can suture the social injury of collective violence. This phantasy imagines the legal order as complete and seeks to 'close' it. For this reason, justice appears as the 'final' term of the signifying chain, which gives meaning to its other discursive elements and operates as the axiological foundation of the legal form.

The phantasy of justice is not individual but is what Drucilla Cornell calls a 'social fantasy', which consists of socially shaped ideas that give meaning and substance to symbols.[107] This phantasy consists of an affective identification with the idea of justice. As such, the legal form of international criminal law also operates on an ideological level. In the Lacanian Marxist tradition, Slavoj Žižek describes such social fantasies as 'ideology' because of their role in hiding the 'missing' part of this socio-symbolic order and so sustaining that social ordering. As Žižek emphasises, one of the most elementary definitions of ideology is 'a symbolic field which contains [phantasmic] filler holding the place of some structural impossibility, while simultaneously disavowing this impossibility'.[108] The ideological fantasy veils the gap in the socio-symbolic order, giving it consistency and thereby sustaining the socio-symbolic order of international criminal law. The phantasy of justice serves as the ultimate support of international criminal law because it conceals the impossibility of justice in its legal form.

However, in the legal form this fundamental phantasy of justice also 'tells the story of a traumatic event that "continues to not to take place", that cannot be inscribed into the very symbolic space it brought about by its intervention'.[109] The phantasy of justice repeats the very 'gap' in the

---

[107] *The Imaginary Domain*, p. 157.
[108] Slavoj Žižek, *The Plague of Fantasies* (London: Verso, 1997), p. 76.
[109] Slavoj Žižek, *The Fragile Absolute* (London: Verso, 2000), p. 64.

socio-symbolic order that it seeks to veil, because that gap shapes its form. For this reason, the model of justice as the repair of the violation of the socio-symbolic order of law comes to take the form of repetition of that trauma. In phantasy we 'repeat the traumatic situation in a compulsive fashion ... as a way of trying to bind it'.[110] The juridical becomes a symptomatic expression of the traumatic by repeating it in the socio-symbolic structure of legal discourse. The legal form of international criminal law repeats the very terms of the trauma that inaugurates it, namely, the violation of the international legal subject and of global human society. In this way, the trauma persists *in* international criminal law.

Sexual violence cases before the ICTY exemplify this repetition of the originary trauma of the international crime. Vesna Kesić argues that 'war rapes and other forms of violence against women were so tightly enmeshed within the categories of nation and ethnicity, they could only be recognized as a war strategy ... only if they occurred in large numbers ... if they were "systematic" and "followed a pattern," and if they supported the claim of genocide or ethnic cleansing'.[111] When sexual violence can be shown to have a nexus to armed conflict; the intended destruction of a national, ethnic, racial or religious group; or, an attack upon a civilian population, then the conduct becomes an international crime. It otherwise only appears as a numerated offence of rape as a crime against humanity, the archetypal model of wartime rape as the heterosexual penetration of civilian women by combatant men. Given this frame, it is unsurprising that sexual violence becomes most visible in its archetypal form and most legally significant where it is seen as a crime against a victim's community or nation.

This can be seen in the ICTY jurisprudence that comes to characterise sexual violence 'as a crime against a particular community, against women as a form of male property, and not as a crime against the female body, against the woman as an individual', which would be characterised as a domestic crime.[112] This reduction of sexual violence as an

---

[110] Laplanche and Pontalis, *The Language of Psychoanalysis*, p. 472.
[111] Vesna Kesić, 'Muslim Women, Croatian Women, Serbian Women, Albanian Women ...', in Dusan Bjelić and Obrad Savić (eds.), *Balkan as Metaphor* (London and Cambridge, MA.: MIT Press, 2002), p. 317.
[112] Vesna Nikolić-Ristanović, 'The Hague Tribunal and Rape in the Former Yugoslavia', in Vesna Nikolić-Ristanović (ed.), *Women, Violence and War* (Budapest: Central European University Press, 2000), p. 79.

international crime to 'inter-ethnic conflict' can be seen in *Kunarac*, where the ICTY describes how the three Serb soldiers on trial:

> mistreated Muslim girls and women ... *because* they were Muslims. They therefore fully embraced the ethnicity-based aggression of the Serbs against the Muslim civilians, and all their criminal actions were clearly part of and had the effect of perpetuating the attack against the Muslim civilian population.[113]

Such judgements repeat the ethnicised constructions of gender in this armed violence. In doing so, they reinforce the very distinctions of ethnicity, community, and nation that were at stake in the war itself (as discussed in Chapter 3).

The *Kunarac* case thereby reveals the repetition in the phantasmic conception of international criminal justice in the ICTY jurisprudence. It shows how justice imagined as the institution of international criminal law repeats the traumatic event of the 'ethnicity-based aggression of the Serbs against the Muslim civilians' because it necessarily reiterates the ethno-nationalist terms of the attack upon civilians that make it an international crime. It conceives sexual violence in terms of a systematic attack against the *Muslim* civilian population or the persecution of women *of non-Serb origin*. To understand sexual violence as an international crime in this way is to reiterate the very categories of identity which ethnic cleansing sought to constitute and fix.[114] This is because it repeats the very categories of persecution (Muslim, non-Serb) that ethnic cleansing in the Foča region sought to create through an attack on the civilian population. This is a 'structural' repetition of the originary trauma of international criminal law, in which that legal form reproduces the very categories of social differentiation that the conflict itself seeks to construct through violence.

This phantasmic conception of justice determines and fixes international criminal law in an imaginary scene. It structures the justice of international criminal law in relation to its traumatic violation: the international crime. The fundamental phantasy of justice veils the lack in international criminal law, inasmuch as it veils the impossibility of legal justice redressing the injustice of the crime. However, it also sustains and reiterates that lack of justice in international criminal law.

---

[113] *Kunarac et al.*, ICTY-96-23 &23/1-T, Judgement, para. 592.
[114] I am indebted to Mark Cousins for this argument: 'Closing Address', *German Architecture and Its Changing Past* Conference, Architectural Association, 2001.

The Lacanian notion of '[t]rauma implies fixation or blockage. Fixation always involves something which is not symbolised.'[115] This phantasy of the justice of international criminal law symptomatically repeats the traumatic event that is not symbolised in its socio-symbolic order. To symbolise justice as the institution of the existing order of international criminal law entails that it functions as a symptomatic repetition of its originary trauma. It figures international criminal justice as the resolution of subjective and social trauma by the existing legal order. However, it also figures international justice as traumatic because determinate international criminal law suffers the trauma of the impossibility of incalculable justice. This phantasy of the justice of law thereby structures 'international justice' as the traumatic repetition of the *injustice* of collective violence that destroys peoples and societies.

The fundamental phantasy of international justice thereby functions as a defence against the impossibility of international criminal law instituting justice for the destruction of persons and societies. It operates as a phantasmatic suture that covers over the fundamental gap in the socio-symbolic order of international criminal law, namely, the injustice of the crime. As such, it expresses the remainder of injustice that the legal form produces. This phantasy of justice is a symptom of the fundamental contradiction between the determinate legal order of international criminal law and international justice as it is symbolised and imagined in that legal form.

5.5 The Conceptual Contradictions of the Legal Form

Where sexual violence 'surfaces' as a gender-based harm (to use Copelon's terms), it reveals the conceptual problems in the legal categories of international crime, subject, trial, and justice. The conceptual problems include the tensions in the grounds of international criminalisation, the oscillation between individual and collective legal subjects, the unstable foundation of juridical truths, and the gap between international criminal law and international criminal justice. As such, sexual violence as a gender-based harm reveals the immanent contradictions within, and dynamic instability of, the fundamental categories of the legal form.

---

[115] Bruce Fink, *The Lacanian Subject* (Princeton: Princeton University Press, 1995), p. 26.

If justice is imagined as the application of existing international criminal law, it appears to resolve these contradictions and to stabilise the discourse. This is a 'closed' mode of international criminal law, which closes and fixes its discursive operation. In this 'closed' mode, the discourse operates to produce the phantasy of justice, which imagines international criminal justice as the institution of its existing socio-symbolic order. The phantasy of justice sustains the discourse of international criminal law, fixing its elements in place and suturing the 'gap' in its discursive structure. When international criminal law works in this way, the phantasy of international criminal justice covers over the contradictions within the categories of the legal form, by functioning as the imaginary resolution of these conceptual contradictions. It does not shift the legal concepts or phantasmic structure of the legal form or create a new legal social bond.

However, sexual violence as a gender-based crime disrupts both this application of the existing legal form and the phantasy of international criminal justice that supports it. It produces a different relationship to that phantasy, revealing its incompleteness and lack. The legal recognition of these harms involves an acknowledgement of new calls for justice, the creation of a new signification of the gendered harm of sexual violence, the recognition of women as legal subjects, and the construction of new ways of witnessing and judging sexual violence. This recognition of injustice refuses the phantasy that the existing legal form will provide justice. By recognising gendered injustice, international criminal law can operate an 'open' mode, which allows a change in its discursive operation. Rather than being a closed and fixed structure, the legal form becomes 'open' and 'dynamic' in its operation. This process reveals the contradictions (and limits) of the legal form and makes it possible to shift the operation of that discourse. That shift opens the possibility of developing gender justice within international criminal law. It begins with the inclusion of sexual violence as a gender-based harm in the category of international crimes at the establishment of the ICTY and continues in the development of the legal form of international criminal law.

6

The Global Legal Form of International Criminal Law

> It has nothing to do with anything legal. It's a camp, Mr Karadžić. Understand that. It's a concentration camp. All the rules are forgotten there. The domestic legislation, international legislation, all that was forgotten.
>
> Witness KDZ080, *The Prosecutor v.* Karadžić[1]

In the *Karadžić* case, Witness KDZ080 gave evidence on the Bosnian Serb military takeover and persecution of non-Serbs in Prijedor, her detention in the Omarska camp, and the physical and sexual violence against female detainees held there. During her cross-examination by Karadžić, she described the suspension of all law in Omarska. The charges against Karadžić arose from genocide and crimes against humanity committed in 20 municipalities in Bosnia and Herzegovina, including the Prijedor municipality. These charges were brought under international criminal law. They constituted Witness KDZ080 as an international legal subject, her harms as international crimes, and those crimes as injuring an interest of 'international society'. What, then, are the juridical concepts of subject and society in international criminal law? What global social relationships do these juridical concepts express? And under what historical conditions do these global social relationships assume this legal character?

6.1 The Legal Form of International Criminal Law as a Social Order

6.1.1 The 'Biosocial' Structure of 'International Society'

Witness KDZ080 describes what Giorgio Agamben calls the 'state of exception'. Agamben identifies the so-called 'ethnic rape camps' of the former Yugoslavia as profoundly important for understanding this state

---

[1] *Karadžić*, ICTY-95-5/18, Trial Transcript, 26 October 2011, p. 20412.

of exception as 'new biopolitical *nomos* of the planet'.[2] In the modern political order, he argues that the 'normal' political life of the nation-state 'orders forms of life and juridical rules in a determinate space'.[3] In the nation-state, the juridical system divides all material life into the categories of *bios*, the life of the political community, and *zoe*, the state of mere physical existence.[4] It constitutes both categories of political existence and bare life, insofar as it produces and sustains the distinction between them. As such, the juridical produces the 'biopolitical' body of the state through an operation of legal inclusion (as a citizen of the state within the legal order) and exclusion (as a non-citizen without legal existence). Those 'outside' the legal order do not exist in a space of exception to law but in a space of 'exception' in which the law is suspended.

In the state of exception, the suspension of law becomes permanent and comes to characterise the juridico-political order. For Agamben, what is at issue in the state of exception 'is not so much the control or neutralization of an excess as the creation and definition of the very space in which the juridico-political order can have validity'.[5] In the state of exception, 'the realm of bare life – which is originally situated at the margins of the political order – gradually begins to coincide with the political realm, and exclusion and inclusion, outside and inside, *bios and zoē*, right and fact, enter into a zone of irreducible indistinction'.[6] Agamben describes the archetypal figures of this state of exception as 'a Jew in Auschwitz or a Bosnian woman in Omarska'.[7] For Agamben, in Auschwitz and Omarska the distinction between the political and the biological becomes indiscernible. In these 'zones of indistinction', the biological body becomes political, and life itself becomes an object of the political order. As Adam Thurschwell describes, '[i]n this critical moment, normative law, the law of the "normal situation", devolves into a permanent, non-normative state of exception'.[8]

Agamben identifies the state of exception as the 'emergence of a new juridical space at a global level', but nevertheless his model remains

---

[2] Giorgio Agamben, *Homo Sacer* (Stanford: Stanford University Press, 1998), p. 176.
[3] Ibid., p. 175.
[4] Giorgio Agamben, *State of Exception* (Chicago: The University of Chicago Press, 2005), p. 86.
[5] Agamben, *Homo Sacer*, p. 19.
[6] Ibid., p. 9.
[7] Giorgio Agamben, *Means without End* (Minneapolis: University of Minnesota Press, 2000), p. 121.
[8] Adam Thurschwell, 'Specters of Nietzsche', (2003) 24(3) Cardozo L R 1193–1259, 1235.

tied to the juridico-political national order, as Stephen Humphreys describes.[9] In contrast, international criminal law presumes 'international society' rather than the 'determinate space' of the sovereign state and 'universal' values rather than the particularist values of national politics. This is because international criminal law sustains the distinction between the *social* existence of humanity and the bare life of humans at the international level. The legal form of international criminal law constitutes the international legal subject as a particular form of personhood – a specific form of social being – and 'international society' as a particular social order – a specific organisation of social life. It ascribes value to certain categories of global social relations, structuring those relations through the juridical categories of social and physical existence. It functions as a *social* ordering, which distinguishes humanity, a category of social existence, and physical life, a category of physical existence. The first category recognises the social existence of humanity and that social existence attracts legal protection. The second is the category of the physical existence of humans, against which violence may be permissible. The legal form of international criminal law thereby sustains the division between social being (the category of 'humanity', which international criminal law protects) and physical being (the category of physical life, which is subject to legally permissible violence). This structure explains why international criminal law prohibits rape as a crime against humanity (as violence against a woman as a member of 'humanity'), while the killing of that same civilian woman characterised as part of a necessary and proportional military attack may not be (as violence against her physical existence but not her social existence as a member of humanity).

I describe the structure of international criminal law as 'biosocial' because the object of this juridical order is 'global society' rather than the nation-state polity. The legal form of international criminal law sustains the distinction between humanity and bare life by regulating the capacity to destroy the object of this legal ordering: the social existence of 'humanity'. As such, it represents or symbolises norms of conduct necessary that 'are essential for the coexistence of all mankind ... humanity at large cannot hold together without adherence to the standards in question'.[10] At the international level, the legal form of international criminal law thereby constructs social relations as

---

[9] Stephen Humphreys, 'Legalising Lawlessness', (2006) 17(3) EJIL 677–687, 684.
[10] *Tadić*, ICTY-94-1-A, Judgement in Sentencing Appeals, 26 January 2000, para. 40.

juridical and creates the legal social bond as a global social relation. By signifying social existence as global legal bonds and persons as global legal subjects, international criminal law sustains the distinction between humanity and bare life beyond the nation-state. At the level of the subject, the prohibited collective violence suspends the legal social bond, which constitutes the victim as a subject of law and the perpetrator as subject to law, and hence suspends their constitution as international legal subjects. The suspension of the legal social bond is not reducible to the breach of the human rights of the citizen, which excludes the victim from the nation-state polity. Rather, it suspends the social existence of the victims and perpetrators as members of 'human society' beyond the state. As such, it concerns a more fundamental negation of the very category of 'humanity' as a social collectivity.

The legal form of international criminal law therefore does not entrench a state of exception, in which law and life are indistinguishable. This is because international criminal law does not suspend law or define its threshold.[11] Rather, we can describe international criminal law as a *law of exception*, which sustains that threshold between law and life beyond the sovereign. The law of exception is not simply the 'law of the "normal situation"', in which the 'normal juridical order' prevails in a nation-state polity.[12] Instead, it is 'a special kind of law', as Agamben calls it.[13] This 'special kind of law' sustains the distinction between the constitutive inclusionary and exclusionary categories of the *social* order as such, and hence sustains the fundamental division between law and life upon which these categories rest. As Stephen Humphreys describes, law maintains 'their continued separation: a prop against collapse, a barrier to fusion, a conserver of their different identities'.[14]

International criminal law creates and defines the very space in which the juridico-social order has validity beyond the sovereign. It operates as a law of exception, which sustains the distinction between social existence and bare life – what it is to exist as a social subject or to be reduced to physical being – in transnational social relations. As such, it conserves

---

[11] In Agamben's discussion of Guantánamo Bay as the state of exception to the international legal order, the laws of war do not mark a state of exception. Instead, they indicate a state of law, which when suspended give rise to the state of exception. Agamben, *State of Exception*, pp. 3–4.
[12] Thurschwell, 'Specters of Nietzsche', 1235.
[13] Agamben, *State of Exception*, p. 4.
[14] Stephen Humphreys, 'Nomarchy', (2006) 19(2) Cambridge Review of International Affairs 331–351, 342.

the fundamental categories of law and life in 'international society'. This international law of exception institutes and sustains these categories by signifying social life in terms of the juridical order. It constructs the legal social bond as a fundamental category of global social relations, sustaining the juridical distinction between humanity, as a category of social existence, and bare life, as a category of physical existence.

Accordingly, international criminal law operates as a legal social bond, which sustains the legal subject and relations that construct 'international society' at the transnational level. More precisely, we might call this 'global human society', in that it is conceived as a society of all persons, which extends beyond national boundaries and polities. International criminal law symbolises those minimal ties between persons necessary to sustain global social relations and thereby operates as the foundational legal bond of this 'international society'. This legal discourse sustains the distinction between global human society and bare life by constructing the legal ties between persons necessary to sustain the category of global human society. It criminalises violence that is seen to profoundly disrupt the legal social bonds of the 'international society', figured as all human society. The concept of global human society is therefore a relational notion, in which each person exists in legal relations to others because they are members of that juridical category of all persons. In the legal form, the justice of international criminal law seeks to reinstitute that global legal bond where it has been violated.

The operation of international criminal law names Witness KDZ080, together with the other female witnesses who provided evidence to the court, as a victim of international crimes. In doing so, it names not only the individual victim-witness but also all victims of these crimes as international legal subjects. It establishes victims as existing in legal relations of entitlements and obligations to others and re-symbolises their experience of bare life as a harm that injures the protected interests of international society. By doing so, it constitutes the harms to victims as an injustice and victims as social subjects, that is, as persons having social existence in the international legal order. All victims of those crimes thereby become part of the legal social bond.

International criminal law thereby includes women in the category of social existence at the international level. It recognises them as subjects of international criminal law and their harms as prohibited collective violence. The inclusion of women shifts what international criminal law recognises as an international crime, in that it recognises sexual violence as collective violence, and who it recognises as legal subjects, in that it recognises women as members of humanity. As such, it changes the existing juridical categories of humanity and bare life. At the same time, the witness to this experience of bare life evidences the lack or fault in the existing discourse of international criminal law, as described in Chapter 5. She testifies to the experience of bare life, which is the constitutive but excluded term of the existing global legal form. In doing so, she testifies to the breach of the existing socio-symbolic order of international criminal law, its constitutive limit of bare life. While determinate legal categories create social existence in international criminal law, they also mark the limits of its socio-symbolic order.

The operation of the legal form thereby gives international criminal law a traumatic structure, as discussed in Chapter 5. If international criminal law sustains the distinction between social existence and bare life, then it also produces bare life as a constitutive category of being that is 'outside' social existence in the legal order. It both sustains social existence and creates its excluded other, bare life. In the legal form, 'bare life' functions as a constitutive 'exception' to the category of social existence. As such, it is a 'traumatic kernel' within the legal form, which marks the limits of that socio-symbolic order. As Slavoj Žižek describes, it marks a fundamental antagonism or internal contradiction with a social order that cannot be symbolised.[15] In the legal form, it marks fundamental antagonisms in the global social relations that the legal form expresses. On the one hand, the determinate socio-symbolic order of international criminal law creates humanity as a juridical category of social existence. On the other hand, it also creates the juridical category of bare life as its constitutive exception, understood as the state of physical existence that emerges in the collective violence of patriarchal, capitalist, and imperialist social relations of globalisation. At these limits of international criminal law bare life can be found: that group of persons who become inhuman, who are injured with impunity, and who suffer injustice without redress.

Because the institution of international criminal law cannot provide justice as such for the experience of bare life, it must always appear as a gap in this discourse (as described in Chapter 5). When operating in its closed mode, international criminal law covers over that impossibility with the phantasy of justice. This phantasy imagines that reinstituting the

---

[15] Slavoj Žižek, *The Sublime Object of Ideology* (London and New York: Verso, 1989), p. 51. In Lacan, it marks the real, in Agamben, the potentiality of living beings, and in Marx, class struggle (as Žižek notes).

existing legal order can resolve the injustice of bare life. When the discourse of international criminal law works in this way, it repeats the very breach of the international social order it seeks to repair. It reiterates the constitutive ground of the harms of sexual violence, which involve the making of sexuated and ethnicised bare life through the collective destruction of persons and societies.

6.1.2 The Legal Form as Ethno-Fraternal Social Contract

Where international criminal law resolves its fundamental traumatic structure through the phantasy of the justice of the existing legal order, the legal form operates at an ideological level. It functions as the 'hypothetical social contract which supports subjectivity and sociality' at the transnational level.[16] This operation of international criminal law can be said to 'universalise' the modern liberal Western legal form, and, with it, the modern European subject as a legal subject. It creates an ethnic and sexual contract, whose free and equal exchange relations rest on unequal and unfree relations to others. If we inscribe sexual violence as a gender-based crime into this ideological operation of the legal form, then we see that it produces a masculine subject and establishes social relations of masculine intersubjectivity. As Drucilla Cornell argues of municipal Western legal systems, the legal subject is a hegemonic masculine subject, constituted by paternal identification that also founds his relation to other masculine subjects.[17] I describe this social relation as a fraternal social bond, which replaces older patriarchal forms based in the rule of the father.[18] In this social bond, the hegemonic masculine subject functions as the universal subject. This is not a social contract between men and women as masculine and feminine subjects, since women function in its symbolic economy as objects of exchange rather than as social subjects. Rather, it presumes a fraternal relation between masculine subjects. The modern social bond emerges from this fraternal social tie, with its founding discourse of equality, liberty, and brotherhood. International criminal law produces these same hegemonic masculine subjects and

---

[16] Costas Douzinas, *The End of Human Rights* (Oxford: Hart Publishing, 2000), p, 309.
[17] Drucilla Cornell, *Beyond Accommodation* (New York: Rowman and Littlefield, 1999), p. 53.
[18] See Kirsten Campbell, *Jacques Lacan and Feminist Epistemology* (London and New York: Routledge, 2004). Marie Mies also describes this shift in the patriarchal system but does not name it as such: see *Patriarchy and Accumulation on a World Scale* (London: Zed Books, 1999), p. 37.

social ties, which take the form of the fraternal social bond at the international level.

In its operation as a modern fraternal discourse, international criminal law constructs a sexuated social relation and reproduces a sexuated social order. This sexuated social order figures social existence through fraternal masculinity and bare life through maternal femininity. As Luce Irigaray insists, this social contract includes women as social (sexual) objects, and not as social subjects. This form of social bond produces 'a single problem, in its multiple aspects: the absence of and exclusion of woman/women from the symbolic/social order, their representation as nature'.[19] This representation figures women as maternal or sexual Others.[20] It is unsurprising therefore that modern international criminal law is not sexually indifferent. Instead, it reproduces this sexuate order in its production of legal subjects and their relations to others. In fact, it constructs the legal subject as a universal masculine subject, with its attribution of bodily integrity and psychic autonomy, existing in legal relations of warfare to other combatants but prohibited from waging war upon 'feminised' groups, where they are valued as (sexual and maternal) objects of exchange between men.

At the international level, the fraternal contract is also an 'ethnic' contract connected to the nation-state in the international social order. Carole Pateman argues that because '[m]odern civil societies developed as patriarchal "racial states" ... it is not possible to fully understand or analyse either the major institutions of modern civil societies or the construction of the world system of modern states without reference to both race and sex'.[21] As she describes, 'the sexual and racial contracts have been intimately connected since modern states (civil societies) began to be created in the seventeenth century'.[22] This modern nation-state emerged in the world system in its colonial and then imperialist phases.[23] In the postcolonial period, with its emphasis upon the formal

---

[19] Margaret Whitford, *Luce Irigaray* (London: Routledge, 1991), p. 170.
[20] Drucilla Cornell, *The Imaginary Domain* (London, Routledge, 1995), p. 219.
[21] Carole Pateman, 'Race, Sex, and Indifference', in Carole Pateman and Charles Mills (eds.), *Contract and Domination*, (Cambridge and Malden: Polity, 2007), p. 135. The concept of the racial contract was developed by Charles Mills in the context of racialised state-citizen (non-citizen) relations. I use the term 'ethno-fraternal' contract at the international level for reasons explained below.
[22] Pateman, 'Race, Sex, and Indifference', p. 134.
[23] See Antony Anghie, *Imperialism, Sovereignty, and the Making of International Law* (Cambridge: Cambridge University Press, 2007).

equality of states, the 'state' as a legal concept is formally empty, in the sense that it is defined by formal criteria such as a stable political community supporting a legal order in a defined territory but does not attribute substantive qualities to that population, political community, or legal order.[24] However, in the international state system, based as it is upon the Western European nation-state form, that state comes to be imagined as limited sovereign community, as Benedict Anderson describes.[25] In relation to the question of who constitutes the people of the state, 'modernity answers this question in ethno-nationalist terms: no *liberté* and *égalité* without *fraternité*' in the nation-state.[26] As Anderson explains, the nation is 'imagined as a *community* because . . . the nation is always conceived as a deep, horizontal comradeship. Ultimately, it is this fraternity that makes it possible.'[27] Accordingly, the fraternal national contract is racialised or, in its more recent forms, ethnicised through the attribution of 'race' or 'ethnicity' to its 'imagined communities'. In this modern ethno-fraternal contract, 'ethnicity' is attached to nation (a form of imagined social belonging) and to state (a form of political and legal order).

The ethno-fraternal contract points to the connection in the legal form between the 'state' as a political and legal order and the 'nation' as a collective social identity, in which ideas of race and ethnicity come to mark collective inclusion and exclusion.[28] These same modern ethno-fraternal contracts mark collective inclusion and exclusion at the international level. They shape the development of international humanitarian law,[29] and they are evident in international criminal law in the concepts of state and collective legal subjects. The imagining of state as nation figures women's bodies as the natural material of the nation-state, that is, as a category of bare life, in the legal form of international criminal law. In her classic critique of the nation-state, Nira Yuval-Davis argues, 'gender relations are crucial in understanding and analysing the phenomena of nations and nationalism, and the specific

---

[24] Ian Brownlie, *Principles of Public International Law* (7th edn.) (Oxford: Oxford University Press, 2008), p. 71.
[25] Benedict Anderson, *Imagined Communities* (London and New York: Verso, 2006), p. 7.
[26] Siniša Malešević, *Identity as Ideology* (Basingstoke: Polity, 2006), p. 215.
[27] Anderson, *Imagined Communities*, p. 7.
[28] Floya Anthias and Nira Yuval Davis, 'Introduction', in Nira Yuval-Davis and Floya Anthias (eds.) *Woman-Nation-State* (New York: St. Martin's Press, 1989).
[29] Anthony Anghie and Bhupinder Chimni, 'Third World Approaches to International Law and Individual Responsibility in Internal Conflicts', (2003) 2(1) Chinese JIL 77–103.

boundaries of inclusions and exclusions that they construct'. In particular, 'women come to play crucial roles in biological, cultural and political reproductions of national and other collectivities'.[30] Developing this analysis in the context of the wars in the former Yugoslavia, Yugoslavian feminists questioned how '[p]ractices of nation-building employ social constructions of masculinity and femininity that support a division of labor in which women reproduce the nation physically and symbolically and men protect, defend and avenge the nation'.[31] This ideological content of the 'state' reappears in the phantasy of justice described in Chapter 5, in which the 'Serbian man' and the 'Muslim woman' come to personify the imagined inclusions and exclusions of the nation-states created in the destruction of Yugoslavia.

The ethno-fraternal contract is a social fiction constructed in the phantasy of justice. As discussed in Chapter 3, international criminal law constructs 'fictional' representations of the legal subject. This legal creation or fiction of the legal person is a social fiction, which symbolises or represents what it is to be a person (a subject) and attributes that person with imagined characteristics and qualities (an identity).[32] Social fictions operate as what Judith Butler calls a 'register of regulatory ideality', which constructs hegemonic identities with imagined characteristics of ethnicity and gender.[33] They provide hegemonic representations of what it is to be a subject, as well as to exist in relation to others. These identities are hegemonic in the Gramscian sense, in that they are 'naturalised' ideas of socially dominant groups. We can more precisely describe the ethno-fraternal contract as a social fiction of 'hegemonic masculinity'. As Sara Meger describes, 'hegemonic masculinity is closely associated with political and economic hegemony'.[34] That is, these ideas of masculinity are tied to the construction of social domination within the global social system. In the social fictions of international criminal law, we see a similar process of the construction of the 'identity' of the legal subject, which is given hegemonic content in the social fictions of

---

[30] Nira Yuval-Davis, 'Gender and Nation', (1993) 16(4) Ethnic and Racial Studies, 621–632, 621, 630.
[31] Rada Iveković and Julie Mostov, 'Introduction', in Rada Iveković and Julie Mostov (eds.) *From Gender to Nation* (New Delhi: Zubaan, 2004), p. 10.
[32] See Campbell, *Jacques Lacan and Feminist Epistemology*, pp. 117 ff.
[33] *Bodies That Matter* (London: Routledge, 1993), p. 18.
[34] *Rape, Loot, Pillage* (Oxford: Oxford University Press, 2016), p. 40. As Meger describes, this includes the construction of regional hegemons through collective violence, which are an integral part of the making of this global social order.

militarised masculinities or their subordinate 'feminised' others. These social fictions give particular content to the legal subject, which is too often imagined through the sexist and orientalist 'Balkan' stereotypes in the ICTY jurisprudence described in Chapters 2 to 4.

6.2 International Criminal Law as a Global Legal Form

6.2.1 The Global Legal Form of 'International Society'

At a formal or symbolic level, international criminal law constructs persons as legal subjects, which exist in legal relations to all humanity (rather than the international community of states). It is a *juridical* representation of social relations in terms of a universal legal subject and their legal relations to 'humanity'. It 'creates a universe of formally equal individuals whose concrete social and economic positions do not determine their legal status and capacities'.[35] It figures the social relations between persons as transnational legal relationships of rights and obligations, thereby functioning as a form of social bond beyond the nation-state. The form of the social bond is global because those legal relations construct persons as members of the human social collectivity, 'humanity'. The legal form of international criminal law thereby makes a specific transnational form of legal social bonds.

We can describe the making of the legal form as 'constant process of becoming international', following Frédéric Mégret, because the distinctive values and practices of international justice create the *sui generis* nature of international criminal law.[36] However, this process of becoming international is itself contingent upon a process of becoming global, in that international criminal law expresses the global legal relations of 'humanity' (rather than inter-state relations). The process of becoming 'global', rather than 'international', creates this distinctive legal form. We can now more precisely describe how this legal form shifts from the international scale of inter-state relations and the universal scale of individual human rights to the global scale of transnational social relations. International criminal law is 'global' in three ways that are integral to its legal form. First, it represents persons and their relations as global,

---

[35] Nancy Anderson and David Greenberg, 'From Substance to Form', (1983) 7 Social Text 69–84, 70.
[36] Frédéric Mégret, '"Beyond Fairness"', (2009) 14(1) UCLA Journal of International Foreign Affairs 37–76, 58.

so that persons exist as legal persons in global juridical relations. Second, it expresses the relations of globalising exchange in juridical form. Third, it is an integral element of the processes of globalisation. This process is *'the culmination of the universalizing and abstracting tendencies in international – legal – capitalism ... the universalizing of the legal form.'*[37] This process of universalisation untethers the legal form of international criminal law from the traditional grounds of the legal form of state law, namely, sovereign power (a stable political community) supporting a legal order (the protected interests of a particular society) in a defined territory. International criminal law thereby constitutes a new mode of relationship to the global, and so it can be described as a global legal form.

The global legal form of international criminal law is a constitutive part of globalisation because it functions as a new *legal* form of global social relations. In his reading of Pashukanis, Alan Norrie argues that 'the juridical moment is not antecedent to a prior economic moment, but is a *constitutive part* of it'.[38] The global legal form is not merely a 'lifeless abstraction' that has no concrete existence.[39] Rather, the emergence of this form can be seen in transnational social relations. This is not to simply claim that there is greater enforcement of these norms, which would lead to the familiar problem of the coercive power of international law. Instead, this argument follows Pashukanis in contending that coercion is not the foundation of the legal relation but rather that it is the ordering of social relations that guarantees the existence of the legal form.[40] The making of legal relations in the global legal form is a constituent part of the ordering of global social relations. In the process of 'globalisation', the global legal form thus operates as the juridical element of global social relations.

This approach sustains what Costas Douzinas identifies as the 'crucial distinction between globalisation and universalization'. He argues that this distinction is crucial because '[t]he community of human rights is universal but imaginary: universal humanity does not exist empirically

---

[37] China Miéville, *Between Equal Rights* (London: Pluto, 2005), pp. 267–268. While Miéville makes these comments in relation to states, they are equally applicable to the legal subject of international criminal law.
[38] Alan Norrie, 'Pashukanis and the "Commodity Form" Theory', (1982) 10 Int'l J Soc L 419–437, 423.
[39] Evgeny Pashukanis, *Law and Marxism* (London: Ink Links, 1978), p. 85.
[40] Ibid., p. 89.

and cannot act as a transcendental principle philosophically'.[41] My account of the global legal form does not presume that 'universal humanity' exists empirically or that international criminal law 'reflects' this already existing category of persons. Instead, it insists that the legal form itself creates the 'abstract universality' of humanity, understood as global human society. It contends that the legal form of international criminal law is a constitutive element of the creation of the category of the subject and the social in global social relations.

If international criminal law is a juridical ordering of global social relations, it criminalises collective coercive violence that destroys that legal form of global social bonds. The global legal form governs a space of permissible violence, which may harm or destroy the bare life of humanity, that is, its very material existence. However, it does not permit other forms of coercive collective violence, which are seen to destroy the 'category' of humanity, that category of social existence which international criminal law creates. As such, international criminal law expresses in legal form those social bonds necessary to sustain the juridical relationship between persons *qua* members of global human society in the new relations of globalisation. International criminal law gives these social relations their legal form and in this way mediates global social relations. Its representation of global social bonds is performative in the Austinian sense. International criminal law creates the object it names, the global legal bond, and its legal rules, institutions, and practices instantiate this legal social bond between persons and societies.

International criminal law thereby 'globalises' the legal form by constituting all persons as legal subjects and their relations as legal social bonds. These juridical subjects exist in relations of formal legal equivalence because they are members of the collective community of humanity. As a legal discourse, international criminal law is a *juridical* representation of social relations in 'international society', which it figures as the global society of all human persons, 'humanity'. In the legal form, the 'abstract universality' of global human society determines their legal status and capacities. That legal bond is contingent upon the globalisation of the legal form, which universalises the model of person and of society that it produces. It is for this reason that 'international society' 'appears as an endless chain of legal relations'.[42]

---

[41] *Human Rights and Empire* (Oxford: Routledge, 2007), p. 181.
[42] Pashukanis, *Law and Marxism*, p. 85.

Understood in these relational terms, international criminal law can be said to symbolise the social relationships between persons as members of 'humanity', sustaining the bar between 'humanity' and 'bare life'. This relational framing of international criminal law conceives the international crime as a breach of the legal social bond, rather than the violation of natural or positive law. In this relational model, international criminal law operates as a fundamental structure, which holds the legal subject and its legal social bond together. The potentiality of international criminal law lies precisely in its legal quality – in its capacity to symbolise harm as injustice, to construct that injustice as a legal relation of entitlements and obligations between subjects, and to create just processes for determining those entitlements and obligations. If international criminal law is an integral element of the constitution of the category of 'humanity', then it can function as a minimal knotting that holds this category 'in place' and constructs all persons as members of that set. As such, it functions as that most minimal and necessary of global social bonds between persons. Unlike national legal forms, it does not derive from territory, sovereignty, or peoples but from global social relations. This is the political promise and risk of international criminal law as a global legal social bond.

Without the legal social bond of international criminal law, 'global society' cannot be made in our current historical conditions. In Marxist terms, it involves the struggle to address the 'historically incomplete achievement of full legal personality', which requires 'full proletarianization' of the legal subject at the global level through the inclusion of all those otherwise figured as bare life.[43] When the legal form is not globalised, the legal social bond is not produced, and the global social relations are not constructed. This is because the legal bond makes 'global human society' as such. Accordingly, the substantive criminalisation of international crimes is crucial for the construction of the global legal bond, as it gives the legal form concrete and material existence (as discussed in Chapter 2). Without the process of 'globalising' international criminal law, the unequal global relations between states continue, and the hegemonic ordering of peoples in 'international society' as those who have social existence and those who do not prevails. In that moment, the current fluctuation of forces in global social relations, produced by the uneven and contradictory processes of globalisation, is seemingly

---

[43] Colin Sumner, 'Pashukanis and the "Jurisprudence of Terror"', (1981) 11(1) Insurgent Sociologist 99–106, 105.

resolved by old or new great powers, and the endless chains of legal relations are not produced.

The legal form will then congeal the global ontologies of existence and non-existence in the international social order, as well as the global force relations upon which they rest. On the one side, imperial powers reappear as the sovereign, exempting themselves from being subject to international criminal law. On the other, the bare life of humans appears, condemning persons and societies to collective coercive violence. At the ideological level, the legal form will operate only as an ethno-fraternal contract, producing what Dubravka Žarkov compellingly critiques as hegemonic narratives of 'the "local" victim and perpetrator, on the one hand, and the "international" deliverer of justice on the other' in international criminal law.[44] It will find its legitimation not in justice but in the older colonial forms of 'civilisational' narratives,[45] or in their newer neoliberal forms of 'securitisation'.

This contingent process of the making of international criminal law raises the question of '[h]ow and in what specific historical conditions—does abstract universality become a "fact of (social) life"?'[46] How and under what historical conditions does the regulation of social relationships assume the legal character of international criminal law? If the emergence of the legal form of the modern state is tied to 'capitalism in its monopoly and imperialist phase', as Lacan, Agamben, and Pashukanis suggest, then what happens to the legal form in the new modes of production in our globalised world? How we do explain the connection between the legal form of international criminal law and globalisation?[47]

6.2.2   The Global Legal Form and Globalisation

From the 1970s onwards, it has become clear that the global social system is in a transitional period. I use the idea of the 'global social system' to capture the totality of 'world-scale complex of relational networks or

---

[44] Dubravka Žarkov, 'Ontologies of International Humanitarian and Criminal Law', in Dubravka Žarkov and Marlies Glasius (eds.) *Narratives of Justice In and Out of the Courtroom* (New York: Springer, 2014), p. 18.

[45] Anghie and Chimni, 'Third World Approaches to International Law', 84–86.

[46] Slavoj Žizek, 'Against Human Rights', (2005) 34 New Left Review 115–131, 129.

[47] My aim here is to draw out the connections between the global legal form and these new global social modes of production rather than provide a full account of these social modes of production.

social structures', as discussed in Chapter 1.[48] This idea builds on Wallerstein's important analysis of social relations at a world scale, in which a capitalist world economy produces an international division of labour between core and periphery countries.[49] However, I use the term 'global social system' rather than 'world system' analysis for two reasons. The first reason is to emphasise the complex political, economic, and cultural systems that comprise the totality of all global social relations. I emphasise these interconnected global systems to avoid reproducing four related key limitations of world-system analysis. The first limitation is the well-established problem of its reductionist and economistic causal account of the relationship between the 'modern world system' and the 'capitalist world economy'. The second limitation is that world-system analysis does not adequately address 'cultural' systems in globalisation. Given that international criminal law operates as 'signifying system through which ... a social order is produced, experienced, and explored', then we cannot afford to neglect 'culture' in 'this widest possible sense' as an important dimension of the global social order, as Kate Nash suggests.[50] The third limitation is that world-system analysis does not address the sexual division of labour in its account of the international division of labour, as discussed in Chapter 1. Finally, world-system analysis does not fully address the impact of globalisation upon social relations at a world scale, even while acknowledging that the existing world system is in transition.[51]

The second reason to use the term 'global social system' is to emphasise how the social forces of globalisation shape this transition in global social relations. The very concept of 'globalisation' is highly contentious, with different accounts emphasising economic, political, or cultural globalisation. However, it captures the 'intensification of global interconnectedness',[52] which involves 'flows of goods, capital, people, information, ideas, images and risks across national borders, combined with the

---

[48] Immanuel Wallerstein, 'Structural Transformations of the World Economy', (2016) 39(1) Review 171–194, 171.
[49] Immanuel Wallerstein, *World-Systems Analysis* (Durham and London: Duke University Press, 2006), pp. 23–24.
[50] Kate Nash, *Contemporary Political Sociology* (Oxford: Wiley-Blackwell: 2010), p. 31. See also her important critique of 'culture' in world-systems analysis, pp. 48–49.
[51] See William Robinson, 'Globalization and the Sociology of Immanuel Wallerstein', (2011) 26(6) International Sociology 723–745, and Immanuel Wallerstein, 'Robinson's Critical Appraisal Appraised', (2012) 27(4) International Sociology 524–528.
[52] Mary Kaldor, *New and Old Wars* (Cambridge: Polity, 2002), p. 3.

emergence of social networks and political institutions'.[53] My understanding of globalisation follows Hardt and Negri's argument that contemporary post-Fordist capitalist forms of production intensify and amplify processes of global economic, political, and social exchange.[54] In this approach, 'globalisation' does not indicate the emergence of a singular 'global society', in the sense of a bounded and homogenous structure. Rather, it highlights the dynamic processes that make global social relations, and it emphasises the diffuse and differentiated interdependencies and interconnections that make new forms of global social relations.

These forces of globalisation produce new forms of transnational social relations. For Hardt and Negri, globalisation is a set of processes that constitutes the new social relations of 'global capitalist hierarchy' (or, as Miéville calls it, the 'unequal violence' of the imperialist world order).[55] However, it also constitutes new forms of co-operation, interaction, and association, and, 'ultimately, society itself' at the global level.[56] Accordingly, the dynamic processes of these intensified exchanges produce new transnational social relations that are both connective and conflictual. As Hardt and Negri emphasise, globalisation produces new forms of social interaction and association, some of which are antagonistic, coercive, and conflictual and others that are coalitional, affiliative, and connective. Understood in terms of these framing concepts, the term 'globalisation' can capture these multiple processes involving dynamic and differential intensifications of 'transplanetary social connections'.[57]

The idea of the global social system, understood as the totality of global social relations and its international division of labour (Wallerstein), shaped by changes in the production of new forms of social life in post-Fordist contemporary globalisation (Hardt and Negri), is crucial for considering the relationship between the global legal form and globalisation. To understand the development of the global legal form in the context of a changing global social system, I return to Pashukanis' observation that 'in critical periods, when the balance of forces has

---

[53] Nash, *Contemporary Political Sociology*, p. 43.
[54] Michael Hardt and Antonio Negri, *Multitude* (Harmondsworth: Penguin, 2005), p. xiii.
[55] Michael Hardt and Antonio Negri, *Empire* (Cambridge, MA: Harvard University Press, 2000) p. 134; Miéville, *Between Equal Rights*, p. 293.
[56] Michael Hardt and Antonio Negri, *Assembly* (New York: Oxford University Press, 2017), p. xv.
[57] Jan Aart Scholte, *Globalization* (2nd edn.) (Basingstoke: Palgrave Macmillan, 2005), p. 3.

fluctuated seriously [...] the fate of the norms of international law becomes extremely problematic'.[58] Given the rearticulation of the norms of humanitarian law as international criminal law, how then should we understand the relationship between this legal form and the fluctuation of the balance of forces in global social relations?

The contemporary fluctuation of the 'balance of forces' to which Pashukanis refers should not be reduced to the coercive power of states, nor to the struggle between capitalist states. Rather, it needs to be understood in terms of the processes of globalisation within which that struggle emerges.[59] The idea of the 'balance of forces' becomes analytically very useful if it is re-read using the different paradigm of force offered by Foucault. Unlike Pashukanis, Foucault does not see war as a straightforward relation of violent domination. Rather, Foucault argues that 'war can be regarded as the point of maximum tension, or force-relations laid bare'.[60] In Foucault, the notion of 'force' refers to the 'ability to affect and be affected', so that force is always relational. Violence is a 'concomitant or consequence of force, but not a constituent element'.[61] This approach enables us to understand the contemporary fluctuation of the 'balance of forces' in terms of the emergence of new relations of force in the processes of globalisation, and not only the coercive power of states. In these terms, the war in the former Yugoslavia is these force relations laid bare.

The material conditions that produce the legal form of international criminal law are the conflictual and connective transnational social relations that emerge in the dynamic social forces of globalisation. The global legal form emerges in particular global orders of economic, political, and cultural exchange and the connected value given to the productive capacities of individual and collective life in those global processes. Pashukanis ascribes the origins of the legal form in the bourgeois state to capitalist relations of exchange and describes the legal form as the expression of social relations of commodity exchange as legal relations. As Miéville describes, 'the *generalising* of the legal form can only occur under conditions of generalised commodity exchange' in capitalist societies.[62] The legal form is an integral element of commodity exchange in

---

[58] Pashukanis, *Selected Writings on Marxism and Law* (London: Academic Press, 1980), p. 179.
[59] In Chimni's terms, 'the era of global imperialism': *International Law and World Order* (Cambridge: Cambridge University Press, 2017), p. 506.
[60] Michel Foucault, *Society Must Be Defended* (Harmondsworth: Penguin, 2004), p. 46.
[61] Gilles Deleuze, *Foucault* (London: Continuum, 1999), p. 70.
[62] Miéville, *Beyond Equal Rights*, p. 93.

capitalism, without which that exchange is not possible.[63] If, however, this account is understood as dynamic and historical, then the global changes in the material conditions of production and exchange that Hardt and Negri describe also give rise to new legal forms at the international level.[64] The new global legal form of international criminal law emerges in the transition to new forms of global social relations, both exploitative and emancipatory. The legal form of international criminal law can be ascribed to these global relations of exchange and its systems of value.

The legal form of international criminal law can be understood as a structured process of the confrontation of legal agents thrown up by the dynamics of globalising capitalism, to paraphrase Miéville. This legal form is homologous to the processes of globalising economic, political, and cultural exchange and the values they produce, in that the structure of its legal rules and concepts correspond to the forms of exchange in the global social system. International criminal law can be described as a legal expression of the new global relations of production and exchange. The global legal form of international criminal law is a constitutive part of globalisation because it functions as a new *legal* form of global exchange. The juridical relation makes global exchange possible and is thereby an integral element of a 'globalisation of economic and cultural exchanges' (as Hardt and Negri put it).[65] It makes that exchange possible by creating global legal relations between global legal subjects. Equally importantly, this approach also points to the social antagonisms that produce the global legal form and its potential dialectical quality.

6.2.3 Globalisation, the Socialist Federal Republic of Yugoslavia, and the ICTY

My analysis of the emergence of the global legal form follows Jasmina Husanović in taking the former Yugoslavia 'not as an exception but the norm ... of operative biopolitical regimes',[66] which exemplifies 'the

---

[63] Norrie, 'Pashukanis and the "Commodity Form" Theory', 423.
[64] I follow Norrie's reading of Pashukanis' general theory of law as offering the basis for the study of law in changing forms of capitalist society: ibid..
[65] Hardt and Negri, *Empire*, p. xi.
[66] Jasmina Husanović, 'The Politics of Gender, Witnessing, Postcoloniality and Trauma', (2009) 10(1) Feminist Theory 99–119, 102–103.

universal predicament of the globalising world'.[67] Building on this argument, we can describe the Yugoslavian wars of the 1990s and the ICTY as exemplifying the operation of force relations in globalisation. This is not to argue that globalisation 'created' either these wars or international criminal law. As Saskia Sassen points out, we should not understand globalisation in terms of a single causal model, which would wrongly use effect to explain cause.[68] Rather, the dynamics of the social forces of globalisation produce new forms of conflict and connection, which are the overdetermined conditions of the emergence of the Yugoslavian conflicts and the ICTY. The processes of globalisation traverse and shape these social relations of armed violence, just as they traverse and shape the formation of their international legal regulation. These force relations both restructure older political, economic, and cultural orders and create new political, economic, and cultural relations. In that transition in the global social system, new forms of global social relations emerge.

The first key force relation is the global making of the post-Cold War political world. The emergence of new political forms in the post-socialist global order from the 1980s onwards is central to the conflictual and connective associations of the Yugoslav wars. For example, the declining legitimacy of communist systems and the impact of a multi-party electoral system exposed 'the conflicting political forces in Yugoslav society' that subsequently erupted into armed violence.[69] Equally importantly, the post-socialist and postcolonial context shaped the nation-state building that occurred in this armed violence. The armed conflict was an integral part of completing the desocialisation of Yugoslavia by making capitalist nation-states, as well as the remaking of a multi-ethnic and federal state as postcolonial nations according to the logic of ethnically defined peoples.[70] The collapse of Cold War inter-state relations also facilitated the enforcement of international criminal law against the protagonists of the Yugoslavian wars. Without the collapse of older Cold War power blocs, the emergence of the UN consensus regarding the international prosecutions of war crimes in the Yugoslavian conflict would not have been possible.

---

[67] Jasmina Husanović, *Culture, Community and Activism in Bosnia and Herzegovina* (Tuzla: Off Set Press, 2021), p. 36.
[68] *Territory, Authority, Rights* (Princeton: Princeton University Press, 2008), p. 38.
[69] Paul Hirst, *War and Power in the Twenty-first Century* (Cambridge: Polity, 2001), p. 84.
[70] This trajectory is not unique to Yugoslavia. See the discussion of ethnic violence and postcolonial (capitalist) nation-state formation in Anghie and Chimni, 'Third World Approaches to International Law'.

The second key force relation is the intensification of the economic forces of global capitalist exchange. The global extension of capitalist social relations within the former Yugoslavia was a crucial condition of the Yugoslav wars. Sometimes called 'negative globalisation' (following Zygmunt Bauman), the economic forces of globalising capital have particular and differential impacts upon existing social and political orders, as can be seen in the former Yugoslavia. Yugoslavia was highly, if unevenly, integrated in the global economy from its establishment after World War Two.[71] By the 1970s, Yugoslavia could be accurately described as a periphery state in the world economic system.[72] The neoliberal economic globalisation experienced by Yugoslavia in the 1980s included privatisation, deindustrialisation, and removal of socially protective measures.[73] These economic conditions had crucial political effects in the emergence of war, since the declining legitimacy and strength of the socialist state were combined with a severe economic crisis due to the 'structural adjustment' programme of the International Monetary Fund.[74] Equally importantly, this economic globalisation also shaped the model and implementation of international post-conflict justice, including linking international criminal trials to state reconstruction and state reconstruction to the establishment of the liberal rule of law and 'functional' free-market states.[75]

The third key force is the global reshaping of older patriarchal nation-state orders. From the 1970s onwards, we see global – if uneven and incomplete – shifts in the social roles of women, with their increasing entry into the waged labour force and increasing political and professional participation. This shift can be seen at the 'international' level in the increasing participation of women in international institutions, such as the UN, and globalised professions, such as the international media, as discussed in Chapter 2. At the same time, women's movements also

---

[71] Darko Suvin, *Splendour, Misery, and Possibilities* (Brill, 2016), pp. 39, 179. Susan Woodward, *Balkan Tragedy* (Washington: The Brookings Institution, 1995), pp. 25–29.

[72] Suvin, *Splendour, Misery, and Possibilities*, p. 387.

[73] Tatjana Đurić Kuzmanović, and Ana Pajvančić-Cizelj, 'Economic Violence against Women', (2020) 27(1) European Journal of Women's Studies 25–40.

[74] See Susan Woodward, 'Violence-Prone Area or International Transition?', in Veena Das, Arthur Kleinman, et al. (eds.), *Violence and Subjectivity* (Berkeley: University of California Press, 2000).

[75] Chandra Sriram, 'Justice as Peace?', (2007) 21(4) Global Society 579–591. In the Yugoslavian context, see Nela Porobić Isaković and Gorana Mlinarević, *The Peace That Is Not* (Geneva: Women's International League for Peace and Freedom, 2021).

emerge in this period within nation-states, as well as internationally. In the former Yugoslavia, shifts in women's roles had already begun from World War Two onwards, due to the socialist ideal of women's emancipation, the formal legal equality of women within the Yugoslav state (including rights to abortion, maternity leave, divorce, and property), and the increasing participation of women in education and waged labour, including the legal and judicial professions.[76] From the 1970s onwards, Yugoslavian women participated in the international women's movement, such as the UN Women's Conferences.[77] They also built national feminist movements seeking to change patriarchal Yugoslav society and take on the unresolved 'Woman question' of Yugoslavian socialism.[78] As discussed in Chapter 2, this movement was decidedly 'internationalist' in its outlook and political practices.

These global force relations also restructure older political and social orders. First, the new global relations rearticulate the Yugoslavian political 'settlement' of older global empires.[79] The modern Yugoslavia emerged from the collapse of the Ottoman Empire, the Austro-Hungarian defeat in World War One, and the defeat of the German imperialist occupation of World War Two. The new global shifts undo this settlement. They rearticulate the political and economic legacies of older imperial orders, including Serbia as regional hegemon, the underdevelopment of Bosnia and Kosovo, and European interests in its 'uncivilised' 'lesser Europe'. That rearticulation can also be seen in the mobilisation of regional ethno-nationalist identities in the conflict and Western European use of myths of archaic 'Balkan' hatreds to justify non-intervention by the 'international community'. Second, these global forces also profoundly reshape older political and juridical orders. In the Yugoslavian case, this is most evident in shifts in the inter-state order, from the failure to enforce the UN Charter, the older inter-state legal order established after World War Two, to American and European intervention in the conflict, reflecting the emergence of new inter-state relations after the end of the Cold War. However, the new global orders

---

[76] See Jelena Batinić, *Women and Yugoslav Partisans* (New York: Cambridge University Press, 2015), and Lenard Cohen, 'Judicial Elites in Yugoslavia', (1985) 11(4) Rev Soc L 313–344, 334.

[77] See the important work of Chiara Bonfiglioli, including 'The First UN World Conference on Women (1975) as a Cold War Encounter', (2016) 27(3) Filozofija i društvo 521–541.

[78] See Zsófia Lóránd, *The Feminist Challenge to the Socialist State in Yugoslavia* (Cham: Palgrave Macmillan, 2018).

[79] Pal Ahluwalia, 'Empire or Imperialism', (2004) 10(5) Social Identities 629–645.

also reshape existing legal orders in the former Yugoslavia. For example, European and American engagement with the region framed the making of 'Balkan' transitional justice, ranging from crucial American support for the establishment of the ICTY to subsequent European Union (EU) support for national war crimes prosecutions (most notably in Bosnia). Within this context, we see the emergence of the global legal culture at the ICTY and the replacement of the Yugoslav inquisitorial legal tradition with an Anglo-American legal tradition in war crimes prosecutions by the Bosnian state.

The forces of globalisation 'intensify' ongoing but contradictory shifts in older patriarchal social orders. In the former Yugoslavia, these shifts in gender relations can be seen in the reversal of the political and economic participation of women, deepening gendered political and economic inequalities, and 're-traditionalisation' of gender roles during the 1980s and 1990s.[80] During the war, a further shift in gender relations can also be seen in the mobilisation of women in nationalist political and military movements, as well as their forced mobilisation in civilian defence.[81] At the same time, these shifts also produce the involvement of Yugoslavian women in anti-war movements and feminist movements, as well as their engagement with transnational feminist movements.[82]

Crucially, the force relations of globalisation also produce new social relations. In global processes, new connections between people, communities, and states come to exist within a conflict. For example, in the Bosnian conflict, political and military actors sought to construct new forms of ethnic association, which were in turn instantiated by the Dayton Peace Agreement.[83] Dayton was itself overseen by a new transnational group of states and international organisations visible at a formal level in the Peace Implementation Council. Other transnational affiliations, such as ties of religious community or political solidarity, also brought foreign fighters and humanitarian workers to the war in Bosnia.

---

[80] See Jill Benderly, 'Feminist Movements in Yugoslavia, 1978–1992', in Melissa Bokovoy, Jill Irvine, et al. (eds.), *State-Society Relations in Yugoslavia, 1945-1992* (Basingstoke: Macmillan, 1997); Đurić Kuzmanović and Pajvančić-Cizelj, 'Economic Violence against Women'.
[81] Dubravka Žarkov, *The Body of War* (Durham: Duke University Press, 2007). See also Jasenka Ferizović, 'The Case of Female Perpetrators of International Crimes', (2020) 31 (2) EJIL 455–488.
[82] See Cynthia Cockburn, *The Space between Us* (London and New York: Zed, 1998).
[83] See Dino Abazović, 'Bosnia and Herzegovina: Ten Years after Dayton' (2005) 5(1) European Yearbook of Minority Issues 195–206.

At the same time, intensifying global interconnectedness also produces the new global networks that traverse contemporary conflicts. In the case of Bosnia, these networks included the international media covering the war, alliances between international and national NGOs, and the global flows of fighters, arms, and funds that sustained the conflict itself.[84]

The legal field of international criminal law also emerges from these intensified global connections. In the case of the ICTY, these ranged from transnational political networks, such as the non-governmental organisations that campaigned for war crimes prosecutions, to religious affiliations, such as the pressure from the Islamic Conference Organisation for the protection of Bosnian Muslims, and the significant funding for the ICTY by Muslim-majority countries, such as Malaysia and Pakistan.[85] These new global connections also included communication networks, notably global information circuits such as CNN and the Internet. Such communication networks were important for sustaining Yugoslavian and transnational political networks and building global public pressure on the 'international community' to stop war-time atrocities. Critically, these new forms of transnational relations included Yugoslavian and international women's groups and feminist networks, mobilising around the war generally and conflict-related sexual violence in particular.

6.2.4 *The Global Exchange of Women*

In analysing the force relations of globalisation, it is important to include 'the material/symbolic body that has been de-faced, erased, and/or made violently non-relevant in the operative biopolitical regimes', as Husanović argues.[86] Following this argument requires situating conflict-related sexual violence within the analysis of global processes. Husanović rightly insists that the Bosnian experience of 'bare life' exemplifies the wider global emergence of the state of exception.[87] However, Agamben's theory of bare life does not explain why the body of women come to be figured as the 'natural' material of the nation-state in the Yugoslavian conflicts. It has an 'exclusionary logic [that] writes out the

---

[84] The classic account of globalising processes in the Bosnian conflict remains Kaldor, *New and Old Wars*, chapter 3.
[85] Misha Glenny, *The Fall of Yugoslavia* (London: Penguin, 1996), p. 222.
[86] Husanović, 'The Politics of Gender', 103.
[87] Husanović, *Culture, Community and Activism*, p. 36.

matters of gender, menial labour, and reproduction from the political'.[88] Underlying this exclusionary logic is Agamben's failure to recognise the sexually differentiated social order that underwrites his theory, namely, that '[b]ios is the sphere of politics proper – of the polis ... It is the sphere from which slaves, women and children were excluded, as they were part of life as zoe.'[89] However, gender and sexuality are part of material life and integral to the 'social reproduction of persons' *and* nonpersons, as Butler argues.[90] To address the role of women's domestic, reproductive, and affective labour in the reproduction of social relations in war, I use feminist social reproduction theory to reframe my analysis of global social relations.[91]

This reframing brings into the view the new global form of feminised economy and masculinised politics of pre-war Yugoslavia and its peripheral position in the global social system. In the social reproduction theory of Maria Mies and Silvia Federici, such features are seen as the consequence of patriarchal and imperialist capitalist globalisation,[92] and as the conditions of the emergence of war.[93] In their social reproduction theory, violence against women is an integral part of capitalist accumulation. This is because capitalist accumulation relies on the use of violence of men against women to sustain the sexual division of labour within nation-states and the international division of labour between core and periphery states.[94] However, the 'direct causal connection' between globalisation and conflict-related sexual violence is not as evident as these approaches assume.[95] While it is possible to explain the emergence of the Yugoslavian conflicts in terms of globalisation, it does not explain the *sexual* nature of the violence that took place or why it took this form. It is

---

[88] Judith Butler and Gayatri Spivak, *Who Sings the Nation-State?* (London: Seagull Books, 2007), p. 38.
[89] John Lechte, *Fifty Key Contemporary Thinkers* (London: Routledge, 2007), p. 208.
[90] Judith Butler, 'Merely Cultural', (1997) 52/53 Social Text 265–277, 272.
[91] See Tithi Bhattacharya, 'Introduction', in Tithi Bhattacharya (ed.), *Social Reproduction Theory* (London: Pluto Press, 2017).
[92] See Silvia Federici, *Re-enchanting the World* (Oakland: PM Press, 2019), and Mies, *Patriarchy and Accumulation*.
[93] See Silvia Federici, *Revolution at Point Zero* (Oakland, CA: PM Press, 2012), particularly 'War, Globalisation, and Reproduction', and Maria Mies, '"War Is the Father of All Things" (Heraclitus) "But Nature Is the Mother of Life" (Claudia von Werlhof)', (2006) 17(1) Capitalism, Nature, Socialism, 18–31. While these works offer an important theoretical analysis, their political analysis of the Yugoslavian wars is problematic.
[94] Mies, *Patriarchy and Accumulation on a World Scale*, p. 169.
[95] Silvia Federici, 'Foreword', in Mies, *Patriarchy and Accumulation*, p. xi.

crucial to retain the insight of social reproduction theory that interlocking systems of exploitation form the material conditions of the Yugoslav conflicts. However, it is also important to capture how the forces of globalisation overdetermine both the reshaping of older social relations and the emergence of new social relations and sexual relations within these processes.

If globalisation involves the intensification of economic, cultural, and political exchange, then how does it also involve an exchange of bodies and, in particular, sexual exchange? Sara Meger's important feminist political economic framework draws out the relationship between conflict and sexual violence as a system of commodity exchange between men that enables certain groups to construct themselves as hegemonic masculinities.[96] Crucially, her later work draws out the productive and reproductive nature of collective violence, arguing that '[w]ar is not merely a disruption of social, political, and cultural life, but is itself integrally connected to the generation of symbols, meanings, and values associated with life'.[97] She points out that 'the exchange value generated by conflict-related sexual violence depends on the social and cultural significance of *bodies* themselves'.[98] Drawing on Irigaray, she argues that 'the social relations that Marx claimed to be "mystified" through exchange are only in the first place possible and understandable because of pre-existing relations between men over the control and valuation of women'.[99] For Meger, conflict-related sexual violence involves the ascription of particular values to women's (and men's) bodies in terms of masculinity and femininity and the exchange of these commodified bodies between men through violence.

If feminist social reproduction theory argues that women's reproductive and caring labour is crucial for the reproduction of capitalist systems as a whole, Meger's work suggests that it is necessary to include sexual labour and exchange in that social reproduction.[100] Building on this

---

[96] See Meger, *Rape Loot Pillage*.
[97] Sara Meger, 'The Political Economy of Sexual Violence against Men and Boys in Armed Conflict', in M. Zalewski, Paula Drumond, et al. (eds.), *Sexual Violence against Men in Global Politics* (London and New York: Routledge, 2018), p. 104.
[98] Ibid., p. 106.
[99] Sara Meger, 'A Feminist Political Economy of Global Security', in Antje Daniels, Rirhandu Mageza-Barthel, et al. (eds.), *Gewalt, Krieg und Flucht* (Opladan, Berlin, Toronto: Barbara Budrich Publishers, 2021), p. 61.
[100] Susan Ferguson, *Women and Work* (London: Pluto, 2020), p. 111.

approach, we can characterise sexuality as 'practical human activity',[101] that is, as the productive labour of bodies in making sexuality. As distinct from the animal function of 'procreation' to which Marx refers, sexuality should be understood in the psychoanalytic sense of socially organised sexual drives. In patriarchal capitalist systems, sexuality becomes subject to commodity exchange, becoming part of the capitalist alienation of productive labour (specifically, of the productive sexual labour of bodies).

Considerable feminist work on sexual violence and war has shown that women's bodies have always been given value in conflict. The issue is how to understand what value is given to which gendered bodies in which wars and which societies. If social reproduction includes sexual labour, then it becomes possible to see the value of this labour for social reproduction of capitalist and patriarchal nation-states. Rhonda Copelon points out:

> Women are targets not simply because they 'belong to' the enemy, but precisely because they keep the civilian population functioning and are essential to its continuity. They are targets because they, too, are the enemy - because of their power and vulnerability as women, including their sexual and reproductive power.[102]

The important roles of women in social reproduction have been long recognised in humanitarian law. As Patricia Viseur Sellers points out, the first patriarchal restraints on war-time rape were to preserve 'civil society', the productive elements of the society that the occupier sought to reap the benefits of or the occupied sought to protect.[103]

The Yugoslavian conflicts highlight the particular importance of women's bodies and sexuality to the construction of modern nation-states. This is because women were seen as essential to the biological and cultural reproduction of the 'nation', as discussed earlier. Important Yugoslavian feminist work points to the connection between conflict-related sexual violence against women and the construction of ethnic and national groups. It explains sexual violence as an integral part of building 'hetero-nationality', with the bodies of victims and perpetrators ascribed

---

[101] Karl Marx, *Economic and Philosophical Manuscripts* (New York: Dover, 2007), p. 73.
[102] Rhonda Copelon, 'Surfacing Gender', (1994) 5(2) Hastings Women's L. J 243–266, 262.
[103] Patricia Viseur Sellers, 'The Legal and Cultural Value of Sexual Violence', in Kirsten Campbell, Regina Mühlhäuser et al. (eds.), *In Plain Sight* (New Delhi: Zubaan, 2019), pp. 282–283.

with value as markers of ethnic and national belonging.[104] In this context, women become the objects of sexual exchange between members of groups in a fraternal social contract and between groups in ethnonationalist social contracts. This process of masculinisation produces 'the hegemonic body as intact and powerful, and objectifying the body of the Other', as Žarkov describes it. In this context, men are also vulnerable to sexual 'feminisation', where they appear as symbols of the heterosexual masculinity of an Other, figured as an 'ethnic' or national community.[105] However, men do not generally become visible objects of sexual exchange in this heterosexual economy. Siniša Malešević argues that 'ethnic cleansing' in the Yugoslav context is an integral part of modern 'nation-state building', predicated on linking ethnic and nation-state belonging. Accordingly, we can understand conflict-related sexual violence as a system of value of bodies and sexuality, which derives from the context of nation-state building in the new global order and which emerges from the overdetermined conditions of the forces of globalisation.

This sexual economy of war attributes women's bodies with value for their role in social reproduction, including their reproductive, caring, and sexual labour. That is, these bodies are assigned value as commodities in an exchange economy of violence.[106] Women's bodies are given 'value' as 'reproducers' of the 'biological' or 'cultural' community and as signifiers of communal belonging. This 'value' includes their perceived value to the community, such as the women detained in the Omarska camp, who were targeted because of their prominence as judges or lawyers and their bodies and sexuality given political 'value'.[107] Women's bodies become valued for their material uses, from their use as objects of violence in so-called 'ethnic cleansing' or their literal exchange in the war-time sexual economies of trafficking and forced prostitution. Finally, these bodies also become valued for their libidinal uses, insofar as these bodies become objects of sexual 'enjoyment'. In this heterosexual economy of

---

[104] See, for example, Maria Olujic, 'Embodiment of Terror', (1998) 12(1) Medical Anthropology Quarterly 31–50, 43; and Vesna Kesić, 'Muslim Women, Croatian Women, Serbian Women, Albanian Women ...', in Dusan Bjelić and Obrad Savić (eds.) *Balkan as Metaphor* (Cambridge: MIT Press, 2003).

[105] Žarkov, *The Body of War*, pp. 164–169.

[106] To be clear, they are not valued in the sense of being cared for but in the Marxist sense of assigned exchange value as a commodity.

[107] My thanks to Elma Demir for this important point.

192 SUBJECTIVITY AND SOCIALITY IN INTERNATIONAL CRIMINAL LAW

conflict-related sexual violence, women's bodies become valued as objects of signifying, material, and libidinal exchange, while men's bodies become devalued through their 'feminisation' in these same processes. What we see, then, is an emergence of a sexual economy of intensified exchange of women's bodies, in which these bodies come to take on new exchange value in the collective violence of war. That violence makes possible a new form of 'primitive accumulation', namely the alienation of women from their own productive capacities and the exploitation of those productive capacities by transfers of value from women to hegemonic groups of men.[108] It is these values that the ethno-fraternal contract of international criminal law reproduces.

6.2.5 The Global Exchange between Women

If legal value of rape is integrally tied to the 'cultural value of rape', as Viseur Sellers describes it, then this raises the question of how to explain the resignification of the 'cultural value' of sexual violence in international criminal law described in Chapter 2. This resignification involves both the liberal recognition of women as equal legal subjects at the international level and the feminist reconceptualisation of sexual violence as a gender-based harm. The 'revaluation' of the 'value' of rape shifts it from being understood as a crime committed against the interests of the masculine individual or state to a crime that either discriminates against, or harms, women. This revaluation also needs to be situated in the context of transitions in the global social system. If the force relations of global exchange intensify the sexual exchange of women, they also produce the global exchange between women that gives rise to the 'revaluation' of sexual violence in the legal form.

Global changes in gendered social relations were crucial to the 'revaluation' of conflict-related sexual violence. An important dimension of this process was women's increasing political and professional participation, including the legal profession. In terms of the former Yugoslavia, legal professionals, such as the former magistrate Nusreta Sivac, who testified in *Karadžić*, and the lawyer Jadranka Cigelj, both held in the Omarska

---

[108] On primitive accumulation in the Yugoslavian conflicts of the 1990s, see Jasmina Husanović, 'Traumatic Knowledge in Action', and Jasmin Mujanović, 'The Baja Class and the Politics of Participation', in Damir Arsenijević (ed.), *Unbribable Bosnia and Herzegovina* (Baden-Baden: Nomos, 2014).

Camp, would become crucial in advocating for, and enabling, the prosecution of international crimes committed in the conflict, including rape. Both testified in trials before the ICTY.[109] Changing gender roles also facilitated the increasing participation of women in 'international society', such as the UN and the ICTY. Julie Mertus argues that 'the inclusion of women as (1) gender experts and other staff positions at Tribunal, (2) witnesses in specific cases, and (3) counsel seeking to improve the treatment of rape under international law' led to a significant shift in the Tribunal's treatment of conflict-related sexual violence.[110] To this list, the role of women judges should be added, such as Judge Florence Mumba, Judge Elizabeth Odio Benito, and Judge Gabrielle Kirk McDonald.[111] The importance of including women in these roles is particularly evident in the early leading sexual violence cases, such as *Kunarac*. Working individually and collectively, they were committed to including international crimes against women in international prosecutions.[112]

It is also important to recognise the changes in gender relations globally that enable women to act within and upon the ICTY. This changing global context was crucial for the revaluation of sexual violence in 'international society', and in the perceived mandate of the ICTY as a legal institution.[113] At the level of nation-states, the social context includes the feminist movements of the 1980s and 1990s, which produced a generation of women committed to feminist ideas and who had gained professional experience working on sexual violence prosecutions or human rights at domestic or regional levels. At the international level, it includes the movement of feminist ideas of gender equality into 'international society'. At the global level, it includes the global political

---

[109] See *Calling the Ghosts*, Mandy Jacobson and Karmen Jelinčič (dir), Bowery Productions, 1996.

[110] Julie Mertus, 'When Adding Women Matters', 38(4) (2008) Seton Hall L Rev, 1297–1326, 1299. See also Michelle Jarvis and Najwa Nabti, 'Policies and Institutional Strategies for Successful Sexual Violence Prosecutions', in Serge Brammertz and Michelle Jarvis (eds.), *Prosecuting Conflict-Related Sexual Violence at the ICTY* (Oxford: Oxford University Press, 2016), pp 76–77.

[111] Priya Gopalan, Danielle Kravetz et al., 'Proving Crimes of Sexual Violence', in Brammertz and Jarvis (eds.), *Prosecuting Conflict-Related Sexual Violence*, pp. 145–146.

[112] This was notable in my early ICTY fieldwork in the period 2005–2007, following the first intensive period of sexual violence prosecutions.

[113] See Grace Harbour, 'International Concern Regarding Conflict-Related Sexual Violence in the Lead-up to the ICTY's Establishment', in Brammertz and Jarvis (eds.), *Prosecuting Conflict-Related Sexual Violence*, p. 28, and Jarvis and Nabti, 'Policies and Institutional Strategies for Successful Sexual Violence Prosecutions', p. 74.

and cultural exchange between women in the wider international women's movement, transnational feminist NGOs and women's coalitions, as discussed in Chapter 2.

It could be said that the role of professional women in changing international criminal law underscores why Mies describes 'a feminist middle-class movement, both in the over- and under-developed countries, as an absolute historical necessity'.[114] However, the 'revaluing 'of sexual violence at the international level reveals the historical necessity of a feminist movement drawn from all classes. This is partly because these legal professionals should not be assumed to belong to their national middle class. More importantly, it is also because feminist activists and women drawn from all social classes – both in their countries and in the global social system – played crucial roles in enabling the revaluation of conflict-related sexual violence.

In the former Yugoslavia, women's groups, victims' associations, feminist coalitions, and non-governmental organisations were crucial in supporting survivors and war crimes prosecutions. These groups were often not middle class, professional, or feminist. Some were local, informal, and short lived, while others were formal, larger, 'internationalised', or international. They engaged – and still engage – in a range of practices, including mutual aid and solidarity actions; evidence collection, survivor, and witness support; and advocacy supporting prosecutions before the ICTY or in the successor states.[115] Three leading studies of these groups in Bosnia and Herzegovina by Elissa Helms, Maria O'Reilly, and Husanović show the importance of, and challenges for, these groups in supporting justice claims for women survivors of war.[116] These groups all undertook the collective affective and material work that is a necessary condition of continuing to demand justice, and show the importance of alternative forms of social solidarity and action in sustaining such justice claims. The ICTY itself acknowledged the important role of such groups in supporting its accountability work.[117]

---

[114] Mies, *Patriarchy and Accumulation*, p. 206.
[115] See Maja Korać, 'Linking Arms', *Women and Nonviolence Series*, No. 6 (Uppsala: Life and Peace Institute, 1998).
[116] Elissa Helms, *Innocence and Victimhood* (Madison: University of Wisconsin Press, 2013); Maria O'Reilly, *Gendered Agency in War and Peace* (London: Palgrave, 2018); Husanović, *Culture, Community and Activism*.
[117] See Brammertz and Jarvis (eds.), *Prosecuting Conflict-Related Sexual Violence*, pp. 88–90, 104–105, 149, 326–327.

Within the ICTY, women – and, importantly, some men – struggled to change positive international criminal and procedural law, and the policies and practices of the legal institution, in regard to sexual violence prosecutions. Where they did succeed, it is possible to see shifts in the discursive operation of international criminal law. These shifts can be seen in the two key periods of development of sexual violence prosecutions discussed in Chapter 2, namely, 1993 to 2002 and 2009 to 2017.[118] The first period runs from the establishment of the ICTY in 1993 to 2002, which was a period of significant jurisprudential development of the elements of offences and evidential practices in lower level cases and indictment drafting for later leadership cases. The second period runs from 2009 to 2017, which was a period of refocused attention upon prosecuting sexual violence and jurisprudential development in modes of responsibility and proof in leadership cases.[119] In both periods, shifts in legal rules and practices were facilitated by a significant mass of female staff committed to prosecuting conflict-related sexual violence. They were also facilitated by 'external' international frames focusing on conflict-related sexual violence.

In the first period, the development of sexual violence as an international crime occurred in the context of global feminist movements focusing on sexual violence as a gender-based based crime and their critical engagement with the ICTY and ICTR.[120] It also occurred in the context of wider human rights commitments of the first wave of staff members. Following this period was a 'seven year gap' in appropriately sustaining sexual violence prosecutions.[121] During this time, there was a 'professionalisation' of staff and greater disengagement from earlier

---

[118] This periodisation is developed from my ICTY fieldwork. See also Jarvis and Vigneswaran, 'Challenges to Successful Outcomes in Sexual Violence Cases', pp. 46–53, and Jarvis and Nabti, 'Policies and Institutional Strategies for Successful Sexual Violence Prosecutions', p. 83.

[119] This shift was evident in the course of my ICTY fieldwork. See also Jarvis and Nabti, ibid., pp. 82–83, 103–104.

[120] For example, during this period coalitions of international and regional feminist organisations submitted numerous *amicus curie* briefs and correspondence regarding sexual violence prosecutions.

[121] Jarvis and Nabti, 'Policies and Institutional Strategies for Successful Sexual Violence Prosecutions', p. 104.

social movement commitments in the institution.[122] The attention of the 'international community' and civil society also shifted from Yugoslavia to other conflict zones, and from the ICTY to the ICC.[123] During this period, there was little engagement with sexual violence in policy or scholarship generally. A similar lack of engagement can be seen in feminist practice and scholarship, which also did not actively engage with the ICTY. This arguably reflected a wider ebb in the international feminist movement during this time.

In the second period, the development of sexual violence prosecutions took place in the context of a renewed focus on sexual violence in the UN Women, Peace, and Security Resolutions from 2008 and the Prevent Sexual Violence Initiative from 2012. From 2010 onwards, this focus increasingly framed conflict-related sexual violence as a gender-neutral crime.[124] Within the ICTY, during this period senior female staff in the Office of the Prosecutor led a renewed focus upon the prosecution of male and female sexual violence in leadership cases, supported by the then Chief Prosecutor.[125] Despite the development of this important body of case law, external engagement with the ICTY on the issue of sexual violence continued to be limited, including feminist advocacy.

As a result of all these factors, struggles for gender justice were not sustained across the institution of the ICTY as a whole, nor throughout its operation. Unsurprisingly, these struggles were not shared by all women in the ICTY, nor by the legal institution as a whole.[126] At no point in its 'life course' could the ICTY be described as a feminist institution, whether in terms of its formal or informal values or practices. Moreover, women remained significantly under-represented in all roles, both as a total proportion of judicial actors and staff and as a declining proportion of senior roles on the bench and the Office of the

---

[122] John Hagan, Ron Levi et al., 'Swaying the Hand of Justice', (2006) 31 Law and Social Inquiry, 585–616, 593–594. My ICTY fieldwork also confirms this change in institutional culture.
[123] Jarvis and Nabti, 'Policies and Institutional Strategies for Successful Sexual Violence Prosecutions', pp. 83, 103. Jarvis and Vigneswaran also point to the negative impact of the Completion Strategy: 'Challenges to Successful Outcomes in Sexual Violence Cases', pp. 50–53, itself a reflection of wider international disinterest in the region.
[124] Karen Engle, *The Grip of Sexual Violence in Conflict* (Stanford: Stanford University Press, 2020), pp. 132–136.
[125] This shift was evident during my later period of fieldwork.
[126] See Jarvis and Vigneswaran, 'Challenges to Successful Outcomes in Sexual Violence Cases'.

Prosecution.[127] As a result, the building of new rules, practices, and values within the institution was uneven and varied across its lifetime.[128] For these reasons, feminist shifts in the discourse of international criminal law were themselves uneven and variable.

Despite these difficulties, the moments where it was possible to shift the operation of international criminal law led to crucial developments of justice for sexual violence as a gender-based crime, that is, as a form of gender justice. In these moments, the struggle for gender justice exposes the limits of the existing legal form of international criminal law and resignifies its categories of social existence and bare life. These shifts in international criminal law are important because they changed not only the specific institution of the ICTY but also the rules and practices of international criminal law more generally. By shifting the discursive operation of international criminal law, it became possible to symbolise crimes, subjects, trials, and justice in new ways, as discussed in Chapter 5. However, these struggles also show the difficulty of developing gender justice within the existing form of international criminal law. The shifts in the operation of the legal form addressed the gender injustices of international criminal law as they surfaced but were not sufficient to change international criminal law itself.

6.3 From the Global Legal Form to Transformative Feminist Justice

The reinscription of sexual violence makes visible the social antagonisms of global forces that produce the legal form and reveals the potential dialectical movement in that legal form. This argument should not be mistaken for a functionalist approach in which 'as a "neutral vessel" law will simply *express* struggles, both progressive and reactionary'.[129] Rather, it contends that the social forces of globalisation are contradictory, in that they are both forces of domination (producing bare life) and emancipatory (producing alternative forms of social collectivity). As such, they throw up contradictions within the fundamental legal

---

[127] On female witnesses, see Chapter 4. On female judges, see Kimi King, Eliza Kelly et al., 'Deborah's Voice', (2017) 98(2) Social Science Quarterly, 548–565, 553. On female prosecutors, see Jarvis and Nabti, 'Policies and Institutional Strategies for Successful Sexual Violence Prosecutions', pp. 80–81.

[128] Ibid., p. 103.

[129] Robert Knox, 'Imperialism, Commodification, and Emancipation in International Law and World Order', EJIL Talk!, December 29 2017, p. 5, https://www.ejiltalk.org/imperialism-commodification-and-emancipation-in-international-law-and-world-order/

categories and hence within the determinate form of international criminal law itself. Such an approach insists that international criminal law contains contradictions that express the dynamics of the force relations of globalisation (to follow Negri),[130] and as such, it is a site of political struggle. Framed in these terms, the political question becomes whether it is possible to invent more emancipatory legal forms in the global transitional period. To explore the question of whether it is possible to building a feminist form of international criminal law, I turn next to the feminist approach to justice of the Women's Court.

[130] Antonio Negri, 'Rereading Pashukanis', 2017 5(2) Stasis, 8–49, 45–46.

PART II

The Women's Court and Transformative
Gender Justice

7

The Women's Court and the Feminist Approach to Justice

> We strengthen global feminist-pacifist alliances and coalitions: in order to bring punishment to violence and crimes, to influence the international institutions of justice, to start making documents and resolutions based on everyday experiences of injustice against women and all those with diminished social, economic, and political power.
>
> Women's Court for the former Yugoslavia, 2015[1]

Some 20 years after the establishment of the ICTY and the Dayton Agreement ending the war in Bosnia, the Women's Court took place in Sarajevo, Bosnia and Herzegovina, in 2015. The aim of the Women's Court was to develop a feminist approach to justice for crimes committed in the war in former Yugoslavia and in the post-war period. The Women's Court was the first transitional justice mechanism to be established in the former Yugoslavia and the first women's court to solely consider crimes committed in a European conflict. The Women's Court is now regarded as a leading contemporary example of alternative justice mechanisms.[2] What, then, is the feminist approach to justice that the Women's Court offers? Does this feminist approach offer an alternative model of international justice? And does this approach provide the basis for building an alternative feminist paradigm of international criminal law?

If both the ICTY and the Women's Court aimed to provide justice for international crimes, each had different concepts of harms, subjects, and justice. Like my analysis of the global legal form, my analysis of the Women's Court identifies the fundamental categories of this new paradigm, each of which built new concepts and practices of justice. As with my analysis of the global legal form, my aim is not to provide an

---

[1] http://www.zenskisud.org/en/
[2] Radhika Coomaraswamy, *Preventing Conflict, Transforming Peace, Securing the Peace* (New York: UN Women, 2015), p. 112.

institutional history or ethnography of the Women's Court. Rather, my analysis aims to describe the feminist form of justice in the Women's Court and consider its potential for building a feminist approach to international criminal law. My analysis first examines the models of justice that inform the development of this new paradigm of justice, and then sets out its fundamental categories.

7.1 The Women's Court and the Question of Justice

The Women's Court 'is an umbrella term, a common denominator, for a series of initiatives which differ from the mainstream judicial procedures and have been taking place over a period from the early 1990s to date' and involving some 4,000 participants.[3] During this process, there were different levels of engagement and disengagement by individuals and groups across the region and internationally, as Maria O'Reilly describes in her leading study of the Women's Court.[4] The idea of holding a Women's Court in the former Yugoslavia was first proposed by the Yugoslavian feminist and peace activist Žarana Papić. Papić launched the initiative for a Women's Court with Corinne Kumar, the coordinator of global movement of women's tribunals, at an international conference on 'new paradigms for justice' held in Sarajevo in 2000.[5] After Papić's death in 2002, 'the initiative lay dormant and was postponed owing to other issues, assessed at the time as more pressing'.[6] The initiative was relaunched in 2006, led by Memnuna Zvizdić (Women to Women, Sarajevo), Biljana Kašić (Centre for Women's Studies, Zagreb), and Staša Zajović (Women in Black, Belgrade), who were also involved in the first initiative.[7] The formal organisation of the Women's Court began in 2010, and included members from over 10 non-governmental organisations across the former Yugoslavia, with Women in Black as the lead organisation.[8] The formal preparatory process for the Women's Court included consultations with potential witness participants in the Court

---

[3] Daša Duhaček, 'Women's Court', in Staša Zajović (ed.), *Women's Court: About the Process* (Belgrade: Women in Black and Centre for Women's Studies, 2015), pp. 69, 93.
[4] *Gendered Agency in War and Peace* (London: Palgrave, 2018).
[5] Staša Zajović, 'The Women's Court', in Zajović (ed.), *Women's Court: About the Process*, p. 8.
[6] Duhaček, 'Women's Court', p. 75.
[7] Zajović, 'The Women's Court', p. 8.
[8] 'About the Women's Court', https://www.zenskisud.org/en/o-zenskom-sudu.html.

(witness participants), formal initiative members, and other groups (preparatory process participants) in the region from 2011 to 2014.[9]

My analysis first examines the models of justice that are the conceptual building blocks of the Women's Court. It identifies these models, analyses their perceived significance and limitations, and situates them in their social and political context. The analysis begins by identifying the models of justice in the publications of the Women's Court, focusing on the book *Women's Court: About the Process* (*About the Process*), edited by the lead organisation.[10] The volume describes the preparatory process (Staša Zajović) and analyses the feminist approach to justice (Daša Duhaček) and witness participant testimonies (Rada Iveković). As a result, important contributions to, and debates about, the Women's Court may not be fully visible, and this important history needs to be written. However, my focus here is the operative models in building the feminist approach to justice. These are formal legal justice, transitional justice, and people's justice.

7.1.1 *Formal Legal Justice*

The first model is formal legal justice for international crimes, which is generally described as 'the institutional legal system' in *About the Process*.[11] This term primarily refers to criminal prosecutions before the ICTY from 1994 onwards and then the national courts of the successor states from 2000 onwards. The majority of prosecutions at national courts were undertaken in Bosnia and Herzegovina, after the establishment of the War Crimes Chamber of the State Court in 2005. This is unsurprising given Bosnia has the largest number of war-affected persons and the majority of direct crimes committed in its territory. Prosecutions in successor states also included sexual violence crimes, but with considerable variation in numbers and quality.[12] Bosnia is also the leading state in this regard. Despite challenges in ensuring equitable and effective prosecutions, it has 'tried a significant body of cases' to generally high standards at state level.[13]

---

[9] I did not participate in the preparatory process.
[10] Zajović (ed.), *Women's Court: About the Process*.
[11] Zajović, 'The Women's Court', p. 7.
[12] See Kirsten Campbell, 'Building National and Regional Accountability for Conflict Related Sexual Violence', (2018) 7(2) IHRLR, 201–224.
[13] Jasenka Ferizović and Gorana Mlinarević, 'Applying International Experiences in National Prosecutions of Conflict-Related Sexual Violence', (2020) 18(2) JICJ, 325–348.

Calls for the repression of, and accountability for, international crimes began during the war in the former Yugoslavia (as discussed in Chapter 2). These demands for formal legal accountability were widely supported by feminist and women's groups in the former Yugoslavia.[14] Women's Court preparatory process participants were involved as individuals or organisations in trial monitoring and victim advocacy and support in the successor states. Their engagement with formal legal justice in part reflects the long-standing criminalisation of genocide, war crimes against the civilian population, including the war crimes of rape and forced prostitution, and 'traditional' war crimes, under Yugoslav municipal law since World War Two.[15] The municipal crime of rape was also formally characterised as a serious offence with significant sentence terms under Federal and then state criminal codes.[16]

Criminal justice is an important operative model of justice in the feminist approach to justice. In *About the Process*, witness participants emphasise the importance of criminal accountability and describe criminal sanction for crimes against women as an essential part of justice. They also identify the social recognition of war crimes as central to establishing post-conflict justice for women.[17] In the preparatory consultations undertaken in 2011 and 2012, the majority of participants from all regions identified the ICTY as the only institution that dealt with crimes across the entire former Yugoslavia and described it as 'often the only instrument that serves justice'.[18] National prosecutions of international crimes were also seen as highly important throughout the preparatory process.

However, dissatisfaction with international and national criminal justice was also crucial to building the Women's Court. Zajović and Duhaček identify the death of Milošević without sentence at the ICTY as a crucial factor in relaunching the Women's Court initiative in 2006.[19] Witness participants also expressed their dissatisfaction with ICTY verdicts in the

---

[14] Duhaček, 'Women's Court', p. 74.
[15] See *Criminal Code of the Socialist Federal Republic of Yugoslavia*, 1 July 1977, Chapter 16.
[16] Mira Alinčić, 'Law and the Status of Women in Yugoslavia', (1976) 8(1) Colum Hum Rts L Rev, 345–371, 360. The relevant provisions of the Federal Criminal Code were subsequently incorporated into State criminal codes after the constitutional reforms of 1974.
[17] Zajović, 'The Women's Court', pp. 14, 61, 66; Rada Iveković, 'Violence and Healing', in Zajović (ed.), *Women's Court: About the Process*, pp. 115–118.
[18] Zajović, 'The Women's Court', p. 23.
[19] Zajović, ibid., pp. 8–9; Duhaček, 'Women's Court', p. 75. It should be noted that both were members of the Women's Court Organising Committee.

2011–2012 consultations. However, they also described national prosecutions as highly problematic. These were seen as serving the interests of local political elites and as disconnected from justice for victims or wider social change.[20] In later preparatory consultations held in 2013 and 2014, witness participants expressed 'mistrust toward the institutional legal system, both nationally and internationally'.[21] Witness participants identified six key concerns with criminal justice. These were impunity, the gap between legal norms and application, inadequate state witness protection, institutional and community pressure and intimidation against testifying, stigmatisation and harassment of victim-witnesses of rape, and highly limited reparations awards.[22] In relation to sexual violence crimes, Iveković describes how the testimonies of witness participants demand that the state and its institution acknowledge these crimes, address impunity for them, expedite investigations and prosecutions, standardise 'penal criteria and procedures' and compensation, and provide legal aid and compensation.[23] The views of witness participants largely reflect wider social attitudes across the former Yugoslavia, which emphasise the importance of criminal accountability and characterise retribution as the primary function of criminal trials but also showed increasing dissatisfaction with the ICTY and national prosecutions.[24] The demands for improved sexual violence prosecutions also reflect widespread and long-standing concerns of survivors and feminist activists, as well as the increasing focus on sexual violence prosecutions before national courts during this period, particularly in Bosnia.[25]

Criminal justice, then, is understood as a necessary but problematic component of feminist justice. As described in *About the Process*, '[m]ost often, the institutional legal system does not serve justice'.[26] Criminal trials were seen as privileging the rights of the accused, rather than the victim, such that 'the institutional legal system does not acknowledge or

---

[20] Zajović, 'The Women's Court', p. 23–24.
[21] Ibid., p. 66.
[22] Ibid., pp. 24–25.
[23] Iveković, 'Violence and Healing', pp. 115–117.
[24] See Diane Orentlicher, *Some Kind of Justice* (Oxford: Oxford University Press, 2018). However, there is considerable variation as to who should be held criminally accountable for what and whether by international or national courts between the successor states, and 'ethnic' communities within states.
[25] See Gabi Mischkowski and Gorana Mlinarević, *And That It Does Not Happen to Anyone Anywhere in the World* (Cologne: Medica Mondiale, 2009).
[26] Zajović, 'The Women's Court', p. 7.

sanction violence against women'.[27] However, even if fair trials were possible, they 'do not imply justice for victims'.[28] This is because criminal trials were described as unable to meet the wider needs of survivors or create a just peace. As Duhaček explains, existing criminal justice processes were not seen as having enabled collective social change, which requires 'a full scope of measures, well beyond the legal procedures'.[29] Feminist justice was necessary to 'satisfy the needs that the institutional justice does not fulfil'.[30]

7.1.2 Transitional Justice

The second operative model is transitional justice. In *About the Process*, transitional justice is described as the most important attempt to overcome the limitations of international and national criminal justice.[31] From the establishment of the ICTY onwards, there were proposals for the creation of a truth commission, informed by the South African model of political transition.[32] Initial unsuccessful initiatives focused on Bosnia and were primarily driven by external international actors.[33] However, the Women's Court draws on a wider concept of transitional justice than truth-telling. Duhaček describes transitional justice as consisting of non-legal processes and mechanisms, such as 'truth and reconciliation committees, lustration, opening secret police dossiers, rehabilitation of political prisoners, reparations, public apologies, archives, memorials and museums'.[34] This wider understanding of transitional justice reflects the subsequent development of the concept to respond to 'complex questions of negative heritage from the past, and to the constant challenges of structural injustice'.[35] In particular, it draws on new ideas emerging in the 1990s about the role of justice in enabling countries to transition from war to peace.

---

[27] Zajović, ibid., p. 7; Duhaček, 'Women's Court', pp. 72–73.
[28] Zajović, ibid., p. 7.
[29] Duhaček, 'Women's Court', p. 88.
[30] Zajović, 'The Women's Court', p. 26.
[31] Ibid., p. 7.
[32] Jasna Dragović-Soso, 'History of a Failure', (2016) 10/2 Int J Transitional Justice 292–310, 295.
[33] See Nela Porobić Isaković and Gorana Mlinarević, *The Peace That Is Not* (Geneva: Women's International League for Peace and Freedom, 2021), p. 88ff.
[34] Duhaček, 'Women's Court', p. 88.
[35] Zajović, 'The Women's Court', p. 7.

In the next decade, the idea of transitional justice as part of post-conflict social reconstruction become the context for a renewed push to establish truth commissions in the region. By the mid-2000s at the international level, transitional justice came to be seen as a liberal peace-building project, becoming part of UN policy on rule of law.[36] In 2005, the UN Development Programme (Bosnia) supported the establishment of a Bosnian truth and reconciliation commission, which again was led by international external actors and did not succeed. The initiative was not supported by Bosnian women's associations because of its failure to consider potential impacts of testifying for sexual violence victims and to address accountability for perpetrators.[37] In 2006, regional civil society groups held the first Regional Forum for Transitional Justice in Sarajevo. The Forum established the first initiative for a regional truth commission, REKOM, in 2008, which has yet to be held.[38] In *About the Process*, Zajović describes how

> [a]lmost all members of the Initiative Board for Women's Court have actively participated in it (and some of them are still very active in the Coalition). REKOM is an exceptionally important regional initiative, but due to its quite broad scope of activities it did not meet the expectation of fulfilling the women's/feminist perspective.[39]

What was needed was the '*inclusion of gender dimension in theory and practice of transitional justice*'.[40] This key limitation of existing transitional justice initiatives is described as the second impetus for establishing the Women's Court.

The model of transitional justice was an important operative concept of justice in the development of the feminist approach to justice.[41] *About the Process* describes participating witnesses as 'mostly advocating for non-criminal sanctions – for the restorative justice (healing, reconciliation, trust, symbolic reparations), and then for the institutional reforms (lustration, material reparations, rule of law)'.[42] However, as Duhaček argues, the concept did not include a 'gender perspective', which

---

[36] See Kirsten Campbell, 'Reassembling International Justice', 2014 8(1) Int J Transitional Justice 53–74.
[37] Dragović-Soso, 'History of a Failure', 307. See also Porobić Isaković and Mlinarević, *The Peace That Is Not*, chapter 5.
[38] https://www.recom.link/en/sta-je-rekom/
[39] Zajović, 'The Women's Court', p. 9.
[40] Ibid., p. 12.
[41] Ibid.
[42] Ibid., p. 24.

feminists sought to remedy following the Yugoslavian wars of the 1990s.[43] To address the need for *feminist* social change required more than 'adding women' to existing models. Rather, it involved changing the very concept of transitional justice so that it could address the injustice experienced by women in the past and enable the building of a more gender-just society in the future.[44] Because the Women's Court had wider socially transformative aims than existing models of transitional justice, it became apparent that the Court would have to develop a new 'feminist approach to justice'.[45]

7.1.3 People's Justice

The third operative model is 'people's justice'. This model is based on ideas of justice for the people, which involve informal and non-state justice processes that aim to create social justice for all. The model contains two interconnected ideas. The first idea is 'people's courts', which involve informal, non-legal bodies seeking justice for wrongs not recognised or addressed by formal legal systems.[46] The idea of 'people's courts' also draws on Yugoslavian socialist legal and political culture, including the model of Yugoslav 'self-management courts'.[47] While the 'self-management courts' involved 'labour relations', it is important to note how Yugoslav socialist political culture of 'self-managing socialist democracy' informed the Women's Court. These include the ideas of participatory democratic decision-making of 'worker's self-management' and social 'self-organisation', the internationalist orientation of the non-aligned movement to the global South, and broader ideas of 'social ownership' and 'social and human solidarity'.[48] Finally, this idea of people's courts also draws on international people's tribunals, such as the first International Women's Tribunal on Crimes against Women held in 1976 (and discussed in the preparatory process).[49] The 1976 Women's

---

[43] Duhaček, 'Women's Court', p. 88.
[44] Iveković, 'Violence and Healing', p. 106.
[45] Zajović, 'The Women's Court', p. 12.
[46] Ljupka Kovačević, Marija Perković et al. (eds.), *Zenski Sud: Feministicki pristup pravdi.* [*Women's Court: Feminist Approach to Justice*] (Belgrade and Kotor: Anima and Women in Black, 2011). See also O'Reilly, *Gendered Agency in War and Peace*, pp. 155–158.
[47] O'Reilly, ibid., p. 158.
[48] Iveković, 'Violence and Healing', pp. 119–120.
[49] Diana Russell and Nicole Van de Ven (eds.), *Crimes against Women* (Berkeley: Russell Publications, 1990).

Tribunal subsequently informed the international women's courts and tribunals movement in the 1990s.

This second idea of women's courts and tribunals was central to the development of the feminist approach to justice. The so-called 'Courts of Women' movement was initiated by the Asian Women's Human Rights Council in 1991 and became a global movement through El Taller, an international non-governmental organisation, and its sister organisation.[50] Women from the former Yugoslavia participated in a number of these women's courts as feminist activists and witnesses, including the Global Tribunal on Violations of Women's Human Rights held in Vienna in 1993 and the World Court of Women against War, for Peace held in Cape Town in 2001. As *About the Process* describes, the World Court included the 'participation of women witnesses and activists from BiH', who would become instrumental in initiatives for the Women's Court.[51] This international exchange with the Courts of Women movement continued in the preparatory process for the Court.[52], Duhaček describes the Courts of Women as a 'global movement, that seeks to relook at rights and *other notions of justice from the lives and life visions of women* – particularly from the global South', citing El Taller and emphasising its new model of justice.[53]

The Courts of Women offered a 'new paradigm' for the Women's Court.[54] It provided both a conceptualisation of justice that centralised women's experiences and a model of alternative justice mechanisms in the form of women's courts. As Duhaček describes, citing El Taller, '[t]he Courts of Women are public hearings ... in which we hear individual testimonies of survival and *resistance* that guide us in our search *for new paradigms of knowledge and justice*'.[55] Duhaček identifies three basic principles of women's courts. First, they are led by women's groups and organisations, and they are 'marked by the process through which they are being built'.[56] Second, the process centres on women who have suffered injustice and the recognition of their rights. Third, women's

---

[50] Duhaček, 'Women's Court', p. 70.
[51] Zajović, 'The Women's Court', p. 8. See also O'Reilly, *Gendered Agency in War and Peace*, p. 170.
[52] Duhaček, 'Women's Court', p. 77.
[53] Ibid., p. 70.
[54] Ibid. See also Biljana Kašić, 'How to Radicalize Responsibility, Feminism and Rape', (2009) 10, DEP Deportate, esuli, profughe, 168–181.
[55] Duhaček, 'Women's Court', p. 74.
[56] Ibid., p. 71.

courts consist of public hearings of women's testimonies, and 'these proceedings, besides personal stories, also include a relevant political analysis which provides a context for these individual testimonies'.[57] They also include a body like a jury that provides a public judgement condemning the injustice, making recommendations and calling for action.

During the Women's Court preparatory process, it became clear that 'this region needed to build its own, context specific approach', including addressing the different contexts of participants from each successor state.[58] To build this approach, feminist 'principles of work' were developed in the preparatory process. These were the principles of 'the horizontal and democratic character of work'; the principle of autonomy of each state to organise their participation in the Court according to their needs; and the 'feminist ethics of care and responsibility', based on the principle of supporting participants and witnesses.[59] These principles aimed to support feminist solidarity amongst participants, to enable the building of new knowledge about the war from women's experiences, and to assist women to work collectively to design the Women's Court.

The preparatory process revealed 'numerous challenges and difficulties', particularly in relation to regional dynamics.[60] First, it revealed the specific challenges of organising the Court in each country, particularly for sexual violence survivors in Bosnia, Croatia, and Kosovo. These challenges included lack of security, poor socio-economic conditions, political use of victims, general social disinterest, lapse of time since the war, deepening ethnic division, and the failure of state institutions.[61] Second, it revealed the challenges of building feminist coalitions across the Yugoslav region.[62] The challenges included 'internal' political differences concerning the goals and organisation of the Court; 'regional' differences in capacities, resources, and concerns; and different war-time and post-war experiences, including war-time and post-war construction of state, nation, and ethnicity.[63] These challenges in part

---

[57] Ibid., p. 73.
[58] Ibid., pp. 77, 93.
[59] Zajović, 'The Women's Court', pp. 11–16, 64.
[60] Zajović, ibid., p. 22; Duhaček, 'Women's Court', pp. 93-94.
[61] Zajović, ibid., pp. 32–35.
[62] Ibid., pp. 22–23; Duhaček, 'Women's Court', p. 93.
[63] For an important account of these challenges in Bosnia, see O'Reilly, *Gendered Agency in War and Peace*.

reflected the significant post-war differences in the situation of witnesses and activists in the successor states, with those from Bosnia and Kosovo facing particular organisational, resource, and political challenges and also having distinctive concerns, perspectives, and experiences of the conflicts. Unlike other transitional processes, the feminist politics that informed the organisation of the Women's Court necessarily exposed these challenges and their political importance. These important challenges are likely to be more fully addressed by feminists in the former Yugoslavia, who acknowledge it to be an important question for continuing the work of the Women's Court in a productive way for future feminist politics in the region.[64]

Writing before the Women's Court was held, Duhaček described how its establishment 'will be against all odds' and a 'political miracle'.[65] Contested internal politics is a standard constitutive feature of both established institutions and new ones undergoing a precarious process of being built, such as the Women's Court. Such difficulties were also faced by other transitional justice initiatives in the region, such as REKOM, which have not yet been able to successfully establish an alternative justice mechanism to date. Ultimately, against all odds, the preparatory process participants decided to establish the Women's Court. They identified seven key reasons for doing so:

> To make the continuity of violence against women committed in peace and in war visible
>
> To give voice to individual experiences of women and to include women's experience in public memory
>
> To acknowledge the victims' sufferings, to establish the facts and to put pressure on community and the institutional system
>
> To understand the context (social, economic, family, cultural, personal, and political) in which violence against women is happening and in which that violence is made possible
>
> To satisfy the needs that the institutional justice does not fulfil and to make space for the creation of new approaches to justice
>
> To empower women and to create networks of international women's solidarity

---

[64] On the challenges of continuing the work of the Women's Court, see Staša Zajović, 'Witnesses at the Women's Court', in Staša Zajović and Miloš Urošević (eds.), *Women's Court: About Event in Sarajevo and About Continue the Process* (Belgrade: Women in Black, 2017), pp. 65–68.

[65] Duhaček, 'Women's Court', p. 94.

> To prevent future crimes and to establish a just peace for future generations through the facing with crimes from the past and the illuminating of social mechanisms that made them possible.[66]

The participants decided to develop a model of the Women's Court that combined elements of both women's courts and tribunals: '[t]he women's court allows more space for testifying, healing of trauma and regeneration of relationships, but it is necessary to put pressure on the institutional legal system through the WC [Women's Court]'.[67] The identification of potential witnesses, collection of testimonies, and selection of the 'thematic crimes' were also undertaken during the preparatory process, as well as choosing to hold the Court in Sarajevo, the 'most Yugoslav city'.[68] It was agreed that the Court would address 'violence committed during the 1990s [and] after the wars of the 1990s' because of the 'continuity of injustice and violence, starting from the wars of the 1990s and connect[ing] the war and the post-war period'.[69]

The Women's Court was a new model of justice, rather than being a 'mechanic application of known models', as Zajović describes. This new model was developed because of the 'needs of the participants in the process, and primarily of potential witnesses'.[70] Zajović notes that 'the process of organizing the WC indicated a necessity for joint creation of a different model of justice'.[71] Recognising that the 'women witnesses are the leading subjects of the Women's Court', this new paradigm of justice should be seen as the outcome of their collective work and their creation of the Women's Court as an idea and as a concrete institution.[72] It represents their highly significant contribution to regional and international feminist politics and peace-building. Most importantly, it represents their demand for justice.

---

[66] Zajović, 'The Women's Court', pp. 26-27.
[67] Ibid., pp. 25-26.
[68] Ibid., pp. 29-31, 38-43; Duhaček, 'Women's Court', pp. 91-93.
[69] 'Women's Court: Feminist Approach to Justice', 7-10 May 2015, Sarajevo, Three Fold Brochure, on file with the author (Women's Court Three Fold Brochure).
[70] Zajović, 'The Women's Court', p. 17.
[71] Ibid., p. 25.
[72] Women's Court: Feminist Justice: Preliminary Decisions and Recommendations, Judicial Council, 9 May 2015, Women's Court, Sarajevo, (Women's Court Preliminary Decision), p. 1.

7.2 The Women's Court: The Paradigm of Feminist Justice

The Women's Court was held in Sarajevo in 2015. There were two days of hearings on 8 and 9 May and four days of public events held between 7 and 10 May. The hearings were organised into five panels of women's testimonies, each focused on the following 'thematic crimes':

(1) 'War against the civilian population (militaristic/ethnic/gender-based violence)';
(2) 'Woman's body – a battlefield (sexual violence in war zones)';
(3) 'Militaristic violence and women's resistance';
(4) 'Persecution of those who are different, in war and in peace (ethnic violence)';
(5) 'An undeclared war (social and economic violence, women's resistance)'.[73]

Thirty-six victim witnesses and twelve expert witnesses from the former Yugoslavia testified before some five hundred people attending the Court proceedings and the Judicial Council of the Court.[74] The Judicial Council consisted of seven international and regional experts. It delivered its preliminary decisions and recommendations orally on 10 May, and in written form in September that year, with the full judgement to be delivered at a later date.[75] The edited transcripts of witness testimonies and expert witness testimonies were published in 2017 in *Women's Court: About Event in Sarajevo and about Continue the Process* (*About the Event*), edited by the lead organisation.[76] *About the Event* also includes Court documents, such as the Women's Court Rules and Preliminary Decision, together with analyses of the Court by Latinka Perović and Staša Zajović and reviews of the event by Dragica Vujadinovic and Adriana Zaharijević. The feminist approach to justice is understood as an ongoing process that does not end with the proceedings of the Women's Court.[77] The lead organisation for continuing the process after the Court, Women in Black, identifies key activities as

---

[73] Women's Court, Program May 7–10, 2015, Bosnian Cultural Centre, Sarajevo, on file with the author.
[74] Latinka Perović, 'The Surviving Victims of Violence as Subjects of Justice', in Zajović and Urošević, (eds.), *Women's Court: About the Event*, p. 9.
[75] Women's Court Preliminary Decision.
[76] Zajović and Urošević, (eds.), *Women's Court: About the Event*. The published proceedings can be found at pp. 79–271 (Women's Court Proceedings).
[77] Zajović, 'Witnesses at the Women's Court', p. 24 ff.

including 'regional encounters of the Women's Court witnesses', reflection on the Sarajevo event and current political and social events (such as regional transitional justice processes), legal and psychological assistance to witnesses, feminist therapeutic activities, and specific events on the Women's Court.

The feminist approach to justice built its new ideas and practices of justice in the concrete institution of the Women's Court. These ideas and practices fall into five key categories: (1) transformative feminist justice; (2) gender-based harms; (3) feminist justice proceedings; (4) feminist judgement; and (5) subjects of justice. To describe these categories, I draw on Court information materials and formal documents, the Preliminary Decision of the Women's Court, *About the Process*, and *About the Event*. My analysis also draws on my contemporaneous notes on the proceedings, as well as my field work in Bosnia and Herzegovina during this period.

7.2.1 The Category of Transformative Feminist Justice

Like the global legal form, the idea of 'justice' serves as the axiological foundation of the feminist approach of the Women's Court. However, the Women's Court develops a new concept of justice, which Duhaček argues has two distinctive characteristics. The first is that its concept of justice is 'grounded in addressing (concrete) injustice', rather than 'the (abstract) concept of justice'.[78] It begins with the 'concrete realities of social life',[79] rather than the abstract concepts of justice that ground the global legal form. The feminist approach to justice seeks to address the concrete injustices suffered by victims and grounds its conceptualisation of justice 'in the particular circumstances of social life that give rise to concrete claims of justice'.[80] The second characteristic is that the concept of justice is necessarily normatively oriented to a future gender-just society. The Women's Court aimed 'to prevent future crimes and to establish a just peace for future generations through the facing with crimes from the past and the illuminating of social mechanisms that

---

[78] Duhaček, 'Women's Court', p. 79.
[79] Mari Matsuda, 'Liberal Jurisprudence and Abstracted Visions of Human Nature', (1986) 16(3) N M L Rev 613–630, 613.
[80] Iris Marion Young, *Justice and the Politics of Difference* (Princeton: Princeton University Press, 1990), p. 4.

made them possible'.[81] As such, its conceptualisation of justice emphasises the building of future just societies. Duhaček emphasises that unlike transitional justice models, the feminist approach to justice resists restoring a society that was unjust to women or rebuilding a post-conflict society through 'remasculinisation'.[82] Instead, it aims to shape 'new possibilities in the present for the future'.[83]

Accordingly, the Women's Court develops a concept of transformative feminist justice. The Women's Court has been described as a key example of transformative justice, in that it seeks to move beyond the prosecutions of criminal justice and the rights violations of transitional justice in order to 'address the structural inequalities and vulnerabilities created by systems of war or repressive rule that affect women in disproportionate numbers'.[84] Jelke Boesten and Polly Wilding argue that ideas of 'transformative justice' first emerge in transitional justice debates in 2014, where it referred to the need to address socio-economic change and include 'bottom up' social change in transitional justice paradigms. As they point out, these ideas rarely addressed 'gender' as such.[85] However, feminist scholars have long argued for transformative gender justice, which links justice for gendered harms to the social transformation of gender inequalities.[86] Such feminist approaches argued that 'gender justice' necessarily involves social transformation that changes the subordination of women that exists prior to, and after, conflict.[87] As Ivekovic describes of the Women's Court, '[t]he most important conclusion from the tribunal will relate to the women's *demands in view of* the building of a future just and democratic society that includes gender justice'.[88]

The concept of 'gender justice' captures the focus of the Women's Court upon transforming unjust gendered social relations, rather than restoring a society that was unjust for women. However, it does not fully

---

[81] Zajović, 'The Women's Court', p. 27.
[82] Duhaček, 'Women's Court', pp. 88–89.
[83] Ibid., p. 73.
[84] Coomaraswamy, *Preventing Conflict*, p. 110.
[85] Jelke Boesten and Polly Wilding, 'Transformative Gender Justice', (2015) 51 Women's Studies International Forum, 75–80, 76-77.
[86] See Fionnuala Ní Aoláin, 'Transformative Gender Justice?', in Paul Gready and Simon Robins (eds.), *From Transitional to Transformative Justice* (Cambridge: Cambridge University Press, 2019).
[87] See Susan Rimmer, 'Sexing the Subject of Transitional Justice', (2010) 32(1) AFLJ 123–147.
[88] Ivekovic, 'Violence and Healing', p. 106.

encompass its wider conceptualisation of justice that seeks 'to challenge fundamentally unjust power relations within society; power relations that are often at the heart of the conflict itself'.[89] In the feminist approach to justice of the Women's Court, these power relations include different forms of militaristic, patriarchal, ethno-nationalist, and socio-economic violence against women in war and post-war societies. As such, this idea of justice shifts away from focusing upon changing unjust gender relations. Instead, it aims to transform the social relations that produce these different forms of violence against women in order to build a more just society for all. For this reason, it is more appropriate to describe the approach that the Women's Court seeks to develop as transformative feminist justice rather than transformative gender justice.

Transformative feminist justice conceptualises justice as a collective social good for all members of society. As Jasmina Husanović describes, the feminist approach to justice faces the challenge of how to conceptualise feminist justice as socially owned, that is, as the collective labour and property of all persons.[90] This is because transformative feminist justice conceptualises justice not as the property of the individual rights-holder but as the collective good of all members of a society. Similarly, for Iveković, 'the feminist struggle is the one that has the prospect to *create a broader space of equality for all*'.[91] This idea of justice involves building of an emancipatory society with and for all its members,[92] and it draws on Yugoslavian 'socialist values, such as solidarity, equality, collective good, and social ownership'.[93] Accordingly, any attempt to build transformative forms of justice cannot only be individual but must involve the collective building of a new emancipatory society. Transformative feminist justice is not based upon the ideas of the nation-state or of the international society that shape the current form of international criminal law. Rather, it is based upon the feminist struggle to build new social relations that are both regional (beyond ethnic or national community) and global (beyond the nation-state).

---

[89] Nahla Valji, 'Gender Justice and Reconciliation', in Kai Ambos, Judith Large et al. (eds.), *Building a Future on Peace and Justice* (Berlin: Springer, 2009), p. 219.

[90] Jasmina Husanović, personal communication, 2020.

[91] Iveković, 'Violence and Healing', p. 134.

[92] Jasmina Husanović, 'Resisting the Culture of Trauma', in Marlies Glasius and Dubravka Žarkov (eds.), *Narratives of Justice In and Out of the Courtroom* (New York: Springer, 2014), pp. 158–159.

[93] Nela Isaković and Gorana Mlinarević, 'Sustainable Transitions to Peace Need Women's Groups and Feminists', (2019) 72(2) Journal of International Affairs, 173–190, 175.

7.2.2 The Category of Harm

Though at first the Women's Court appeared to focus upon building a feminist approach to justice, nevertheless 'it became clear that this approach is centred round *injustice*'.[94] This concept of injustice builds on the feminist standpoint epistemology used by women's courts, which construct their knowledge of the social world from the experiences of subordinated groups. The methodology of the Women's Court privileges the standpoint of women's experiences – 'the lives and life visions of women' – as sources of knowledge of injustice. [95] It does so because these experiences of injustice had not been fully heard or addressed. Following this principle, the Women's Court does not define injustice in the abstract. Instead, it builds this concept from the concrete experiences of injustice by women, as they identify and describe them. By building its concept of harm from women's experiences of violence, the feminist approach to justice understands harms as based in gender relations rather than being gender-neutral. As such, it conceives these harms as gender-based harms or injustices.

To identify these harms, the Women's Court collected descriptions of concrete injustices from women participating in the preparatory process. These injustices encompass a range of physical, emotional, economic, and social harms and are not narrowly defined. Taken collectively, these testimonies described the 'experiences of many women' of injustice.[96] As such, these testimonies were seen as describing the collective experiences of women as a group. Rather than assuming that all women experienced the same injustices, this approach sought to identify the different injustices that these women experienced. The personal testimonies of the 'individual experiences of women' formed the 'subjective' elements of the thematic crimes presented at the Court.[97]

The individual testimonies were then used collectively as the basis for identifying 'the most frequent forms of violence' within each country and then regionally.[98] The process thereby shifts from individual to collective experience. Again, the approach does not envisage all women as experiencing the same form of violence but rather that women experience specific forms and effects of violence. From these collective personal

---

[94] Duhaček, 'Women's Court', p. 78.
[95] Ibid, p. 70.
[96] Zajović, 'The Women's Court, p. 42.
[97] Ibid., p. 26.
[98] Ibid., p. 45.

experiences, the participants developed categories that could name these 'most frequent forms of violence'. The categories of violence were identified as ethnic violence, military violence, gender-based violence, and economic violence.[99] They were clearly understood as collective and systemic in their nature and are described as 'structural injustice' or 'structural violence'.[100] These categories of violence formed the 'objective' element of the thematic crimes presented at the Court. They provide both the substantive 'themes' or content of the 'thematic crimes' and their collective and 'structural' conceptualisation in terms of social, economic, familial, and cultural contexts and causes.

This feminist approach to justice involves a process of building new concepts of harms rather than assuming these are known in advance. The process 'gives' voice to the individual experience of violence but also names it as a collective experience. The different forms of violence are identified from concrete experiences of injustice described from women's perspectives. As such, the approach methodologically and substantively conceptualises harms as gendered injustice. The new concepts of harms are then used as the basis to develop new categories of substantive crimes against women, which form the thematic crimes of the Women's Court. The thematic crimes can be seen as having two elements. The first is the subjective element, consisting of the individual experience of violence. The second is the objective element, and consists of the collective crime, together with its 'structural' context and cause.

7.2.3 The Category of Feminist Justice Proceedings

7.2.3.1 Methodology and Structure of Proceedings

The aim of the Women's Court proceedings was to create a space that enabled women's experiences of war-time and post-war violence to be heard and acknowledged publicly.[101] Creating this space included 'a number of alternative commemorative practices' both in the city of Sarajevo and in the Bosnian Cultural Centre, where the proceedings were held.[102] These included a press conference, opening ceremony, and women's peace march in Sarajevo, together with 'artistic-activist'

---

[99] Women's Court Three Fold Brochure.
[100] Zajović, 'The Women's Court, p. 15; Duhaček, 'Women's Court', pp. 82–84; Iveković, 'Violence and Healing', p. 105.
[101] Women's Court Three Fold Brochure.
[102] O'Reilly, *Gendered Agency in War and Peace*, pp. 154–155.

performance and exhibition.[103] The proceedings took place before a large public audience. The physical form of the proceedings reflected the democratic and 'horizontal' nature of the proceedings.[104] Each panel was held on a raised stage at the front of the auditorium, with witnesses and expert witnesses seated on the side of the stage and moving to the front to give testimony at a lectern. The Judicial Council were seated in the front row of the audience, and they came to the stage to deliver their oral judgement on the final day of the Court.

'Given the lack of an already existing set of rules to conduct procedures in this Court', the organising committee provided a set of procedural rules at the Court hearings (Women's Court Rules).[105] These set out the role of the Court, witnesses, and Judicial Council; the thematic crimes; the form and subject of witness and expert witness testimony; and the records of the Court. The structure of the proceedings, and the role of participants within them, adapted the methodology of the women's courts movement: 'What does the WC [Women's Court] procedure look like? WC methodology links a subjective text (a woman's testimony) with the objective analysis of political, social-economic and cultural context of the violence that took place.'[106] The proceedings consisted of the presentation of women's testimonies (the subjective text) followed by the expert witnesses (the objective analysis) in each panel. The roles of testimonial and expert witnesses were typical of women's courts. In the place of an international and/or national jury, the Women's Court had an international judicial council, comprised of both Yugoslav and international experts. As such, the proceedings had a four-party structure: the witnesses, the expert witnesses, the Judicial Council, and the public audience. The new form of justice proceedings aimed to support new forms of witnessing and judging within this process and to create new public knowledge about crimes committed against women.

7.2.3.2 The 'Subjective Text' of Testimonial Witnesses

The subjective text of women's testimonies is the foundation of the Court proceedings. Rule 1 states that the 'Women's Court shall hear testimonies

---

[103] Zajović, 'Witnesses at the Women's Court', p. 19.
[104] 'Women's Court: Feminist Approach to Justice', Sarajevo 7–10 May 2015', directed by Filip Marković and produced by Women in Black, video, https://www.zenskisud.org/en/filmovi.html.
[105] 'Rules of the Women's Court', Brochure, Women's Court, Sarajevo, 7 May 2015, on file with the author (Women's Court Rules).
[106] http://www.zenskisud.org/en/Metodologija.html.

of women about the crimes and violence committed against them'. Rule 4 directed witnesses to testify about crimes and violence committed during the war, the long-term effects of those crimes, and their experience of violence in the post-war period. They were also asked to 'testify about individual and/or organised resistance of women against all forms of violence'. Rule 5 requested that 'witnesses shall testify in public, and always in person', and all witnesses did so. The Women's Court Rules did not contain any specific provisions for sexual violence testimonies. However, during proceedings, journalists and photographers were 'not allowed to make recordings or take pictures'.[107]

Thirty-six witnesses testified before the Court. The witnesses came from across the former Yugoslavia, were all women, and were all of a wide age range. Eleven witnesses testified on panel one (war against the civilian population), four witnesses on panel two (woman's body – a battlefield), seven witnesses on panel three (militarist violence), eight witnesses on panel four (ethnic violence), and six witnesses on panel five (undeclared war).[108] The panel banners included names of witnesses and the town or region in which they lived during the war (which should not be confused with ethnicity or nationality). The second panel, 'Woman's Body – A Battlefield – Sexual Violence in War Zones', consisted of four victim-witnesses testifying to sexual violence to themselves and to others. As Maria O'Reilly describes, this was the smallest panel of the Court. The victim-witnesses were from Eastern Bosnia and Kosovo, with all describing the perpetrators as Serbian forces or paramilitaries.[109] A fifth witness from Croatia on panel four also testified to sexual violence against herself by unidentified paramilitaries, as well as the disclosure of rape by a Bosnian friend. Two other witnesses from Croatia in the first and fourth panels reported sexual violence against neighbours or family members by unidentified perpetrators.

The witnesses were able to choose how they wished to bear witness to their experiences. The testimonies varied in terms of form and content, with the majority of testimonies given for about 20 minutes.[110] During the proceedings, witnesses explained that they had chosen to testify about an experience that was significant to them or decided to speak about an event during the proceedings. For example, after the hearings, one sexual

---

[107] Zajović, 'Witnesses at the Women's Court', p. 40.
[108] Ibid., p. 19.
[109] O'Reilly, *Gendered Agency in War and Peace*, p. 161.
[110] As agreed in the preparatory process: Zajović, 'The Women's Court', p. 30.

violence victim-witness described how this was *'the first time, twenty years later, that I spelled out the whole truth that was weighing upon me'*.[111] In their testimonies, witnesses spoke of how they felt about these experiences or about testifying. For example, one witness to sexual violence described how her experience of war-time rape made her feel, while another described how she felt better for speaking. Others were clearly overcome by emotion and were unable to complete their testimony.

The witness testimonies were all '[f]irst person testimonies from survivors'.[112] As discussed in Chapter 4, these witnesses testified as *'superstes ...* a person who has lived through an event from beginning to end and can therefore bear witness to it'.[113] These testimonial texts share a narrative structure, as can be seen in the witness testimonies to sexual violence. The witnesses spoke of their pre-war lives, and then what happened during the war to them, their families, and their communities, and then after the war. The victim-witnesses described multiple acts of sexual violence over time by multiple perpetrators and being targeted as members of particular ethnic communities. The witnesses testified not only to harms to themselves but also to harms to others – their families, their communities, and the destruction of Yugoslav society. For example, four sexual violence victim-witnesses testified to sexual violence not only to themselves but also to others. The victim-witnesses did not isolate this experience from their other experiences of the war, but instead they situated it in the context of a range of other harms they experienced in the war, such as loss of employment, housing and education; inadequate medical care and food; armed attack on their village or town; and armed displacement and detention.

The witnesses testified to the ongoing psychological and physical impact of their war-time experiences. They also testified to the struggle to survive in their post-war societies in which 'the wars brought destruction of property, infrastructure and natural resources, and were accompanied by economic recession and hyperinflation [and] total institutional breakdown and violence', particularly in Bosnia and Kosovo.[114] Reflecting high poverty rates amongst survivors and the lack of economic

---

[111] Zajović, 'Witnesses at the Women's Court', pp. 35–36.
[112] O'Reilly, *Gendered Agency in War and Peace*, p. 154.
[113] Giorgio Agamben, *Remnants of Auschwitz* (New York: Zone, 1999), p. 17.
[114] Tatjana Đurić Kuzmanović and Ana Pajvančić-Cizelj, 'Economic Violence against Women', (2020) 27(1) European Journal of Women's Studies, 25–40, 30.

or psycho-social support sexual violence survivors received in all successor states, the witnesses described how 'our own authorities haven't done anything for us women, who have been left to cope on our own'.[115] All the witnesses censured the failure of institutions and society to support them or to punish and condemn the perpetrators of this violence.

The witnesses spoke not only of their experiences of harm but also of their experiences of solidarity and struggles for justice. The witnesses described being helped by, or helping, others during the war, such as nursing premature infants or a supportive friendship with another rape victim.[116] They also described the importance of the support and empowerment they received from women's organisations during the war and post-war period. Maria O'Reilly highlights the 'focus on survivors' active efforts to recover and rebuild their lives' in the testimonies.[117] These efforts include the struggle for justice, whether in the form of prosecutions and civil claims against perpetrators or their attempts to legally claim redress or enforce their rights in actions against the state. The testimonies ended with calls for justice and/or for a different future.

While the testimonies were given in the first person, they had a collective structure. Testifying was a collective practice rather than individual. Witnesses emphasised the importance of the group process of preparing for, and giving, testimony.[118] In the proceedings, the witnesses did not testify alone but sat together for each panel, with each witness supported by other witnesses, the witness supporter, and expert witnesses. This collective practice involved building 'mutual support and solidarity' between witnesses.[119]

Witnessing itself had a relational structure. The first relation is between the witness and other victims of the war. Like many other witnesses before the ICTY and successor state courts, witnesses explained that they felt a responsibility to bear witness on behalf of others. In the case of the Women's Court, this responsibility included bearing witness for other women. For example, in the post-court consultations, a witness described how *'the process gave us ... power not be there alone, to be the*

---

[115] Witness EK, Session 2, 'The Woman's Body – A Battlefield – Sexual Violence in the War Zones', Women's Court Proceedings, p. 136.
[116] Witness JC, Session 2, Women's Court Proceedings, pp. 132–133.
[117] O'Reilly, *Gendered Agency in War and Peace*, p. 159.
[118] Zajović, 'The Women's Court', pp. 37–41.
[119] Ibid., pp. 36–37.

voice of others as well. I am privileged to have lent my voice to other women.'[120] This sense of responsibility included testifying to ensure that other women do not suffer the same experiences in the future. The second relation was between the witness and her wider society. The witnesses call for justice and for a just peace. Like the victim-witnesses at the ICTY described in Chapter 4, these witnesses give testimony 'in order to *address* another, to impress upon a listener, to *appeal* to a community' for justice.[121] In their testimonies, the witnesses highlight how 'no one assumes responsibility for the criminals' or for their experiences of injustice.[122] Their call for justice therefore concerns not only individual accountability but also social accountability. The connection between individual and social accountability can found in the 'social solidarity' that Gabriela Mischkowski describes:

> [s]ocietal solidarity forms the matrix for an individual to reassemble what is left of one's life and to be-think oneself of one's own capabilities, hopes, and aspirations to draw up courage for a new life after. Solidarity is justice. To prosecute the wrongdoers means to affirm that wrong was indeed done. It means to show solidarity with the victims and to revoke solidarity from those who committed the crimes.[123]

In this mode of witnessing, the witnesses commit their personal testimony of their experience to others, so that others take responsibility for the 'general (non-personal) validity and consequences' of that testimony for society.[124] The witness testimonies are addressed to all society, insisting that it is a collective responsibility of all to acknowledge the validity of the testimony and that these crimes have occurred and to take responsibility for the consequences of acknowledging these crimes by providing justice for them and building a more just peace.

7.2.3.3 The 'Objective Analysis' of Expert Witnesses

In keeping with the methodology of women's courts, the Court had expert witnesses in each panel, all from the former Yugoslavia. The

---

[120] Zajović, 'Witnesses at the Women's Court', p. 41.
[121] Shoshana Felman and Dori Laub, *Testimony* (New York and London: Routledge, 1992), p. 204.
[122] Witness NT, Session 2, Women's Court Proceedings, p. 139.
[123] Gabriela Mischkowski, 'The Trouble with Rape Trials: The Prosecution of Sexual Violence in Armed Conflict from the Perspectives of Female Witnesses', The Bangladesh Genocide and the Issue of Justice, International Conference Heidelberg 4–5 July 2013, p. 6.
[124] Felman and Laub, *Testimony*, p. 204.

evidential role of the 12 expert witnesses was to 'assist the Women's Court in fully understanding the context within which the crimes and violent acts were committed'.[125] As described in the methodology of the Women's Court, 'the expert witnesses at WCs explain the political, gender, social-economic, ethnical-racial and cultural context of violence, analysing its causes and consequences and formulating the context for individual testimonies, which clearly shows the significance of personal testimony intertwined with political analysis'. They provide an 'objective' political analysis of the violence collectively described by the 'subjective' testimonies and the economic, social, and political causes and context of these crimes.[126]

The expert witness in panel two, 'Woman's Body – A Battlefield', was Marijana Senjak, a highly regarded feminist psychologist and therapist from the former Yugoslavia. Senjak established and led Medica Zenica and has worked with women victims of war, including sexual violence survivors, since 1992.[127] She begins by describing how

> the feminist approach to justice is much broader than legal provisions. In addition to the sanctioning of the perpetrator, it also implies recognising the suffering and the damages, compensation and recovery of survivors ... it is supposed to restore confidence and instil hope for peace with justice.[128]

Senjak situates the individual experiences of sexual violence in the context of wider collective violence in the war, including patterns of sexual violence and crimes against women, such as murder, deportation, and forced labour, and wider criminal campaigns of war crimes and genocide. Based on her extensive clinical experience, 'the most frequent patterns' of sexual violence include 'mass rapes and other forms of sexual abuse in detention camps, group and multiple rape in occupied places, where women and girls were held captive in houses and apartments, enslavement and sexual slavery in conditions of detention in camps, and murders of women following the crime of war rape'.[129]

---

[125] 'Structure of the Women's Court', in Zajović and Urošević (eds.), *Women's Court: About the Event*, p. 289.
[126] 'Methodology of Work', https://www.zenskisud.org/en/Metodologija.html.
[127] 'Structure of the Women's Court', p. 291.
[128] Marijana Senjak, 'The Women's Body as a Battlefield', Expert Witness, Session 2, Women's Court Proceedings, pp. 140–148 (Senjak, Women's Court Proceedings).
[129] Ibid., p. 141.

These crimes 'are aimed against women', Senjak argues.[130] Situating these crimes in their social causes and contexts, she describes rape as 'an extreme demonstration of the imbalance of power wielded by men in patriarchal society'.[131] Senjak characterises war-time rape as a form of violence against women, which is not an aberration of war but an 'extreme manifestation' of 'individual, structural, and interpersonal violence in peace time'.[132] Senjak's analysis emphasises the '**continuity of gender rooted violence**' in 'crimes in war and peace time'.[133] Her analysis understands the harm of sexual violence not only as a breach of the human rights of the individual victim-witness. Rather, she also connects the individual harm to the collective harms of gender injustice, which shapes the continuity of gender violence in war and peace. Sexual violence is seen as a collective crime, in the sense that it is characterised as collective violence against women as a group. The structural context of this crime is patriarchal social values and orders.

Senjak's objective analysis identifies the consequences of these crimes for women, including their physical and psychological impact, and the difficulties they faced in obtaining support from the state and wider society.[134] She links individual and social recovery and argues that a comprehensive approach to recovery at all levels of society is necessary. Senjak identifies reparations in their widest sense as being crucial to this process of the recovery. The 'lessons learned in the region' form the basis of her policy recommendations, which are directed to the development of better UN policies that can address the failure of the state to prevent war crimes and protect its female citizens, provide resources for individual and social recovery from war, and strengthen the 'structural response' to sexual violence in war and peace.[135]

7.2.3.4 The Collective Witnessing of the Public

The public audience also played a crucial role in this mode of transformative witnessing. The audience were not disinterested observers but played an active role in the proceedings. For example, when a witness testifying to sexual violence described her fight for justice, the audience

---

[130] Ibid., p. 142.
[131] Ibid., p. 140.
[132] Ibid., p. 144.
[133] 'Women's Court for the Ex Yugoslavia', (Women's Court Leaflet), on file with the author.
[134] Senjak, Women's Court Proceedings, pp. 142, 144–146.
[135] Ibid., pp. 146–147.

responded with cheers and claps. Audience members were openly moved by the testimonies. The 'public' was not an already existing community but was constituted as such in the Women's Court proceedings. Latinka Perović, Judicial Council member and Yugoslavian historian and politician, describes how the audience of the Women's Court 'was made up of representatives of women organizations from numerous countries worldwide: the "Network of Women Solidarity"', as well as participants in the preparatory process for the Women's Court, victims associations, non-governmental organisation, and the Judicial Council members. The Court itself 'was closed to the public ... Public reactions came "from within", from the women who were involved in it.'[136] The public reactions to the testimonies created the audience members as active interlocutors in the proceedings. They became an 'attentive audience', which shaped the witnesses' experience of the Women's Court as *'the only place where we were listened to and heard'*.[137] After the hearings, the witnesses themselves described the public witnessing of their testimony as an important aspect of their experience of the Women's Court.[138] In the acts of listening and hearing, the audience took up the role of public and collective witnessing. As Zajović describes, through the Women's Court '[i]njustice and grief transcended the private sphere and ... become part of social reality and collective memory'.[139]

7.2.4 The Category of Feminist Judgement

The International Judicial Council consisted of seven people, four members from the former Yugoslavia and three international members, including myself. At the Court hearings, the organising committee provided a set of rules setting out the principles of judgement. In essence, the Women's Court Rules required that the Council 'shall carefully hear and record the testimonies ... shall also establish political and civic responsibility of perpetrators, appeal to judicial institutions with its requests and proposals, and monitor the response of the said institutions' (Rule 12). The role of the Judicial Council was not to 'determine individual criminal responsibility for war crimes and violence committed against women, nor the responsibility for compensation for damages' (Rule 2). In keeping

---

[136] Perović, 'The Surviving Victims of Violence', p. 9.
[137] Zajović, 'Witnesses at the Women's Court', p. 41.
[138] Ibid., pp. 35–36.
[139] Ibid., p. 35.

with Rule 8 requiring the delivery of a public verdict, the Women's Court Preliminary Decision and Recommendations were delivered orally at the conclusion of the proceedings of the Court 'to give you our first impressions immediately after listening to the witnesses [and] the Court adopts these with the view to preparing the comprehensive and conclusive judgment in due time'.[140]

The Women's Court Preliminary Decision begins with the recognition of women as subjects of justice. The first paragraph recognises that women created the Court and that the witnesses 'are the leading subjects of the Women's Court'.[141] The Preliminary Decision developed its concepts of injustice from the five thematic crimes that were identified in the preparatory process and from the evidence presented in these categories to the Court. The evidence was the subjective text of women's testimonies, which described their experience of harms as well as the objective analysis of the expert witness testimonies that provided context for those crimes. The Preliminary Decision described and named these experiences as public categories of individual and collective violence and linked them to their wider social causes and consequences before, during, and after the war.[142] It connected the individual 'subjective' experiences of harm and the 'objective' political analysis of the expert witnesses to the five key forms of systemic and structural violence of the thematic crimes. For each of these thematic crimes, the Preliminary Decision provided a list of numerated acts that constituted international crimes (crimes against peace, war crimes, genocide, and crimes against humanity) and rights violations under international law. These numerated acts also identified and described new gendered harms not yet explicitly characterised as international crimes or human rights violations within the existing international legal framework.

An example of this approach can be seen in the thematic crime of 'using women's bodies as a battlefield'.[143] The description of gender-based crimes and rights violations in the thematic crime drew on the witness and expert testimonies given in panel two, which focused on sexual violence. The acts numerated under the thematic crime were described by testimonial witnesses, whose accounts of their experiences did not focus on sexual violence in isolation but situated it in their

---

[140] Women's Court Preliminary Decision, p. 1.
[141] Ibid.
[142] Women's Court Leaflet.
[143] Women's Court Preliminary Decision, p. 2.

experience of many crimes of war. The characterisation of these acts also drew on the objective analysis of the expert witness in this panel. The Women's Court Preliminary Decision noted that 'these crimes are intersecting, and the testimonies showed that these crimes crossed and moved beyond the given categories'.[144] Accordingly, the description of the acts included under the thematic crime also drew on other descriptions of the use of women's bodies as a battlefield given in other panels both by testimonial and by expert witnesses.

The Women's Court Preliminary Decision situated the thematic crimes in forms of system criminality. As the Preliminary Decision describes, 'the testimonies reveal that these crimes were made possible by systems of criminality, which reinforce and intensify unequal power relations between men and women'.[145] Drawing on the concept of system criminality developed at Nuremberg, the Preliminary Decision identified eight key elements of war as a form of system criminality:

> political, military, economic and security leadership and intellectual elites; militaries, paramilitaries and other armed groups; the media; war profiteers; senior government and administrative officials; religious institutions and leaders; international institutions and other governments.[146]

Following Rule 11, the Preliminary Decision aimed to 'establish political and civic responsibility of perpetrators'. The Preliminary Decision described individual responsibility for participation in systemic crimes, organised at group and state levels, and state and international responsibility for failing to protect citizens. It attributed legal and political responsibility for these crimes to the 'nationalist political and military regimes formed on the territory of the former Yugoslavia in the 1990s'.[147] 'Responsibility' was not restricted to the commission of thematic crimes. Rather, the Preliminary Decision also attributed 'public civil responsibility' to those 'who supported, condoned, or turned a blind eye to the commission of the crimes'.[148] The '[r]esponsibility for these crimes continues into the current failure to recognize and offer redress for these crimes, and to redistribute resources and power for a more just society'.

[144] Ibid., p. 1.
[145] Ibid., p. 5.
[146] Ibid.
[147] Ibid., p. 4.
[148] Ibid., p. 6.

The Preliminary Decision emphasised that 'women must be active and meaningful participants in the creation of such a society'.[149]

The Women's Court Preliminary Decision characterised building feminist justice as an ongoing process and as a collective social responsibility rather than being limited to a final public verdict on individual perpetrator responsibility for crimes. It included a set of general preliminary recommendations for individuals, institutions, and governments, which identified actions to address the thematic crimes against women and construct more just societies. The recommendations included giving participants in the Women's Court proceedings the collective responsibility of publicising the findings of the Women's Court at national and global levels. Under the Women's Court Rules, the Judicial Council itself was given responsibility for addressing judicial institutions with the 'requests and proposals' from the Women's Court and ensuring that they have been acted upon.

7.2.5 The Category of Feminist Subjects

The key aim of the Women's Court is to enable women to become subjects of justice. The feminist approach to justice understands the feminist justice process as building two new interconnected forms of subject positions for women. The first subject position is the agent of feminist justice. As Perović describes, through the feminist justice process, witnesses shifted from their position as victims to 'subjects writing and editing their own testimonies and speaking out loud in front of an audience'.[150] The witnesses emphasise the importance of this shift in their position from being victims to actors in this justice process.[151] In the feminist approach to justice, women survivors of war can become agents of justice working with other women to design the justice process, decide their testimony, and determine their demands for justice. Senjak observed that '[t]he witnesses were at the centre of everything, without being an instrument of evidentiary proceedings, but rather actors of that process'.[152] This collective political work and construction of a new justice process produces the victim-witness not as the object of patriarchal forms of criminal law but as a subject of feminist justice. In

---

[149] Ibid.
[150] Perović, 'The Surviving Victims of Violence', p. 11.
[151] Zajović, 'Witnesses at the Women's Court', pp. 40–41.
[152] Ibid., p. 45.

undertaking this process, the testimonial and expert witnesses were able to build a new paradigm of feminist justice.

The second, and related, position is that of political subject. The feminist approach to justice aims to build a justice process that can enable women survivors of war to become political agents and part of collective processes of social change. Their act of giving public testimony offers evidence of collective injustices, names publicly unacknowledged gender-based harms, and connects those harms to ethno-nationalist patriarchal orders in war and peace.[153] The political act of naming these collective violences positions the witness as an agent who claims justice from their society, state, and international community. As a witness describes: '*I had the feeling I was creating a new state abiding by the rule of law and governed by justice.*'[154] The position of political subject offers a new subject position for sexual violence survivors and an important alternative to the silent victimhood or ethno-nationalist co-option offered by the post-war political settlement.[155]

The creation of this new political subject position is not only individual but also collective. It is collective in the sense that the feminist approach to justice aims to build new relationships of solidarity between women of the former Yugoslavia and to build more just social relations in the wider society. Social solidarity and justice are seen as the basis for a feminist rebuilding of a more just peace. This feminist justice process therefore aimed to enable all those engaged in and with the Women's Court, as well as witnesses, to become political subjects engaged in collective social change.

7.3 The Feminist Form of Justice in the Women's Court

7.3.1 The Feminist Form of Justice

The Women's Court builds a new paradigm of justice. The general concepts of the paradigm can be drawn from the practice (that is, the process and hearings) of the Women's Court. Following the Women's Court participants, I call this model 'the feminist approach to justice'. This is not to suggest it is the only feminist approach to justice that can be developed but rather to describe this distinctive form of feminist justice.

---

[153] Ibid,, p. 73.
[154] Ibid,, p. 25.
[155] See Elissa Helms, *Innocence and Victimhood* (Madison: University of Wisconsin Press, 2013).

This form of feminist justice consists of the fundamental categories of (1) transformative feminist justice; (2) gender-based injustice; (3) feminist justice proceedings; (4) feminist judging; and (5) feminist subjects.

The first and foundational category is transformative feminist justice. It conceptualises justice as a collective social good, which contributes to making an emancipatory society for all. However, it does not conceptualise justice as the application of existing forms of legal or transitional justice, because they have not provided justice for women or changed unjust national or international social orders. Rather, justice is 'the very dimension of events irreducibly to come', which requires 'the transformation, the recasting or refounding of law and politics'.[156] This concept of justice is predicated upon the transformation of existing unjust social relations in the present. Justice does not yet exist but must be made by building new social bonds and values that can refound law and politics.

The second category of gender-based injustice names the different forms of violence experienced by women. The feminist approach to justice builds the category from the concrete experiences of violence described by women. Taken collectively, these experiences describe gender-based harms, in that these harms target or disproportionately affect women as a group. The category of gender-based injustice conceives these harms as structural and systemic collective violence. It names the harms as injustice, to which the feminist approach to justice is addressed.

The third category is feminist justice proceedings. The category consists of practices that aim to enable women to become agents of justice. The justice proceedings consist of the subjective text of the experiences of violence and resistance of the testimonial witness, the objective analysis of the context and causes of these experiences by the expert witnesses, and the collective witnessing of the public that recognises these experiences as a political and social matter.

The fourth category is feminist judgement. The category consists of practices of judging that connect the subjective texts of witnesses and the objective analysis of the expert witnesses, and from these testimonies it builds new concepts of crimes against women that capture their systemic nature. On the basis of the evidence of these forms of violence, feminist judging establishes legal, civic, and political responsibility for these crimes, and collective responsibility for social transformation. This concept of feminist judging is predicated upon the recognition of

---

[156] Jacques Derrida, 'Force of Law', in Drucilla Cornell, Michel Rosenfeld et al. (eds.), *Deconstruction and the Possibility of Justice* (New York: Routledge, 1992), p. 27.

women as subjects of justice and an ongoing responsibility to engage in building feminist justice.

The fifth category is feminist subjects, which are created in these justice processes. The feminist approach to justice aims to build a justice process that can enable women survivors of war to become political agents and part of collective processes of social change. The position of political subject offers a new subject position for survivors of these crimes. The creation of this new political subject position is not only individual but also collective. It is collective in the sense that the feminist approach to justice aimed to enable all those engaged in and with the Women's Court, as well as witnesses, to become political subjects engaged in collective social change.

The categories of the feminist approach to justice construct subjects and their relations in terms of the values of feminist justice. Unlike the global legal form of international criminal law, this feminist approach does not conceive subjects and their relations as juridical exchange between abstract, free, and equal subjects. Rather, it sees concrete persons existing in unequal and unfree social relations. This form of justice conceives crime as a gendered injustice that harms women and their societies rather than injury to the possessive subject of rights or to 'international society'. Because the Women's Court is a 'necessary and effective political form that is neither a state nor a social institution', the feminist approach to justice does not aim to reconstruct existing unjust national and international social order.[157] Rather, it rests upon the symbolisation of gendered injustice and the building of just social relations, which are based in the values of social emancipation (rather than capitalist values of possessive individualism and nation-state sovereignty). As such, the form of feminist justice does not exist in the present but is a possibility that must be made through productive co-operation. For this reason, this feminist form of justice involves collective action that must make a future emancipatory society in the concrete social relations of the present.

7.3.2 The Women's Court as a Feminist Discourse

Iveković situates the challenge of building a feminist approach to justice in the wider feminist problem of building a critique of the 'entire

---

[157] Iveković, 'Violence and Healing', p. 128.

symbolic system' and undertaking an *'epistemological revolution'*.[158] To describe how the feminist approach to justice develops a critique of the socio-symbolic order of existing models of justice and how it produces new knowledges of violence and justice, I build on my earlier account of modern fraternal and feminist discourses as discussed in Chapters 5 and 6. This theory describes the 'symbolic asymmetrical inequality of sexes' that modern fraternal social orders produce but also recognises that a feminist epistemological revolution is necessary to create new socio-symbolic orders, as Iveković suggests.[159] In my earlier analysis of feminist discourses, I argued that feminist movements undertake this epistemological revolution. This is because the collective practices of these movements produce new knowledges about the social world, which produce new discourses of subjects and sociality.[160]

I use this approach to analyse the discursive operation of the form of feminist justice and how it produces new subjects and social bonds. The feminist approach to justice begins with the critique that existing models of international justice, namely, criminal and transitional justice, fail to provide justice for women. Because the feminist approach to justice is grounded in women's experience of concrete injustice, it generates new knowledges about gender-based injustices. In seeking to address those concrete injustices, the feminist form of justice reveals that gender-based harms are not symbolised in existing forms of justice. This is because the concrete injustices are not represented in their socio-symbolic systems. Accordingly, the feminist approach to justice reveals the gaps or missing elements in existing discourses of international justice. Gender-based injustices appear as constitutive faults in these discourses, because they are excluded from their hegemonic representations of the social order (the patriarchal nation-state and the international society of humanity) and the phantasies of (masculine fraternal) subjects and (ethno-national) sociality that sustain them. These faults appear in the existing socio-symbolic order of international justice as an unrepresentable trauma at the symbolic level but are rearticulated as the hegemonic content of the phantasy of justice at the imaginary level.

Rather than veiling or covering over this absence, the feminist approach to justice reveals that experiences of gender-based harms are

---

[158] Ibid., p. 133.
[159] Ibid., pp. 132-133.
[160] Kirsten Campbell, *Jacques Lacan and Feminist Epistemology* (London and New York: Routledge, 2004).

not 'outside' the socio-symbolic order of international justice but are produced by it. Because of its orientation to concrete injustice, the feminist approach to justice necessarily confronts the limits of this socio-symbolic order. In this confrontation, it becomes no longer possible to 'identify' with the phantasy that the existing forms of justice are just. Instead, it becomes necessary to traverse these phantasies of justice to reveal their injustices. Traversing the phantasy 'unfreezes' the discursive structure and opens the space for the creation of new discourses of justice.

What, then, is the structure and operation of this new discourse of feminist justice? The first element of the discourse is a, or the 'gap' or 'missing' element in the modern ethno-fraternal discourses of justice described above. In the feminist discourse of justice, there is an identification with the injustice of the reality of the social experience of women of gender-based harms (the excluded term of ethno-fraternal discourses). There is an identification with feminist justice as an ideal, as an idea of an emancipatory justice that includes women but which does not yet exist (the justice that ethno-fraternal discourses cannot provide). This is the 'cause' of the discourse of feminist justice, in the sense that it inaugurates the feminist approach to justice.

The second element of the feminist discourse of justice is S_1, that is, the symbolic element that represents injustice. This symbolic element (or signifier) is created in the concrete institution and practices of the Women's Court. In the feminist approach to justice, the process and proceedings of the Women's Court describe gender-based harms and names them as injustices. The collective practices of the feminist justice process and proceedings can be described as epistemic practices, that is, as practices that generate knowledge. This knowledge forms the basis of the 'judgement of existence' of gendered injustice, that is, the affirmation that an entity exists by symbolising it.[161] This judgement of existence symbolises women's experiences of injustice, symbolically affirming that these injustices exist. The act of symbolisation involves the creation of new signifiers for harms, subjects, justice proceedings, and judgement that symbolise persons and social relations through ideas of an emancipatory society.

The collective practices of feminist movements, such as the Women's Court, enable this creation of a new signifier. By describing harms and

---

[161] For further discussion, see Campbell, ibid., pp. 108–109.

naming them as injustices, the collective feminist practices of the feminist approach to justice construct new symbolic elements that can represent gendered injustices. The new signifiers symbolise experiences of concrete injustice that are otherwise not represented in the existing socio-symbolic order. The feminist approach to justice creates a new symbolisation of the injustices that women testify to. Like the legal symbolisation of gender-based harms in the *Kunarac* case discussed in Chapter 5, this involves an act of nomination, which 'invents' a new symbolic element to describe and name gender-based harms as injustices. However, unlike that legal discourse, the feminist form of justice does not seek to repair the fault in the existing legal order. It does not involve an identification with the existing order of law but with a future transformative feminist justice. As such, this radical act of symbolic creation invents new ways of symbolising justice, by constructing new symbolic elements from feminist knowledges and values. The building of each new category of harm, subject, justice proceedings, and judgement in the feminist approach to justice involves an act of symbolic creation.

The third element is S_2, the new symbolic network of signifiers that is created in the feminist approach to justice. This symbolic network links the new signifiers created in the justice process and proceedings, so that they form new signifying chains connected together as a symbolic network. The new network of signifiers creates a new discourse of feminist justice. Feminist values and practices structure the new discourse, articulating the relation between subjects as political practices. This structure does not entail that the relation between subjects is necessarily ethical or political but that feminist politics and action construct their social relations in terms of feminist values. In the discourse, 'feminism' is not pre-given or singular but is a set of values emerging from collective feminist struggles. As Zajović describes, '[a]lthough the witnesses claimed that they do not know feminism "theoretically", it is quite clear that they have been practising feminism in action, both in the private and in the public sphere. For them, there are many forms of feminism and feminist struggle, combining gender, ethnic, class and social elements.'[162] Accordingly, these feminist political standpoints are not achieved by an individual knower but are the outcome of a *'collective* critical take' that involves political solidarity, engagement, debate, and action.[163]

---

[162] Zajović, 'Witnesses at the Women's Court', p. 42.
[163] Kum-Kum Bhavnani and Donna Haraway, 'Shifting Subjects', in Kum-Kum Bhavnani and Ann Phoenix (eds.), *Shifting Identities, Shifting Racisms* (London: Sage, 1994), p. 37.

The next term in the feminist discourse of justice is S, the position of the subject. The feminist approach to justice links the signifier of injustice to the creation of a new position for women as speaking subjects. In the operation of this discourse, the signifier of injustice creates a new speaking position for the victim-witness, because it provides the basis for their claim of justice. With this claim, the victim-witness can become a subject of justice, speaking of the injustices that they have experienced and demanding justice for them. As such, the creation of the new signifier of injustice provides the basis for a new representation of the victim-witness as subject of justice. It provides a new way of naming their subject position as well as their experience. As such, the discourse of feminist justice provides the possibility of what Iveković describes as 'new political subjectivation', that is, the making of new political subjects.[164]

The feminist form of justice, then, aims to change subjects and their social relations. It produces a model of the subject that does not assume any qualities of the person other than their capacity for political action. The political subject is made through collective work that enables an identification with feminist values (but not necessarily feminist movements or feminism as such) rather than being an a priori assumed identity.[165] This is a relational, rather than individual, model of the subject. It conceives the subject as coming into being through their relation to a set of feminist values and other subjects in political struggle. Moreover, it seeks to change the social relations within which that political struggle takes place.

The feminist form of justice aims to transform the very idea of 'society' as it exists. It does not seek to restore national or international social orders, which it characterises as fundamentally unjust. Unlike other approaches to justice, the feminist approach to justice sees patriarchal, ethno-nationalist, and capitalist global social relations as integral to the creation of collective violence. As a result, it aims to transform rather than reproduce these social relations by contributing to the making of more just societies in the present. This struggle is not limited to the nation-state but is seen as part of a movement for global justice, which refuses to consign some to bare existence in global exchange but instead grants all social existence. This feminist form of justice emerges from the struggle to resist reproducing the capitalist, patriarchal, and

---

[164] Iveković, 'Violence and Healing', p. 128.
[165] For further discussion, see Campbell, *Jacques Lacan and Feminist Epistemology*, pp. 146–148.

ethno-nationalist values of existing discourses of justice and to create justice as a social good for all.

The Women's Court participates in building the 'epistemological revolution' necessary to create new forms of justice by enabling women to become epistemological subjects. Following Irigaray, 'the women's movement, in drawing attention to the male subject of enunciation, has staked a claim for the right of the female subject to be an epistemological subject too'.[166] The feminist approach to justice creates 'the female subject of enunciation' by positing women as speaking subjects, that is, as subjects who are capable of symbolisation and of knowing. In this way, the feminist approach to justice addresses the 'epistemic injustice' faced by witnesses described in Chapter 4, which 'wrongs someone in their capacity as a subject of knowledge'.[167] In positing women as knowers, the feminist approach to justice can represent the (excluded) experience of women, posit women as speaking subjects, and articulate the relation between women as speaking subjects. This collective work of building a feminist approach to justice creates new practices of knowing and new knowledges.

The emancipatory potential of the feminist form of justice is to produce a new representation of social relations and to build those relations in concrete institutions and practices. It gives acts and persons new meanings and ties persons together as social subjects in new ways. It thereby creates a new socio-symbolic order that gives acts and subjects new political (feminist) meanings. This is because it constructs feminist subjects of justice and their relations to other subjects according to different values than existing discourses of justice. If existing discourses of justice symbolise ethno-fraternal subjects and social bonds, then the feminist approach to justice builds a symbolisation of feminist subjects and social bonds. It does not represent social relations between hegemonic masculine subjects but social relations between feminist subjects. In this new social bond, women can become social subjects rather than objects of ethno-fraternal exchange.

In the feminist form of justice, building justice is not only symbolic but also material in that it involves the creation of concrete institutions and practices. The feminist approach to justice required creating the new 'institution' of the Women's Court and the new justice practices of the

---

[166] Margaret Whitford, *Luce Irigaray* (London: Routledge, 1991), p. 49.
[167] Miranda Fricker, *Epistemic Injustice* (Oxford and New York: Oxford University Press, 2007), p. 5.

feminist justice process and proceedings. The new justice institution and practices are crucial to the creation of new feminist forms of justice, because they enable the creation of new signifying elements, new subjects, and relations between them in concrete social relations. The building of the practices and institution of the Women's Court gives the feminist form of justice its material existence. This is because the institution and its practices are the material from which feminist justice is made. By creating new justice institutions and practices through collective action, the feminist form of justice can be made in concrete social relations. Like international criminal law, feminist justice must be continually created and given material existence in values, practices, and institutions.

7.4 The Global Feminist Form of Justice

> In this process, we have seen how personal is not only political, the personal is also international...[168]

Like the ICTY, the Women's Court sees itself as part of a movement for international justice. However, unlike the ICTY, the Women's Court characterises itself as being part of an alternative 'bottom up' and transformative vision of global justice.[169] As Perović describes, the witnesses '[b]y testifying about their own experience in the local context ... gradually decided to participate in a global context, an important dimension of which is feminist justice'.[170] The Women's Court aimed to 'strengthen global feminist-pacifist alliances and coalitions in order to bring punishment to violence and crimes, to influence the international institutions of justice'.[171] Women's organisations from around the globe participated in the process and proceedings of the Women's Court, which included a specific event on 'the power of internationalist women's solidarity'.[172] The Women's Court situated itself within the global movement of women's courts and as part of internationalist feminist movements.

Accordingly, the Women's Court develops a feminist approach to justice that is global. It builds on transnational feminist movements and aims to contribute to those movements for justice for all.

---

[168] Zajović, 'The Women's Court', p. 15.
[169] Zajović, 'Witnesses at the Women's Court', p. 20, pp. 47–48.
[170] Perović, 'The Surviving Victims of Violence', p. 10.
[171] https://www.zenskisud.org/en/index.html
[172] Zajović, 'Witnesses at the Women's Court', p. 20.

Moreover, the justice claims of the Women's Court exceed the nation-state frame. These justice claims describe international crimes, identify the responsibility of states and international organisations, and call for redress at regional and international levels. They cannot take the modern territorial state for granted because the state of Yugoslavia no longer exists, the conflict itself was 'internationalised', and the post-war political settlements were regional and international. In those post-war settlements, the successor states as well as 'international society' failed to provide justice for women's experiences of injustice. Accordingly, the feminist approach to justice moves beyond the 'Keynesian-Westphalian frame [that takes] for granted the modern territorial state as the appropriate unit and its citizens as the pertinent subjects'.[173] It emphasises the importance of building justice beyond the nation-state and takes the global as its frame.

Just as the legal form of international criminal law emerges from shifts in global social relations, so too does the feminist form of justice. If the legal form of international criminal law can be understood as a structured process of the confrontation of legal agents thrown up by the dynamics of global social relations, so too this feminist form of justice can be understood as a structured process of the co-operation of political agents thrown up by these dynamics. In its description of war-time and post-war violence against women, the feminist form of justice expresses the injustices of the collective violence of war and the post-war social injustices produced by the intensification of neoliberal globalisation in the former Yugoslavia. It describes the coercive violence of the Yugoslav wars and the structural violence of post-war neoliberal globalisation as gendered injustices, symbolises these gendered injustices as crimes, and assigns individual, political, and social responsibility for those crimes. As a participant in the Women's Court describes, the witnesses *'exposed the hierarchy in the power relations in society, they perceive from the feminine perspective the key influential processes, nationalistic violence, post-socialist transformations in the neo-liberal globalisation, which did not define only their lives and traumas, but also their families'.*[174]

Like the global legal form, the feminist form of justice expresses the collective violence that produces the experience of bare life – as evidenced by the testimonial and expert witnesses of the Women's Court and described in the thematic crimes and Women's Court

---

[173] Nancy Fraser, *Fortunes of Feminism* (Verso, London, 2013), p. 190.
[174] Zajović, 'Witnesses at the Women's Court', p. 45.

Preliminary Decision. It too draws on the affective and material collective work of women's groups, victims' associations, and feminist activism in sustaining the justice claims of women. Unlike the global legal form, the feminist approach to justice connects this violence to unjust social orders at national and global levels, thereby politicising this experience of bare life. By doing so, the feminist form of justice also opens the possibility of co-operation of political agents thrown up by these processes. As such, it can be said to emerge from the productive capacities of women acting as collective political agents to build other forms of collective social life. In the feminist approach to justice, it is possible to see what Husanović describes as an emancipatory trajectory, that is, 'a particular trajectory of resistance/transformation which is politically effective and sustains an emancipatory drive by rendering political acts, subjectivisations and agents to which they relate into a phenomenon of the Negrian constituting power irreducible to sovereign order'.[175]

The feminist form of justice expresses the alternative possibilities of political solidarity and social emancipation that emerge in the processes of globalisation. As discussed in Chapter 6, the conflictual and connective forces of globalisation that produced the Yugoslavia war and the ICTY also produced the networks of feminists and women survivors that first mobilised around the war, and specifically around war crimes against women, in the early 1990s, and were part of a global feminist movement. These networks would go on to play an important role in the Women's Court. From its establishment, the Women's Court drew on these global networks and models, particularly from the Global South. This in part reflected the earlier internationalist politics of the non-aligned movement of Yugoslavia. It also reflected an ongoing political project of building transnational feminist coalitions.

The feminist approach to justice can be described as an alter global movement emerging within the social antagonisms of globalisation itself. In the preparatory process, the participants situate the Women's Court within the alter-globalisation movement, understood as 'just, democratic, non-violent globalisation' from below, as opposed to the 'globalisation from above' 'political, financial and military power'.[176] They saw the global women's court movement as building feminist alternatives to neoliberal globalisation, and this idea is integral to the feminist approach

---

[175] Jasmina Husanović, *Culture, Community and Activism in Bosnia and Herzegovina* (Tuzla: Off Set Press, 2021), p. 76.
[176] Kovačević, Perković et al. (eds.), *Zenski Sud*, p. 180.

to justice. We might describe the feminist approach to justice as expressing the 'emergence of collective or proto-socialist relations within capital itself', in that these 'collective forms [are] already latent in the capitalist present: they are not merely desirable (or ethical), nor even possible, but also and above all inevitable, provided we understand the bringing to emergence of that inevitability as a collective human task and project'.[177]

In the feminist alter-global approach to justice, there is an attempt to build a different value for women, not as objects of global exchange but as political subjects producing new forms of justice. This form of feminist justice can be seen as a homologous expression of these alternative collective forms in globalisation. This is because the socio-symbolic form of this model of justice constructs subjects and their social relations around the public goods of global social existence. As such, it points to the possibilities of other forms of justice produced by the contradictory dynamics of our changing globalising world.

---

[177] Fredric Jameson, *Archaeologies of the Future* (New York: Verso, 2005), pp. 250, 252.

8

Building a Feminist Approach to Justice for International Criminal Law

Political Challenges and Conceptual Foundations

> I will fight for justice to be done.
>
> Witness EK, Women's Court, 2015[1]

The Women's Court offers an alternative feminist approach to justice for crimes committed against women in the war and post-war period in the former Yugoslavia. This alternative model consists of new feminist justice practices and categories, which produce a feminist form of justice. 'Institutional legal justice' has an important but problematic role in this feminist approach to justice, and the Women's Court does not develop a feminist approach to law. What, then, are the implications of this approach to justice for feminist engagements with international criminal law? And does it potentially offer an alternative feminist approach to the global legal form of international criminal law?

8.1 'The Institutional Legal System' in the Feminist Approach to Justice

8.1.1 The Role of the Institutional Legal System in the Feminist Approach to Justice

The Women's Court has an ambivalent relation to 'the institutional legal system'.[2] Institutional legal justice is necessary for feminist justice but at the same time does not provide it. As described in the previous chapter, participants clearly identified their concern with the failure of existing

---

[1] Witness EK, 'The Woman's Body – A Battlefield - Sexual Violence in the War Zones', Session 2, in Staša Zajović and Miloš Urošević, (eds.), *Women's Court: About Event in Sarajevo and about Continue the Process* (Belgrade: Women in Black, 2017), p. 136. The published proceedings can be found at pp. 79–271 (Women's Court Proceedings).

[2] My thanks to Amal Treacher for drawing my attention to this structure.

legal systems, but they also emphasised the importance of legal sanctions and remedies. This issue was specifically raised from the first consultations on establishing the Court, where, for example, participants in Bosnia emphasised the importance of ensuring that the Court made an impact upon the legal system.[3] These concerns were also reiterated throughout witness testimonies in the Court. For example, the four sexual violence victim-witnesses ended their testimony with calls for accountability for crimes committed against not only themselves but also others. Their concern is not only individual but also collective impunity, because of its impact upon the wider society. In this context, impunity refers to the failure to prosecute and to punish.[4] For the Women's Court witnesses, like other witness from the former Yugoslavia, criminal justice provides public witnessing to the crimes that took place; acknowledges and stigmatises the harms of these crimes, holds perpetrators accountable, and punishes them; and prevents future violence by removing perpetrators from the community.[5]

The witnesses also call for the institutional legal system to provide not only criminal sanction but also individual and social redress for these crimes. As described by witnesses, the institutional legal system has not provided reparative justice.[6] As discussed in Chapter 5, reparative justice consists of those remedies that seek to 'repair' the consequences of the individual and social harms caused by those crimes. Witnesses call for compensation for their material and physical harms; restitution, such as return of property, employment, and rights of residence; rehabilitation, such as psycho-social and physical care; and satisfaction for 'immaterial' damages, such as public declarations of responsibility, public apology, and 'right to truth' about missing persons.[7] They also emphasise the

---

[3] 'Report on Implemented Activities, January–December 2011, Women's Court: Feminist Approach to Justice', (Belgrade: Women in Black, 2012), p. 55.
[4] Staša Zajović, 'Witnesses at the Women's Court', in Zajović and Urošević (eds.), *Women's Court: About the Event*, pp. 62–65.
[5] See Gabi Mischkowski and Gorana Mlinarević, *And That It Does Not Happen to Anyone Anywhere in the World* (Cologne: Medica Mondiale, 2009), pp. 53–59; Kimi King, and James Meernik, *The Witness Experience* (Cambridge: Cambridge University Press, 2017), p. 60; Diane Orentlicher, *Some Kind of Justice* (New York: Oxford University Press, 2018), pp. 91-110.
[6] Zajović, 'Witnesses at the Women's Court', p. 62.
[7] These demands echo the remedies and reparations provided under Basic Principles and Guidelines on the Right to a Remedy and Reparation for Victims of Gross Violations of International Human Rights Law and Serious Violations of International Humanitarian Law, adopted by General Assembly Resolution 60/147(2005).

importance of the removal of perpetrators from civil institutions, political activities, and public life and of guarantees of non-repetition of these crimes. The witnesses highlight the unequal and ineffective access to justice for victims and the inadequate, ineffective, or delayed provision of reparative remedies. The Women's Court participants called for not only individual but also collective reparation, and not only individual but also collective remedies. Such remedies and reparations are identified by Marijana Senjak as a crucial element of the recovery of affected societies.[8]

Because of the importance of criminal and reparative justice, the Women's Court explicitly adopted the aim of creating different legal practices and influencing the 'institutional legal system'.[9] This attachment to legal justice shaped the institutional design of the Court, with its combination of the more 'legalistic' elements of women's tribunals and the more 'alternative' and informal elements of women's courts, 'to put pressure on the institutional legal system through the WC [Women's Court]'.[10] It was also reflected in the Women's Court Rules, which referred to the Women's Court and the Judicial Council 'appealing to judicial institutions with its requests and proposals' (Rules 8 and 11). This important role of law in the feminist approach to justice continues to be visible in the follow up activities of the Court, in which 'the participants acknowledge the importance of institutional justice, and are resolved to make an impact in changing this system'.[11] Zajović identifies important activities for witnesses as including 'psychological and legal support' in legal proceedings, including individual compensation and restitution claims. Notably, she describes the difficulty of providing legal support as 'indicative of a general climate of impunity in the entire region. It was therefore concluded that it is necessary to create a stronger network of legal assistance – at both regional and international levels.'[12]

The role of 'institutional legal justice' becomes clearly visible at the Women's Court, which exemplifies the important but problematic role of law in the feminist approach to justice. This is not because Yugoslavia is 'exceptional'. Rather, understanding the role of 'institutional legal justice'

---

[8] Marijana Senjak, 'The Women's Body as a Battlefield', Expert Witness, Session 2, Women's Court Proceedings, pp. 142–144 (Senjak, Women's Court Proceedings).
[9] https://www.zenskisud.org/en/index.html.
[10] Staša Zajović, 'The Women's Court', in Staša Zajović, (ed.) *Women's Court: About the Process* (Belgrade: Women in Black and Centre for Women's Studies, 2015), pp. 25–26.
[11] Zajović, 'Witnesses at the Women's Court', p. 65.
[12] Ibid., p. 49.

in the Yugoslavian context helps us to see why it becomes important for a feminist approach to justice. Three important features of this context are legal culture, post-conflict transition, and rebuilding post-conflict society.

The important role of criminal law in the legal culture of the former Yugoslavia is the first critical context. That criminal sanction is the appropriate response to crimes committed in the war is a widely held view in the region and reflects the long-standing criminalisation of international crimes and rape in the Yugoslavian legal system (as discussed in the previous chapter). On the one hand, the criminalisation of these offences could be said to be typical of many European countries. Domestic rape provisions were similar to those in other European continental law systems. Similarly, like other Nazi-occupied European countries following World War Two, Yugoslavia participated in the Nuremberg trials of major war criminals and prosecuted war crimes in national trials against German and Italian military personnel, including sexual violence.[13] On the other hand, the Socialist Federal Republic of Yugoslavia was the first country to incorporate these international crimes into domestic law in 1951, which specifically included sexual violence offences. This reflected the experience of brutal occupation and collaboration, which was to become a crucial part of Yugoslavia's formation as a state. Moreover, the importance of criminal justice also reflects the explicit social role of criminal law in the legal culture, which was understood to have a 'protective function' for society and to express Yugoslavian socialist 'social values'.[14]

More generally, it reflects the widespread role of criminal law in proscribing the use of physical force in municipal legal systems of modern states. In this role, criminal law systems are seen as an integral part of the state's claim on the monopoly on individual and collective violence, and its corollary, 'internal' pacification.[15] As the actual and then formal state of the former Yugoslavia ceased to exist, so too did its monopoly on coercive violence. As the Women's Court witness testimonies describe, '[o]vernight, any kind of legal order disappeared'.[16]

---

[13] See Dan Plesch, Susana SáCouto et al., 'The Relevance of the United Nations War Crimes Commission to the Prosecution of Sexual and Gender-Based Crimes Today', (2014) 25 (1–2) Crim L F 349–381.

[14] See, for example, *Criminal Code of the Socialist Federal Republic of Yugoslavia* 1 July 1977, Art. 1.

[15] See Charles Tilly, *Coercion, Capital, and European States, AD 990–1992* (Oxford: Blackwell; 1992), Chapter 3.

[16] Rada Iveković, 'Violence and Healing', in Zajović, (ed.) *Women's Court: About the Process*, p. 104.

Rama Mani notes, this 'rampant legal injustice ... is a common symptom preceding and during most conflicts'.[17]

The role of law in post-conflict transition in the former Yugoslavia is the second and related context. As in many other post-conflict states, transition in the Yugoslavian successor states was integrally tied to 'legal justice', that is, to the (re)establishment of legal systems and the formal rule of law. The legal frameworks of the transition from (active) war to (negative) peace included international legal recognition of states, (re)establishment of national legal systems, rule of law requirements of EU accession (including war crimes prosecutions), and the adoption of public international and European legal regimes.[18] The legal framing of post-conflict transition was particularly visible in Bosnia, where an integral part of transition was the reconstruction of the state as a legal entity and re-establishing the rule of law and the legal system, in the context of the legal framework of the Dayton Peace Agreement and a new constitution, together with ongoing administration by the Office of the High Representative. This pivotal role of law in the (re)construction of the post-conflict societies of the former Yugoslavia exemplifies the role of legal justice in post-conflict transitions generally.

The rebuilding of post-war society in the region is the third context. The Women's Court shows that legal settlements are a crucial part of post-war gender settlements, because these legal relations grant entitlements or impose obligations that materially affect the lives of women after the war. If conflict-related sexual violence is understood as a gender-based harm, which is a 'manifestation of historically unequal power relationships between men and women', then failing to address that gender-based harm further deepens those unequal power relationships.[19] As the Women's Court expert witnesses on 'gendered violence against women' describe: '[a]s demonstrated in the personal accounts of women witnesses, such dynamics of patriarchal restructuring is omnipresent'.[20] The post-war legal settlements did not remake the legal social bonds

---

[17] Rama Mani, *Beyond Retribution* (Cambridge: Polity, 2002), p. 5
[18] See Kirsten Campbell, 'Reassembling International Justice', 2014 8(1) Int J Transitional Justice 53–74.
[19] Rashida Manjoo, 'Normative Developments on Violence against Women in the UN System', in Rashida Manjoo and Jackie Jones, (eds.) *The Legal Protection of Women from Violence* (London and New York: Routledge, 2018), p. 73.
[20] Vjollca Krasniqi, Rada Iveković et al., 'The Banality of Evil', Expert Witnesses, 'War Against the Civilian Population (Militaristic/Ethnic/Gender based... Violence)', Session 1, Women's Court Proceedings, p. 120 (Krasniqi et al., Women's Court Proceedings).

destroyed in the war but entrenched masculine ethno-nationalist interests to the cost of all women.[21] As the expert witnesses describe, the patriarchal and ethno-nationalist restructuring of the post-conflict state meant '[t]he war legacy has imprinted the justice system in the new states, leaving them full of shortcomings', resulting in a 'flawed justice system'.[22] Institutional legal justice became a central issue for the feminist approach to justice because it is an integral part of the (re)production of patriarchal and ethno-nationalist power relations in these post-conflict societies, just as it is for other post-conflict contexts.[23]

The Women's Court shows that institutional legal justice is centrally important to feminist struggles to build more gender-just societies after the collective violence of war. This is because legal social bonds are a constitutive element of building that collective social life. The testimonies of the Women's Court highlight how institutional legal justice builds 'our relation to others', reproducing or transforming social inclusion or exclusion, and hierarchical relations of domination and subordination. Critical race feminists, such as Patricia Williams, have long pointed to the importance of legal social bonds for constructing the social existence of persons and their relations to others:

> [F]or the historically disempowered, the conferring of rights is symbolic of all the denied aspects of their humanity: rights imply a respect that places one in referential range of self and others, that elevates one's status from human body to social being [...] It is the magic wand of inclusion and exclusion, of power and no power. The concept of rights, both positive and negative, is the maker of citizenship, our relation to others.[24]

Like critical race feminism, the feminist approach to justice claims the rights of women survivors of war as social beings and as full members of their societies.

While the feminist approach to justice claims citizenship rights for women survivors of war, it also poses the problem of institutional legal justice in wider terms of social justice. As Iris Marion Young describes: 'social justice means the elimination of institutionalized domination and

---

[21] See Gorana Mlinarević and Nela Porobić Isaković, 'If Women Are Left out of Peace Talks', (2015) 50 Forced Migration Review, 34–37.
[22] Krasniqi et al., Women's Court Proceedings, pp. 120–121.
[23] See Fionnuala Ni Aoláin, Dina Haynes et al., *On the Frontlines* (Oxford: Oxford University Press, 2011).
[24] Patricia Williams, *The Alchemy of Race and Rights* (Cambridge, MA: Harvard University Press, 1991), p. 164.

oppression ... The concept of social justice includes all aspects of institutional rules and relations insofar as they are subject to potential collective decision.'[25] The question of social justice and 'collective decision' is crucial for the feminist approach to justice because collective harms of war affect all of society, and institutional legal justice is an integral element of rebuilding collective social life as such. As Marijana Senjak describes, '[w]ar trauma arises in a social context; **the recovery from the consequences of war trauma requires interventions on all social levels.**'[26] Because concrete collective injustices require concrete collective justice, it is necessary to address them at the level of social collectivity. Institutional legal justice is integral to the making of shared collective lives, and so it is an integral part of building collective justice. Such legal justice may be material, such as witness protection or reparations, or immaterial, such as the acknowledgement of crimes and their public sanction and stigmatisation.

Building collective social relations requires collective resources and organisation. The collective violence of war produces collective harms to the society, in that it destroys shared social bonds, as well as material and immaterial individual and collective goods. To construct new social bonds and goods requires collective material and symbolic capacities and resources. It also requires the organisation of those capacities and resources at a collective level. Individual or informal justice is important but insufficient to build such social collectives, as the feminist approach to justice itself acknowledges.[27] It confronts the post-war condition in which the capacities and resources of institutional legal justice and the state have been destroyed (in Bosnia, for example) or deformed (in Serbia, for example). It also confronts the failure to construct just collective forms of institutional legal systems and state, and the Women's Court witnesses testify to the collective consequences of the failure to build more just forms of legal justice.

The feminist approach to justice reveals both the necessity and the problem of institutional legal justice and the state as forms of organising collective social life. Unlike other transitional justice mechanisms, the feminist form of justice does not take the state as the unproblematic foundation of building collective social life for two reasons. First, it rejects

---

[25] Iris Marion Young, *Justice and the Politics of Difference* (Princeton: Princeton University Press, 1990), pp. 15–16.
[26] Senjak, Women's Court Proceedings, p. 143.
[27] Zajović, 'Witnesses at the Women's Court', pp. 62–65.

the patriarchal nation-state as the basis for building just societies. As Rada Iveković describes: '[i]t is only once *gender and nation* have been separated (instead of being purposely interconnected and mutually supportive in the masculinist hegemony of physical force), that it is possible to open *the space of justice and of truth*.'[28] Second, the feminist approach to justice aims to build 'transnational' legal justice beyond the state, as feminist justice has regional, international, and global dimensions.

The idea of regional justice is crucial for the feminist approach to justice. The Women's Court was organised for women from all the successor states of the former Yugoslavia. It required regional feminist justice because crimes were committed against women across the region as a whole and could not be dealt with if limited to successor states in isolation. Providing accountability and reparations for those crimes is not possible without regional institutional legal justice. Such regional justice also recognised that the destruction of the former Yugoslavia was a collective loss for all its citizens and that therefore new social bonds had to be built at a regional level.[29] Accordingly, new forms of justice for all citizens of the former Yugoslavia need to be built across the 'region'.

International justice is also an important element of the feminist form of justice for three reasons. First, there is the practical problem of prosecuting international crimes such as sexual violence in national jurisdictions, as the Women's Court shows. National criminal justice systems too often do not provide accountability for sexual violence crimes in peace time, and prosecutions of international crimes in national courts frequently reproduce these same failings. Such difficulties are worsened in post-conflict contexts, where national legal systems may be dysfunctional, captured by ethno-nationalist elites, or operate in divided communities. Moreover, national prosecutions do not engage with the wider criminal conduct of the war across the region. In this context, international courts can become the only instrument of justice, as the Women's Court participants describe the ICTY.

Second, such crimes have an important 'international' dimension. To characterise these harms as 'ordinary' crimes or individual civil wrongs under domestic law does not capture the context of the collective violence of war. So, for example, Witness MS describes how she fought

---

[28] Iveković, 'Violence and Healing', p. 127.
[29] As could be seen in the moving singing of Yugoslavian songs by the audience and witnesses at the Women's Court hearings on the Victory over Fascism Day, marking the capitulation of Nazi Germany on 9 May.

to have the killing of her neighbours by Croatian soldiers requalified from the domestic offence of 'murder out of the lowest motives' to the international offence of 'war crime'.[30] Characterising these experiences as international crimes emphasises their systemic quality, as well as their context of the collective violence of attacks on civilian populations, genocidal campaigns, or the illegal conduct of war. Without this characterisation, sexual violence crimes are not adequately included in the public narratives of the conflict or provide the public recognition of 'victims as right-holders entitled to redress' due to their experience of the conflict.[31]

Third, characterising this conduct as an international crime attributes social existence to victims not only as citizens of the state (that is, as rights-holders entitled to redress) but also as persons having social existence in the international legal order. In particular, characterising gender-based harms as international crimes sees 'women as equal and worthy members of "humanity". Prosecuting sexual violence against women in these authoritative institutions is an important expression of women's full membership in the global citizenry.'[32] The inclusion of women in the prohibitions upon international crimes gives rise to their 'social 'existence' in 'international society' and hence reorders those global social relations. It gives rise to responsibility for gender-based crimes, including obligations of prevention, prosecution, and reparation under international law, and of 'international society' to 'protect those under their care', as the Women's Court Preliminary Decision describes it.[33] As the Preliminary Decision sets out, both national states and the UN failed to protect the citizens of the former Yugoslavia. Such international responsibilities are seen as crucial for feminist justice, and the consequences of the failure to comply with these responsibilities can be seen in Women's Court testimonies. Without the status of social

---

[30] 'The Persecution of the Different at Wartime and Peacetime Alike – ethnic violence', Session 4, Women's Court Proceedings, pp. 228-229.

[31] See Nela Porobić Isaković and Gorana Mlinarević, *Concept and Framework for Development of a Gender Sensitive Reparations Framework for Civilian Victims of War in Bosnia and Herzegovina* (Geneva: Women's International League for Peace and Freedom, 2015), p. 9.

[32] Doris Buss, 'International Criminal Courts', in Jill Steans and Daniela Tepe-Belfrage (eds.), *Handbook on Gender in World Politics* (Cheltenham and Northampton MA: Edward Elgar, 2016), p. 165.

[33] Women's Court: Feminist Justice: Preliminary Decisions and Recommendations, Judicial Council, 9 May 2015, Women's Court, Sarajevo (Women's Court Preliminary Decision), p. 5.

existence in the international legal order, those subject to such collective violence are left to suffer as bare life. Such a position refuses international solidarity with global struggles against armed domination, which emerge with reactionary forces in the global social system.

Finally, the feminist approach to justice emphasises the importance of global justice. Because the global legal form is a constituent part of the making of international society, the feminist approach to justice confronts the problem of how to construct alternative forms of transnational legal social bonds that can build global emancipatory social relations. It seeks to contribute to the global feminist movement for justice for all and so needs to build alternative legal social bonds that are not based on the possessive individualism or state sovereignty of the global legal form. Instead, it needs to develop global legal social bonds based on the public goods necessary for the emancipatory social existence of all, which can then become a constituent element of the building of another global society. As such, the feminist approach to justice confronts the challenges of how to build institutional legal justice as part of the broader struggle for global justice.

In the feminist approach to justice, the institutional legal system has an important role in constructing just transnational social relations because it produces legal subjects and their relations to others. It reveals how legal social bonds are a constituent element of social reproduction, that is, the reproduction of the totality of social relations. This includes the reproduction of global social relations in their dominating and emancipatory forms. If gender relations are an essential part of the reproduction of the existing unjust social order, and institutional legal systems are in turn a constituent element of reproducing those inequitable power relations, then two challenges for the feminist approach to justice follow. First, it must engage with institutional legal systems if it is to change these forms of social reproduction. Second, it must change those systems so that they can operate as a constituent element of building just social relations. For this reason, the feminist approach to justice reveals the necessary but highly problematic task of engaging with institutional legal justice as a constituent element of the struggle to build emancipatory forms of regional, international, and global collective social life.

8.1.2 The Double Bind of the Global Legal Form of International Criminal Law

The Women's Court's ambivalent relationship to law reveals the double bind of the global legal form of international criminal law for feminist approaches to justice. On the one hand, international criminal law recognises victims as having social existence (as members of global society) rather than being bare life (as having mere physical existence). On the other hand, it also produces these very categories of humanity and bare life that shape the exclusions from global society that those victims suffer. The justice of law remains that which these victim-witnesses 'cannot not want to inhabit and yet must criticise'.[34]

This double bind echoes long-standing feminist debates in municipal jurisdictions concerning whether to reform or refuse law, particularly in the area of criminal law and sexual violence. The question has now sharply re-emerged in recent feminist debates on international criminal justice, which also broadly coalesce around two similar positions. The first position argues feminists should refuse to engage with international criminal law, and is exemplified by the work of Karen Engle and Janet Halley. It argues that feminist engagements with international criminal law inevitably become part of the exercise of governmental power. It describes such feminist engagements as 'governance feminism', which it claims now dominates international criminal law.[35] The argument rests on earlier Foucauldian critiques of national law and state, which contend that law is an inevitably disciplinary mechanism that reproduces normative identities and the repressive powers of the sovereign state.[36] The argument transposes this theory to the international level, arguing that 'governance feminism' participates in global forms of governmentality.[37] In essence, the argument concludes that feminism should not engage with international criminal law because to do so reproduces, rather than transforms, existing global power structures.

However, the 'refusal' position faces two fundamental problems. The first problem concerns its empirical and political assumptions. Empirically, it assumpes that governance feminism dominates international criminal law. However, it is incorrect to make this assumption for the ICTY. It neither focused upon sexual violence prosecutions nor

---

[34] Gayatri Chakravorty Spivak, *Outside in the Teaching Machine* (New York: Routledge, 2009), p. 70.
[35] Karen Engle, *The Grip of Sexual Violence* (Stanford: Stanford University Press, 2020), p. 14.
[36] See Wendy Brown and Janet Halley (eds.) *Left Legalism/Left Critique* (Durham and London: Duke University Press, 2002).
[37] Janet Halley, 'Where in the Legal Order Have Feminists Gained Inclusion', in Janet Halley, Prabha Kotiswaran et al. (eds.), *Governance Feminism* (Minneapolis and London: University of Minnesota Press, 2018), pp. 3–4.

did it characterise sexual violence as a gender-based harm. Feminists of any political view cannot be said to have dominated the ICTY. Politically, it also assumes (North American) ideas of sexual liberation. In this assumption, the argument in fact reproduces the same focus upon sexual violence that it critiques, as shown in its 'decontextualised' approach to consent in Chapter 3.[38] In effect, it privileges its concern with individual sexual liberation over the wider political and social concerns of women witnesses, survivors, and feminist activists in the former Yugoslavia. As a result, the argument fails to engage with the agency of women as subjects of justice, and their capacity for collective action, which are central to the feminist approach to justice.

The second, and related, problem is that feminist disengagement from international criminal law does not shift the existing global legal form or the global power relations of which it is a constituent part. International criminal law already operates to regulate the distinction between permissible and impermissible violence, and so to construct 'international society' as a particular social order. It is not the case that the legal regulation of sexual violence is simply present or absent (as discussed in Chapter 2). What may appear to be an absence of legal regulation in actuality forms a category of permissible violence. As Jennifer Nedelsky argues, law structures both legal accountability and impunity.[39] Law gives force to impunity, creating the space of 'legal impunity' or permissible violence.[40] This problem is particularly evident in the 'area of violence against women', a category of violence traditionally regarded as permissible and impunible.[41] It would be mistaken to understand the international criminalisation of sexual violence as the increasing exercise of sovereign power over a previously existing space of freedom. Rather, this category of conduct is already highly regulated by legal and social norms as to permissible and impermissible violence. It is the reality of socially sanctioned permissible violence against women in war and peace that the feminist approach to justice highlights. Ultimately, refusing international criminal law does not escape its double bind.

The second 'reformist' position argues that feminists should engage with international criminal law, and is exemplified by the work of

---

[38] See also Mara Grahn-Farley, 'The Politics of Inevitability', in Sari Kouvo and Zoe Pearson (eds.), *Feminist Perspectives on Contemporary International Law* (Oxford: Hart, 2011).
[39] Jennifer Nedelsky, *Law's Relations* (Oxford: Oxford University Press, 2011), p. 361.
[40] Ibid., p. 225.
[41] Ibid., p. 361.

Catherine O'Rourke and Fionnuala Ní Aoláin. Like the feminist approach to justice, it sees criminal accountability as important for the recognition of harms and the social stigmatisation of perpetrators and de-stigmatisation of victims and contends that not engaging with state and legal orders only further entrenches gender inequalities.[42] However, it also argues that it is necessary to reform international criminal law, given its patriarchal nature and limited effectiveness in providing gender justice.[43] Accordingly, the argument emphasises the importance of reforming the rules and institutions of international criminal law and of clearly understanding its role in effecting transformative gender justice. In essence, it advocates strategic feminist engagement with international criminal law.[44]

However, the 'reformist' position faces two crucial problems. First, feminists have struggled to reform international criminal law. Second, where such reforms have been possible, they provided uneven and incomplete gender justice (as discussed in Chapter 6). Such reforms involved limited changes to substantive offences such as sexual violence rather than changing customary international norms as a whole. They were also unevenly developed within particular institutions, such as the ICTY, rather than implemented in all national and international prosecutions of international crimes. These struggles raise the question of whether it is possible to develop feminist strategies that can change the existing form of international criminal law as such.

The question of legal strategies is central to the 'reform or revolution' debate in recent Marxist international legal theory and can be said to mirror the 'reform or refuse' problem within feminist debates.[45] The recent Marxist debates emerge with the resurgence of interest in Pashukanis, following the publication of China Miéville's *Between Equal Rights*. For Miéville, '[t]o fundamentally change the dynamics of the system, it would be necessary not to reform the institutions but to

---

[42] See, for example, Ni Aoláin, Haynes et al., *On the Frontlines*; Catherine O'Rourke, *Gender Politics in Transitional Justice* (Abingdon and New York: Routledge, 2014).

[43] Fionnuala Ní Aoláin, 'Gendered Harms and Their Interface with International Criminal Law', 16(4) (2014) International Feminist Journal of Politics, 622–646, 623.

[44] Catherine O'Rourke, *Women's Rights in Armed Conflict under International Law* (Cambridge: Cambridge University Press, 2020), p. 25.

[45] Robert Knox, 'Marxist Approaches to International Law' in Anne Orford and Florian Hoffmann (eds), *The Oxford Handbook of the Theory of International Law* (Oxford: Oxford University Press, 2016), p. 325.

eradicate the forms of law'.[46] Accordingly, to change the global social system requires revolution against global capitalism. However, as Chimni observes, it seems 'foolhardy to refuse to seek "reform" of the international legal system at a time when world revolution is pipe dream'.[47] Indeed, Lenin's analysis of the 'infantile disorder' of 'left-wing communism' is instructive here.[48] As Paul Hirst describes, the problem here is that 'the key Leninist criterion for evaluating political practices in relation to the state, the thesis of its "withering away", is postulated as a necessity of the process of transition to communism rather than as an objective to be pursued in struggle'.[49]

Pashukanis himself followed the Leninist strategy of using 'legal opportunities' according to the concrete historical context and did not reject the use of law for revolutionary purposes, as Robert Knox points out.[50] Pashukanis describes this strategy as 'the recognition of the real significance of a type of legal form which is used in a specific situation, and as a well-known and very necessary method of struggle'.[51] Both feminist engagements with international criminal law and the feminist approach to justice of the Women's Court also recognise that strategic use of law as a very necessary method of feminist struggle. However, they also show that it is not possible to simply use international criminal law in its existing form. Rather, if feminists are to use international criminal law in this way, then they must also seek to change it.

Accordingly, the strategic use of law raises the question of transitional legal forms, which concerns whether it is possible to develop legal forms that can be used as part of the struggle to create emancipatory social relations. The transitional legal form is a long-standing problem in Marxist theory and politics. It concerns the form of law and state in 'transitional' revolutionary and socialist periods between capitalism and 'complete communism', when it is posited that the state and law will wither away. Pashukanis does not offer an alternative theory of socialist forms of justice, other than to advocate non-legal principles of social

---

[46] China Miéville, *Between Equal Rights* (London: Pluto, 2005), p. 318.
[47] Bhupinder Chimni, *International Law and World Order* (Cambridge: Cambridge University Press, 2017), p. 521.
[48] Vladimir Lenin, *'Left-Wing' Communism* (Moscow: Progress, 1968).
[49] Paul Hirst, *On Law and Ideology* ((London: Macmillan, 1979), p. 6.
[50] Robert Knox, 'Marxism, International Law, and Political Strategy', (2009) 22(3) LJIL 413–436, 429.
[51] Evgeny Pashukanis, *Selected Writings on Marxism and Law* (London: Academic Press, 1980), p. 139.

protection and rehabilitation.[52] He rejected ideas of 'proletarian law' in the period of socialist transition. However, he also acknowledged the importance of the legal form, and its dialectical nature, in this transitional process.[53] If law was to be used 'during the transition, then it had to be refashioned to keep it open to new matrixes of freedom that class struggle could determine'.[54] The transitional role of law in the struggle to construct a socialist society remained a central but unresolved theoretical problem in Pashukanis' work (and the political problem for which he was executed by Stalin). The transitional role of law was also a crucial problem for the anti-Stalinist Yugoslavian state, which emphasised that the socialist state and law should themselves be understood as transitional, in that they should be seen as part of the transition to a fully communist society.[55] In this transitional period, the Yugoslavian Constitution and Criminal Code emphasised the 'socially protective' role of law.[56] Both criminal law and international law were seen as important areas of socialist law, and crimes under international law were recognised from the establishment of the Yugoslavian state onwards.

The problem of legal and social transition confronts the feminist approach to justice. As Iveković describes, the Women's Court attempts to construct a feminist approach to justice in the context of transition: '1. after the war, peace; 2. after socialism, capitalism'.[57] The Women's Court is situated in two moments of transition. The first transition is the destruction of the Yugoslavian state and society in war and the emergence of the successor states in post-war (negative) 'peace'. This is a transitional period of crisis in state and society, and their rebuilding after the war. The second transition is from socialism to capitalism and the intensification of global capitalist social relations in the former Yugoslavia. Both these transitions emerge in the shifting global force relations described in Chapter 6. Iveković describes the transition to peace and capitalism as being mutually contradictory, and this critique should be read in the context of the Yugoslavian idea of transitional

---

[52] Evgeny Pashukanis, *Law and Marxism* (London: Ink Links, 1978), pp. 185–188.
[53] Ibid., p. 63.
[54] Antonio Negri, 'Rereading Pashukanis', 2017 5(2) Stasis, 8–49, 46.
[55] See Ivo Lappenna, *State and Law* (London: Athlone, 1964).
[56] *Criminal Code of the Socialist Federal Republic of Yugoslavia* 1 July 1977; Constitution of the Socialist Federal Republic of Yugoslavia, 21 February 1974. The idea of protection of the 'socialist self-management social system' also gave rise to the most repressive aspects of Yugoslavian state security and criminal law.
[57] Iveković, 'Violence and Healing', p. 131.

socialism. She also argues that the Women's Court adds a third important meaning to this problem of transition: '3. *after patriarchy – its dissolution*'.[58] Accordingly, the political problem of transition must engage with 'the intertwinement of those three elements (sex, class, and nation) this would predict the much-anticipated exit from the existent order'.[59] In the struggle to create a transition from the existent order to new forms of collective social life, the feminist approach to justice emerges.

The transitional period in the former Yugoslavia can be described as a situation of 'dual power' – of social and state crisis and emerging counterpowers – that can emerge in the contradictory dynamics of the changing globalising world.[60] On the one side, there is the failure of state power, with the collapse of the state in war at the national level, and changing inter-state relations and shifting global forces at the international level. On the other side, there is the emergence of new forms of collective co-operation, providing the conditions for the creation of (anti-capitalist, imperialist, patriarchal) values and (non-state) organisation of the Women's Court. The feminist approach to justice can be seen as a transitional dual power strategy, which 'breaking away from neoliberal governance and developing practices of counterpower ... create[s] institutions of being and producing together'.[61] However, the feminist approach to justice does not follow the militaristic dual power theory of the Marxist tradition. Rather, it develops practices of counterpower through the creation of an institution based in self-governing, democratic, and feminist values, which enable alternative ways of 'being and producing together'.

In our concrete historical conjuncture, the appropriate framing of a feminist approach to international criminal law is neither reform nor revolution. Rather, it is 'transition' in the socialist sense of the struggle to create the conditions for the emergence of new forms of social organisation. Within this frame, it becomes possible to more accurately describe feminist struggles for gender justice in international criminal law as 'non-reformist reform', following Nancy Fraser. Such institutional reforms

---

[58] Ibid.
[59] Ibid.
[60] On contemporary dual power theory, see Slavoj Žižek (ed.), *Fredric Jameson, An American Utopia* (London and New York: Verso, 2016).
[61] Michael Hardt and Antonio Negri, *Assembly* (New York: Oxford University Press, 2017), p. 245.

have a 'double face': 'on the one hand they engage people's identities and satisfy some of their needs as interpreted within existing frameworks of recognition and distribution; on the other hand, they set in motion a trajectory of change in which more radical reforms become practicable over time.'[62] In these terms, gender justice struggles achieved non-reformist reform by engaging with women's identities and satisfying some of their needs within the existing framework of international criminal law. These non-reformist reforms not only involved the strategic use of the existing framework but also changing international criminal law itself. By developing new gender justice rules, practices, and values in the ICTY, feminist struggles changed the existing framework of international criminal law. In this way, they set in motion a trajectory of change, which 'alters the terrain on which later struggles will be waged [and] expand the feasible set of options for future reform'.[63] As such, these struggles provided a necessary condition for building new feminist strategies for more radical reform of international criminal law. It is now essential to use the political possibilities opened by such feminist non-reformist reforms and take the next step of building a feminist approach to international criminal law.

To take this next step involves refashioning international criminal law to keep it open to new matrixes of freedom that feminist struggle can determine (to paraphrase Negri). It requires a feminist transitional strategy of building new global legal social bonds, as part of the struggle to create the conditions for the emergence of new emancipatory forms of social organisation and life. This is because every transitional conjuncture is as much global as it is national. If the global legal form of international criminal law constructs 'international society' through the categories of social existence and bare life, and hence is an integral part of the making of 'international society', then it becomes necessary to consider how to construct alternative forms of global legal bonds. The feminist approach to justice challenges us to consider how such global legal bonds might contribute to the building of a global society based on the public goods necessary for social existence of all. Within this frame, the feminist approach to justice can be seen as a practice of counterpower that seeks to co-operatively build new justice institutions and new forms of global

---

[62] Nancy Fraser, 'Social Justice in the Age of Identity Politics', in Nancy Fraser and Axel Honneth (eds), *Redistribution or Recognition?* (London and New York: Verso, 2003), p. 79.
[63] Ibid., pp. 79–80.

legal bonds as part of a wider struggle for global justice. It points to the possibilities of other forms of legal justice produced by the contradictory dynamics of our changing globalising world.

8.2 Building a Feminist Conceptual Framework for International Criminal Law

How, then, to develop a feminist approach to international criminal law? The feminist approach to justice does not provide an alternative model of legal social bonds. Rather, it is necessary to develop such a model from the general concepts of the feminist approach to justice. Accordingly, I develop its feminist concepts of harms, subjects, justice proceedings, and justice as legal concepts. The feminist legal concepts of crime, legal subjects, legal proceedings, and international criminal justice can then serve as the basis for building an alternative framework for a feminist approach to international criminal law.

8.3 Towards a Feminist Concept of Gender-Based Harms as International Crimes

To construct the alternative feminist legal framework, I begin by developing a 'feminist injustice' model of international criminalisation. The model builds on the thematic crimes of the Women's Court. To do this, I use Adrian Howe's 'social injury' strategy, which aims to address the group dimensions of gender-based harms, to develop the thematic crimes as a model of international criminalisation. Howe first develops the idea of 'social injury' as a feminist strategy for describing gender-based harms as legally cognisable claims and obtaining legal redress or remedy.[64] She argues that within legal discourse, we should focus on 'the distinctive aspect of women's experiences ... of our injuries: we should envalue them, politicise them, and, when necessary demand that they become actionable or even that they be criminalised.'[65] While Howe's strategy focuses on civil claims (that is, civil actions against persons or state), it is also useful for feminist strategies in international criminal law. It enables the shift from current ideas of harms to the individual person or to international society in international criminal law and to develop the

---

[64] Adrian Howe, 'The Problem of Privatised Injuries', in Martha Fineman (ed.), *At the Boundaries of Law* (London, Routledge: 1990), p. 154.
[65] Adrian Howe, '"Social Injury" Revisited', (1987) 15 Int'l J Soc L 428–438, 434.

collective and structural idea of injustice in the feminist approach to justice.

The concept of social injury reconceptualises violence against women as socially created harms, which are group-based and gender-specific. The social injury strategy captures the 'social dimension of women's experience' by focusing upon how subordination harms women as a group. Like the feminist approach to justice, the idea of social injury is a 'materially grounded concept because it is based in the materiality of women's gender-specific injuries'.[66] This materially grounded concept has three elements. The first is the criminological concept of 'aggregate social harm', which is

> 'those injuries, diseases and material losses that are suffered by individuals and are a consequence of deliberate policy or intentional behaviour'. It is conduct which is 'collective' and foreseeable 'in an objective sense' even if there is no direct connection between the perpetrator and the ultimate damage.[67]

The second is the idea of group-based injury, that is, injuries to members of a group. These are harms to a class of persons, who become members of the group because they suffer the aggregate social harm produced by the wrongful conduct. The third element is the idea of gender-specific injury, where injury is constructed by gender relations. These are injuries that are constructed by structural and systemic forms of wrongful conduct. I build on this social injury strategy to develop the feminist injustice model of international crimes, which consists of three components: (1) concrete injustice, (2) social injury, and (3) system violence.

8.3.1 Concrete Injustice

The feminist approach to justice begins from concrete injustice, in the sense of wrongful damage or injury to persons and their collective social life. It builds new concepts of crimes by (1) identifying concrete descriptions of injustice by women, (2) recognising the different forms of violence in these descriptions, and (3) analysing these forms of violence as structural injustices. In contrast, the global legal form constructs international crimes through abstract ideas of harm to the person (namely, physical integrity, human dignity, sexual autonomy, and

---

[66] Adrian Howe, 'The Problem of Privatised Injuries', p. 163.
[67] Ibid., p. 161.

equality of persons) and harm to the abstract protected interests of international society (namely, the breach of positive international law and the violation of universal values that harm global human society), as described in Chapter 2. It conceives criminality as harm to the abstract qualities of persons and the abstract entity of 'international society', disconnected from actually existing global social relations.

Instead of beginning with abstract ideas of harm, the feminist approach to justice is anchored in concrete social life. It begins from women's experiences of concrete injustice, which can be described as the 'injuries, diseases, and material losses' of social harms outlined in the social injury strategy. The feminist approach to justice describes these injustices as encompassing a range of physical, emotional, economic, and social harms. It characterises these injustices not only as gender-based harms, which concern the adverse (or discriminatory) treatment of women in war. Rather, it understands them more broadly as gendered injustices, which recognises how social and political power shapes the gendered experience and effects of war. The feminist approach to justice connects these experiences of injustice not only to power within the nation-state but also to power relations within the existing global order.

In essence, international criminalisation should capture these concrete injustices. To conceptualise concrete injustice as the ground of criminality involves four elements. The first is to include women's experiences of the injustices of war. The second is to use the descriptions of these experiences of injustice to identify the range of harms that women experience. The third is to use the descriptions of concrete injustice as the conceptual basis for generating collective categories of violence. The fourth is to use these categories of violence as the basis for generating crime categories and for legally characterising these harms as crimes.

8.3.2 Social Injury

The feminist injustice model of criminalisation describes concrete injustices as social injuries. Accordingly, the second component of the model is social injuries, which harm classes of persons individually and collectively. They are aggregate social harms, in the sense that they not only comprise multiple incidents of individual harms but also combine them together to form a 'whole' class of harms, which have distinctive properties or characteristics. As such, these concrete injustices necessarily have a collective dimension, and are group-based injuries. They are harms to a class of persons, who become members of the group because they suffer the aggregate social harm produced by the wrongful conduct.

The feminist injustice model understands gender-based harms as injuring persons as members of social groups, building on Howe's idea that 'social injuries' produce their victims as subordinated social groups. In the context of national legal systems, Howe's social injury strategy describes how social inequalities produce injuries to groups: 'harms to women [are] injuries endured by virtue of membership of a minority status social group.'[68] Harms to women are associated with their status as a subordinated social group. In the context of international crimes, collective violence remakes that social group, a process that involves the distinctive use of violence to create *and* destroy classes of persons. This distinctive use of violence harms the social subjectivity of persons, as it makes them into members of particular subordinated groups and refuses them social existence on this basis. Accordingly, the harm involves injuries to persons as social as well as physical subjects. As such, the collective violence of war makes new socially subordinated groups. It constitutes that class of persons as a group with particular characteristics and as a group affected by wrongful conduct.

In the context of international crimes, gender-based harms injure a class of persons, who as a group suffer 'inhibited status' due to an attack or disproportionate effect upon them (to use the language of CEDAW).[69] As the Women's Court testimonies show, these harms injure 'the status, safety, and value of women as a group'.[70] Like 'adverse distinction' in humanitarian law, gender-based harms consist of the adverse treatment of a class of persons that creates their secondary social status. The social injuries are gender-specific, because they produce hierarchical sexual differentiation between men and women. For example, conflict-related sexual violence constructs persons as groups with particular characteristics, such as 'Muslim women', and as a class of persons suffering particular injuries, such as physical or social harm. As such, it makes social groups through the iterative injuries of sexual violence. The feminist injustice model therefore reconceptualises gender-based harms as the production of victims as a gender class, understood as a class of persons

---

[68] Adrian Howe, and Maureen Cain, 'Introduction', in Maureen Cain and Adrian Howe (eds.) *Women, Crime and Social Harm* (Oxford: Hart, 2008), p. 3.
[69] Fionnuala Ní Aoláin, 'Exploring a Feminist Theory of Harm in the Context of Conflicted and Post-Conflict Societies', (2009) 35(1) QLJ 219–244, 224.
[70] Ibid.

sexually differentiated by social relations of domination and subordination and subjected to violence on that basis.

The feminist injustice model emphasises that the social injuries of collective violence produce not only social groups of victims but also social groups of perpetrators. Dubravka Žarkov insists that 'the "ethnic war" in the Balkans should not even be conceptualised as a war *between ethnic groups*, but rather as a war that produced *ethnic groups*' of both victims and perpetrators.[71] This is because the symbolic and material structures of collective violence produce group patterns of perpetration as well as victimisation. For example, two victim-witnesses at the Women's Court describe how a small group of armed soldiers detained them with other family members, before holding them separately for sexual assault and release.[72] These assaults might be described as so-called 'opportunistic' rapes, that is, unplanned and individually motivated sexual violence. However, to do so would be inaccurate. The so-called 'opportunistic' rape occurs in the context of the collective organisation of violence, which produces collective action (perpetrators who are armed because of their group membership) and meaning (victims targeted as members of an 'enemy' group), and collectively sanctioned violence. The feminist injustice model understands such concrete injustices as social injuries, which involve collective victimisation and perpetration. These concrete injustices create collective victims and perpetrators through system violence.

8.3.3 System Violence

The third component of the feminist injustice model is system violence. The Women's Court Preliminary Decision characterises the thematic crimes as forms of structural violence and injustice, which are collective and systemic in their nature. The feminist injustice model builds on this idea and develops it as a concept of system violence. System violence consists of systemic oppression and domination, where that system consists of interacting structures of collective violence. This is because '[f]eminism must not settle with revealing gender violence only, since feminism also deals with the entire structural violence. Women's

---

[71] Dubravka Žarkov, 'Feminism and the Disintegration of Yugoslavia', 2003 24(3) Social Development Issues 59–68, 66.
[72] Witness JC, pp. 125–127; Witness EK, pp. 133–135, 'The Woman's Body – A Battlefield - Sexual Violence in the War Zones', Session 2, Women's Court Proceedings.

testifying about intertwining of various forms of violence is also feminist. During this process, women never talked about just one form of violence' in the Women's Court.[73]

8.3.3.1 Systemic Oppression and Domination

To develop this account of system violence, I take up Daša Duhaček's argument that Iris Marion Young's concern with 'the structural problems of oppression and domination as defining issues of injustice ... comes very close to the concepts of Women's Court'.[74] For Marion Young, injustice consists of oppression and domination that 'immobilise or diminish a group', through institutional constraints on self-development or self-determination.[75] Oppression and domination can be said to produce social injuries to groups by constraining their self-development or self-determination. However, Marion Young only provides a schematic description of rape as a form of violence and warfare as a form of oppression and domination.

How then might we capture the structural and systemic nature of the thematic crimes of the Women's Court? Marion Young's later concept of 'structural injustice' develops her idea of the structural and systemic character of oppression and domination:

> Structural injustice, then, exists when social processes put large groups of persons under systematic threat of domination or deprivation of the means to develop and exercise their capacities, at the same time that these processes enable others to dominate or to have a wide range of opportunities for developing and exercising capacities available to them ... Structural injustice occurs as a consequence of many individuals and institutions acting to pursue their particular goals and interests.[76]

Marion Young describes structural injustice as 'ordinary injustice', 'for the most part within the limits of accepted rules and norms', and explicitly distinguishes ordinary injustice from 'systematically perpetuated genocide', which is not.[77] Nevertheless her concept of structural injustice is very useful for understanding international crimes, because it

---

[73] Zajović, 'The Women's Court', p. 15.
[74] Daša Duhaček, 'Women's Court', in Zajović, (ed.), *Women's Court: About the Process*, p. 85.
[75] Marion Young, *Justice and the Politics of Difference*, p. 42, p. 37.
[76] Iris Marion Young, *Responsibility for Justice* (Oxford: Oxford University Press, 2010), p. 52.
[77] Ibid., p. 93.

emphasises how social processes create the systemic domination and deprivation of capacities of groups of persons while enabling other groups of persons to dominate and develop their capacities. Building on this concept, the system violence of the Women's Court thematic crimes can be understood as the systemic domination and deprivation of capacities of groups of persons, which enable other groups to dominate or exercise their capacities. Accordingly, the feminist injustice strategy focuses on understanding the 'power relationships and structures' that produce groups through the systemic deprivation and exercise of capacities in collective coercive violence rather than understanding their 'social identity' as the core cause of conflict.[78] In this approach, war itself is a form of system violence that creates structural injustice.

8.3.3.2 Coercive Collective Violence

The Women's Court Preliminary Decision describes this system violence as the 'context of the crimes: war as systemic criminality'. The Preliminary Decision identifies eight forms of system violence, which involve both physical and symbolic violence. These interacting structures include (1) political, military, economic, and security leadership, (2) intellectual elites, (3) militaries, paramilitaries, and other armed groups, (4) media, (5) professions (such as law and medicine), (6) government and administration, (7) religious institutions and leaders, and (8) international institutions and states.[79] In addition, other systems could also include industry and business, and political parties (as was the case in the Nuremberg Control Law No. 10 trials).

In the feminist injustice model, these forms of system violence share three characteristics. First, system violence includes different forms of violence, ranging from physical violence (such as the direct force that kills persons) to symbolic violence (such as ideologies of social inclusion and exclusion). Second, it involves violence that is both collective and coercive. Charles Tilly argues that collective violence 'involves at least two perpetrators of damage and some coordination between perpetrators. Below that threshold, we call violence individual.'[80] For Tilly, forms of collective violence are coercive if they involve 'interactions

---

[78] Dubravka Žarkov, 'Intersectionality – A Critical Intervention', in Kirsten Campbell, Regina Mühlhäuser et al. (eds.), *In Plain Sight* (New Delhi: Zubaan, 2019), p. 223.
[79] Women's Court Preliminary Decision, p. 5.
[80] Charles Tilly, *The Politics of Collective Violence* (Cambridge: Cambridge University Press, 2003), p. 13.

which produce direct damage to persons and objects'.[81] He calls these forms of collective violence 'co-ordinated destruction', which is the co-ordinated 'deployment of coercive means [to] undertake programs of actions that damages persons and/or objects'.[82] It involves the organisation of collective violence, which combines the activation of symbolic and material resources and the incorporation of multiple social actors. Forms of collective violence include war, genocide, colonialism, and terrorism (and state violence in his earlier work).

System violence, then, is a form of coercive collective violence. Drawing on the Foucauldian idea of violence discussed in Chapter 6, we can more precisely say that this form of coercive collective violence has a particular capacity to affect through force. For Foucault, violence is 'a relationship', which 'acts upon a body or upon thing; it forces, it bends, it breaks, it destroys, or it closes off all possibilities'.[83] It is relational because it is an action upon a person or thing, which turns them into an object through the direct application of force. In these terms, violence is the capacity to change or destroy the object, which is the capacity to affect through force. If system violence is the capacity of an action to affect through force, then its efficacy lies in the intensity of forces in the action. It creates a relation to the object, and the capacity to do so in turn draws upon on a plurality of forces. This approach suggests system violence takes different forms, which have different capacity to change or destroy, and have different objects.

System violence should be understood as a continuum of collective violence, which consists of relations of forces ranging across a spectrum of intensity, form, object, and actors. Different violent acts involve different relations of force to, and capacities to affect, the object of violence. The concept of a continuum of collective violence provides an alternative conceptualisation of the 'international' element of international crimes. International criminality lies not in the degree of organisation or scale of violence but in the creation of systems of coercive collective violence that increase the capacity to act directly upon individuals and collectives. System violence intensifies the forces in the coercive action of violence, that is, the capacity to change or destroy the object upon which the force acts. Rather than consisting of a single act of an

---

[81] Charles Tilly, *From Mobilization to Revolution* (New York: Random House, 1978), p. 177.
[82] Tilly, *The Politics of Collective Violence*, p. 103.
[83] Michel Foucault, 'The Subject and Power', in James Faubion (ed.), *Power* (London: Penguin, 2000), p. 340.

individual upon an object, system violence involves collective actors, processes, and resources. This intensifies and amplifies the capacity to directly change or to destroy the objects of violence. The generative force of violence produces the aggregate harms of social injuries, the groups of victims that suffer them, and the groups of perpetrators that enact them. The criminality of system violence lies in its creation of systems of collective coercive violence that create structural injustice.

Reinscribing sexual violence as a gender-based harm into the concept of system violence reframes it through feminist theories of the gendered continuum of violence against women. With this reframing, it also becomes possible to describe system violence more precisely as a gendered continuum, which has two dimensions. First, system violence consists of different forms of gendered violence. This concept of system violence builds upon feminist arguments that sexual violence is a part of a wide range of violence against women, in which the violence is structured through (heteronormative) gender norms and relations.[84] These forms of violence (re)produce hierarchical gender norms (ideas of what it is to be a man or a woman) and gender relations (the economic, political, and social organisation of relations between men and women). Accordingly, violence against women 'is situated along a continuum both in terms of time and space, and the varied forms and manifestations reflect this'.[85] Second, these different forms of violence against women reflect a continuum of gendered violence between war and peace. This concept of system violence builds on feminist arguments concerning the connections between gender relations and gender violence in peace and war and emphasises the continuity of peace-time and war-time gendered violence. As Cynthia Cockburn argues, gender relations and violence persist across 'preconflict, conflict, peacemaking, reconstruction', and these gender relations shape the different forms and effects of violence in the continuum of collective violence.[86] Drawing on these ideas, we can describe the thematic crimes described by the Women's Court as a gendered continuum of system violence.

---

[84] Caroline Moser, 'The Gendered Continuum of Violence and Conflict', in Caroline Moser and Fiona Clark (eds.), *Victims, Perpetrators or Actors?* (New York: Palgrave Macmillan, 2001), pp. 36-7. This idea was first developed by Liz Kelly.
[85] Rashida Manjoo, 'The Continuum of Violence against Women and the Challenges of Effective Redress', (2012) 1(1) Int'l Hum Rts Rev 1-29, 27.
[86] Cynthia Cockburn, 'The Continuum of Violence', in Wenona Giles and Jennifer Hyndman (eds.), *Sites of Violence* (Berkeley: University of California Press, 2004), p. 43.

8.3.3.3 Social (Re)Production in System Violence

System violence is an integral part of the production and reproduction of structural injustice, that is, social relations of oppression and domination.[87] The Women's Court Preliminary Decision describes how, '[t]ogether, the testimonies reveal that these crimes were made possible by systems of criminality, which reinforce and intensify unequal power relations between men and women'.[88] For example, the Preliminary Decision describes the militarisation of women's lives and '[m]aking women the symbolic and material carriers of burdens of war, including the reinforcement of gendered stereotypes and the disproportionate impact on women of loss of family members, unemployment, and intolerant exclusionary social structures' as part of the system criminality of war.[89] Its description of the thematic crimes reveals how conflict reproduces and amplifies social structures of gendered oppression and domination, that is, the structural injustice of peace-time 'patriarchal systems of ... beliefs, values, and relationships'.[90] It shows that patriarchal ideas and relationships are part of the social process of war, revealing 'the ideal types of "masculinity" and "femininity" as they constituted in a patriarchal society in a state of war'.[91]

The concept of the gendered nature of system violence shows how it (re)produces patriarchal social relations. If we understand patriarchy as a sex/gender system, as Gayle Rubin suggested in her earlier work, then the subordination of women is seen as a 'product of the relationships by which sex and gender are organized and produced'.[92] Gendered system violence (re)produces this sex/gender system, producing the subordination of women in violence. As Catia Confortini argues, violence is integral to the construction of 'hegemonic masculinity ... Since gender is a practice produced and reproduced through social relations, violence can be seen as a method for the reproduction of the "gender order"'.[93] As such, gender relations are integral to violence, because '[v]iolence and

---

[87] My thanks to Marina Veličković and Gorana Mlinarević for our discussions of structural violence.
[88] Women's Court Preliminary Decision, p. 5.
[89] Ibid., p. 2.
[90] Cynthia Enloe, *The Big Push* (Berkeley: University of California Press, 2017), p. 21.
[91] Marina Blagojević, 'Preface', in Vesna Nikolić-Ristanović (ed.), *Women, Violence and War* (Budapest: Central European University Press, 2000), p. xi.
[92] Gayle Rubin, *Deviations* (Durham, NC: Duke University Press, 2011), p. 47.
[93] Catia Confortini, 'Galtung, Violence, and Gender' (2006) 31(3) Peace & Change, 333–367, 353.

gender are involved in a relationship of mutual constitution'.[94] System violence creates not only social groups of women (and men) as feminised victims of these injustices but also social groups of men as masculinised 'agents of collective patriarchal destruction'.[95] Because of its collective and coercive nature, system violence reinforces and intensifies the peacetime structural injustice of patriarchal power relations between men and women. It enables the creation of the systemic domination and deprivation of capacities of groups of (sexed and gendered) persons and enables other (sexed and gendered) groups to dominate or exercise their capacities through collective violence. Because systems of collective patriarchal violence increase the capacity to act directly upon individuals and collectives, they intensify and amplify the (re)production of the existing gender order.

Such gendered system violence, then, complicates the conceptual dichotomies between what Galtung calls direct violence (the intentional physical violence of individual actors upon others) and indirect violence (the violence of social structures that harm persons).[96] As Rashida Manjoo describes, violence against women is 'a continuum that spans interpersonal and structural violence'.[97] System violence is both direct, as it involves physical and symbolic violence that directly acts on its object, and indirect, in that it consists of systemic social structures that produce structural injustice. As such, it displaces Marion Young's distinction between direct physical violence ('the wrongful action of an individual agent or the repressive policies of a state') and structural injustice (the social structures that deprive or enable large groups to exercise and develop their capacities). Rather than reproducing these dichotomies, the concept of system violence can capture how 'direct violence is a tool used to build, perpetuate, and reproduce structural violence', including patriarchal gender orders such as those described by the thematic crimes of the Women's Court.[98]

---

[94] Ibid., 355.
[95] Blagojević, 'Preface', p. xi.
[96] Johan Galtung, 'Violence, Peace, and Peace Research' (1969) 6(3) Journal of Peace Research, 167–191, 170. Galtung later develops a third category of cultural violence, that is, symbolic violence that legitimates direct or structural violence: Johan Galtung, 'Cultural Violence', (1990) 27(3) Journal of Peace Research 291–305. Nevertheless, the distinction between direct and structural violence remains. My thanks to Maria O'Reilly for our discussion of Galtung.
[97] Manjoo, 'The Continuum of Violence against Women', 27.
[98] Confortini, 'Galtung, Violence, and Gender', 350.

The same conceptual dichotomies inform Marion Young's critique of liberal 'liability' models of crimes that focus on individual actors rather than seeing 'structure as the subject of justice'.[99] They also reappear in important critiques of the liberal legal form of international criminal law. These critiques argue that international criminal law only criminalises individual actors engaged in 'exceptional violence' rather than the 'structural' or 'slow' violence of political and economic structures that produce these crimes and accordingly does not change those structures.[100] However, system violence is not an effect but is an integral part of structural violence. Building on Confortini's work, David Graeber argues:

> [i]n all these formulations, 'structural violence' is treated as structures that have violent effects, whether or not actual physical violence is involved ... the ultimate problem with Galtung's approach ... is that it views 'structures' as a free floating entities, when what we are referring to here are material *processes*, in which violence, and the threat of violence, play a crucial, constitutive role.[101]

Crucially, the concept of system violence captures how systems of collective violence are material processes that play a crucial constitutive role in the (re)production of social relations, including their production of systemic injustice. As Iveković argues:

> The testimonies, to start with, cannot easily be categorised as dealing separately with economic, ethnic, sexual or militarist violence. We then claim that a great deal of such long-term, diverse and brutality has been turned into constant *structural violence* so that we nowadays live in violent societies. The first thing that we observe is that there is a continuity between those supposedly separate forms of violence, and that *all, each and every one* of them, can be classified as political, but also as social, in addition to the specific qualification of each of them. Another continuity that we observe is the one between the war and the post-war violence.[102]

---

[99] Marion Young, *Responsibility for Justice*, p. 97ff. Although Marion Young does not refer to Galtung, her idea of 'structural injustice' can be considered analogous to Galtung's understanding of structural violence as social injustice.

[100] See, for example, Tor Krever, 'International Criminal Law', (2013) 26(3) LJIL 701–723; Sarah Nouwen, 'As You Set Out for Ithaka', (2014) 27(1) LJIL 227–260; and Mark Drumbl, 'Collective Violence and Individual Punishment', (2005) 99(2) NWULR 539–610.

[101] David Graeber, 'Dead Zones of the Imagination', (2012) 2(2) HAU: Journal of Ethnographic Theory, 105–128, 114.

[102] Iveković, 'Violence and Healing', p. 105.

System violence should not be seen as an effect of structural or slow violence but as an integral part of the (re)production of the global social system, including the patriarchal, capitalist, neoliberal social relations of globalisation described in Chapter 6. Taken together, the thematic crimes of the Women's Court describe interlocking systems of violence, which form an integral part of (re)production of these social relations in the Yugoslavian conflicts and post-conflict former Yugoslavia.

8.3.3.4 International Criminalisation as the Prohibition of System Violence

The concept of system violence provides the basis for developing an alternative understanding of criminalisation under international law. It does not reduce the criminalisation of 'international' violence to notions of armed conflict, that is, wars between or within states, and so recognises that it is possible to commit international crimes in times of 'peace' as well as war. Instead, it conceptualises the proper object of international criminalisation as system violence, which involves collective coercive physical or symbolic violence that intensifies the capacity to change or destroy the objects upon which it acts and which creates forms of structural injustice. The approach reconceptualises the 'international' dimension of international crimes, namely, the existence of an armed conflict, attack on a civilian population, or destruction of a protected group, as structural injustice. These are interacting systems of coercive collective violence that put groups of persons under systematic threat of domination or deprivation of the means to develop and exercise their capacities while also enabling other groups to dominate or benefit from developing and exercising capacities available to them because of their participation in those systems. From this social perspective, the protected interest of international criminal law is not the individual rights of persons or of 'international society' but the production of structural injustice by coercive collective violence.

8.3.4 Reconceptualising Conflict-Related Sexual Violence through the Feminist Injustice Model

The feminist injustice model provides three theoretical strategies for reconceptualising conflict-related sexual violence as a gender-based crime. These strategies reframe sexual violence through the concepts of gender relations, gendered injustice, and gendered system violence.

The first theoretical strategy is to understand conflict-related sexual violence in terms of *gender relations* rather than understanding gender as an individual or group characteristic. This approach reframes the concept of sexual violence in terms of Butler's theory of gender. In her theory, the construction of gender norms over time by the repetition of acts continually makes the category of 'gender'.[103] In other words, 'gender' is made by doing or 'performing' particular acts that bring into existence 'gender norms'. In Butler's terms, the 'regulatory norms of "sex" work in a performative fashion to constitute the materiality of bodies, and more specifically, to materialize the body's sex, to materialise sexual difference in the service of the consolidation of the heterosexual imperative'.[104] The 'regulatory ideal' (or gender norm) that structures sexuality in terms of sexual difference is in actuality a heterosexual norm, for it defines ideas of masculine and feminine sexuality in terms of sexual desire for the *opposite* sex.[105]

Building on this concept of gender, sexual violence can be better understood as the enactment of norms of masculinity and femininity through violence. The act *produces* sexual difference through its repetition of those norms by force upon the bodies of both men and women. Inger Skjelsbæk argues that sexual violence is 'the form of violence which most clearly communicates masculinisation and feminisation'.[106] Following this important argument, sexual violence is a performative act that instantiates categories of gender. For Butler, 'a performative act is one which brings into being or enacts that which it names, and so marks the constitutive power of discourse'.[107] 'Sexual violence' materialises ideas of masculinity and femininity – ideas of what it is to be a man or a woman – through its repetition of norms of sexual practices – what sexual acts are considered appropriate to men or women – which in turn relies upon notions of 'biological' sexual difference – what it is to have a male or female body. Sexual violence ties together 'biological' bodies and 'social' roles, such that it produces bodies as male or female, upon which it inscribes masculine or feminine gender norms through violence. For example, in the Yugoslavian conflicts, particular forms of sexual violence

---

[103] Judith Butler, *Frames of War* (London: Verso, 2010), p. 168.
[104] Judith Butler, *Bodies That Matter* (London: Routledge, 1993), p. 2.
[105] Judith Butler, *The Psychic Life of Power* (London: Routledge, 1997), pp. 138–140.
[106] Inger Skjelsbaek, 'Sexual Violence and War', (2001) 7(2) European Journal of International Relations 211–237, 227.
[107] Judith Butler, 'For a Careful Reading', in Judith Butler, Seyla Benhabib et al., *Feminist Contentions* (London and New York: Routledge, 1995), p. 134.

can be seen as reproducing 'the ideal types of "masculinity" and "femininity" as they are constituted in a patriarchal society in the state of war', by constructing the body of a male victim as a feminised 'homosexual' subordinate and the body of a female victim as an object of sexual exchange and ethno-national reproduction.[108]

Conflict-related sexual violence constructs bodies through force, making and marking categories of ethnicity, religion, and nation through categories of sexual difference. The categories are themselves made through violence in the context of conflicts in which those persons were often not previously ascribed those identities and where those identities are at stake in the conflict itself. Sexual violence constitutes these identities, making persons into the social categories of the perpetrator – so that, for example, a Yugoslavian citizen becomes a Muslim woman. In coercive collective violence, sexual violence instantiates and solidifies these categories. An integral part of the harm is to reduce persons to social identities defined by the violence of the perpetrator – and in particular to their *sex* in the case of sexual violence. For example, if women play important roles in reproducing ethnicity, nation, and state and signify the difference and boundaries of collectivities, as Nira Yuval-Davis argues, then categories of sexual difference become crucial to the categories of ethnicity, religion, and nation that are contested in conflict itself.[109]

In the 'relational gender' model of conflict-related sexual violence, masculinity and femininity are hegemonic norms that are constituted in hierarchical relation to each other. For example, in the context of the Yugoslavian conflicts, we see that male sexual assault most often involves the feminisation of its victims – 'you are not a man' – while female sexual assault reduces women to the subordinate non-masculine role of femininity – 'you are a woman'. As such, 'masculinity' and 'femininity' are relational terms, in which each term is given hierarchical meaning in relation to the other. Moreover, these relational terms are filled with imaginary content according to hegemonic gender norms in specific social contexts, such that in a given particular context, this is what it is imagined to be a man, with a male body and masculine sexuality, and this is what it is imagined to be a woman, with a female body and feminine sexuality. Sexual violence is the process of constituting persons, bodies, and practices as sexual through hierarchical gender norms of sexual

---

[108] Blagojević, 'Preface', p. ix.
[109] See Nira Yuval-Davis, *Gender and Nation* (London: Sage, 1997).

difference through violence. It constructs the sexual subjectivity of both perpetrators and victims in those acts of violence. As Monique Plaza puts it: 'it is *social sexing* which underlies rape ... Rape is sexual essentially because it rests on the *very social* difference between the sexes.'[110] To identify the specific harms of sexual violence in particular conflicts, it is therefore necessary to identify how notions of sexual difference and violence are made meaningful in that social context.

The second theoretical strategy is to understand the harm of sexual violence as gendered injustice. This gendered injustice involves the imposition of sexual subjectivity through system violence. If 'sexual violence' is a category that describes a wide range of acts, these acts all share the common characteristic of being violence structured around gender norms of sexual subjectivity, ranging from forced nudity to sexual penetration. These acts involve sexuation, the organisation of persons through categories of sexual difference, and sexualisation, the construction of bodies and practices as sexual. Sexual violence consists of acts of sexuation and sexualisation through force. What these categories of acts share is the 'inhibiting of the very possibility of sexual self-making'.[111] In Marion Young's terms, such violence limits the development and exercise of the bodily, communicative, and relational powers of subjects. It constrains the sexual capacities of persons by the imposition of gender norms by violence upon bodies. In this way, war-time system violence amplifies the structural injustice of patriarchal peace-time gender relations by producing the aggregate harms of conflict-related sexual violence and creating the 'inhibited status' of those who suffer it. Conflict-related sexual violence produces structural injustice because it puts groups of persons under systemic oppression and domination and deprives them of their capacities, including sexual capacities, while also enabling other groups of persons to dominate and develop their capacities, including sexual capacities, as discussed in Chapter 6. Conflict-related sexual violence thereby harms persons not only by directly acting upon them as individuals but also by creating them as members of subordinated groups through interacting systems of violence. As such, patriarchal sex/gender systems become an integral part of the systems of violence.

---

[110] Monique Plaza, 'Our Damages and Their Compensation', (1981) 1(2) Feminist Issues, 25–35, 29.
[111] Linda Alcoff, *Rape and Resistance* (Cambridge: Polity, 2018), p. 145.

The approach necessarily situates conflict-related sexual violence in the wider gender dynamics and structures of conflict and contextualises it within these interacting systems of violence. It links sexual violence to non-sexual forms of violence against women and situates it in wider structural gender inequalities of masculine status and identity, in the context of which men engage in a range of forms of hostility against women to preserve or increase their 'domains of masculine mastery'.[112] In this conceptualisation, the interacting systems of violence in conflict are not mere reflectors of gendered roles created elsewhere but work as important mechanisms for (re)producing both gender inequality and gender identity. As such, conflict and conflict relations are active shapers of sex/gender systems. Accordingly, conflict-related sexual violence is an important mechanism for (re)producing gender inequality and identity in conflict. This approach shows how sexuality is part of the domain of 'masculine mastery' of war, including the making of ethno-nationalist belonging in system violence. In the gender dynamics of systemic domination in coercive collective violence, particular groups are able to dominate and develop their capacities. As described in Chapter 6, this process involves the alienation of women from their productive capacities and the exploitation of those productive capacities by transfers of value from women to hegemonic groups of men, in which that hegemony is established through collective violence.

In the feminist injustice model, conflict-related sexual violence is a form of gender-based harm, connected to other gendered harms of conflict, and part of a wider gendered continuum of system violence. Different forms of sexual violence repeat over time (the duration of the conflict) and space (the conflict region), producing differentiated social patterns of sexual violence and aggregated harms. The different patterns of sexual violence are linked to different forms of coercive collective violence, including different forms of gendered system violence, such as the thematic crimes described by the Women's Court.

8.4 Towards a Feminist Concept of Legal Subjects

The global legal form resolves the tensions in its concepts of individual and collective legal subjects by constructing a masculine subject, which it imagines as a possessive individual given rights and duties. In contrast,

---

[112] Vicki Schultz, 'Reconceptualizing Sexual Harassment', (1998) 107(6) Yale LJ 1683–1805, 1761.

the feminist approach to justice emphasises the importance of recognising women as subjects of justice, and subjects of justice as collective subjects. To develop this approach as a concept of legal subjects, it is not helpful to follow the 'identity' strategy that currently dominates critiques of international criminal law.[113] The strategy argues that particular identities, such as female perpetrators or male victims, are 'missing' or 'excluded' from international criminal law and that therefore it is politically strategic to include them in its operation. Leaving aside the questionable accuracy of this claim, the strategy assumes that such identities have identifiable and pre-existing attributes but fails to recognise that these attributes are products of histories and politics, including of conflicts themselves. It also fails to recognise that such identities are further entrenched by the operation of the global legal form itself. Accordingly, simply adding more categories of reified victim and perpetrator identity will reinforce these identities rather than changing the legal subject as such. The feminist approach to justice offers an alternative strategy, which is to develop concepts of legal subjects that can capture the *formation* of subjects in processes of victimisation, perpetration, and justice.

8.4.1 Victimisation

The feminist approach to justice begins by conceptualising women as subjects of justice rather than as victims of injustice. It does not attribute pre-existing ontological qualities to the subject of justice but instead sees the political work of feminism as producing that subject. This political work can be seen, for example, in the preparatory process and justice proceedings of the Women's Court, which aimed to enable women to be subjects, and not objects, of justice. Two related implications follow for developing a feminist concept of legal subjects. The first is including women as individual legal subjects within the existing legal order is a necessary but insufficient condition of creating a feminist legal subject. Simply including women in an unchanged legal order captures them in its problematic of (masculine) possessive individualism (as many feminist legal scholars have argued). The second is that it is politically problematic to construct feminist legal subjects on the basis of pre-existing 'characteristics' of women as subjects of justice. To do so will

---

[113] See Kirsten Campbell, 'Producing Knowledge in the Field of Sexual Violence in Armed Conflict Research', (2018) 25(4) Social Politics, 469–495.

instantiate already existing hegemonic and hierarchical ideas of masculinity and femininity, rather than building new justice practices that enable women to take up new positions as legal subjects.

Instead, a feminist approach to international criminal law shifts from focusing upon victim groups to the victimisation produced by system violence. It does not *begin* by identifying protected 'gender' groups, who are identifiable as individual rights-bearers, and where the violation of rights constitutes discrimination. Rather, it emphasises how system violence produces classes of persons who suffer injury because they are constructed as members of that class of persons. These harms are 'aggregate' because they harm not only individuals but also groups of individuals and the society to which they belong. The aggregate social harms are gender-specific because they injure a class of harmed persons, who as a group suffer social injury. As such, this approach focuses upon how system violence produces aggregate social harms that injure a class of persons, who as a class suffer 'inhibited status'.

8.4.2 Perpetration

The feminist approach to justice also shifts from the decontextualised model of the perpetrator as an autonomous individual in international criminal law, to instead focus upon participation in structural injustice. It rearticulates responsibility for structural injustice in terms of participation in the structural violence of conflict. The Women's Court Preliminary Decision describes structural injustices as the 'context of the crimes: war as systemic criminality'. This approach focuses on participation in military, political, and economic regimes and widens responsibility to include the role of states and the 'international community'. It builds on existing doctrinal concepts of organisational and 'system criminality', which involves individual responsibility for participation in systems of criminal conduct discussed in Chapter 3. The concept of responsibility seeks to identify these systems, whose aims, and means of accomplishment of those aims, are criminal.

Building on this approach, the model of the feminist legal subject moves away from conceptualising the perpetrator as an individual legal subject, with its corollary of an already existing victim group. Instead, it assesses responsibility in terms of the construction of the perpetrator group through the structural injustice of system violence. If system violence produces not only social groups of victims but also social groups of perpetrators, then it is necessary to develop a concept of criminal responsibility that can capture how perpetrators mobilise symbolic and material structures of violence to construct themselves *as a group*. At a conceptual level, this approach follows the sociological idea of perpetrator 'groups' as constructed categories.[114] Taking the crime of genocide as an example, Martin Shaw emphasises that it involves '*an attempt to destroy a group of people, regardless of how far groups defined by perpetrators correspond to "real" groups*'.[115] The analytic reframing focuses upon the construction of persons as groups of perpetrators participating in collective violence, rather than upon the targeting of already existing victim groups, whether defined by gender or ethnicity. The concept of perpetration examines how actors use system violence (the types of violence normally applied only to armed enemies, as Martin Shaw puts it) to construct themselves as a hegemonic group of perpetrators. As such, it captures how perpetrators construct relations to each other as members of that group, and to victim groups, the object built by systems of collective violence. As a model, it focuses our analysis upon how collective violence constructs a category of persons (perpetrators) existing in relations of system violence to other categories of persons (victims). It does not presuppose that men or women are perpetrators but offers a frame through which to capture their roles as collaborators, organisers, and enforcers of patriarchal and ethno-nationalist ideologies in system violence. Accordingly, the reconceptualisation of the subjects and objects of collective violence enables legal ideas of perpetration to capture how hegemonic categories of social subordination, such as 'gender' or 'ethnicity', become an integral part of collective coercive violence.

This idea of perpetration reframes the legal concept of criminal responsibility. It centres the concept of responsibility upon the intent and actions of perpetrators in constructing themselves as a group through violence in relation to other (victimised) groups, where that relation of violence is grounded in discrimination against, or destruction of, those victim groups. It focuses the construction of perpetrator groups through collective violence rather than upon victim groups as the objects of violence. An example of the problems raised by the latter focus can be seen in the *Mladić* and *Karadžić* cases, which typically of ICTY cases describe perpetrator groups as 'Bosnian Serb' or 'Serb forces' but inconsistently describe victimised groups as 'non-Serb' 'Croats' and/or

---

[114] Martin Shaw, *What Is Genocide?* (Cambridge and Malden, MA: Polity, 2007), p. 110.
[115] Ibid., pp. 103–104.

'Muslims'. The perpetration-focused approach more accurately captures criminal responsibility by focusing upon the perpetrator's intent to construct a 'Serb' group through system violence rather than whether 'non-Serb' victimised groups are the object of persecution or genocide. It focuses on the ideological, material, and organisational system violence that constructs (hegemonic) collectivities. In this approach, criminal responsibility captures how persons participate in the (symbolic and material) violence that constructs them as a group, which shares the prohibited aim of dominating or oppressing victimised persons through the prohibited means of collective violence. It examines how perpetrators participate in system violence that creates them as members of a dominating group and that enables them to dominate or exercise their capacities through coercive collective violence.

8.4.3 The Feminist Legal Relations Model

The new concepts of victimisation, perpetration, and criminal responsibility constitute a new feminist legal relations model of legal subjects. It focuses upon enabling all persons to become subjects of justice by building new legal relations that capture the social injuries of structural violence. Given that legal relations, the bundles of rights and duties attributed to persons, constitute perpetrators and victims as legal subjects, then to change the legal subject requires building new forms of legal relations. The model focuses upon building new legal relations that articulate individual and collective rights and obligations rather than upon including existing identities in international criminal law. As such, it aims to build new legal relations that can capture victimisation and perpetration as system violence and hence as an international crime.

8.5 Towards a Feminist Concept of Legal Proceedings

The feminist approach to justice emphasises the importance of building justice processes and institutions that enable women to become subjects of justice. It emphasises the importance of criminal justice processes and institutions in transitional societies, showing how they are the concrete condition of building just legal social bonds and an integral part of the struggle to build new forms of collective social life. At the same time, it provides a strong critique of existing forms of international criminal justice proceedings, showing both how they do not provide participatory parity to women and how their gendered narratives of international crimes negatively impact upon societies 'in transition'.

Accordingly, the feminist approach to justice shows the importance of ensuring that legal systems are not discriminatory and do not prevent women's participation in justice processes. As Maria O'Reilly describes, this approach requires recognising and challenging 'the "status subordination" affecting many survivors of wartime violence' within criminal and transitional justice processes, as well as their wider society.[116] In legal terms, it requires identifying and removing institutional and social obstacles to the participation of victims 'as full partners' in legal proceedings.[117] However, the feminist approach to justice also requires moving beyond participation in existing forms of criminal proceedings, due to its wider transformative aim of enabling women to become subjects of justice. Rather, it also requires building new models of legal proceedings on the basis of feminist practices and values, which can provide an alternative to the 'global legal culture' of international criminal law.

Accordingly, I develop a legal concept of 'feminist justice proceedings', which builds upon the feminist approach to justice. Following the feminist approach, it emphasises the importance of creating justice practices that will enable all persons to participate in, and become subjects of, justice. To develop this concept, I draw on the concrete example of the justice practices of the Women's Court proceedings. Its new form of justice proceedings aims to support witnesses and their demands for justice. The proceedings have an inquisitorial structure, with the 'court' functioning as an inquiry aiming to ascertain the truth of the witness's experience and the gendered nature of system violence in and after the conflict. Crucially, they develop a new feminist methodology for witnessing and judging international crimes against women. In developing the legal concept of feminist justice proceedings, I focus upon this feminist methodology of fact-finding, which offers new feminist modes of witnessing and judging.

8.5.1 Feminist Modes of Victim-Witness Testimony

The feminist approach to justice offers a mode of 'transformative' witnessing that shifts the position of sexual violence survivor from that of victim-witness to testimonial and political agent. The feminist mode of

---

[116] Maria O'Reilly, *Gendered Agency in War and Peace* (London: Palgrave, 2018), p. 66.
[117] Ibid.

victim-witness testimony places women as witnesses at the centre of justice processes, instead of reproducing a juridical model that focuses upon the perpetrator. It privileges women as knowing subjects, displacing 'law' as the 'site of epistemic privilege' of truth and objectivity.[118] It assumes that women are reliable and credible witnesses in the legal sense of being accurate and trustworthy witnesses but also in the wider social sense of being legitimate and authoritative knowers. The feminist mode of victim-witness testifying enables the sexual violence survivor to become a testimonial agent rather than being the passive victim-witness subjected to patriarchal processes of criminal justice. As testimonial agent, they can become the author of their own testimony, which is given in a particular context that is designed to support the testimony in the form in which they wish to tell it. They can also testify to their experiences of rebuilding their lives and pursuing justice and not only their experiences of victimisation. In this mode of testimony, witnesses testify as political subjects and agents of social change.

The feminist mode of victim-witness testifying is created through a range of procedural practices, which aim to empower women to testify and to support the construction of the 'subjective' text of witness testimony. They include pre-hearing, hearing, and post-hearing practices. The first set of practices aim to support women prior to giving testimony. These include identifying potential witnesses through public, community, and NGO engagement; enabling witnesses to collaboratively decide the content and to prepare and present their testimony in an extensive preparatory process; providing individual and group psychological support during the preparatory process; and building collective mutual support of witnesses. The second set of practices aim to support witness agency during the proceedings. These practices include positioning witnesses as central to the organisation of the court setting and proceedings; enabling witnesses to decide the content and form of their public testimony, and to show feeling and engagement in their testimony and to explain what harm and justice mean to them. The third set of post-proceedings practices aim to support all witnesses and not only those who testify. These include ongoing activities with witnesses; psychological and legal support in the period after the proceedings; witness participation in the preparation of the publication of testimonies; and trial monitoring.

---

[118] Regina Graycar and Jenny Morgan, *The Hidden Gender of the Law* (Sydney: Federation Press, 2002), p. 56.

8.5.2 Feminist Modes of Collective Witnessing

The feminist approach to justice links the experiences of individual victim-witnesses to the systemic violence of war and its consequences. In her discussion of the Women's Court, Iveković makes the important observation that an '"objectivised" trans-Yugoslav narrative of the country's falling apart ... is in a way nevertheless suggested through diverse *individual* testimonies that paint *together* a complex mosaic'.[119] This 'complex mosaic' is built from a collective, rather than individual, mode of testimony. The feminist approach to justice connects the testimonial mode of the individual victim-witness, which focuses on the subjective text of the witness, to the testimonial mode of collective witnessing, which focuses upon collective testimonies to systemic and structural violence. It links individual and collective testimony through the use of the 'objective' texts of expert witnesses to frame the social and political context of individual testimonies and through the 'objective' analysis of evidential totality of these testimonies by the Judicial Council in the Women's Court Preliminary Decision. In this context, 'objective' indicates collective knowledge claims about the social and political causes, context, and consequences of and responsibility for this violence. Linking testimonial modes in this way creates an alternative model of collective witnessing.

In this model, collective testimonies, in which multiple witnesses testify to multiple harms to multiple victims, create a new 'evidential totality', understood as the total body of evidence (as described in Chapter 4). This new 'evidential totality' is built from the perspective of women's experience of harms in and after war. For example, taken as a whole, individual testimonies of sexual violence describe collective harms and aggregate social injuries. The evidential totality of the testimonies makes visible how sexual violence is part of wider gendered systems of violence, involving collective patterns of harms, victimisation, and perpetration. The feminist mode of collective witnessing thereby makes visible the connections between individual experiences of harm and collective experiences of structural injustice. With this framing, it becomes possible to connect individual testimony of sexual violence to the collective harms of gender injustice.

Collective testimonies also evidence the responsibility of participants in the system criminality of war. Seen as an evidential totality, the

---

[119] Iveković, 'Violence and Healing', p. 103.

testimonies evidence the collective nature of the violence the women experience. For example, they show that sexual violence is a form of collective violence in its perpetration and objects. They reveal not only that individuals perpetrated sexual violence but that they did so as participants in systems of violence, such as military and political organisations. As an evidential totality, collective testimonies evidence collective responsibility for the system criminality of conflict. They show not only the criminal responsibility of individuals and of the political and military regimes in which they participated but also the wider legal and political responsibility of states and the international community that enable these crimes to occur.

8.5.3 Feminist Judging

In the global legal form, the 'international community' appoints the international judge according to their professional expertise, 'high moral character, impartiality and integrity' (Art. 13, ICTY Statute). The role of the judge is to act as neutral arbiter, who sits 'outside' the society they are judging. In contrast, the feminist approach to justice 'situates' judges in the justice process and uses a different model of judicial selection and expertise. First, it involved the 'bottom up' selection of judges by those seeking to build the alternative justice mechanism. All those selected were women, in contrast to the ICTY's historical under-representation of female judges. Second, the judges had substantive non-legal expertise in the humanities and social sciences, gender and feminist theory, and feminist and political activism, as well as international law. Three members were from the former Yugoslavia, with two 'international' members having long-standing connections to the 'region'.

The feminist approach to justice offers an alternative understanding of the position of the judge as 'legal knower' and of the construction of legal knowledge in legal processes. The legitimacy of feminist judging derives from a commitment to feminist justice, however defined. Feminist judges are given, and accept, responsibility for addressing the concrete injustices that the justice process describes and for changing the wider social relations from which these concrete injustices emerge. As such, judges are not seen as 'value-free' arbiters removed from the justice process. Rather, they are seen as engaged political actors, responsible for judging according to feminist values as well as the ongoing responsibility to build feminist justice. Accordingly, the legal knower is situated within social relations, and their legal knowledge expresses social values. This does not imply that feminist judging is partial or biased, but that it acknowledges and accounts for values in judging, including feminist values. Ideas of 'legal objectivity' as value-free and neutral judgement have traditionally been used to exclude social values and interests that differ from the world view of dominant social groups, to paraphrase Sandra Harding.[120] In contrast, feminist judging requires accounting for our social and cultural values in the act of judgement, including our methods of constructing legal knowledge. As such, it provides a stronger model of impartial and unbiased judging.

The feminist approach to justice offers the basis for developing a new model of feminist judging as an epistemic and political practice. It understands feminist judging as a form of 'strong objectivity' (as Harding describes it), which acknowledges the situated and limited view of the legal knower, develops legal knowledge from women's lives, and accepts political and epistemic responsibility for its accounts of the world.[121] In this model, feminist judging involves building 'strong objectivity' through feminist legal methods or epistemic practices. I describe 'feminist legal methods' as epistemic practices to emphasise that these are regulatory norms for constructing and evaluating legal knowledge (as outlined in Chapter 4). Communities of knowers regulate epistemic practices, which reflect the values of the epistemic community concerning the most appropriate methods of inquiry and justification of knowledge. These regulative standards are the normative criteria by which members of the community of inquiry determine which practices 'will advance our cognitive aims' and political goals.[122] Accordingly, we can describe feminist judging as an epistemic and political practice. It is an epistemic practice that involves constructing and evaluating legal knowledge, according to the regulative standards developed by feminist epistemic communities. It is also a political practice that feminist values inform and for which knowers are politically accountable. These feminist values are not pre-given but emerge from political struggles.

In the feminist approach to justice, we can identify five new epistemic feminist practices for judging international crimes, as described in Chapter 7. The first practice is recognising women testifiers and expert

---

[120] Sandra Harding, *Whose Science, Whose Knowledge?* (New York: Cornell University Press, 1991), p. 143.
[121] For further discussion, see Campbell, 'Producing Knowledge'.
[122] Helen Longino, 'Feminist Epistemology as a Local Epistemology', (1997) 71 The Aristotelian Society (Supplementary Volume) 19–35, 33–4.

witnesses as co-producers of knowledge about war and as agents of social change. The second is the naming and describing of individual and collective harms on the basis of women's testimonies. The third practice is connecting these social harms to gendered system criminality. The fourth practice of feminist judging describes those harms as legally articulable claims and identifies individual and collective responsibility for those crimes. The fifth practice is the ongoing political and epistemic responsibility of judges for feminist justice.

8.5.4 Feminist Public Witnessing

The feminist approach to justice suggests a fourth important component of feminist justice proceedings, which is public witnessing to these crimes. This 'collective' public can be described as the fourth party to feminist justice proceedings. In taking up public and collective witnessing, the audience to the proceedings becomes what Shoshana Felman calls a 'community of witnessing', which builds collective cultural frames of reference and perceptions of events.[123] Damir Arsenijević and Jasmina Husanović et al. argue that Bosnia lacks a 'public language of grief' (as does the Yugoslavian region generally), because the suffering of war and genocide is not communicated in an 'expressly public language' but instead remains 'hegemonically ethnic or private'.[124] Given this social and political context, the building of a witnessing 'public' was crucial for the feminist approach to justice. It was an integral element of building social solidarity with victims and revoking it from perpetrators, as described by both Mischkowski and Senjak in Chapter 7. It was also an integral element of building a public language of grief. Building such language requires, as Arsenijević describes, recognising that 'suffering, which results from war and genocide, is the effect of societal injustice, and is, as such, a *par excellence* public matter', and that justice claims must move past 'the interests of any particular identity ... to claims for a more equitable sociality for everyone'.[125] The feminist justice proceedings of the Women's Court sought to both publicly recognise crimes

---

[123] Shoshana Felman and Dori Laub, *Testimony* (New York and London: Routledge, 1992), p. 279.
[124] Damir Arsenijević, Jasmina Husanović et al., 'A Public Language of Grief', in Vlad Beronja and Stijn Vervaet (eds.), *Post-Yugoslav Constellations* (Berlin: de Gruyter, 2016).
[125] Damir Arsenijević, 'Mobilising Unbribable Life', in Andy Mously (ed.), *Towards a New Literary Humanism* (London: Palgrave Macmillan, 2011), p. 178.

against women and claim justice for all. As such, this dimension of feminist justice proceedings should be seen as a form of social witnessing that builds a public language of grief. Such witnessing involves all of society in affirming that crimes were committed and that all society has a social responsibility to provide for justice for them.

8.6 Towards a Feminist Concept of Relational Legal Justice

The feminist approach to justice does not understand it as enforcing the existing global form. Rather, it suggests that justice must address concrete social injustices and be part of the wider struggle to transform (patriarchal, capitalist, imperialist) social relations of domination and exploitation in the global social system. The feminist approach to justice reframes justice for international crimes as part of the struggle to transform global social relations. Building on the feminist approach to justice, legal justice for international crimes needs to both address the concrete injustices of the present and build more just social relations in the future. Such a model of legal justice emphasises its role in producing new representations of social relations and building those relations in concrete institutions and practices.

I describe this model as relational legal justice, because it builds justice practices in institutional legal systems in relation to social injury and social transformation. Understood in these relational terms, international criminal justice is not an *a priori* expression of abstract legal norms nor of an 'international society' founded upon 'humanity'. Instead, international criminal justice builds global legal bonds, which are a constitutive component of building global social relations. As such, relational legal justice understands international criminal justice as requiring social responsibility and accountability, and not only individual responsibility and sanction, and as linking building global legal relations to the struggle to build emancipatory forms of collective social life. In the relational model, international criminal justice can be said to have three components. The first is the symbolisation of the injustices of system violence as legal claims. The second is the construction of just processes for determining those claims. The third is the linking of legal accountability to wider transformative justice processes.

A feminist concept of relational justice necessarily addresses gender justice, in that it aims to provide justice for gender-based harms. A relational model of gender justice focuses upon providing adequate remedy and redress for the social injuries of gender-based harms.

However, if gender injustice is social, then so too must be its redress and remedy. Accordingly, a relational model of gender justice focuses upon how justice practices address gender-based harms of conflict and whether they work to create more gender-just societies. It emphasises the potential of justice to transform social relations of domination and oppression, and not only provide redress for individual wrongs or harms. As such, it focuses on the relation between justice practices and the transformation of social relations. This relational model should be understood as a form of transformative feminist justice that seeks to build a more just society for all.

8.7 A Feminist Approach to International Criminal Law

The feminist approach to justice offers the basis for building a feminist approach to international criminal law. First, it offers the basis for building new legal concepts for an alternative feminist legal form of international criminal law. The legal concepts are developed from feminist justice practices, knowledges, and institutions, which are themselves structured through feminist values. As such, they provide the basis for transforming the legal categories of the global legal form. Second, it shows that a feminist approach to international criminal law needs to be built in legal rules, practices, and institutions. Building these new justice practices enables the production of new discourses of international criminal law and hence new legal social bonds. Third, it reconceptualises a feminist approach to international criminal law as a 'transitional strategy'. Transitional strategies involve the strategic use of international criminal law for political struggles in concrete historical situations. They use the productive contradictions within the global legal form to open new possibilities for justice. Such strategies focus upon the role of international criminal law in political and social transition and recognise its importance in the transitional periods that can emerge in the contradictory dynamics of our globalising world. Transitional strategies emphasise the dialectical role of law in building legal social bonds as constituent elements of global social relations, as part of the struggle to create the conditions for building new forms of global collective life. I turn to the challenge of building such a feminist approach to international criminal justice in practice in the next chapter.

9

Building a Feminist Justice Approach to International Criminal Law in Practice

Strategies for Change

It is my wish to see justice served, rather than law being enforced.[1]

Women's Court participant, 2016

The challenge of building more just 'institutional legal systems' remains an important but unresolved question in the feminist approach to justice. How, then, might we build a feminist approach to international justice in practice? How can we create a feminist approach to international criminal law that can serve as a form of justice rather than simply enforcing the global legal form?

This chapter explores two key interconnected strategies for building a feminist approach to international criminal law in practice, using the example of conflict-related sexual violence. These are feminist 'transitional' strategies that use international criminal law for political struggles in concrete situations and build upon new legal opportunities opened by previous feminist struggles for gender justice. The first strategy develops an alternative framework of international legal norms that can serve as the basis for building feminist legal social bonds. The second strategy applies this legal framework in practice by developing framework principles for sexual violence prosecutions and an international convention on sexual violence as an international crime. Using conflict-related sexual violence as the basis for developing this feminist approach to international criminal justice also usefully illustrates potential strategies and challenges for addressing other gender-based crimes.

The aim of outlining these strategies is to open discussion of alternative directions for the collective feminist work of building new forms of international criminal justice. As such, they indicate potential plans of

---

[1] Staša Zajović, 'Witnesses at the Women's Court', in Staša Zajović and Miloš Urošević, (eds.), *Women's Court: About Event in Sarajevo and about Continue the Process* (Belgrade: Women in Black, 2017), p. 65.

action for building a feminist approach to international criminal law. Such strategies are necessarily collective in both their development and realisation and are contingent upon the collective processes of building alternative forms of feminist justice for international crimes. They are not intended to be an exhaustive or complete feminist project for international criminal law. Rather, they indicate potential areas of feminist work, which can be fully developed and realised only in collective feminist projects.

STRATEGY ONE: BUILDING A FEMINIST LEGAL FRAMEWORK FOR INTERNATIONAL CRIMINAL LAW

The first strategy is to build an alternative feminist legal framework for sexual violence as an international crime. This involves developing feminist legal concepts in four key areas: (1) substantive offences; (2) criminality responsibility and the legal subject; (3) legal proceedings and institutions; and (4) relational legal justice.

9.1 Building Feminist Substantive Norms for Sexual Violence as an International Crime

Following the feminist injustice model outlined in Chapter 8, the first element of this strategy is to describe and name gender-based violence and harms as legally articulable claims. The strategy involves describing and naming gender-based violence (the act of violence) and the gender-based harms it produces (the consequences of the act of violence), as a gender-based crime (the legally prohibited conduct). Accordingly, this strategy requires developing a feminist model of the substantive legal norms of the international crime of sexual violence that can describe and name sexual violence as gender-based violence and harm. To develop this model, I focus on building alternative legal concepts of the criminal act, the international crime, and criminal intent.

9.1.1 *The Criminal Act*

Building on the legal concept of feminist injustice outlined in the previous chapter, it is possible to identify four new conceptual elements of the international crime of sexual violence:

(1) Sexual violence is a category of acts.
(2) These acts are characterised by the imposition of sexual subjectivity through violence.

(3) This conduct produces aggregate social harms.
(4) Such conduct is internationally wrongful because it is an impermissible form of system violence.

9.1.1.1 Element One: Sexual Violence Is a Category of Acts

The first element is that 'sexual violence' should be understood as a *category* that describes a wide range of criminal acts, ranging from forced nudity to sexual penetration. The category consists of a continuum of coercive sexual acts in conflict. The continuum of sexual violence captures the variation between these different acts and the patterns in which they occur, as well as their commonalities in the gendered continuum of violence of conflict. The acts that fall in this category will vary according to how notions of 'sexual difference' are given meaning in a given concrete social context of conflict. Accordingly, it is necessary to develop the category of acts for each conflict through a gender analysis that builds on victims' description of their experience of sexual violence and expert witness analysis of sexual violence as gendered system violence.

9.1.1.2 Element Two: Sexual Violence as the Imposition of Sexual Subjectivity

The second element is the imposition of sexual subjectivity in the process of sexualisation and sexuation outlined in Chapter 8. These acts are criminalised because they injure the sexual self-determination and capacities of persons, through the imposition of hierarchical and heteronormative norms of sexual difference through system violence. The consequential harm is the making of this 'inhibited status' *per se*, from which other physical, emotional, familial, economic, and social harms may follow. This concept of sexual violence focuses on the consequences of the crime, which concerns the injury it causes, rather than the circumstances in which it occurs, which concerns the form of the act or the consent of the victim. The reformulation of the offence of sexual violence as a 'consequentialist' crime builds on the important work of Peter Rush and Alison Young.[2] Rush and Young argue that rape is currently conceived as a crime of 'circumstances', which

> predicates its criminal liability on proof of the circumstance in which the accused acts and the prohibited mentality with regard to that prohibited

---

[2] Peter Rush and Alison Young, 'A Crime of Consequence and a Failure of Legal Imagination', 1997 9(1) AFLJ 100–133.

circumstance ... the prohibited circumstance is the absence of consent by the complainant and the prohibited mentality is intention or recklessness as to that circumstance of non-consent.³

Instead of treating rape as a crime of circumstance, Rush and Young argue that it should be treated as a 'consequentialist' crime like other offences against the person, such as murder. As Rush describes, characterising the crime of rape in this way 'follows the architecture of general principles of criminal responsibility used in offenses against the person, in as much that it focusses on the prohibition of the consequences of the accused's conduct and the mentality of the accused in relation to those consequences'.⁴ Accordingly, rape is understood as 'sexual injury rather than as a non-consensual sexual activity'. Using this 'sexual injury' model, Rush provides a useful definition of rape as follows:

> A person who
> (a) sexually penetrates another person, and
> (b) causes injury to that other person
> (c) with the intention of causing injury or with recklessness as to causing injury is guilty of the offence of rape.⁵

This approach reconceptualises rape as a sexual injury, in which the injurious conduct is the sexual violence of the perpetrator and the prohibited consequence is the 'inhibited status' of the sexual subjectivity of the person. This approach does not rely on the person suffering specific harms as a consequence of sexual violence, which would further entrench highly problematic ideas of the 'damaged' rape survivor for whom rape is 'the worst experience' that they survive.⁶ Rather, it describes sexual violence as such as wrongful and the consequence of that wrongful act as the injury to the exercise of the capacities of the person, and accordingly to their self-development and self-determination. It conceptualises sexual violence as a 'consequentialist' crime, like other international crimes. It recognises the injury to the status of the subject as a sexual and social being, following approaches that reformulate sexual violence in terms of violations of sexual autonomy. However, it does not draw on the contractual models of sexual subjectivity of the global legal form, which have consent as an element of

---

³ Peter Rush, 'Jurisdictions of Sexual Assault', (2011) 19(1) FLS 47–73, 67–68.
⁴ Ibid., 68.
⁵ Ibid.
⁶ See Karen Engle, and Annalise Lottman, 'The Force of Shame', in Clare McGlynn and Vanessa Munro (eds.), *Rethinking Rape Law* (Abingdon and New York: Routledge, 2010).

the offence. In contrast to consent models, the feminist injustice model allows the reformulation of the offence of sexual violence as a crime of consequence rather than circumstance.

The approach raises the question of whether there should be a distinction between rape, defined by penetration, and other forms of sexual violence. As discussed in Chapter 2, this distinction has been criticised for its mirroring of masculine models of sexuality, because of its privileging of penetration in sexual offences. This critique led to the development of the so-called 'desexualisation' model in many jurisdictions, such as Australia and Canada, which emphasises the violent rather than sexual component of the crime. In substantive terms, this approach shifts from gender-specific to gender-neutral definitions of the offence and aims to remove the distinction between (1) sexual and non-sexual assault on the person and/or (2) penetrative and non-penetrative sexual assault.

At the international level, it is important to retain the sexual component of these offences to capture the specific characteristics of sexual violence as a consequential injury, the harm of penetration that victims describe, and the specific relational status subordination of women that is a consequence of rape as a gender-based harm in conflict. Accordingly, sexual violence should be conceptualised as a category of sexual acts, including rape, committed in coercive circumstances and articulated as a series of offences. While penetration marks the distinction between this offence and other sexual violence offences, it only does so to adequately specify the consequential injury that is the grounds for criminalisation (as should be the case for all other sexual violence offences) but not to mark it as the paradigmatic sexual injury.

9.1.1.3 Element Three: Sexual Violence Produces Aggregate Harms

The third element is that sexual violence is a category of acts that produces social injuries, that is, aggregate social harms. The conduct produces aggregate social harms that injure a class of persons, who suffer 'inhibited status', or secondary social status. It produces hierarchical and heteronormative sexual differentiation between men and women through system violence and creates the secondary social status of the class of persons subjected to it. The approach emphasises the consequentialist harm both to the individual and to the group. It recognises that conflict-related sexual violence as a gender-based harm produces aggregate harms to that class of persons, which creates the inhibited status of its members. Because these aggregate harms intensify hierarchal gender norms and relations, they also produce inegalitarian social relations. For this reason, the consequential harm is not only to the individual and the group but also to the society that experiences the gendered system violence of sexual violence. Using collective testimonial and expert evidence, it is possible to legally describe these harms, identify affected classes of persons, and assess the impact of these harms on a society.

9.1.1.4 Element Four: An Impermissible Form of System Violence

The fourth conceptual element is that conflict-related sexual violence is an impermissible form of system violence (that is, of coercive collective force). Conflict-related sexual violence can be seen as a category of sexual acts that are a criminalised form of system violence. The coercive collective violence provides the basis for international criminalisation, defining the so-called 'contextual' or 'international' elements of the core international crimes (as discussed in Chapter 8). These are all forms of system violence, which involve collective coercive physical or symbolic violence that intensifies the capacity to change or destroy the objects upon which it acts and which create forms of structural injustice. We can legally conceptualise such system violence as a minimal threshold, which has a collective character of sufficient intensity and organisation to distinguish it from sporadic and isolated incidences of violence.[7] The connection to system violence, rather than the legally and conceptually confusing idea of 'conflict', can be said to characterise sexual violence as an international crime. Accordingly, the 'conflict-related' aspect of sexual violence is reconceptualised as the 'international' or contextual element of the crime.

The approach builds upon the customary international rule that prohibits sexual violence as a war crime, crime against humanity, and genocide while also drawing on the existing legal model of sexual violence as a category of sexual acts committed in coercive circumstances. However, it also shifts away from the existing individualised model of sexual violence, with its focus upon the individual violence of the perpetrator and consent of the individual victim ('threat of force, force', etc., as in the ICC), to focusing on sexual violence as a form of system violence. In this approach, the context of the coercive circumstances of system violence criminalises sexual violence as an international crime (rather than being a domestic offence). The legal concept of sexual violence

---

[7] *Tadić*, ICTY-94-1-T, Judgment, 7 May 1997, paras. 561–568.

focuses on the coercive circumstances in which sexual violence takes place rather than the consent of the individual victim. Kiran Grewal makes the useful comparison of the treatment of consent in sexual violence and forcible transfer offenses,[8] which assess the coercive environment of the displaced group in determining the 'absence of genuine choice'.[9] Rather than focusing on the models of consent in these cases, we should instead use the concept of the 'coercive environment' that affects not only individual victims but groups of persons. Given that this approach was developed from the concept of 'coercive circumstances' in the *Kunarac* case, there is a strong doctrinal argument for its use in the legal conceptualisation of the 'international' component of sexual violence. Building on this approach, sexual violence as an international crime can be defined as an act of sexual violence committed in the coercive circumstances of armed conflict, crimes against humanity, or genocide.

9.1.2 The International Crime

The international crime is understood as an impermissible form of system violence, which puts groups of persons under systematic domination or deprivation while also enabling others to dominate or benefit from this violence. This concept of the international crime shifts the legal conceptualisation of each of the core crime categories.

9.1.2.1 War Crimes, Crimes against Humanity, and Genocide

In terms of war crimes, the feminist injustice model reconceives armed conflict as a form of gendered collective coercive violence. This reconceptualisation requires re-evaluating the prohibited means and methods of warfare (the means and methods of system violence), the protective regime for civilians and non-combatants (the rules protecting persons from system violence), and the regulatory focus upon active hostilities (rather than other forms of system violence).[10] To undertake this re-evaluation involves shifting the masculine legal subject ('the experience of combatants and male civilians') and the neglect of the 'differential impact on men and women' of gendered system violence in

---

[8] Kiran Grewal, 'The Protection of Sexual Autonomy under International Criminal Law', (2012) 10(2) JICJ 373–396, 392–393.
[9] *Mladić*, MICT-13-56-A, Judgement, 8 June 2021, para. 356.
[10] See Helen Durham and Tracey Gurd (eds.), *Listening to the Silences* (Leiden and Boston: Martinus Nijhoff, 2005), Chapters 10 and 11.

humanitarian law.¹¹ It also involves developing the underlying humanitarian principles of this body of law to address gendered system violence, such as interpreting the principle of proportionality to include the value of women's lives, rather than privileging male combatants or military objectives in assessing the legality of the conduct of conflict.¹²

In terms of crimes against humanity, the reconceptualisation focuses on the prohibited use of system violence to attack civilian society. It builds on the feminist approaches of the Women's Court and the important work of Nela Porobić Isaković and Gorana Mlinarević on the gendered harms of the war. These feminist approaches show how this form of gendered system violence attacks civilian society as such (rather than the civilian population as a group). The Women's Court links gender, ethnic, and militaristic violence in 'the crime of war against the civilian population',¹³ and emphasises that all these forms of system violence attack civilian society.¹⁴ Porobić Isaković and Mlinarević develop two important components of the concept of an attack on a civilian society.¹⁵ First, their gendered harms analysis describes the attack upon the 'society', in the sense of those 'public goods' held in common by all persons in civilian life, ranging from material infrastructure to civic resources. Second, it refers to the attack on the civilian nature of society. Similarly to the Women's Court, they describe that attack as involving the 'forced militarisation' of civilian life, which includes ideological violence such as the 'forced ethnification of society', the forced mobilisation of civilians for civil defence or in war efforts, and the use of force against civilians. Building on these approaches, the feminist concept of

---

[11] Judith Gardam, 'The Silences in the Rules That Regulate Women during Times of Armed Conflict', in Fionnula Ní Aoláin, Naomi Cahn, et al. (eds.), *The Oxford Handbook of Gender and Conflict* (Oxford: Oxford University Press: 2018), p. 39.

[12] Judith Gardam and Michelle Jarvis, *Women, Armed Conflict, and International Law*, (The Hague: Kluwer Law International, 2001), p. 128ff.

[13] Women's Court: Feminist Justice: Preliminary Decisions and Recommendations, Judicial Council, 9 May 2015, Women's Court, Sarajevo, (Women's Court Preliminary Decision), p. 2.

[14] Vjollca Krasniqi, Rada Iveković et al., 'The Banality of Evil', Expert Witnesses, 'War Against the Civilian Population (Militaristic/ Ethnic/ Gender-based... Violence)', Session 1, in Zajović and Urošević, (eds), *Women's Court: About the Event*, p. 118. The published proceedings can be found at pp. 79–271 (Women's Court Proceedings).

[15] Nela Porobić Isaković and Gorana Mlinarević, *Concept and Framework for Development of a Gender Sensitive Reparations Framework for Civilian Victims of War in Bosnia and Herzegovina* (Geneva: Women's International League for Peace and Freedom, 2015), pp. 51–53.

crimes against humanity is that it prohibits system violence that attacks the public goods and civilian nature of society.

Both the Women's Court thematic crimes and the gendered harm analysis identify a specific form of attack upon civilian society, which involves the creation of 'groups' through coercive collective violence. The Women's Court describes 'the crime of persecution of those who are different in war and peace', which involves '[t]he violent creation and imposition of differences, based on communitarian, ethnic, religious, gender, sexuality, age, disability, and similar group constructions. These differences were used to divide people and legitimate violent practices of exclusion'.[16] In their gendered harms approach, Porobić Isaković and Mlinarević also identify 'identity imposition' as a specific harm arising from the forced militarisation of society.[17]

The feminist approaches above describe the intertwined patriarchal and ethno-nationalist systems that are crucial components of coercive collective violence and how that violence imposes identity upon, or creates difference within, civilian societies. They identify the discriminatory creation of groups through militarised violence as an attack on civilian society as such. This violence not only imposes identities upon civilians but destroys the civilian society by dividing it into 'collective' identities of communal inclusion or exclusion. As described in these approaches, this system violence is gendered in its structure, operation, and effect. The feminist framing enables us to describe more precisely the criminalisation of persecution as a crime against humanity. From this feminist perspective, persecution as a crime against humanity can be reconceived as the discriminatory creation of groups through the use of system violence to deprive those persons of fundamental rights.

In terms of genocide, the feminist concept of the persecutory attack on civilian society also helps to describe the grounds of criminalisation of genocidal acts more precisely. If genocide is a process of constructing dominant and subordinate groups through the structural injustice of collective violence (as outlined in Chapter 8), then following the feminist reframing of persecution, the criminality of genocidal conduct can be redescribed as the exclusion of classes of persons from social life (and from social existence) and the destruction of their existence within society (reducing them to bare life). Rather than characterising the protected group as the object of prohibited violence, genocide can be

---

[16] Women's Court Preliminary Decision, p. 3.
[17] Porobić and Mlinarević, *Concept and Framework*, p. 52.

reconceptualised as the creation of classes of persons through system violence, with the aim of destroying the existence of that class of persons as members of society. It involves the use of system violence to destroy the social co-existence of persons as members of society. The criminalised conduct uses system violence to destroy peaceful co-existence as a form of social life. Understood as such, genocide is a prohibited form of system violence that destroys the social co-existence of all persons.

9.1.2.2 Crimes against Peace

In both the Women's Court proceedings and the gendered harms analysis, crimes against peace also emerge as an important category of crimes. As Porobić Isaković and Mlinarević describe '[f]orced militarisation of a society is essentially a violation of the right to peace'.[18] Similarly, the Women's Court Preliminary Decision describes war itself as systemic criminality and concludes that '[t]he testimonies showed all the nationalist political and military regimes on the territory of the former Yugoslavia committed crimes against peace and were engaged in an aggressive war'.[19] However, the ICTY did not include the crime of aggression in its Statute and failed to capture 'state' systems and structures in collective criminality (as discussed in Chapter 4). Moreover, the ICJ judgements on state responsibility for genocide only established what could be called 'passive' responsibility for failing to prevent genocide, rather than 'active' responsibility for committing genocide.

Like the feminist approaches to crimes against peace, Frédéric Mégret also highlights the importance of the core crime category of crimes against peace. He also connects aggression to attacks on citizens of states (as both civilians and combatants of the aggressor and aggressed states) and argues that aggression is a violation of the right to peace.[20] Mégret contends that the international crime of aggression has been neglected in contemporary international criminal law and that engaging with the crime is central to reconsidering international criminal law as a 'peace project'. Without the crime of aggression, he suggests, international criminal law only deals with the 'manifestations of a deeper phenomenon that it has found to be off limits and, therefore, fails to understand the

---

[18] Ibid..
[19] Women's Court Preliminary Decision, pp. 2-4.
[20] Frédéric Mégret, 'What Is the Specific Evil of Aggression?', in Claus Kreß and Stefan Barriga (eds), *The Crime of Aggression* (Cambridge: Cambridge University Press, 2017), p. 1443.

very cause of so many of the atrocity crimes that are committed'.[21] All three approaches can be said to reconsider crimes against peace as part of a wider peace project.

However, these reconsiderations of crimes against peace understand it as a breach of the fundamental human right to life. While this is an important shift in reconceptualising the crime of aggression, it focuses upon the criminality of waging war and killing as the prohibited conduct. As such, it retains the central concern with armed conflict by states in the international crime of aggression from the Nuremberg Charter to the Rome Statute. However, the concept of system criminality enables a shift away from this focus upon the state so as to fully conceptualise the protected social interests of crimes against peace and its connection to the protected social interests of the core crime categories. It shows the international crime categories constitute three forms of illegal system violence and protect different social interests in prohibiting this violence. War crimes involve criminal means and aims of armed force. Crimes against humanity attack the civilian nature of a society, while genocide intends to destroy the social co-existence of persons. In all three core crimes, system violence gives the criminal conduct the 'character, gravity, and scale' to constitute the crime against peace.[22] As such, the crime against peace 'contains within itself the accumulated evil of the whole'.[23]

The feminist concept of crimes against peace builds on the idea of 'a collective act of aggression', in which the crime consists of the 'collectivisation' of violence, as described in Chapter 8.[24] The 'collectivisation' of violence into organisational and systemic criminality enables groups of persons to dominate or benefit from developing and exercising capacities available to them because of their participation in system violence and puts groups of persons under systematic threat of domination or deprivation of the means to develop and exercise their capacities. The 'collectivisation' of violence can be said to give rise to leadership responsibility (or the 'over-arching' JCE as the ICTY describes it in the *Mladić* and *Karadžić* cases). By reformulating this 'international' dimension of the core crimes, it then becomes possible to link conflict-related sexual

---

[21] Frédéric Mégret, 'International Criminal Justice as a Peace Project', (2018) 29(3) EJIL 835–858, 857.
[22] Rome Statute, Article 8bis(1).
[23] See Nuremberg Judgment, p. 186.
[24] Robert Cryer, *An Introduction to International Criminal Law and Procedure* (Cambridge: Cambridge University Press, 2019), p. 303.

violence as a prohibited form of system violence to the wider context of the illegal system violence prohibited by crimes against peace.

With this reframing, it becomes possible to develop the legal concept of the crime against peace rather than of aggression as a crime of states. The concept of system violence understands the state as a functional rather than legal category. It thereby reframes the first element of the crime of aggression, namely, that it consists of the use of armed force by the state. Instead of the legal state, it uses a functional category of responsible actors. Accordingly, such actors would include not only states but also other international actors, such as private military contractors, corporations, arms suppliers, and so on. The crime is characterised by the capacity to collectivise violence, that is, to construct system criminality, within and across state territories. Understood as a crime against peace rather than aggression, this element of the crime against peace then consists of the use of unlawful coercive collective violence. The unlawfulness of this conduct derives from collective violence that has no other aim or means of accomplishing those aims other than through the violation of international legal norms (following Nuremberg).

In the feminist model, crimes against peace protect non-state interests of peaceful co-existence. In contrast, the crime of aggression protects state interests of sovereignty, territorial integrity, or political independence and accordingly prohibits the use of armed force against another state under the second element of the offence. This feminist concept of peace draws on Marxist anti-imperialistic traditions in international law, which characterise it as a breach of peaceful global co-existence. Its roots lie in Marxist conceptions of the war of aggression by Nazi imperialism in World War Two. The Yugoslav socialist concept of the crime against peace included an anti-hegemonic right to self-determination and emphasised the importance of 'geopolitical emancipation', understood as the struggle against domination and oppression in an unequal (imperial) global social order.[25] As such, we can say that the Yugoslavian idea of crimes against peace rejected both ethno-national and imperial state orders as the basis of peaceful global co-existence.[26]

Building on the Marxist tradition, system violence as a crime against peace directs our attention to those who suffer the consequences of these

---

[25] See Zoran Oklopcic, 'Redeeming the Triple Struggle? The Yugoslav Accounts of Non-alignment', in Luis Eslava, Michael Fakhri et al., (eds.), *Bandung, Global History, and International Law* (Cambridge: Cambridge University Press, 2017).

[26] See Gal Krin, *Partisan Ruptures* (London: Pluto Press, 2019), Chapters 3 and 5.

forms of domination and oppression. Both the feminist approaches and Mégret describe these 'affected groups', which include citizens of all successor states in the region (as the feminist approaches describe) or 'populations' of states (as Mégret describes). Importantly, they also recognise the militarised society of both the aggressor and the aggressed collectivity as affected groups. To shift from state-centred aggression to non-state crimes against peace, it is important to build on these insights, but also to shift from making the affected group contingent on state membership. Rather, the affected group is the collectivity of all those who are directly affected by such system violence, which we can describe as the 'affected collectivity'. What is affected is their right to peaceful global co-existence, whether through the internationally illegal use of armed force (war crimes), the attack on civilian society (crimes against humanity), or the destruction of social co-existence (genocide). The right to peace is individually and collectively held by the affected group.[27] With this approach, the criminalisation of conflict-related sexual violence becomes clearly linked to crimes against peace, and hence to the wider feminist aim of reinterpreting international criminal law as a peace project.

9.1.3 Criminal Intent

The feminist injustice model refocuses the concept of sexual violence as an international crime upon the context of the conflict and the conduct of the defendant, rather than the consent of the complainant. It defines criminal intent by whether the accused intended to cause injury or was reckless as to whether injury would occur rather than their belief or otherwise in the consent of the victim to the sexual act. 'Consent' is no longer an element of the offence to be established by the prosecution, which is instead considered as an evidential matter (discussed in Section 9.3.2).

The approach provides a consistent conceptual basis for criminal intent for the international crime of sexual violence. Sexual violence as an international crime becomes structurally consistent with other international crimes, since the criminal intent for the underlying offence is not predicated on consent of the victim. Moreover, it better captures the relationship between the underlying offence and its contextual elements, given that leadership cases typically do not concern direct perpetration

---

[27] Mégret, 'What Is the Specific Evil of Aggression?', 1445; Hilary Charlesworth and Christine Chinkin, *The Boundaries of International Law* (Manchester: Manchester University Press, 2000), p. 273.

but rather the responsibility of the accused for the consequences of these acts to victims. In this way, the feminist injustice model aligns the concept of intent of the underlying offence of sexual violence and the intent of the 'international' element.

Given the general conceptualisation of *mens rea* in the contextual elements of international crimes as intent, knowledge, or recklessness, the feminist injustice model is also helpful in describing the harm of sexual violence as a consequence of intentional or reckless acts in 'collective' modes of liability. This approach is useful in demonstrating intent in common purpose doctrines, such as the ICC, to show that the group intended to cause the consequences of the crime or were aware that it would occur. It is also useful where knowledge or recklessness is tied to the test of the foreseeability of the crime, such as in command responsibility, or in 'extended' joint criminal perpetration (JCEIII).

The reconceptualisation of sexual injury as an aggregate social harm also enables the development of the idea of sexual violence as a consequential crime. It characterises sexual violence as an aggregate social harm, which is '"a consequence of deliberate policy or intentional behaviour". It is conduct which is "collective" and foreseeable "in an objective sense" even if there is no direct connection between the perpetrator and the ultimate damage.'[28] The model shifts from typical 'proximate harm' models of individual perpetrators and victims of sexual violence, which assume causal connection between direct perpetration and harm. Instead, it offers a consequential model of harm causation that does not rely on proximity (a key problem in sexual violence leadership cases, as discussed in Chapter 4).

The feminist injustice model thereby addresses the particular difficulties of persuading fact finders that sexual violence is an intended or foreseeable consequence of the contextual criminal conduct of the accused, particularly in leadership cases. The approach should not be misunderstood as imposing a 'negligence' model of civil liability. Rather, it should be understood in the context of the standards of intentional behaviour, imputation of knowledge, and foreseeability already existing in international criminal law. Central to the idea of aggregate social harm is consequential injury, which is injury as a consequence of intent or recklessness. As such, these consequences can be foreseen and therefore

---

[28] Adrian Howe, 'The Problem of Privatised Injuries', in Martha Fineman (ed.), *At the Boundaries of Law* (London, Routledge: 1990), p. 161.

prevented from occurring. In these terms, sexual violence is a preventable harm, as has long been recognised by military forces.

9.2 Building Feminist Substantive Norms of Criminal Responsibility and Legal Subjects

The second element of the feminist strategy is reconceptualising criminal responsibility and legal subjects. The feminist 'legal relations' model of legal subjects outlined in Chapter 8 emphasises the importance of reconstructing criminal responsibility so that it can capture gendered patterns of system violence (perpetration) and social injury (victimisation). Such an approach focuses upon understanding perpetration and victimisation in terms of responsibility for system violence and its consequential harms. It requires shifting focus from individual legal persons to collective subjects and objects of system violence and on building new legal relations or norms that can construct these legal subjects.

The legal 'liability model of responsibility' can be said to identify 'individual or collective agents whose actions can be causally linked to a harm and who do not have valid excuses for those actions' (because their actions are not within the limits of accepted rules and norms).[29] Building on this description, criminal responsibility can be said to arise from participation in the collective action of system violence, which can be causally linked to the harms of social injuries and which involves aims, and means of implementing those aims, which violate international criminal norms. The collective action involves the domination or deprivation of capacities in system violence (patterns of perpetration), which produces the aggregate social harms of social injustices (patterns of victimisation), and those who participate in system violence are responsible for the consequent injustices it creates. This system violence is criminal in its aims and involves criminal conduct in their implementation.

To ascribe criminal responsibility involves identifying the systems that are the constituent components of any given structured whole of system violence, that is, 'the whole pattern of criminality'.[30] Components of this

---

[29] Iris Marion Young, *Responsibility for Justice* (Oxford: Oxford University Press, 2010), p. 180. Young argues that this liability model should not be used to capture structural injustice because no agent can be said to be responsible for them. However, this is not the case with system violence.
[30] *Tadić*, ICTY-94-1-A & -*Abis*, Sentencing Judgement, 26 January 2000, Separate Opinion of Judge Cassese, para. 14.

system violence may include political, military, economic, and security leadership, with interacting systems that are ideological (intellectual elites and media); military (including paramilitaries and armed groups); professional (legal, medical, scientific), governmental (including administration and policing); religious (including leaders and institutions); economic (including war profiteering as well as corporations, industry, and finance); political (including political parties); and international (including institutions and organisations, such as the UN, EU, and states). The systems may take the concrete form of collective entities or associations, such as groups, organisations, associations, or institutions. Such component systems are, in effect, the 'middle link' in the chain of causation of harm between leadership and direct perpetrators in system violence. Such an approach does not reintroduce notions of collective responsibility but instead contends that 'responsibility should not (only) be located at individual level, but should also address the system within which individual behaviour is embedded'.[31] Criminal liability arises from participation in these 'systems' of collective coercive violence and responsibility for the collective action that is causally linked to consequential harms. It builds on the current erosion of the traditional customary distinction between international and internal conflicts and extends the application of the protective principles underlying international criminal law across all forms of system violence. It contends that these prohibitions should apply to all actors participating in system violence, whether in war or peace, and these protections should apply to all victims of these crimes, regardless of their group status or membership.

Importantly, the approach contextualises criminal responsibility for sexual violence within the interlocking systems of collective violence. It links patterns of sexual violence to 'the whole pattern of criminality', contextualising it within the different forms of system violence in a gendered continuum of system violence. Criminal liability for conflict-related sexual violence arises from the 'causal link' between sexual and system violence. These systems of violence have gendered structures (the components of system violence), operation (implementation), and effect (consequential harms). Three important shifts in the conceptualisation of criminal responsibility for such victimisation follow. The first is that an analysis of system violence should not begin by identifying victim groups

---

[31] André Nollkaemper, 'Introduction', in Harmen van de Wilt, André Nollkaemper et al. (eds.), *System Criminality in International Law* (Cambridge: Cambridge University Press, 2009), p. 3.

but instead by describing patterns of victimisation and the classes of person that they create. The second is that these consequential harms are aggregate, and not only individual. The third is that victimisation includes breaches of collectively held rights, including social and economic rights, and destruction of collective 'public goods', the collectively held 'goods' in common to all persons in a society (rather than only breaching individual civil and political rights). Such an approach situates sexual violence victimisation in the system violence that creates it and links its consequential harms to the wider collective harms of that system violence.

9.3 Building Feminist Criminal Justice Institutions and Proceedings

The third element of the strategy is to build feminist institutional and trial practices and values as an alternative to the 'global legal culture' of international criminal law. Following the 'feminist justice proceedings' model outlined in Chapter 8, the strategy focuses on building feminist institutional and trial norms. The strategy develops key feminist practices and values of the model as generalised norms, acting as practical concepts to guide action. It does not aim to set out a programme of institutional reform. Rather, the aim is to identify and describe key tactical areas of feminist collective work that can serve as the basis for building a feminist approach to the legal processes and institutions of international criminal law.

9.3.1 Building Feminist Legal Institutional Norms

The feminist justice proceedings model highlights four key areas for developing feminist practices and values as feminist institutional norms. These are: (1) feminist justice mandates; (2) feminist judging; (3) feminist justice accountability; and (4) feminist justice prosecutions.

9.3.1.1 Feminist Justice Mandates

The first key area is building a feminist justice mandate for legal institutions. At the international level, the idea of 'mandate' refers to the core functions given to international criminal justice mechanisms. Building feminist justice mandates involves constructing institutional core functions in terms of feminist values. It moves beyond the 'gender justice mandate' attributed to the ICC, which consists of limited statutory provisions and policies within ICC organs but does not apply across the institution as a whole.[32] These provisions and policies emphasise formal equality, such as removing discriminatory obstacles to the equal treatment of individual victims or providing for fair representation of female and male judges. They do not provide substantive equality, such as addressing the concrete status subordination of victims as a class of persons or the concrete hierarchies between nation-states in global social order.[33] As such, they provide formal justice (the equal opportunity to participate in justice processes) rather than substantive justice (enabling all persons to become subjects of justice).

In contrast, the feminist approach to justice makes substantive gender justice a foundational principle of justice mechanisms. It aims to recognise the subordinated status of women as a gendered class of persons, to address their concrete experience of injustice, and to place them at the centre of these justice processes. Accordingly, it centres the need to recognise and address 'gender' as a form of hierarchical power relations, including the power relations of the global social system. Accordingly, a feminist justice mandate makes substantive gender justice an integral part of institutional design, which shapes institutional functions, practices, and values. It recognises the subordinated status of victims of gender-based crimes as a class of persons, addresses their experience of concrete injustices, and enables their participatory parity in justice processes. Such mandates make substantive gender justice a core function of international criminal justice and explicitly task the institution with its implementation in all its sections.

To build a feminist justice mandate in practice requires not only 'equal access to justice' policies, which remove obstacles to equal participation in justice processes, but also 'substantive access to justice' policies, which actively create the concrete conditions that enable the participatory parity of all. Such policies need to address not only individuals, but also the affected collectivity. This is because system violence creates large numbers of complex cases, destroys state infrastructure, de-legitimises criminal justice systems, and displaces or impoverishes the affected population. For this reason, gender justice mandates need to develop appropriate collective 'access to justice' policies that address the material

---

[32] Louise Chappell, *The Politics of Gender Justice at the International Criminal Court* (Oxford: Oxford University Press, 2016), p. 32.
[33] See Catharine MacKinnon and Kimberlé Crenshaw, 'Reconstituting the Future', (2019) 129 Yale LJF 343–364.

conditions that operate as structural barriers to participation in justice processes. Such policies may range from free legal information and representation to providing medical and economic assistance and building national legal capacity.

A feminist justice mandate also recognises the gendered barriers to women, and particularly sexual violence victims, to becoming subjects of justice. It acknowledges that where conflict deepens gender structural inequalities, it also deepens the gendered impact of material and social conditions upon participation in justice processes. So, for example, Brammertz and Jarvis observe, '[i]nadequate infrastructure, including insufficient witness protection systems, can present a particular barrier to effective sexual violence prosecutions in national systems recovering from conflict'.[34] These barriers prevent participatory parity in international prosecutions and universal jurisdiction prosecutions in other countries, as well as in national systems. Accordingly, feminist justice mandates address the wider material and social infrastructure necessary to enable victims to participate in justice processes, which ranges from adequate healthcare and housing to financial support to travel or pay for childcare. In effect, feminist justice mandates recognise and address the interconnected social and legal status subordination of sexual violence victims. As such, they address all members of this subordinated class of persons. To do so requires careful contextual analysis of existing and consequent social stratification within that class of persons. It also requires engaging with all victims of this crime, including male victims or persons targeted on sexuality grounds, who may also face gendered status subordination.

9.3.1.2 Feminist Justice Judging

The second key area is feminist justice judging. The feminist approach to justice emphasises the role of 'judges acting as agents for "gender justice"'.[35] The agentic concept of feminist judging is particularly important

---

[34] Serge Brammertz, Michelle Jarvis et al., 'Using the OTP's Experience with Sexual Violence as a Springboard for Building National Capacity', in Serge Brammertz and Michele Jarvis (eds.), *Prosecuting Conflict-Related Sexual Violence at the ICTY* (Oxford: Oxford University Press, 2016), p. 338. See also Radhika Coomaraswamy, *Preventing Conflict, Transforming Peace, Securing the Peace* (New York: UN Women, 2015), Chapter 5.

[35] Rosemary Grey, and Louise Chappell, '"Gender-Just Judging" in International Criminal Courts', in Susan Harris Rimmer and Kate Ogg (eds.), *Research Handbook on Feminist Engagement with International Law* (Cheltenham and Northampton: Edward Elgar Publishing, 2019), p. 213.

for international criminal law for two reasons. First, serving judiciary are likely to be responsible for developing and implementing a wide range of policies in international courts, which may range from evidential rules to sentencing guidelines, or the interpretation and application of international norms in domestic legal systems. Second, judicial decisions play a particularly important role in the development of customary norms in international criminal law. This includes addressing the normative gaps that are particularly pronounced in the case of gender-based crimes, as shown by the analysis of the judicial development of the offence of sexual violence in Chapter 2. Patricia Viseur Sellers' observation of the ICC holds equally true of all courts: '[e]ach must share the responsibility to vigilantly gauge whether adverse gender discrimination results from the application or interpretation of substantive or procedural international laws.'[36] Feminist justice judging describes this responsibility as accountability to feminist values in judicial decision-making and includes in those feminist values substantive gender justice as well as gender inequality.

In this model, feminist justice judging is a set of practices that build substantive gender justice. It emphasises four key practices of feminist judging that enable the building of new legal rules, principles, and jurisprudence for gender-based crimes such as sexual violence (as outlined in Chapter 8). The first practice is recognising women testifiers and expert witnesses as co-producers of knowledge about war. The second is naming and describing of individual and collective harms on the basis of women's testimonies. The third is connecting sexual violence to gendered system violence. The fourth is describing those harms as legally articulable claims. All four practices are crucial for building new legal norms and jurisprudence for gender-based crimes. These practices are collective (and not only individual), which the values and culture of the legal institution itself supports (or limits).

The development of these practices rests upon appropriate judicial selection and expertise, as the feminist judging of the Women's Court shows. It is now commonplace to assert the need for gender parity and competence as selection criteria for international judges. It is important to advocate for under-represented groups as candidates on international courts and equal representation of men and women. It is also important to ensure gender competence at the international level, which enables

---

[36] Patricia Viseur Sellers, 'Gender Strategy is Not a Luxury for International Courts', (2009) 17(2) Am UJ Gender Soc Pol'y & L 301–323, 315.

judges to bring a gender perspective to their work, as well as addressing the discriminatory values they may also bring. However, the model of feminist justice judging challenges current understandings of judicial gender representation and competence as addressing gender inequality. In contrast, feminist justice judging aims to address substantive gender justice (and not only discriminatory practices and values). Accordingly, feminist justice judging emphasises the importance of developing judicial and institutional practices that build substantive gender-just legal proceedings.

Developing these practices of feminist judging should be seen as a collective feminist responsibility, as well as the responsibility of individual judicial actors and legal institutions. The analysis of the process of building new legal knowledges of sexual violence at both the ICTY and the Women's Court shows the importance of feminist engagement with judicial practice, which ranged from submitting *amicus curie* briefs to developing feminist legal arguments on sexual violence as an international crime. Building on this analysis, it is possible to identify three key tasks for the collective feminist work of developing appropriate practices and models of feminist judging. The first is developing feminist legal arguments and norms in legal scholarship. This work provides conceptual and political resources for feminist judging and can also serve as the writing of 'highly qualified publicists' (and hence as a source of customary international law). The second is developing appropriate models of substantive expertise in gender as a field of knowledge for feminist judging in international criminal law. The third is developing appropriate models of the strong legal objectivity outlined in Chapter 8, which can address contextual social values in the construction of legal knowledge. This includes developing feminist legal methods and reasoning that can serve as the basis for feminist judicial decisions.

9.3.1.3 Feminist Accountability

The third key area for developing institutional norms can be described as feminist accountability. The feminist approach to justice rests upon two interconnected ideas of accountability – namely, giving an account of, and making accountable for, crimes against women. It links accountability for gender-based crimes to the transformation of gendered relations in conflict and post-conflict societies. Such accountability is necessary to include these crimes in public narratives of the conflict, to ensure their public stigmatisation, and to provide public recognition of victims as right-holders entitled to redress. Feminist accountability is an important concept for building gender-just criminal justice proceedings. It can be said to have two elements. First, to accurately characterise gender-based crimes ('giving accounts of') and, second, to appropriately sanction those responsible ('making accountable for').

In terms of criminal justice, the first element of feminist accountability involves giving accurate and meaningful accounts of gender-based crimes. This approach acknowledges that international criminal law operates as a socio-symbolic system, which interprets and communicates social meaning through the legal process (as described in Chapters 4 and 5). The operation of international criminal law is not only expressive but is also productive of legal subjects and relations. Accordingly, how justice proceedings construct crimes, conflict, and responsibility for them is a crucial issue for building feminist accountability. As such, the disparity between the richly described gender-based crimes in the Women's Court and narrower narratives in the ICTY calls for a feminist reconsideration of how international criminal law can more meaningfully capture the experiences of women in war. A key challenge for building a feminist approach to international criminal law is to develop justice proceedings that can produce meaningful accounts of gender-based crimes. This challenge does not only concern individual testimonies or cases. Rather, as the analysis of the ICTY has shown, it needs to be taken up across the criminal justice system as a whole, including the selection of accused, charges, cases, witnesses, and sentencing.

The second element of feminist accountability concerns appropriate sanction. This primarily concerns the failure to prosecute crimes, as well as sentencing and release. The Women's Court participants identify impunity, low sentences, and early release of perpetrators as a key source of dissatisfaction with institutional legal justice. Laurel Baig's important review of ICTY sentencing for sexual violence crimes also identifies sentencing, plea agreements, rehabilitation, post-conviction release, and compensation and restitution procedures as neglected areas of institutional policies, leading to generally poor practice in this area.[37] Feminist accountability requires developing feminist models of sanction, both penal (sentencing) and non-penal (compensation and restitution), and rehabilitation. This challenging task requires collective feminist work.

The feminist approach to justice points to the potential usefulness of the idea of 'social protection' in the Marxist tradition for undertaking this

---

[37] Laurel Baig, 'Sentencing for Sexual Violence Crimes', in Brammertz and Jarvis (eds.), *Prosecuting Conflict-Related Sexual Violence*, Chapter 8.

task (as discussed in Chapter 8). A feminist concept of 'social protection' emphasises the role of criminal law in protecting society and its effect on the offender and on social relations. However, it rejects the idea of social protection as 'social defence', in which the role of law is to defend the socialist state and which gave rise to the most repressive forms of state 'administration' in socialist systems.

The feminist concept of social protection can be seen as having two components. The first emphasises the protection of society through sanction, which removes the perpetrator from society, protects social values, and reintegrates victims into society. Sanction is penal, in the form of imprisonment, and non-penal, in the form of compensation and restitution to individual and collective victims. Non-penal sanction should include seizure of all assets and profits accrued through the perpetrator's participation in war-time activities. The second component emphasises the effect of criminal justice on the offender and on the affected society. This effect arises from sanction, insofar as penal sanction removes perpetrators from political power and non-penal sanction removes their economic power. Sanction can then operate to disrupt the economic and political systems of criminality that otherwise continue into the post-war period. This social effect also arises from the 'social' rehabilitation of perpetrators, which in post-conflict societies includes their acknowledgement of crimes, remorse, and social reconciliation, as well as important post-conviction matters, such as conditional release and victim notification. Such an approach builds on the feminist ideas of social solidarity with victims (and withdrawal from offenders) and victim-witness calls for criminal sanction that stigmatises the harms of the crimes, holds perpetrators accountable, and removes perpetrators from the community, as well as for non-criminal sanction of compensation, restitution, and public acknowledgement of crimes.

The feminist approach to justice also makes visible the 'public' dimension of feminist accountability, because it sees justice as a public good, to be collectively owned by all, and as an essential part of social transformation. The question of public accountability in international criminal justice has been largely neglected, despite its clear importance.[38] Public accountability consists of '*a social relationship in which an actor feels an obligation to explain and to justify his or her conduct to some significant*

---

[38] With the exception of Mark Findlay and Ralph Henham, *Beyond Punishment* (Basingstoke: Palgrave Macmillan, 2010).

other'.³⁹ At a formal level, international legal institutions are accountable to 'international society', given that criminal prosecutions are undertaken on behalf of 'international society', and legal institutions report to the UN. However, this raises the question as to whether that international society is understood only as the 'society of states', given their concrete form in the UN, which risks capturing 'public accountability' in the geopolitical interests of the global social system.

Importantly, international prosecutions are also understood to be undertaken on behalf of the affected society (as discussed in Chapters 4 and 5). International criminal justice institutions typically characterise engagement with this public constituency as 'outreach', which involves public information and education. For example, the ICTY describes the establishment of its 'Outreach' programme as part of fulfilling its mandate of building peace and reconciliation in the former Yugoslavia.⁴⁰ Brammertz and Jarvis describe 'community education' about the nature of crimes and the facts established about the conflict as crucial to effective sexual violence prosecutions.⁴¹ The ICTY showed that such public information and education programmes are essential for effective, legitimate, and peace-building international criminal justice institutions.

However, Refik Hodžić argues that such a concept of 'outreach' is too narrow to capture 'the role that it [the ICTY] had in terms of its responsibility to its constituents in the former Yugoslavia and the impact that it had on the ground'. Instead, it needs to capture the responsibility of the legal institution to the survivors of international crimes, as well as to 'core affected communities'.⁴² Accordingly, the 'public' constituency of the ICTY can be seen as all affected persons and communities of the former Yugoslavia. However, that idea of responsibility also raises the issue that neither survivors nor affected societies are homogenous 'publics'. The international legal institution faces multiple publics in post-war contexts, which may be more or less visible to the institution, affected in different ways, or in conflict between each other or the

---

[39] Mark Bovens, 'Public Accountability', in Ewan Ferlie, Laurence E. Lynn Jr et al. (eds.), *The Oxford Handbook of Public Management* (Oxford: Oxford University Press, 2007), p. 184.

[40] 'Outreach Programme', https://www.icty.org/en/outreach/outreach-programme.

[41] Brammertz, Jarvis et al., 'Using the OTP's Experience', in Brammertz and Jarvis (eds.), *Prosecuting Conflict-Related Sexual Violence*, p. 361.

[42] Frédéric Mégret, 'The Legacy of the ICTY As Seen through Some of Its Actors and Observers', (2011) 3(3) GoJIL 1011–1052, 1036–7. See also Hodžić, 'A Long Road to Reconciliation', in Richard Steinberg (ed) *Assessing the Legacy of the ICTY* (Leiden: Brill, 2011).

institution itself. The gendered nature of the institutional (non-) recognition of public constituents is readily apparent in the experiences of the Women's Court witnesses.

Developing a concept of feminist public accountability is an important task of building a feminist approach to international criminal law. In feminist justice proceedings, women victims of war are seen as constituents to which justice mechanisms are accountable. If women are to be subjects of justice, then an international criminal justice institution must be accountable to them as persons making justice claims – as individual witnesses participating in justice proceedings and as right-holders entitled to redress. However, the institution owes this accountability not only to individuals but also to collectives, namely, groups of affected victims, and the affected societies on whose behalf criminal prosecutions are undertaken. Building on the social model of public accountability, it is possible to describe five characteristics of feminist public accountability: '(1) public accessibility of the account giving ... (2) explanation and justification of conduct ... (3) the explanation should be directed at a specific forum (4) the actor must feel obliged to come forward ... and (5) there must be a possibility for debate and judgment—and not a monologue without engagement.'[43]

At the same time, feminist justice proceedings emphasise the importance of giving public accounts of gender-based crimes and of building a public that witnesses those crimes. It emphasises the importance of collective public witnessing for including women's experiences in public memory, acknowledging the facts of what happened to them, stigmatising gender-based crimes, and undertaking to change the social relations that made that violence possible. In this approach, building a public language of injustice and justice is crucial for legal social bonds to become part of affected societies. Accordingly, feminist justice proceedings include 'the public' as a fourth party to proceedings (as discussed in Chapter 8). The witnessing public is not seen as pre-existing feminist justice proceedings. Rather, it must be built through the practices of the justice mechanism. Feminist public accountability involves building witnessing 'publics' by using practices that enable it to give meaningful public accounts of gender-based crimes. As such, it is an active form of accountability that seeks to build its 'public' through institutional practices. Accordingly, feminist public accountability shifts the model of

---

[43] Bovens, 'Public Accountability', p. 185.

public education and information programmes from top-down information knowledge transmission to active and dialogical engagement.

To build feminist accountability, criminal justice institutions must engage with women war survivors as part of their public constituencies. In post-conflict contexts, women as civilian survivors of war may face many more challenges in gaining institutional recognition and engaging in collective political action than men as ex-combatants, as was the case in the former Yugoslavia. Accordingly, feminist institutional accountability involves developing practices that actively recognise and enable women as persons making justice claims, whether as witnesses or rights-holders, and that enable institutions to become accountable to them. It also requires designing and undertaking wider feminist accountability practices, such as substantive public and community information and education programmes that address the gender dimensions of prosecutions of international crimes. Following the feminist approach to justice, such programmes need to include women's experiences of war, recognise and stigmatise gender-based crimes, and address the gendered social relations that made that violence possible. These forms of feminist public accountability are particularly important for societies that experience the intensification of patriarchal gender relations in post-war periods, such as the former Yugoslavia. Accordingly, developing principles, practices, and methodologies of feminist public accountability that include women victims of war and provide public accounts of gender-based crimes is an important collective feminist project.

9.3.1.4 Building Feminist Justice Prosecutions

The fourth area is feminist justice prosecutions. Building on the concept of feminist accountability, feminist justice prosecutions have two characteristics. They are (1) meaningful prosecutions that accurately characterise gender-based crimes and (2) provide appropriate sanctions on that basis. Feminist justice prosecutions provide redress for the gender-based crimes that occur in a given conflict, following the relational feminist justice model outlined in Chapter 8. They are meaningful prosecutions that accurately characterise and appropriately sanction gender-based harms, such that there is a legal relation between harms and the prosecutions of them.

To build feminist justice prosecutions involves capturing gendered patterns of criminality in a specific conflict in criminal cases and charges. For example, if prosecutions are to accurately reflect the patterns of sexual violence in a particular conflict, then charges and cases need to capture those specific patterns of illegality. If sexual violence assumes different patterns in conflict, then the cases chosen and charges laid should reflect those patterns. The approach focuses feminist efforts upon developing prosecutorial and judicial policies that capture gendered perpetration and victimisation in conflict, rather than upon widening definitions of offences to include specific groups of sexual violence victims. It also displaces the municipal law analogy from feminist engagements with international criminal law, which gives rise to the problematic idea of international justice as the individualised criminal trial of a direct perpetrator for each victim-witness.

Feminist justice prosecutions instead use a model of collective crimes, which involve perpetration through participation in system criminality and which produce victimisation by harming classes of victims. In this model, each case involves charges against classes of perpetrators according to their role in a specific system of criminality that produces harms to classes of victims, living and dead. As such, feminist justice prosecutions aim to capture patterns of perpetration and victimisation through the selection of cases and charging. Accordingly, feminist justice prosecutions involve institutional strategies and policies that enable prosecuted cases to capture patterns of perpetration (with their respective systems of criminality and classes of perpetrators) and victimisation (with their respective harms and classes of victims) across a given conflict.

Building feminist justice prosecutions requires that institutional policies and strategies consider whether prosecutions represent different forms of illegal system violence in a given conflict, and not only perpetrators who are most responsible for the worst crimes. The approach raises the classical problem of whether it is possible to retain the penal function of a judicial body – to punish all that break the law – with a policy of selective prosecution at the international level. However, all international criminal prosecutions necessarily involve selective prosecution and the exercise of prosecutorial discretion and strategy (as discussed in Chapter 5). The issue is not whether there should be selective prosecution, which is an integral part of prosecuting international crimes. Rather, it concerns the appropriate criteria for selection of prosecutions and for court management of trial proceedings, such as judicial confirmation of charges. It also concerns the appropriate basis for developing wider institutional policy on case selection, management, and completion, such as the ICTY Completion Strategy. Feminist justice prosecutions only make transparent the reasons for such policies.

An explicit policy of representative prosecution accepts an appropriate ground of case selection is that prosecutions represent patterns of illegality in conflict, including patterns of illegality of gender-based crimes such as sexual violence. Similarly important are judicial principles that recognise such public policy considerations as relevant to judicial decision-making in trial proceedings, such as confirmation of charges. Representative prosecutions should be distinguished from thematic prosecutions, which focus on sexual violence crimes, for example. Thematic prosecutions play an important part in addressing 'gaps' in prosecutions or current law (as described above). However, they also risk failing to properly contextualise sexual violence in wider patterns of crimes.[44] Accordingly, it is necessary to contextualise thematic prosecutions within wider policies of representative prosecutions.

Feminist justice prosecutions consider not only who and what will be prosecuted but also when those prosecutions will take place. Usually thought of as a question of prosecutorial strategy and institutional policy, as it was at the ICTY, the issue of the timing of prosecutions has wider implications for feminist justice. The example of the ICTY shows that the timing of prosecutions, whether undue delay or overhasty completion, can have detrimental effects on gender justice outcomes in criminal proceedings. It also has wider social importance, which is well illustrated by the Women's Court participants' concerns at the delay in undertaking and completing prosecutions some 25 years after the end of the war. Because building legal bonds is important to constructing new social relations, the timing of prosecutions comes to have particular significance in transitional periods. As such, gender justice policies should aim to expedite prosecutions as soon as possible during or after the conflict. It is clear that 'timeliness' of investigation and commencement and completion of proceedings are crucial elements of building feminist justice prosecutions.

Building feminist justice proceedings is an important way to establish feminist public accountability in legal institutions. The legal institution explains what it is doing and why it is doing it in the context of meaningful engagement with its public constituencies. It builds accountability to its publics, including women victims of war, and provides meaningful public accounts of crimes, including gender-based crimes.

---

[44] Michelle Jarvis and Najwa Nabti, 'Policies and Institutional Strategies for Successful Sexual Violence Prosecutions', in Brammertz and Jarvis (eds.), *Prosecuting Conflict-Related Sexual Violence*, pp. 86–87.

Building feminist justice prosecutions in this way also has three further crucial consequences. The first is that it enables the integration of international prosecutorial and judicial policies concerning which cases proceed against whom and on what grounds with regional and national accountability strategies for international crimes. It thereby strengthens 'vertical' accountability between international and national criminal justice systems and 'horizontal' accountability between national courts. Second, by strengthening transnational accountability strategies, it also becomes possible to identify 'justice' gaps in legal redress, such as prosecutions, and legal remedies, such as individual compensation or collective reparations, for all victim classes. Legal redress and remedies flow to all members of these victim classes, whether or not they appear as trial witnesses. Accordingly, identifying 'justice gaps' in legal redress and remedy makes it possible to develop appropriate forms of legal relations and mechanisms to address them beyond the individual criminal trial.

Finally, publicly explaining the role of the international criminal justice institution makes clear that its function is to build the legal relations of international criminal law, which are a necessary condition of wider changes in social relations. However, it also makes clear that international criminal law structurally cannot provide justice *per se*, in the sense that there will always be gaps in the justice it provides. Building feminist justice prosecutions through the frame of feminist accountability thereby opens the space for affected communities to identify these wider justice gaps and address them by developing other collective mechanisms for building post-conflict justice.

9.3.2 Building Feminist Trial Norms for Criminal Justice Proceedings

For the feminist approach to justice, the principle of enabling women to become subjects of justice is at the centre of designing feminist justice proceedings. To enable women to become subjects of justice, its model of feminist justice proceedings offers new concepts of witnessing and fact-finding. These are feminist modes of victim-witness testimony and collective witnessing and feminist fact-finding. Developed as feminist trial norms, these concepts provide the basis for building new forms of evidencing and warranting the injustices of gender-based harms.

9.3.2.1 Feminist Modes of Victim-Witness Testimony

That witnesses to gender-based based harms confront discriminatory gender stereotypes and bias that create gender inequality in judicial systems is well known, particularly in relation to sexual violence offences. In the former Yugoslavia, key reviews by Medica Mondiale, the OSCE BiH, and the ICTY make important recommendations for addressing these discriminatory practices and norms, and building 'formal' equality for witnesses in prosecutions of international crimes.[45] Most recommendations simply require the non-discriminatory implementation of existing legal norms, such as adequate investigation of sexual violence or fair labelling of sexual violence offences. Other recommendations develop institutional and legal norms that focus on the needs and rights of war rape survivors, such as using a 'witness centred' approach and provision of legal and health services, or improving the witness experience of proceedings, such as improving judicial practice on defence questioning and strengthening protective measures. The implementation of the existing recommendations would significantly contribute to addressing the concerns identified by the Women's Court participants and must be undertaken as a matter of urgency in the successor states of the former Yugoslavia. This should also be seen as an urgent matter for all prosecutions of international crimes before national and international courts.

Moving from specific recommendations, the model of feminist justice proceedings underscores the importance of having gender-just procedural and evidential frameworks. The recent Model Legislative Provisions developed by the UN is an important step forward in this regard.[46] However, it focuses upon individual victim's rights in criminal procedure in national jurisdictions and does not develop non-discriminatory international norms for international criminal procedure and evidence. The feminist justice proceedings model suggests a wider approach, which for example addresses restrictive forms of presenting testimonial evidence; the conduct of judges, defence, and prosecution towards witnesses; and

---

[45] See Gabi Mischkowski and Gorana Mlinarević, *And That It Does Not Happen to Anyone Anywhere in the World: The Trouble with Rape Trials* (Cologne: Medica Mondiale, 2009), 93ff; OSCE BiH *Towards Justice for Conflict-Related Sexual Violence in Bosnia and Herzegovina (2014–2016)* (Sarajevo: OSCE, 2016), p. 88 ff; Brammertz and Jarvis (eds), *Prosecuting Conflict-Related Sexual Violence*, chapters three to five.

[46] Model Legislative Provisions and Guidance on Investigation and Prosecution of Conflict - Related Sexual Violence, Office of the Special Representative of the Secretary-General on Sexual Violence in Conflict, 18 June 2021 (Model Legislative Provisions).

the standards of evaluation used to assess that evidence. From this model, it is possible to identify three key areas for development of non-discriminatory procedural and evidential norms. The first area concerns discriminatory evidentiary rules. It builds on existing international practice of specialist provisions prohibiting the discriminatory treatment of sexual violence witnesses, such as allowing consent as a defence, imposing corroboration requirements, or admission of prior sexual conduct of the victim (such as Rule 96 ICTY RPE). Such prohibitions should be regarded as procedural norms of fair trials under customary international law and, as such, accord fair trial rights to victims equivalent to those of the accused.

Following this 'fair trial' principle, and the consequentialist concept of sexual violence, the issue of consent should be treated as an evidential issue to be established by the defence (as it is in forcible transfer cases), rather than an element of the offence to be established by the prosecution. Such a defence should only be allowed as a judicially reviewed exception where it is raised in the form of 'affirmative consent', as Grewal suggests.[47] Clarifying the elements of the offence together with the evidential status of 'consent' arguments in the rules of evidence and procedure would address the current problematic approach to consent.

The second area concerns procedural rules regarding particular defence challenges to witness credibility or reliability. Highly damaging and evidentially unwarranted defence challenges should also be prohibited by procedural rules, again with provision for judicially reviewed exception. For example, as can be seen in the Women's Court testimonies, the testifying witnesses refer to the importance of therapeutic treatment and/or the personal support from victims' associations, NGOs, and other informal organisations. However, these forms of support have been used by defence as the grounds for challenging witness reliability (in the case of therapeutic treatment) and/or credibility (in the case of participation in 'advocacy' organisations), as can be seen in the *Furundžija* case discussed in Chapter 4. Such defence challenges should be prohibited as breaches of victims' fair trial rights.

The third area concerns procedural rules regarding expert witness evidence on sexual violence and other gender-based crimes and the presentation and evaluation of witness testimony. Expert witnesses have a crucial role in addressing common 'rape myths', not only in terms of

---

[47] Grewal, 'The Protection of Sexual Autonomy under International Criminal Law', 392–393.

the evaluation of evidence by the court but also in terms of educating the wider society about those myths. This is particularly important in prosecutions of international crimes, which are often highly public and contested trials. Moreover, while expert witness testimony of sexual violence generally has not been accepted as evidence on patterns of sexual violence, as discussed in Chapter 4, it is also crucially important in establishing patterns of aggregate social harms. In this regard, the role of such expert witnesses should be seen as analogous to the widely accepted use of military or historical expert witnesses. The expert witnesses in the Women's Court showed the importance of providing 'objective' structural and contextual analyses of gender-based crimes. This expert evidence is crucial for understanding the gendered shaping of system criminality, rather than relying on the limited interpretation of the 'social facts' of patriarchy by judges or fact witnesses, as seen in the *Krstić*, *Mladić*, and *Karadžić* cases. Accordingly, procedural and evidential rules should provide for the standard use of such expert evidence on sexual violence in criminal trials.

Importantly, the feminist approach to justice also seeks to move beyond ideas of formal gender equality to ideas of substantive justice, as defined by women as agents of justice. To do this requires considering the form of trial proceedings and the role of witnesses within them. As discussed in Chapter 8, the feminist approach to justice includes a range of pre-hearing, hearing, and post-hearing practices that aim to empower women to testify and can be used as the basis for further developing these approaches in the context of legal proceedings. The first set of practices aim to support women in being able to testify. These include identifying potential witnesses through public, community, and NGO engagement; enabling witnesses to be active participants in preparing their testimony in a full preparatory process; providing psychological support during the preparatory process; and enabling witnesses to provide mutual support to each other (without risking contamination of evidence). The second set of practices aim to support witness agency during the proceedings. These practices include positioning witnesses as central to the organisation of the court setting and proceedings; working collaboratively with witnesses to decide the content and form of their testimony, and enabling witnesses to show emotion and engagement in their testimony, and explaining what harm and justice mean to them. The third set of practices concerns post-proceedings. These include ongoing activities with witnesses; psychological and legal support in the period after the proceedings; consistent rules on redaction, anonymisation, and publication of testimony developed in consultation with witnesses; and institutional trial monitoring.

These feminist practices also raise the broader question of how to design justice proceedings in which the sexual violence survivor can become a testimonial agent. The feminist approach to justice underscores the importance of providing equal access to justice for female witnesses, meaningful witness support in all phases of the criminal process (before, during, and after trial), and links to reparations and specialised support programmes. It also draws on the inquisitorial legal tradition in emphasising the active role of witnesses in justice proceedings and the witness support that enables this role. In the context of international criminal trials, such witness support needs to be both psycho-social, in the form of a specified (qualified) person supporting the witness, and legal, in the form of a victim-witness representative, and provided throughout the legal process. While the inquisitorial legal tradition also informs the ICC victim participation provisions, these measures do not establish fair trial rights for victims as parties to the proceedings or to have a legal representative as such. While there are practical challenges for developing an active role for witnesses and victims in the context of international trials, developing international procedural norms for the legal participation and representation of victims and witnesses is nevertheless crucial. Giving victims and witnesses an active role in criminal proceedings is an essential element of enabling them to become testimonial agents.

9.3.2.2 Feminist Modes of Collective Witnessing

An important challenge in building feminist justice proceedings is to address the collective evidencing of sexual violence as gender-based harms, as discussed in Chapter 4. As the feminist approach to justice shows, collective witnessing is crucial to evidencing sexual violence as a form of collective violence, as discussed in Chapter 8. The feminist approach to justice provides a model of collective witnessing that makes visible the connections between individual experiences of gender-based harm and collective experiences of structural injustice and identifies the patterns of victimisation and perpetration in gendered system violence. Building on this model, it is possible to develop an evidential methodology to capture such patterns of gender-based victimisation and perpetration.

The methodology consists of a sequential 'gender analysis' of evidence, social injury, and aggregate harm. The *gender analysis of evidence* identifies women's experiences of harms in a given conflict. It does so by identifying experiences of harms as women survivors identify and describe them, as other witnesses identify and describe the experiences of women (including the experiences of missing or dead victims) and as expert evidence describes those experiences across the affected society as a whole (such as social and demographic studies). The gender analysis of evidence ensures the inclusion of gender-specific harms, such as sexual violence, in the totality of evidence of system violence.

The *gender analysis of social injuries* examines the harms that this group suffers across the totality of evidence. It analyses the evidence to identify the range of harms experienced by women as a class of persons. It does so by identifying the distinct patterns of experiences, such as rape, sexual enslavement, and sexual trafficking, together with their distinctive configurations, such as social group membership (such as the sexual trafficking of young women) or conflict context (such as detention settings following military occupation). This analysis captures different patterns of gender-based victimisation.

The *gender analysis of aggregate harms* captures the gender-based injury to women as a class of persons. It examines how these individual experiences of harms 'aggregate' or combine together to form a category of harm characterised by its distinctive properties or characteristics, such as sexual violence. It identifies the category of harm by identifying the shared characteristics of these practices and how they repeat over time and space, such as sexual violence victimisation across the duration of the conflict and the conflict region. The 'aggregate' harms are group-based injuries and consist of collective status subordination experienced by this class of persons.

The gender analysis shows how the totality of individual evidence of sexual violence describes the collective experience of aggregate social injuries, defined as injuries to a class of persons. It shows these group experiences in the totality of evidence of sexual violence, thereby making it possible to identify patterns of gendered harm (the different types of sexual violence) in terms of its patterns of victimisation (the targeting of women) and effects (the disproportionate impact on women). That analysis serves as the basis for describing the collective or group nature of gender-specific injuries. With the description of gender-specific injuries, it then becomes possible to evidence sexual violence as a gender-based form of system violence, which produces the gendered status subordination of women.

Equally importantly, the methodology also enables an analysis of the collective evidence of gendered patterns of perpetration, by linking aggregate gender-based harm to the gendered system violence in which they occur. This involves a sequential 'gender analysis' of the collective evidence of perpetration, which examines perpetrator violence, collective violence, system violence construction, system violence components, and perpetrator groups. The *gender analysis of perpetrator violence* describes the violence in which perpetrators participate. It involves analysing different types of perpetrator violence that correlate to the range of harms experienced by women as a class of persons. It identifies distinct forms of perpetration, such as rape and other offences, and their distinctive configurations, such as social group membership (for example, paramilitary affiliation and gender) and conflict context (such as detention settings in a given area). Accordingly, it identifies different patterns of perpetration and groups of perpetrators.

The *gender analysis of collective violence* identifies the distinctive forms of collective violence committed by these perpetrators. It examines how these individual acts combine or 'aggregate' together to form a distinctive category of perpetration, such as sexual violence. Conceptually equivalent to the aggregate harms of victims, the category describes the aggregate violence of perpetrators. It identifies the category of perpetration by identifying the shared characteristics of these practices and how they repeat over time and space, such as sexual violence perpetration across the duration of the conflict and the conflict region.

The *gender analysis of system violence construction* examines the building of the forms of collective violence through the organisation of actors and symbolic and material resources. It identifies the means of 'collectivising' violence by analysing the organisation of actors and resources into systems of coercive force. For example, the construction of sexual violence as a form of system violence involves the organisation of actors (such as militaries and local police), material resources (such as arms, supplies, and buildings), and cultural resources (such as symbols, ideas, and ideals) into systems of coercive force.

The *gender analysis of system violence components* identifies the component systems of the collective violence. It involves describing the 'systems' of collective violence that create the domination or deprivation of capacities of groups of persons while enabling other groups to dominate and develop their capacities. These interacting structures may include: (1) political, military, economic, and security leadership; (2) intellectual elites; (3) militaries, paramilitaries, and other armed groups; (4) media; (5) professional groups (such as legal and medical professionals); (6) government and administration; (7) religious institutions and leaders; (8) industry and business; (9) political parties; and (10) transnational organisations and states.

The *gender analysis of perpetrator groups* analyses how the system violence produces classes of persons, whose members participate in the domination or deprivation of the capacities of other groups of persons. The social injuries of collective violence produce not only social groups of victims but also social groups of perpetrators. Accordingly, the gender analysis of perpetrator groups examines how the structures of collective violence produce group patterns of perpetration. It examines how system violence constructs groups of perpetrators, by establishing them as a class of persons predicated upon the domination of victimised groups and characterised by their participation in system violence.

9.3.2.3 Feminist Fact-Finding

The feminist concepts of victim-witness testimony and collective witnessing show the importance of developing feminist models of fact-finding on gender-based harms. They show that the feminist methods and proceedings that establish facts are two important components of such a model. The first question is how to build new feminist epistemic models of legal methods and methodologies. Despite Hilary Charlesworth's pathbreaking work in this area, it is a surprisingly neglected area in feminist scholarship on international criminal law.[48] If the determination of legal facts, and the evaluation of evidence upon which it rests, necessarily draws upon particular models of knowledge, then developing new models of feminist fact-finding is an important collective feminist aim (as discussed in Chapter 8).

To generate stronger legal objectivity requires addressing the interlinked questions of method (techniques for gathering evidence), methodology (a theory and analysis of how legal fact-finding does or should proceed), and epistemology (a theory of legal knowledge that answers questions about who can be a knower, what tests beliefs must pass in order to be legitimated as knowledge, and what kinds of facts can be known) (to adapt Harding).[49] The task involves building new feminist epistemic practices that can serve as regulatory norms for constructing

---

[48] Hilary Charlesworth, 'Feminist Methods in International Law', (1999) 93(2) AJIL, 379–394. An exception is Eithne Dowds, *Feminist Engagement with International Criminal Law* (Oxford: Hart, 2019), pp. 18–19.

[49] Sandra Harding, 'Introduction', in Sandra Harding (ed.), *Feminist and Methodology* (Bloomington: Indiana University Press, 1987), pp. 2–3.

and evaluating legal knowledge. Helen Longino argues that '[t]he complete set of regulative standards, inclusive of theoretical virtues, guiding a community's epistemic practices could be called its epistemology'. These regulative standards are the normative criteria by which members of the community of inquiry determine which practices 'will advance our cognitive aims' and political goals.[50] This involves developing 'transformative, responsible, and responsive epistemic practices' as feminist regulative standards of legal fact-finding.[51]

The second challenge is how to design more just proceedings for gender-based crimes, such as sexual violence. Given the different structure and purpose of fact-finding processes in inquisitorial and common law traditions, it is necessary to consider the implications of these different legal systems for witness experiences and fact-finding in gender-based crimes, such as sexual violence. For example, commentators describe the adversarial trial process adopted by the ICTY as being highly problematic for victim-witnesses generally, and sexual violence witnesses in particular.[52] In contrast, the Women's Court justice process has a similar structure to inquisitorial proceedings, as discussed in Chapter 8. Given that international criminal law is a hybrid legal system, it is important to consider how to develop mixed legal systems that can provide more just proceedings for the gendered injustices of war. Part of this challenge is to engage with global legal traditions and pluralist legal cultures in considering the design of truly global feminist justice proceedings.[53]

To build new feminist models of legal fact-finding requires building transnational 'webs of connection called solidarity in politics and shared conversations in epistemology'.[54] We can describe these 'webs of connection' as epistemic communities (the groups that generate knowledge about gender or law, for example). Given the traditional domination of the international legal profession by white, Western, and male global

---

[50] Helen Longino, 'Feminist Epistemology as a Local Epistemology', (1997) 71 Aristotelian Society, 19–35, 33–34.
[51] Lorraine Code, *Ecological Thinking* (Oxford: Oxford University Press, 2006), p. xi.
[52] See Julie Mertus, 'The Politics of Memory and International Trials for Wartime Rape', in Paul Gready (ed.), *Political Transition* (London: Pluto Press, 2003).
[53] On the Yugoslav context, see Fionnuala Ni Aoláin, 'The Fractured Soul of the Dayton Peace Agreement', (1998) 19(4) Mich J Int'l L 957–1004. On the global context, see Coomaraswamy, *Preventing Conflict, Transforming Peace, Securing the Peace*, pp. 119–121.
[54] Donna Haraway, *Simians, Cyborgs, and Women* (London: Free Association, 1991), p. 191.

elites, it is important that such feminist epistemic communities do not reproduce these power relations. Instead, it is necessary to undertake the collective feminist work of democratising the membership of the epistemic communities of international criminal law and building the conditions that enable global participation in these shared conversations in legal epistemology.

9.4 Building Feminist Relational Legal Justice

Feminist relational legal justice seeks to build legal social bonds in relation to social injury *and* social transformation. It recognises that international criminal justice does not exist as an abstract concept but must be given concrete existence in legal rules, practices, and institutions. It also recognises that feminist legal social bonds are built in concrete social situations, which are the social conditions of war-affected societies and the global social system. Accordingly, its legal relations must be built in war-affected collectives and in transnational social relations. The Women's Court shows the importance of building 'institutional legal justice' for sexual violence and other gender-based international crimes in the struggle to build more emancipatory social relations in the Yugoslav region. However, it also shows the struggle to build these legal relations in the concrete social situation of the former Yugoslavia.

The struggle began with the General Framework Agreement for Peace in Bosnia and Herzegovina in 1995 (Dayton Peace Agreement) and continues into the present. The Dayton Peace Agreement does not in fact provide a framework for building justice for international crimes.[55] Instead, it provides fragmented provisions that establish disconnected rights, duties, and mechanisms, with insufficient provision for implementation or enforcement. These highly limited accountability mechanisms and collective obligations created a 'justice gap' for international crimes, which was not addressed in the course of its implementation.

The first justice gap involves international criminal justice. Provision for criminal accountability in the Dayton Peace Agreement is limited to the obligation to co-operate with the ICTY (Article IX) and the establishment of Bosnian State jurisdiction for international crimes under the

---

[55] For an important feminist analysis of the Dayton Peace Agreement, see http://peacewomen.org/sites/default/files/DPA-report-FINAL.pdf. My thanks to Nela Porobić Isaković and Gorana Mlinarević for my invitation to this workshop, where I developed this analysis.

State Constitution. At the level of the Bosnian State and its constituent entities, it does not establish obligations to prosecute international crimes (other than as part of limited lustration and vetting measures) or provide remedies for their violations (other than individual rights of return and property rights) (Annexes 4, 7, and 8). It does not require the Bosnian State (or its constituent entities) to build what I describe as 'positive international complementarity' with the ICTY, which involves a 'proactive policy of cooperation aimed at promoting' both national *and* international criminal proceedings.[56] Nor does the Agreement establish such obligations for the 'regional' successor states (as parties to the conflict). The Agreement also does not address the potential role of the UN – or the Peace Implementation Council of Dayton – in building positive international complementarity.[57] Finally, the Agreement does not address the potential regional role of the ICTY in building international criminal justice across the former Yugoslavia, despite its mandate to contribute to the restoration and maintenance of peace. The importance of this role in supporting regional prosecutions is evident following the establishment of 'specialised organs for war crimes investigations and proceedings' in the successor states from 2003 onwards, particularly in Bosnia.[58]

The second gap is 'transitional justice'. The Dayton Peace Agreement established only limited 'transitional rights and obligations' of the Bosnian State in the form of limited individual rights of refugees and displaced persons to return to their prior residence and reclaim property, limited co-operation on missing persons, the protection of common cultural property, lustration of the police, military, and public service (Annex 7 and 8), and barring participation in elections and public office of those convicted or indicted but failing to appear before the ICTY under the Bosnian State Constitution (Article 9). However, it does not establish other transitional justice measures or wider collective

---

[56] ICC, Office of the Prosecutor, Prosecutorial Strategy, 2009–2012 (February 2010), p. 5. See also Kirsten Campbell, 'Building National and Regional Accountability for Conflict-Related Sexual Violence', (2018) 7(2) IHRLR 201–224.
[57] See Diane Orentlicher, *Some Kind of Justice* (New York: Oxford University Press, 2018).
[58] Brammertz and Jarvis et al., 'Using the OTP's Experience with Sexual Violence as a Springboard for Building National Capacity', p. 344. On the DPA and the ICTY, see Ní Aoláin, 'The Fractured Soul of the Dayton Peace Agreement'. On sexual violence prosecutions, see Jasenka Ferizović and Gorana Mlinarević, 'Applying International Experiences in National Prosecutions of Conflict-Related Sexual Violence', (2020) 18(2) JICJ 325–348.

obligations of peace-building at the level of the Bosnian State, its constituent entities, or at the 'regional' level of the successor states. At a regional level, there were no obligations to develop transitional justice policies. Of the successor states, it was only Bosnia that would develop a 'transitional justice' strategy. However, this 'gender neutral' strategy has yet to be adopted.[59]

The third justice gap is gender justice. The Dayton Peace Agreement made no provision to address the specific gender-based effects of the war or the post-war situation of women. No women were involved in the final negotiations.[60] The ethno-nationalist division of Bosnia in the Dayton Peace Agreement amplified this gender injustice. The gender justice gap is exemplified by the failure to fully prosecute or provide reparations for sexual violence as an international crime. In her highly prescient analysis of the Dayton Peace Agreement in 1997, Ustinia Dolgopol argued that the failure of the international community and Bosnian State entities to fulfil their obligations to survivors of sexual violence would have profound consequences for those women and their society.[61] To this analysis, I would add the successor states. While Bosnia remains the leading state in its efforts to improve criminal prosecutions, to provide civil compensation, and to recognise sexual violence survivors as civilian victims of war, these efforts have nevertheless been delayed, uneven, and insufficient.

This is the gender justice gap that the Women's Court witnesses are still living with, and attempting to change, across the former Yugoslavia some 25 years after the formal end of military violence in the Dayton Agreement. While prosecutions of conflict-related sexual violence are clearly supported by victims and the wider society in the former Yugoslavia, they were not connected to other gender-based harms or crimes or understood as a form of gender justice. Moreover, they were not connected to other elements of gender justice, such as reparative or transitional justice, which were necessary to address the individual material and social needs of sexual violence survivors and the broader

---

[59] The Programme for Victims of Sexual Violence in Conflict was subsequently developed in 2012 by the UNDP and the Ministry for Human Rights and Refugees and has yet to be adopted.

[60] For an important feminist analysis of the gendered nature and impacts of the Dayton Peace Agreement, see Nela Porobić Isaković and Gorana Mlinarević, *The Peace That Is Not* (Geneva: Women's International League for Peace and Freedom, 2021).

[61] Ustinia Dolgopol, 'A Feminist Appraisal of the Dayton Peace Accords' (1997) 19(1) Adel L Rev 59-71, 66-71.

collective challenge of transforming gendered inequalities.[62] The feminist approach to justice shows that the legal relations of international criminal justice play a crucial part in this wider transformation of social relations of domination and oppression. However, it also shows the need to connect criminal justice to other forms of reparative and transitional justice for international crimes and situate all forms of justice within a transformative feminist frame.

With this analysis, it is possible to describe more precisely the gender justice gap in 'institutional legal justice' that the Women's Court reveals. It consists of the failure to provide redress, remedy, and reconstruction for gender-based crimes in concrete justice institutions, mechanisms, and practices.[63] The feminist approach to justice reveals the importance of all three forms of justice. The first is criminal justice, which provides redress in the form of criminal accountability. The second is reparative justice, which provides remedies for the harms that flow from those crimes. These remedies are both individual and collective and include restitution, right of return, and reparations. Such remedies must be social and economic, as well as civil and political. The third is reconstructive justice, which aims to address the political, economic, and social legacies of war in affected societies. On the one hand, it 'deals with the past', working through the past conflict by using transitional justice mechanisms and practices, ranging from lustration to truth commissions. On the other, it 'deals with the future', by reconstructing the political, economic, and social arrangements that gave rise to the conflict as well as the political, economic, and social arrangements that emerge from it. None of these forms of justice seek to repair or restore the pre-conflict society. Rather, they are forms of relational justice that aim to both address social injuries and effect social transformation. Accordingly, building a feminist approach to international criminal law requires constructing the transnational legal relations of international criminal justice for gender-based crimes and linking it to reparative and reconstructive justice for gender-based harms.

---

[62] For an important feminist analysis of this challenge, see Porobić Isaković and Mlinarević, *Concept and Framework*.

[63] This approach builds on the important work of Rami Mani, particularly *Beyond Retribution* (Cambridge and Malden: Polity, 2002). For further discussion, see Kirsten Campbell, 'Reassembling International Justice', (2014) 8(1) Int J Transitional Justice 53–74, 66–67.

To effectively build these forms of justice in the concrete social situations of war-affected societies, and the transnational social relations that produce them, is conditional upon embedding them in post-war political settlements. As can be seen in the example of the Dayton Peace Agreement, redress, reparation, and reconstruction need to be an integral part of peace agreements, processes, and implementation. It shows that justice is an integral part of peace, where peace is understood as an ongoing process of social justice that aims to transform individual and structural relations of subordination and exploitation, and not only as a political agreement that ends armed conflict. Building on the experience of the gender justice gap in the former Yugoslavia, it is possible to identify five 'international justice' principles to build these forms of justice in the concrete conditions of conflict and post-conflict social situations.

The first principle is the meaningful and active participation of women in all levels of peace talks and decision-making mechanisms, as well as in all criminal and civil justice institutions, and any bodies responsible for framework implementation.[64] The second principle is the inclusion of positive international complementarity for international, regional, and state criminal justice systems. The third principle is the inclusion of mechanisms for criminal, reparative, and reconstructive justice in peace agreement frameworks. The fourth principle is the integration of criminal, reparative, and reconstructive justice mechanisms and their national, regional, and international implementation. The fifth principle is the inclusion of a 'gender justice relational review' of all existing justice mechanisms at national, regional, and international levels. Gender justice relational review compares patterns of gender-based harms in a given conflict to the justice mechanisms provided for them and examines whether they provide justice for those harms. Such a review involves identifying justice gaps in existing provision and developing appropriate justice mechanisms for gender-based harms.

These 'international justice' principles should be seen as necessary conditions for the development of the framework principles for sexual violence set out in the next section. Both these and the framework principles draw on the experience of seeking justice for conflict-related sexual violence as a gender-based crime in the former Yugoslavia.

---

[64] On feminist peace-building in the Yugoslavian context, see Nela Porobić Isaković and Gorana Mlinarević, 'Sustainable Transitions to Peace Need Women's Groups and Feminists', (2019) 72(2) Journal of International Affairs, 173–190.

As such, the principles are not templates to be applied regardless of context. Instead, they are generalised transitional strategies, and concrete historical situations will determine their development and application.

STRATEGY TWO: BUILDING A FEMINIST APPROACH TO SEXUAL VIOLENCE AS AN INTERNATIONAL CRIME IN PRACTICE

The second strategy applies the feminist legal framework to legal practice and positive international criminal law, using the example of sexual violence as an international crime. Building on the feminist legal framework, the strategy develops a set of principles for developing feminist justice prosecutions of sexual violence (that is, legal practice) and for developing a draft international convention on conflict-related sexual violence (that is, positive legal norms). These principles provide strategic policy and legal frameworks to build a feminist approach to sexual violence as an international crime in practice.

9.5 Policy Framework Principles for Prosecutions of Sexual Violence as an International Crime

Building on the feminist legal framework, it is possible to identify six key principles that can serve as the basis for building substantive gender justice in the prosecution of sexual violence as an international crime.

Principle 1: Develop appropriate concepts of gender and gender-based crimes for international criminal law.

This involves developing new concepts of gender and gender-based crimes for conflict-related sexual violence, which are appropriate for capturing the gendered nature of conflict and gender harms in specific conflict contexts.

Principle 2: Undertake doctrinal development of legal norms of sexual violence as an international crime, particularly in relation to substantive elements and modes of liability.

This involves the development of legal concepts, doctrines, and rules at the international level that can provide comprehensive definitions of sexual violence as a gender-based crime covering all conflicts by all actors at all levels of responsibility.

Examples of the application of this principle include:

- prosecutorial strategies that undertake jurisprudential development and representative cases;
- appropriate judicial engagement with jurisprudential development; and
- further development of international customary norms concerning gender-based crimes.

Principle 3: Identify and address gender norms and power biases in the values, design, culture, and established practices of legal institutions.

This involves identifying institutional cultures and practices that affect sexual violence prosecutions and the design of policies and practices that address these norms and biases in appropriate ways for each specific institutional and conflict context.

Examples of the application of this principle include:

- assessment of individual, cultural, and legal gender values of legal professionals and institutions and development of appropriate policies to address these values;
- normative and legal gender review of existing legal cultures, such as identifying discriminatory provisions or practices in legal systems;
- the harmonisation of standards (international legal norms) and best practice (legal and institutional) between international and national courts;
- mechanisms for regular institutional review of gender-based crimes patterns of prosecution, trial practices, and sentencing; and
- developing feminist justice mandates.

Principle 4: Integrate gender analysis of system violence into criminal and civil justice processes.

This involves capturing the different patterns of sexual violence as an international crime to ensure the development of appropriate legal responses to those patterns. The application of the principle enables the development of appropriate criminal justice responses, such as identification of the gendered elements of core crimes and gender-based crimes in each specific conflict context, as well as building appropriate civil justice responses, such as reparation programmes.

Examples of the application of this principle include:

- accurate analysis of the gendered nature of system violence;
- integration of gender analysis into investigative and legal strategies;
- accurate charging of offences as gendered elements of core crimes and gender-based crimes;
- inclusion of proportionate numbers of victims reflecting the different patterns of gendered harms;
- appropriate sentencing and release programmes; and
- development of appropriate forms of restitutionary remedies for gendered harms, such as gender-sensitive individual compensation and collective reparation programmes.

Principle 5: Provide significant and active victim participation and protection in the criminal process.

This involves developing victim-centred justice processes, which enable participatory parity for men and women, and meaningful victim participation. The application of the principle provides the basis for building accurate legal accounts of the gendered experience of conflicts.

Examples of the application of this principle include:

- inclusion of numbers of witnesses proportionate to different gendered patterns of crimes;
- development of evidential standards and courtroom practices to give the testimonies of these witnesses equal value and weight and to support witnesses in fully testifying to their experiences;
- improvement of the witness experience in the legal institution (including practices such as legal representatives for witnesses);
- development of new models of witness protection on the basis of individual and collective needs for support;
- provision of psycho-social and economic witness support; and
- co-ordinated gender review of proportion of male and female witnesses, witness support, and witness experience in all sections of the judicial institution.

Principle 6: Actively linking criminal, reparative, and reconstructive justice.

This principle aims to build engagement with post-conflict societies as an integral part of any international criminal justice process. The engagement should begin with the inauguration of any criminal justice processes (whether instituting proceedings or establishing institutions) in order to avoid the significant disadvantages associated with administrative or *ad hoc* models of engagement.

Examples of the application of this principle include:

- active engagement with existing national legal cultures and criminal and civil justice systems;
- active development of positive international complementarity;
- active integration of criminal justice with reparative and reconstructive justice processes and mechanisms; and
- developing feminist accountability strategies.

9.6 Legal Framework Principles for an International Convention on Sexual Violence as International Crime

The policy framework principles identify the doctrinal development of substantive and procedural norms of sexual violence as an important area for building feminist justice prosecutions. Such doctrinal development is crucial to addressing the ongoing failure to prosecute sexual violence as an international crime effectively and fully. While there is wide recognition of this failure, three different approaches to addressing it have recently emerged. The first calls for more effective implementation of existing rules, while the second seeks to progressively 'codify' existing rules. The third approach, following the policy framework principles, calls for the development of new international rules.

The first approach argues that 'existing provisions are adequate for this purpose and that priority should be given to applying them more effectively'.[65] The major policy review of the Prevent Sexual Violence Initiative by the British government took this position in response to my proposal for a new convention on conflict-related sexual violence in 2015. The ICRC takes a similar position in relation to humanitarian law.[66] In this approach, existing substantive and procedural norms serve as an adequate basis for undertaking sexual violence prosecutions. More recently, a second approach is to develop a model code of substantive offences governing sexual violence offences, which in effect codify

---

[65] Select Committee on Sexual Violence in Conflict Sexual Violence in Conflict: A War Crime, Report, 12 April 2016, HL Paper 123, para. 85.
[66] ICRC, 'Resolutions of the 32nd International Conference of the Red Cross and Red Crescent (2015)' (2016) 900 International Review of the Red Cross, 1389.

existing international rules.⁶⁷ This is the approach taken by the Model Legislative Provisions, which draw heavily on the ICC Elements of Crimes but do not substantively develop the crimes. For example, the crime of genocide in the Model Legislative Provisions mirrors that of the ICC provisions and does not include sexual violence as an enumerated act of genocide.⁶⁸

Enforcing international criminal norms is clearly a crucial element of building a feminist approach to international criminal justice. Similarly, model codes that 'codify' existing standards provide useful clarification and progressive interpretation of current law, which is important given the existing doctrinal debates concerning sexual violence as an international crime. However, it is not sufficient to implement existing legal frameworks. To do so simply implements all the problems identified in my earlier analysis of the existing form of international criminal law. Both approaches build on existing legal frameworks and do not develop feminist legal norms, practices, and values that could form the basis of a new feminist legal framework.

Accordingly, a third approach is necessary that builds a new feminist legal framework in an international instrument, such as a convention on the prohibition, prevention, and punishment of sexual violence as an international crime. It should take the form of a general multilateral treaty agreed to by state parties and supported by the UN. Such a treaty would establish generalisable rules, which would have the status of the general practice of states supporting the existence of customary rules. The proposed convention would enable the creation of progressive customary norms for all prosecutions of sexual violence as an international crime and address the fragmented nature of the existing legal framework by developing a comprehensive definition of the offence of sexual violence covering all conflicts by all actors at all levels of responsibility. It would enable the development of sexual violence as a specified offence under international law, as well as the development of international procedural and evidential norms for sexual violence offences. It would also incorporate a full range of implementation, enforcement, and referral policies and mechanisms needed to support sexual violence prosecutions.

The aim of developing an international convention on sexual violence as an international crime is to create rules that are generally accepted

---

[67] See, for example, Dowds, *Feminist Engagement with International Criminal Law*.
[68] Model Legislative Provisions, Article 35, p. 24.

norms at the international level, obligations to prevent and prosecute these crimes, and mechanisms to build compliance with these rules. The proposed convention would be similar in operation to the Geneva Conventions of 1949 and the grave breaches enforcement obligations. The suppression measures would include obligations to incorporate the proposed conventions' provisions in domestic criminal and military codes, to prosecute or extradite for prosecution those accused of these crimes, and to provide instruction to armed forces and make the proposed convention known to the public.

The proposed convention would set out sexual violence as a differentiated, specified, and serious category of offences under international criminal law. The definition of this category would build on the conceptual definition of the offence outlined earlier in this chapter, namely:

(1) an act of a sexual nature
(2) that causes injury through its commission in the coercive circumstances of conflict, crimes against humanity, or genocide and
(3) is committed with the intention of causing injury or with recklessness as to causing injury;
(4) where that act involves sexual penetration of another person or causing the sexual penetration of another person, it shall be qualified as the offence of rape.

Building on this approach, the convention would specify the different forms of perpetration of conflict-related sexual violence. It differentiates between sexual violence crimes according to the core crime categories that give the conduct its character as an international crime, which would include: (1) armed conflict, (2) an attack upon a civilian population, or (3) the destruction of a protected group. Those international elements are conceptualised as different forms of coercive collective violence, as described earlier in this chapter. This approach would thereby enable the development of sexual violence offences as part of general crime categories, as well as a distinct offence rising to the level of an international crime.

The proposed convention would set out the elements of the offence, criminal responsibility and liability, and procedural and evidential norms, including:

(1) the category of acts of a sexual nature prohibited under international law (the elements of sexual violence offences);
(2) the modes of commission of the acts in the coercive circumstances of genocide, crimes against humanity, or armed conflict, whether

internal or international (the contextual elements of international crimes);
(3) the criminal responsibility of state and non-state actors, including UN peace-keeping forces, private military companies, and paramilitaries;
(4) the modes of liability of military and civilian leadership and their responsibility for other armed actors, regardless of their relationship to state parties to the conflict;
(5) the application of these norms to all victims, whether or not they belong to any party to the conflict; and
(6) specific procedural and evidential international norms governing sexual violence offences.

The proposed convention would also set out compliance, enforcement, responsibility, and reparation obligations of equivalent gravity to other serious violations of international criminal law and draw on existing obligations under this legal regime. By recognising the *jus cogens* status of sexual violence as an international crime prohibited in all circumstances and prohibited against all actors, states would be subject to the positive obligations arising from this status. The recognition of the prohibition of sexual violence as a *jus cogens* norm is important because it provides the basis for state obligations to prosecute (or extradite) these crimes under the principle of universal jurisdiction. Moreover, the convention should include positive state obligations of prevention, protection and so on, similar to that of the Genocide Convention or the Draft Articles on the Prevention and Punishment on Crimes against Humanity.[69]

To strengthen implementation, the instrument should include mechanisms and measures such as the following:

(1) obligations to suppress and prosecute, including the obligation to establish universal jurisdiction provisions and incorporate international substantive and procedural norms into national law;
(2) review mechanisms and standards for prosecutions, including review of conflict-related sexual violence patterns of prosecution, trial practices, and sentencing; and
(3) public accountability and information programmes, including education in all relevant sectors, such as criminal justice systems and military forces, as well as civilians.

---

[69] See Report of the International Law Commission on the Work of Its Seventy-First Session, U.N. Doc A/74/10, (2019).

Finally, the implementation of the proposed convention should be overseen by an independent body within the UN system. It should enable the participation of affected persons and feminist non-governmental organisations according to the principles of feminist public accountability.[70]

The aim of setting out these strategic frameworks is to open, rather than to end, the important discussion of strategies for building new feminist approaches to international justice beyond the state and the global legal form. This is a collective feminist project, which is contingent upon the collective feminist work of building coalitions, generating knowledge, and engaging in political action. It is also an internationalist project, which must be anchored in the principles of transnational solidarity and of collective struggle for global political, economic, and social emancipation for all. The building of such feminist transnational social relations is a crucial third strategy for building a feminist approach to international criminal justice. This strategy is perhaps the most difficult and urgent of all. Just as the earlier Yugoslav and internationalist feminists did, we need to insist that international criminal justice in its existing global legal form does not provide justice for all and that it is possible to build other forms of international justice. To this end, it is again time for a World Women's Conference. At a practical level, such a conference would provide the opportunity to draft a convention on sexual violence as an international crime and, more widely, to address the existing lacuna for gender-based international crimes in international legal regimes. At a political level, it would provide the opportunity to identify wider feminist strategies for engaging with international justice, law, and the international system. Given the apparent current 'crisis' in transnational feminist politics from international criminal law to 'Women, Peace, and Security', and the current structural transitions in the global social system, developing such strategies is now more crucial than ever.

This book has explored why international criminal law is an important transitional strategy for feminist struggles for global justice. However, it has also shown that the global legal form, and its ideas of subjects and society, do not serve justice. If 'justice' is a human activity, which

---

[70] My thanks to Gorana Mlinarević for our discussions of the proposed Policy and Legal Framework Principles, implementing body and World Women's Conference.

expresses the relations and values of human society, then it is possible to build other forms of justice that express feminist relations and values that seek to transform 'international justice' as a form of global social relations. The Bosnian and Syrian peace activists and feminists who met in 2014 are still fighting for justice. It is imperative that all those committed to global social emancipation join that fight, and the other struggles for global justice yet to come.

BIBLIOGRAPHY

References

Abazović, D. 'Bosnia and Herzegovina: Ten Years after Dayton', (2005) 5(1) European Yearbook of Minority Issues 195–206.

Adams, P. *The Emptiness of the Image: Psychoanalysis and Sexual Differences* (London: Routledge, 1996).

Agamben, G. *Homo Sacer: Sovereign Power and Bare Life* (Stanford: Stanford University Press, 1998).

Means without End: Notes on Politics (Minneapolis: University of Minnesota Press, 2000).

Remnants of Auschwitz: The Witness and the Archive (New York: Zone, 1999).

State of Exception (Chicago: The University of Chicago Press, 2005).

Ahluwalia, P. 'Empire or Imperialism: Implications for a New "Politics" of Resistance', (2004) 10(5) Social Identities 629–645.

Alcoff, L. *Rape and Resistance* (Cambridge: Polity, 2018).

Alinčić, M. 'Law and the Status of Women in Yugoslavia', (1976) 8(1) Colum Hum Rts L Rev 345–371.

Anderson, B. *Imagined Communities: Reflections on the Origins and Spread of Nationalism* (London and New York: Verso, 2006).

Anderson, N. and Greenberg, D. 'From Substance to Form: The Legal Theories of Pashukanis and Edelman', (1983) 7 Social Text 69–84.

Anghie, A. *Imperialism, Sovereignty, and the Making of International Law* (Cambridge: Cambridge University Press, 2007).

Anghie, A. and Chimni, B. 'Third World Approaches to International Law and Individual Responsibility in Internal Conflicts', (2003) 2(1) Chinese JIL 77–103.

Anthias, F. and Yuval-Davis, N. 'Introduction', in N. Yuval-Davis and F. Anthias (eds.), *Woman-Nation-State* (New York: St. Martin's Press, 1989), pp. 1–15.

Aoláin Ni, F. 'Radical Rules: The Effect of Evidential and Procedural Rules on the Regulation of Sexual Violence in War', (1996–1997) 60(3) Alb L Rev 883–906.

'The Fractured Soul of the Dayton Peace Agreement: A Legal Analysis', (1998) 19(4) Mich J Int'l L 957–1004.

'Rethinking the Concept of Harm and Legal Categorizations of Sexual Violence during War', (2000) 1(2) Theo Inq L 307–340.

'Exploring a Feminist Theory of Harm in the Context of Conflicted and Post-conflict Societies', (2009) 35(1) QLJ 219-244.

'Gendered Harms and Their Interface with International Criminal Law', (2014) 16(4) International Feminist Journal of Politics 622-646.

'Transformative Gender Justice?', in P. Gready and S. Robins (eds.), *From Transitional to Transformative Justice* (Cambridge: Cambridge University Press, 2019), pp. 150-171.

Aoláin Ni, F. and Haynes, D. *On the Frontlines: Gender, War and the Post-conflict Process* (Oxford: Oxford University Press, 2011).

Arrighi, G., Hopkins, T. et al. *Antisystemic Movements* (New York: Verso, 1989).

Arsenijević, D. 'Mobilising Unbribable Life', in A. Mously (ed.), *Towards a New Literary Humanism* (London: Palgrave Macmillan, 2011), pp. 166-180.

Arsenijević, D., Husanović, J., et al. 'A Public Language of Grief', in V. Beronja and S. Vervaet (eds.), *Post-Yugoslav Constellations: Archive, Memory, and Trauma in Contemporary Bosnian, Croatian and Serbian Literature and Culture* (Berlin: de Gruyter, 2016), pp. 259-277.

Baig, L. 'Sentencing for Sexual Violence Crimes', in S. Brammertz and M. Jarvis (eds.), *Prosecuting Conflict-Related Sexual Violence at the ICTY* (Oxford: Oxford University Press, 2016), pp. 262-298.

Baig, L., Jarvis, M., et al. 'Contextualising Sexual Violence: Selection of Crimes', in S. Brammertz and M. Jarvis (eds.), *Prosecuting Conflict-Related Sexual Violence at the ICTY* (Oxford: Oxford University Press, 2016), pp. 172-219.

Bass, G. *Stay the Hand of Vengeance: The Politics of War Crimes Tribunals* (Princeton: Princeton University Press, 2000).

Bassiouni, M. C. *The Law of the International Criminal Tribunal for the Former Yugoslavia* (New York: Transnational, 1996).

'The Protection of "Collective Victims" in International Law', in M. C. Bassiouni (ed.), *International Protection of Victims* (Siracusa: Association International de droit penal, 1988), pp. 181-198.

Sexual Violence: An Invisible Weapon of War in the Former Yugoslavia (International Human Rights Law Institute, De Paul University College of Law, 1996).

'The Sources and Content of International Criminal Law', in K. Koufa (ed.), *The New International Criminal Law* (Athens: Sakkoulas, 2003), pp. 29-207.

Batinić, J. *Women and Yugoslav Partisans: A History of World War II Resistance* (New York: Cambridge University Press, 2015).

Benderly, J. 'Feminist Movements in Yugoslavia, 1978-1992', in M. Bokovoy, J. Irvine, et al. (eds.), *State-Society Relations in Yugoslavia, 1945-1992* (Basingstoke: Macmillan, 1997), pp. 183-209.

Bhattacharya, T. 'Introduction: Mapping Social Reproduction Theory', in T. Bhattacharya (ed.), *Social Reproduction Theory* (London: Pluto Press, 2017), pp. 1-20.

Bhavnani, K. K., & Haraway, D. 'Shifting the Subject: A Conversation Between Kum-Kum Bhavnani and Donna Haraway', in K. K. Bhavnani and A. Phoenix (ed.), *Shifting Identities, Shifting Racisms* (London: Sage, 1994), pp. 19–39.

Blagojević, M. 'Preface', in V. Nikolić-Ristanović (ed.), *Women, Violence and War: Wartime Victimization of Refugees in the Balkans* (Budapest: Central European University Press, 2000), pp. ix–xiv.

Boas, G. 'A Code of Evidence and Procedure for International Criminal Law? The Rules of the ICTY', in W. Schabas and G. Boas (eds.), *International Criminal Law Developments in the Case Law of the ICTY* (Leiden and Boston: Martinus Nijhoff, 2003), pp. 1–33.

Boas, G., Bischoff, J. et al.. *International Criminal Law Practitioner Library* (Cambridge: Cambridge University Press, 2007).

Boesten, J. and Wilding, P. 'Transformative Gender Justice: Setting an Agenda', (2015) 51 Women's Studies International Forum 75–80.

Bonfiglioli, C. 'The First UN World Conference on Women (1975) as a Cold War Encounter', (2016) 27(3) Filozofija i društvo 521–541.

Boon, K. 'Rape and Forced Pregnancy under the ICC Statute: Human Dignity, Autonomy, and Consent', (2001) 32(3) Colum Hum Rts L Rev 625–675.

Bourdieu, P. 'The Force of Law: Toward a Sociology of the Juridical Field', (1986–1987) 38(5) Hastings LJ 814–853.

Bovens, M. 'Public Accountability', in E. Ferlie, L. Lynn Jr, et al. (eds.), *The Oxford Handbook of Public Management* (Oxford: Oxford University Press, 2007), pp. 182–208.

Brammertz, S. and Jarvis, M. (eds.), *Prosecuting Conflict-Related Sexual Violence at the ICTY* (Oxford: Oxford University Press, 2016).

Brammertz, S., Jarvis, M., et al. 'Using the OTP's Experience with Sexual Violence as a Springboard for Building National Capacity', in S. Brammertz and M. Jarvis (eds.), *Prosecuting Conflict-Related Sexual Violence at the ICTY* (Oxford: Oxford University Press, 2016), pp. 335–378.

Brouwer, A.-M. *Supranational Criminal Prosecution of Sexual Violence* (Antwerp and Oxford: Intersentia, 2005).

Brown, B., Burman, M., et al. *Sex Crimes on Trial: The Use of Sexual Evidence in Scottish Courts* (Edinburgh: Edinburgh University Press, 1993).

Brown, W. and Halley, J. (eds.), *Left Legalism/Left Critique* (Durham and London: Duke University Press, 2002).

Brownlie, I. *Principles of Public International Law* (7th edn.) (Oxford: Oxford University Press, 2008).

Brownmiller, S. *Against Our Will: Men, Women and Rape* (New York: Fawcett Columbine, 1975).

Bryman, A. *Research Methods and Organisation Studies* (London: Routledge, 1989).

Buckel, S. *Subjectivation and Cohesion: Towards the Reconstruction of a Materialist Theory of Law* (Leiden and Boston: Brill, 2021).

Buss, D. 'Going Global: Feminist Theory, International Law, and the Public/Private Divide', in S. Boyd (ed.), *Challenging the Public/Private Divide: Feminism, Law, and Public Policy* (Toronto and Buffalo: University of Toronto Press, 1997), pp. 360–384.

'Women at the Borders: Rape and Nationalism in International Law', (1998) 6(2) FLS 171–203.

'Sexual Violence, Ethnicity, and Intersectionality in International Criminal Law', in E. Grabham and D. Cooper et al. (eds.), *Intersectionality and Beyond: Law, Power and the Politics of Location* (London and New York: Routledge-Cavendish, 2008), pp. 105–123.

'Rethinking "Rape as a Weapon of War"', (2009) 17(2) FLS 145–163.

'Performing Legal Order: Some Feminist Thoughts on International Criminal Law'. (2011) 11(3) Int CLR 409–423.

'Knowing Women: Translating Patriarchy in International Criminal Law', (2014) 23(1) S&LS 73–92.

'International Criminal Courts', in J. Steans and D. Tepe-Belfrage (eds.), *Handbook on Gender in World Politics* (Cheltenham and Northampton: Elgar, (2016), pp. 162–170.

Butler, J. *Bodies That Matter: On the Discursive Limits of 'Sex'* (London: Routledge, 1993).

'For a Careful Reading', in J. Butler and S. Benhabib et al. (eds.), *Feminist Contentions: A Philosophical Exchange* (London and New York: Routledge, 1995), pp. 127–143.

'Merely Cultural', (1997) 52/53 Social Text 265–277.

The Psychic Life of Power: Theories in Subjection (London: Routledge, 1997).

Butler, J. and Spivak, G. *Who Sings the Nation-State? Language, Politics, Belonging* (London: Seagull Books, 2007).

Frames of War: When Is Life Grievable? (London: Verso, 2010).

Cahill, A. *Rethinking Rape* (Ithaca and London: Cornell University Press, 2001).

Cain, M. and Howe, A. 'Introduction', in M. Cain and A. Howe (eds.), *Women, Crime and Social Harm: Towards a Criminology for the Global Age* (Oxford: Hart, 2008), pp. 1–18.

Campbell, K. *Jacques Lacan and Feminist Epistemology* (London and New York: Routledge, 2004).

'The Gender of Transitional Justice: Law, Sexual Violence and the International Criminal Tribunal for the former Yugoslavia', (2007) 1(3) Intl J Transitional Justice 413–432.

'From Legitimacy to Legality: The Problem of the Global Legal Form', in C. Thornhill and S. Ashenden (eds.), *Legality and Legitimacy: Normative and Sociological Approaches* (Baden-Baden: Nomos, 2010), pp. 255–275.

'Reassembling International Justice: The Making of the "Social" in Transitional Justice and International Criminal Law', (2014) 8(1) Intl J Transitional Justice 53–74.

'Building National and Regional Accountability for Conflict Related Sexual Violence', (2018) 7(2) IHRLR 201–224.

'Producing Knowledge in the Field of Sexual Violence in Armed Conflict Research', (2018) 25(4) Social Politics 469–495.

Campbell, K. and Mlinarević, G. 'A Feminist Critique of Approaches to International Criminal Justice in the Age of Identity Politics', in V. Oosterveld and I. Rosenthal et al. (eds.) *Gender and International Criminal Law* (Oxford: Oxford University Press, 2022), pp. 75–98.

Cassese, A. *International Criminal Law* (Oxford: Oxford University Press, 2003).

Chappell, L. *The Politics of Gender Justice at the International Criminal Court* (Oxford: Oxford University Press, 2016).

Charlesworth, H. 'Feminist Methods in International Law', (1999) 93(2) AJIL 379–394.

Charlesworth, H. and Chinkin, C. *The Boundaries of International Law: A Feminist Analysis* (Manchester: Manchester University Press, 2000).

Chimni, B. *International Law and World Order* (Cambridge: Cambridge University Press, 2017).

Chinkin, C. 'Due Process and Witness Anonymity', (1997) 91(1) AJIL 75–79, 78.

Christodoulidis, E. 'Strategies of Rupture', (2009) 20 (1) Law and Crit 3–26, 20.

Cleiren, C. and Tijssen, M. 'Rape and Other Forms of Sexual Assault in the Armed Conflict in the Former Yugoslavia', in R. Clark and M. Sann (eds.), *The Prosecution of International Crimes* (Brunswick: Transaction, 1996), pp. 257–292.

Cockburn, C. *The Space between Us: Negotiating Gender and National Identities in Conflict* (London and New York: Zed, 1998).

'The Continuum of Violence: A Gender Perspective on War and Peace', in W. Giles and J. Hyndman (eds.), *Sites of Violence: Gender and Conflict Zones* (Berkeley: University of California Press, 2004), pp. 24–44.

Code, L. *Ecological Thinking: The Politics of Epistemic Location* (Oxford: Oxford University Press, 2006).

Cohen, L. 'Judicial Elites in Yugoslavia', (1985) 11(4) Rev Soc L 313–344.

Confortini, C. 'Galtung, Violence, and Gender', (2006) 31(3) Peace & Change 333–367.

Coomaraswamy, R. et al. *Preventing Conflict, Transforming Peace, Securing the Peace: A Global Study on the Implementation of United Nations Security Council Resolution 1325* (New York: UN Women, 2015). Available at: https://wps.unwomen.org/pdf/en/GlobalStudy_EN_Web.pdf

Copelon, R. 'Surfacing Gender', (1994) 5(2) Hastings Women's LJ 243–266.

Cornell, D. *The Imaginary Domain: Abortion Pornography and Sexual Harassment* (Routledge, London 1995).

At the Heart of Freedom: Feminism, Sex, and Equality (Princeton: Princeton University Press, 1998).

Beyond Accommodation: Ethical Feminism, Deconstruction, and the Law (New York: Rowman and Littlefield, 1999).

Cryer, R. 'Witness Evidence before International Criminal Tribunals', (2003) 2(3) The Law and Practice of International Courts and Tribunals 411–439.

Cryer, R., Robinson, D. et al. *An Introduction to International Criminal Law and Procedure* (Cambridge: Cambridge University Press, 2019).

Deleuze, G. *Foucault* (London: Continuum, 1999).

Derrida, J. 'Force of Law', in D. Cornell, M. Rosenfeld et al. (eds.), *Deconstruction and the Possibility of Justice* (New York: Routledge, 1992), pp. 3–67.

Dolgopol, U. 'A Feminist Appraisal of the Dayton Peace Accords' (1997) 19(1) Adel L Rev 59–71.

Douzinas, C. *The End of Human Rights: Critical Legal Thought at the Turn of the Century* (Oxford: Hart, 2000).

Human Rights and Empire: The Political Philosophy of Cosmopolitanism (London: Routledge, 2007).

Dowds, E. *Feminist Engagement with International Criminal Law: Norm Transfer, Complementarity, Rape and Consent* (Oxford: Hart, 2019).

Dragović-Soso, J. 'History of a Failure: Attempts to Create a National Truth and Reconciliation Commission in Bosnia and Herzegovina, 1997–2006', (2016) 10(2) Intl J Transitional Justice 292–310.

Drumbl, M. 'Collective Violence and Individual Punishment: The Criminality of Mass Atrocity' (2005) 99(2) NWULR 539–610.

Atrocity, Punishment, and the Law (Cambridge: Cambridge University Press, 2007).

Duhaček, D. 'Women's Court: A Feminist Approach to In/justice', in S. Zajović (ed.), *Women's Court: About the Process* (Belgrade: Women in Black and Centre for Women's Studies, 2015), pp. 68–99.

Durham, H. and Gurd, T. (eds.), *Listening to the Silences: Women and War* (Leiden and Boston: Martinus Nijhoff, 2005).

Đurić Kuzmanović, T. and Pajvančić-Cizelj, A. 'Economic Violence against Women: Testimonies from the Women's Court in Sarajevo', (2020) 27(1) European Journal of Women's Studies 25–40.

Engle, K. 'Feminism and its (Dis)Contents: Criminalising Wartime Rape in Bosnia', (2005) 99(4) AJIL 778–816.

'The Grip of Sexual Violence: Reading UN Security Council Resolutions on Human Security', in G. Heathcote and D. Otto (eds.), *Rethinking Peacekeeping, Gender Equality and Collective Security* (London: Palgrave Macmillan, 2014), pp. 23–47.

'Feminist Legacies', (2016) 110 AJIL Unbound 220–226.
  The Grip of Sexual Violence (Stanford: Stanford University Press, 2020).
Engle, K. and Lottman, A. 'The Force of Shame', in C. McGlynn and V. Munro (eds.), *Rethinking Rape Law* (Abingdon and New York: Routledge, 2010), pp. 76–91.
Enloe, C. *The Big Push: Exposing and Challenging Sustainable Patriarchy* (Berkeley: University of California Press, 2017).
Farmer, L. *Making the Modern Criminal Law: Criminalization and Civil Order* (Oxford: Oxford University Press, 2016).
Federici, S. *Revolution at Point Zero: Housework, Reproduction, and Feminist Struggle* (Oakland, CA: PM Press, 2012).
  Re-Enchanting the World: Feminism and the Politics of the Commons (Oakland: PM Press, 2019).
Felman, S. and Laub, D. *Testimony: Crises of Witnessing in Literature, Psychoanalysis, and History* (New York and London: Routledge, 1992).
Felman, S. 'Forms of Judicial Blindness: Traumatic Narratives and Legal Repetitions', in A. Sarat and T. Kearns (eds.), *History, Memory, and the Law* (Ann Arbor: University of Michigan Press, 1999), pp. 23–93.
  The Juridical Unconscious (Cambridge and London: Cambridge University Press, 2002).
Ferguson, S. *Women and Work: Feminism, Labour, and Social Reproduction* (London: Pluto, 2020).
Ferizović, J. 'The Case of Female Perpetrators of International Crimes: Exploratory Insights and New Research Directions', (2020) 31(2) EJIL 455–488.
Ferizović, J. and Mlinarević, G. 'Applying International Experiences in National Prosecutions of Conflict-Related Sexual Violence: A Case Study of Application of the ICTY Law, Findings and Practices in Prosecutions before the Court of Bosnia and Herzegovina' (2020) 18(2) JICJ 325–348.
Findlay, M. and Henham, R. *Beyond Punishment: Achieving International Criminal Justice* (Basingstoke: Palgrave Macmillan, 2010).
Fine, R. *Democracy and the Rule of Law: Liberal Ideas and Marxist Critiques* (London: Pluto, 1984).
Fink, B. *The Lacanian Subject: Between Language and Jouissance* (Princeton: Princeton University Press, 1995).
Fitzgerald, K. 'Problems of Prosecution and Adjudication of Rape and Other Sexual Assaults under International Law', (1997) 8(4) EJIL 638–663.
Fletcher, G. *The Grammar of Criminal Law: American, Comparative, and International* (Oxford: Oxford University Press, 2007).
Foucault, M. 'The Subject and Power', in J. Faubion (ed.), *Power* (London: Penguin, 2000), pp. 326–348.
  Society Must Be Defended: Lectures at the College de France, 1975–1976 (Harmondsworth: Penguin, 2004).

Frank, D., Camp, B. et al. 'Worldwide Trends in the Criminal Regulation of Sex, 1945 to 2005', 2010 75(6) American Sociological Review 867–893.

Fraser, N. 'Social Justice in the Age of Identity Politics', in N. Fraser and A. Honneth (eds), *Redistribution or Recognition?* (London and New York: Verso, 2003), pp. 7–109.

Scales of Justice: Reimagining Political Space in a Globalizing World (New York: Columbia University Press, 2009).

Fortunes of Feminism: From State-Managed Capitalism to Neoliberal Crisis (Verso, London, 2013).

Freud, S. 'Why War?', in Albert Dickson (ed.), *Civilization, Society and Religion* (Harmondsworth: Penguin, 1985), pp. 349–362.

Fricker, E. 'The Epistemology of Testimony', (1987) 61 Proceedings of the Aristotelian Society (Supplementary Volumes) 57–83.

Fricker, M. *Epistemic Injustice: Power and the Ethics of Knowing* (Oxford and New York: Oxford University Press, 2007).

Gallagher, M. *An Unfinished Story: Gender Patterns in Media Employment* (Paris: UNESCO, 1995).

Galtung, J. 'Violence, Peace, and Peace Research', (1969) 6(3) Journal of Peace Research 167–191.

'Cultural Violence', (1990) 27(3) *Journal of Peace Research* 291–305.

Gardam, J. 'The Silences in the Rules That Regulate Women during Times of Armed Conflict', in F. Ní Aoláin, N. Cahn, et al. (eds.), *The Oxford Handbook of Gender and Conflict* (Oxford: Oxford University Press, 2018), pp. 35–47.

Gardam, J. and Jarvis, M. *Women, Armed Conflict, and International Law* (The Hague: Kluwer Law International, 2001).

Giddens, A. *The Nation-State and Violence* (Cambridge, Polity Press: 1985).

Glenny, M. *The Fall of Yugoslavia* (London: Penguin, 1996).

Goldman, A. *Knowledge in a Social World* (Oxford: Clarendon, 1999).

Gopalan, P., Kravetz, D. et al. 'Proving Crimes of Sexual Violence', in S. Brammertz and M. Jarvis (eds.), *Prosecuting Conflict-Related Sexual Violence at the ICTY* (Oxford: Oxford University Press, 2016), pp. 111–171.

Goy, B., Jarvis, M. et al. 'Contextualising Sexual Violence and Linking It to Senior Officials', in S. Brammertz and M. Jarvis (eds.) *Prosecuting Conflict-Related Sexual Violence at the ICTY* (Oxford: Oxford University Press, 2016), pp. 220–261.

Graeber, D. 'Dead Zones of the Imagination', (2012) 2(2) HAU: Journal of Ethnographic Theory 105–128.

Grahn-Farley, M. 'The Politics of Inevitability: An Examination of Janet Halley's Critique of the Criminalisation of Rape as Torture', in S. Kouvo and Z. Pearson (eds.), *Feminist Perspectives on Contemporary International Law: Between Resistance and Compliance?* (Oxford: Hart, 2011), pp. 109–129.

Graycar, R. and Morgan, J. *The Hidden Gender of the Law* (Sydney: Federation Press, 2002).
Grewal, K. 'The Protection of Sexual Autonomy under International Criminal Law: The International Criminal Court and the Challenge of Defining Rape', (2012) 10(2) JICJ 373–396.
  'International Criminal Law as a Site for Enhancing Women's Rights? Challenges, Possibilities, Strategies', (2015) 23(2) Fem LS 149–165.
Grey, R. and Chappell, L. '"Gender-Just Judging" in International Criminal Courts: New Directions for Research', in S. Harris Rimmer and K. Ogg (eds.), *Research Handbook on Feminist Engagement with International Law* (Cheltenham and Northampton: Edward Elgar, 2019), pp. 213–239.
Hagan, J. and Levi, R. 'Crimes of War and the Force of Law', (2005) 83(4) Social Forces 1499–1534.
Hagan J., Levi, R. et al. 'Swaying the Hand of Justice: The Internal and External Dynamics of Regime Change at the International Criminal Tribunal for the former Yugoslavia', (2006) 31(3) Law and Social Inquiry 585–616.
Halley, J. 'Rape at Rome: Feminist Interventions in the Criminalization of Sex-Related Violence in Positive International Criminal Law' (2008) 30(1) Mich J Int'l L 1–123.
  'Where in the Legal Order Have Feminists Gained Inclusion', in J. Halley, P. Kotiswaran et al. (eds.), *Governance Feminism: An Introduction* (Minneapolis and London: University of Minnesota Press, 2018), pp. 3–21.
Harari, R. 'The *sinthome*', in L. Thurston (ed.), *Re-Inventing the Symptom* (New York: Other Press, 2002), pp. 45–57.
Haraway, D. *Simians, Cyborgs, and Women: The Reinvention of Nature* (London: Free Association, 1991).
Harbour, G. 'International Concern Regarding Conflict-Related Sexual Violence in the Lead-up to the ICTY's Establishment', in S. Brammertz and M. Jarvis (eds.), *Prosecuting Conflict-Related Sexual Violence at the ICTY* (Oxford: Oxford University Press, 2016), pp. 19–32.
Harding, S. *The Science Question in Feminism* (Ithaca, and London: Cornell University Press, 1986).
Harding, S., 'Introduction: Is There a Feminist Method?', in Sandra Harding (ed.), *Feminism and Methodology* (Bloomington: Indiana University Press, 1987), pp. 1–14.
  Whose Science, Whose Knowledge? Thinking from Women's Lives (New York: Cornell University Press, 1991).
Hardt, M. and Negri, A. *Labor of Dionysus: A Critique of the State Form* (Minneapolis: University of Minnesota Press, 1994).
  Empire (Cambridge: Harvard University Press, 2000).
  Multitude: War and Democracy in the Age of Empire (Harmondsworth: Penguin, 2005).

Assembly (New York: Oxford University Press, 2017).
Hegel, G.W.F., *The Philosophy of Right* (London: Oxford University Press, 1967).
Helms, E. *Innocence and Victimhood: Gender, Nation, and Women's Activism in Postwar Bosnia-Herzegovina* (Madison: University of Wisconsin Press, 2013)
Hirsh, D. *Law against Genocide: Cosmopolitan Trials* (London: Glasshouse Press, 2003).
Hirst, P. *On Law and Ideology* (London: Macmillan, 1979).
  War and Power in the Twenty-first Century: The State, Military Conflict and the International System (Cambridge: Polity, 2001).
Hodžić, R. 'A Long Road to Reconciliation: The Impact of the ICTY Upon Reconciliation and Victims' Perception of Justice', in R. Steinberg (ed), *Assessing the Legacy of the ICTY* (Leiden: Brill, 2011), pp. 115–119.
Houge, A. and Lohne, K. 'End Impunity! Reducing Conflict-Related Sexual Violence to a Problem of Law', (2017) 51(4) Law and Society Review 755–789.
Howe, A. '"Social Injury" Revisited: Towards a Feminist Theory of Social Justice' (1987) 15 Int'l J Soc L 423–428.
  'The Problem of Privatised Injuries: Feminist Strategies for Litigation', in M. Fineman (ed.), *At the Boundaries of Law* (London, Routledge, 1990), pp. 148–167.
Howe, A. and Cain, M. 'Introduction: Women, Crime and Social Harm', in M. Cain and A. Howe (eds.), *Women, Crime and Social Harm: Towards a Criminology for the Global Age* (Oxford: Hart, 2008), pp. 1–18.
Humphreys, S. 'Legalising Lawlessness: On Giorgio Agamben's State of Exception', (2006) 17(3) EJIL 677–687.
  'Nomarchy: On the Rule of Law and Authority in Giorgio Agamben and Aristotle', (2006) 19(2) Cambridge Review of International Affairs 331–351.
Husanović, J. 'The Politics of Gender, Witnessing, Postcoloniality and Trauma' (2009) 10(1) Feminist Theory 99–119.
  'Resisting the Culture of Trauma in Bosnia and Herzegovina: Emancipatory Lessons for/in Cultural Production', in M. Glasius and D. Žarkov (eds.), *Narratives of Justice in and out of the Courtroom: Former Yugoslavia and Beyond* (New York: Springer, 2014), pp. 147–162.
  'Traumatic Knowledge in Action', in D. Arsenijević (ed.), *Unbribable Bosnia and Herzegovina: The Fight for the Commons* (Baden-Baden: Nomos, 2014), pp. 145–153.
  Culture, Community and Activism in Bosnia and Herzegovina: Emancipatory Trajectories (Tuzla: Off Set Press, 2021).
Inal, T. *Looting and Rape in Wartime: Law and Change in International Relations.* (Philadelphia: University of Pennsylvania Press, 2013).

International Committee of the Red Cross, 'Resolutions of the 32nd International Conference of the Red Cross and Red Crescent (2015)' (2016) 900 International Review of the Red Cross 1389–1426.

Customary International Humanitarian Law, Volume One: The Rules (Cambridge: Cambridge University Press, 2009).

Iveković, R. 'Violence and Healing: The War and Post-war Period from the First Generation and Beyond', in S. Zajović, (ed.) *Women's Court: About the Process* (Belgrade: Women in Black and Centre for Women's Studies, 2015), pp. 100–136.

Iveković, R. and Mostov, J. 'Introduction: From Gender to Nation', in R. Iveković and J. Mostov (eds.), *From Gender to Nation* (New Delhi: Zubaan, 2004), pp. 9–25.

Jackson, J. and Doran, S. 'Evidence', in D. Patterson (ed.), *A Companion to Philosophy of Law and Legal Theory* (Oxford.: Blackwell, 1996), pp. 172–183.

Jameson, F. *Archaeologies of the Future: The Desire Called Utopia and Other Science Fictions* (New York: Verso, 2005).

Jarvis, M. 'Overview: The Challenge of Accountability for Conflict-Related Sexual Violence Crimes', in S. Brammertz and M. Jarvis (eds.), *Prosecuting Conflict-Related Sexual Violence at the ICTY* (Oxford: Oxford University Press, 2016), pp. 1–18.

Jarvis, M. and Nabti, N. 'Policies and Institutional Strategies for Successful Sexual Violence Prosecutions', in S. Brammertz and M. Jarvis (eds.), *Prosecuting Conflict-Related Sexual Violence at the ICTY* (Oxford: Oxford University Press, 2016), pp. 73–110.

Jarvis, M. and Vigneswaran, K. 'Challenges to Successful Outcomes in Sexual Violence Cases', in S. Brammertz and M. Jarvis (eds.), *Prosecuting Conflict-Related Sexual Violence at the ICTY* (Oxford: Oxford University Press, 2016), pp. 33–72.

Kaldor, M. *New and Old Wars: Organized Violence in a Global Era* (Cambridge: Polity, 2002).

Kapidžić, D. and Daidžić, A. 'BISER: A Conversation with Bosnian Women Living in Exile', (1994) 5(1) Hastings Women's L.J. 53–67.

Kašić, B. 'How to Radicalize Responsibility, Feminism and Rape', (2009) 10 DEP Deportate, esuli, profughe 168–181.

Kelsen, H. *Law and Peace in International Relations* (Cambridge: Harvard University Press, 1942).

Kesić, V, 'Muslim Women, Croatian Women, Serbian Women, Albanian Women ...', in D. Bjelić and O. Savić (eds.), *Balkan as Metaphor: Between Globalization and Fragmentation* (London and Cambridge: MIT Press, 2002, pp. 311–321).

King, K., Kelly, E. et al. 'Deborah's Voice: The Role of Women in Sexual Assault Cases at the International Criminal Tribunal for the Former Yugoslavia', (2017) 98(2) Social Science Quarterly 548–565.

King, K. and Meernik, J. *The Witness Experience: Testimony at The ICTY and Its Impact* (Cambridge: Cambridge University Press, 2017).

Klabbers, J. 'The Concept of Legal Personality', (2005) 11 Ius Gentium 35–66.

Knox, R. 'Marxism, International Law, and Political Strategy', (2009) 22(3) LJIL 413–436.

 'Marxist Approaches to International Law', in A. Orford and F. Hoffmann (eds), *The Oxford Handbook of the Theory of International Law* (Oxford: Oxford University Press, 2016), pp. 306–326.

Korać, M. 'Women's Groups in the Former Yugoslavia: Working with Refugees', 14(8) (1995) Refuge 16–18.

 'Linking Arms: Women and War in Post-Yugoslav States', 6 *Women and Nonviolence Series* (Uppsala: Life and Peace Institute, 1998).

 'Feminists against Sexual Violence in War', (2018) 7(10) Social Sciences 182–195.

Kovačević, L., Perković, M. et al. (eds), *Zenski Sud: Feministicki pristup pravdi* (Belgrade and Kotor: Anima and Women in Black, 2011).

Krasniqi, V., Iveković, R., et al. 'The Banality of Evil: Gendered Violence against Civilians', in S. Zajović and M. Urošević, (eds), *Women's Court: about Event in Sarajevo and About Continue the Process* (Belgrade: Women in Black, 2017), pp. 117–122.

Kress, K. 'Coherence', in D. Patterson (ed.), *A Companion to Philosophy of Law and Legal Theory* (Oxford: Blackwell, 1996).

Krever, T. 'International Criminal Law: An Ideology Critique', (2013) 26(3) LJIL 701–723.

Krin, G. *Partisan Ruptures: Self-Management, Market Reform and the Spectre of Socialist Yugoslavia* (London: Pluto Press, 2019).

Kuo, P. 'Prosecuting Crimes of Sexual Violence in an International Tribunal', (2002) 34 Case W Res J Int'l L 305–321.

Kutz, C. 'The Difference Uniforms Make: Collective Violence in Criminal Law and War', (2005) 33(2) Philosophy and Public Affairs 148–180.

Lacan, J. *The Four Fundamental Concepts of Psycho-Analysis* (London: Peregrine, 1986).

 Freud's Papers on Technique, 1953-1954, Book I (New York: Norton, 1991).

 'A Theoretical Introduction to the Functions of Psychoanalysis in Criminology', (1996) 1(2) Journal for the Psychoanalysis of Culture and Society 13–26.

 Encore: On Feminine Sexuality, the Limits of Love and Knowledge, 1972-1973, Book XX (New York and London: Norton, 1998).

 The Other Side of Psychoanalysis, 1969-1970, Book XVII (New York and London: Norton, 2007).

The Sinthome, 1975-1976, Book XXIII (Cambridge: Polity, 2016).
Lacey, N. *Unspeakable Subjects: Feminist Essays in Social and Legal Theory* (Oxford: Hart, 1998).
　'Historicising Criminalisation: Conceptual and Empirical Issues', (2009) 72(6) MLR 936–960.
　In Search of Criminal Responsibility: Ideas, Interests, and Institutions (Oxford: Oxford University Press, 2016).
Lambek, M. 'The Past Imperfect: Remembering as Moral Practice', in P. Antze and M. Lambek (eds.), *Tense Past: Cultural Essays in Trauma and Memory* London and New York: Routledge, 1996), pp. 235–254.
Laplanche, J. and Pontalis, J-B. *The Language of Psychoanalysis* (New York and London: Norton, 1973).
Lappenna, I. *State and Law: Soviet and Yugoslav Theory* (London: Athlone, 1964).
Lechte, J. *Fifty Key Contemporary Thinkers* (London: Routledge, 2007).
Lees, S. *Ruling Passions: Sexual Violence, Reputation and the Law* (Buckingham: Open University Press, 1997).
Lenin, V. *'Left-wing' Communism: An Infantile Disorder* (Moscow: Progress, 1968).
Longino, H. 'Feminist Epistemology as a Local Epistemology' (1997) 71 The Aristotelian Society (Supplementary Volume) 19–35.
Lóránd, A. *The Feminist Challenge to the Socialist State in Yugoslavia* (Cham: Palgrave Macmillan, 2018).
MacKinnon, C. 'Defining Rape Internationally: A Comment on Akayesu', (2006) 44(3) Colum J Transnat'l L 940–958.
　'Rape Redefined', (2016) 10(2) Harv Law & Pol'y Rev 431–478.
MacKinnon, C. and Crenshaw, K. 'Reconstituting the Future: The Equality Amendment', (2019) 129 Yale LJF 343–364.
Maier, M. 'Offender Rehabilitation in International Criminal Justice', (2021) 53(1–2) Case W Res J Int'l L 269–328.
Malešević, S. *Identity as Ideology* (Basingstoke: Polity, 2006).
　Nation-States and Nationalisms: Organisation, Ideology, and Solidarity (Cambridge: Polity, 2013).
Mani, R. *Beyond Retribution: Seeking Justice in the Shadows of War* (Cambridge: Polity, 2002).
Manjoo, R. 'The Continuum of Violence against Women and the Challenges of Effective Redress', (2012) 1(1) Int'l Hum Rts Rev 1–29.
　'Normative Developments on Violence against Women in the United Nations System', in R. Manjoo and J. Jones (eds.), *The Legal Protection of Women from Violence: Normative Gaps in International Law* (London and New York: Routledge 2018), pp. 73–106.
Manjoo, R. and Jones, J. (eds.), *The Legal Protection of Women from Violence: Normative Gaps in International Law* (London and New York: Routledge, 2018).

Marx, K. *Economic and Philosophical Manuscripts* (New York: Dover, 2007).

Matsuda, M. 'Liberal Jurisprudence and Abstracted Visions of Human Nature', (1986) 16(3) NML Rev 613–630.

Meger, S. *Rape, Loot, Pillage: The Political Economy of Sexual Violence in Armed Conflict* (Oxford: Oxford University Press, 2016).

'The Political Economy of Sexual Violence against Men and Boys in Armed Conflict', in M. Zalewski, P. Drumond, et al. (eds), *Sexual Violence against Men in Global Politics* (London and New York: Routledge, 2018), pp. 102–116.

'A Feminist Political Economy of Global Security', in A. Daniels, R. Mageza-Barthel et al. (eds.), *Gewalt, Krieg und Flucht: Feministische Perspektiven auf Sicherheit* (Opladan, Berlin, Toronto: Barbara Budrich, 2021), pp. 43–69.

Mégret, F. '"Beyond Fairness: Understanding the Determinants of International Criminal Procedure', (2009) 14(1) UCLA Journal of International Foreign Affairs 37–76.

'The Legacy of the ICTY As Seen Through Some of Its Actors and Observers', (2011) 3(3) GoJIL 1011–1052.

'What Is the Specific Evil of Aggression?', in C. Kreß and S. Barriga (eds), *The Crime of Aggression: A Commentary* (Cambridge: Cambridge University Press, 2017), pp. 1398–1453.

'The Subjects of International Criminal Law', in P. Kastner (ed.), *International Criminal Law in Context* (London and New York: Routledge, 2017), pp. 28–45.

'International Criminal Justice as a Peace Project', (2018) 29(3) EJIL 835–858.

Mertus, J. 'The Politics of Memory and International Trials for Wartime Rape', in P. Gready (ed.), *Political Transition: Politics and Cultures* (London: Pluto Press, 2003), pp. 227–245.

'Shouting from the Bottom of the Well: The Impact of International Trials for Wartime Rape on Women's Agency', (2004) 6(1) International Feminist Journal of Politics 110–128.

'When Adding Women Matters: Women's Participation in the International Criminal Tribunal for the former Yugoslavia', (2008) 38(4) Seton Hall L Rev 1297–1326.

Mibenge, C. *Sex and International Tribunals: The Erasure of Gender from the War Narrative* (Pennsylvania: University of Pennsylvania Press. 2013).

Mies, M. *Patriarchy and Accumulation on a World Scale: Women in the International Division of Labour* (London: Zed Books, 1999).

'"War Is the Father of All Things" (Heraclitus) "But Nature Is the Mother of Life" (Claudia von Werlhof)', (2006) 17(1) Capitalism, Nature, Socialism 18–31.

Miéville, C. *Between Equal Rights: A Marxist Theory of International Law* (London: Pluto, 2005).

Minow, M. *Breaking the Cycles of Hatred: Memory, Law, and Repair* (Princeton, NJ: Princeton University Press, 2002).

Mischkowski, G. and Mlinarević, G. *And That It Does Not Happen to Anyone Anywhere in the World: The Trouble with Rape Trials* (Cologne: Medica Mondiale, 2009). Available at: https://www.medicamondiale.org/fileadmin/redaktion/5_Service/Mediathek/Dokumente/English/Documentations_studies/medica_mondiale_and_that_it_does_not_happen_to_anyone_anywhere_in_the_world_english_complete_version_dec_2009.pdf

Mladjenović, L., Kesić, V. et al., 'Voices from a War', (1993) 23(5) Off Our Backs 6–9, 12–15.

Mlinarević, G. and Porobić Isaković, N. *Concept and Framework for Development of a Gender Sensitive Reparations Framework for Civilian Victims of War in Bosnia and Herzegovina* (Geneva: Women's International League for Peace and Freedom, 2015). Available at: https://wilpf.org/wp-content/uploads/2018/04/Gender-Sensitive-Reparations-Program.pdf

'If Women Are Left Out of Peace Talks', (2015) 50 Forced Migration Review 34–37.

The Peace That Is Not: Twenty Five Years of Experimenting with Peace in Bosnia – Feminist Critique of Neoliberal Approaches to Peacebuilding (Geneva: Women's International League for Peace and Freedom, 2021). Available at: https://www.wilpf.org/wp-content/uploads/2022/01/WILPF_The-Peace-That-is-Not_final.pdf

Morgan, J. and Graycar, R. *The Hidden Gender of the Law* (Sydney: Federation Press, 2002).

Morris, V. and Sharf, M. *An Insider's Guide to the International Criminal Tribunal for the Former Yugoslavia* (New York: Transnational, 1995).

Moser, C. 'The Gendered Continuum of Violence and Conflict', in C. Moser and F. Clark (eds.), *Victims, Perpetrators or Actors? Gender, Armed Conflict and Political Violence* (New York: Palgrave Macmillan, 2001), pp. 30–51.

Mühlhäuser, R. 'You Have to Anticipate What Eludes Calculation', in K. Campbell, R. Mühlhäuser et al. (eds.), *In Plain Sight: Sexual Violence in Armed Conflict* (New Delhi: Zubaan, 2019), pp. 3–29.

Mujanović, J. 'The Baja Class and the Politics of Participation', in D. Arsenijević (ed.), *Unbribable Bosnia and Herzegovina: The Fight for the Commons* (Baden-Baden: Nomos, 2014), pp. 135–144.

Naffine, N. 'The Body Bag', in N. Naffine and R. Owens (eds.), *Sexing the Subject of Law* (Sydney: Sweet and Maxwell: 1997), pp. 79–93.

'The Legal Structure of Self-Ownership: Or the Self-Possessed Man and the Woman Possessed' (1998) 25(2) JL & Soc'y 193–212.

'Who are Law's Persons? From Cheshire Cats to Responsible Subjects', (2003) 66(3) MLR 346–367.

Law's Meaning of Life: Philosophy, Religion, Darwin and the Legal Person (Oxford: Hart, 2009).

Naffine, N. and Owens, R. 'Sexing Law', in N. Naffine and R. Owens (eds.), *Sexing the Subject of Law* (Sydney: Sweet and Maxwell: 1997), pp. 3–21.

Nash, K. *Contemporary Political Sociology: Globalization, Politics and Power* (Oxford: Wiley-Blackwell: 2010).

Nedelsky, J. 'Communities of Judgment and Human Rights' (2000) 1(2) Theo Inq Law 245–282.

Law's Relations: A Relational Theory of Self, Autonomy, and Law (Oxford: Oxford University Press, 2011).

Negri, A. 'Rereading Pashukanis: Discussion Notes', 2017 5(2) Stasis 8–49.

Neier, A. 'Rethinking Truth, Justice and Guilt after Bosnia and Rwanda', in C. Hesse and R. Post (eds.), *Human Rights in Political Transitions: Gettysburg to Bosnia* (New York: Zone, 1999), pp. 39–52.

Nesiah, V. 'Gender and Forms of Conflict', in F. Ní Aoláin, N. Cahn et al. (eds.), *The Oxford Handbook on Gender and Conflict* (Oxford University Press 2018), pp. 288–301.

Neumann, F. *Behemoth: The Structure and Practice of National Socialism* (London: Victor Gollancz, 1942).

Nijman, J. *The Concept of International Legal Personality: An Inquiry into the History and Theory of International Law* (The Hague: TMC Asser, 2004).

Nikolić-Ristanović, V. 'The Hague Tribunal and Rape in the Former Yugoslavia', in V. Nikolić-Ristanović (ed.), *Women, Violence and War: Wartime Victimization of Refugees in the Balkans* (Budapest: Central European University Press, 2000), pp. 79–83.

'Sexual Violence, International Law and Restorative Justice', in D. Buss and A. Manji (eds.), *International Law: Modern Feminist Approaches* (Oxford: Hart, 2005), pp. 273–293.

Nikolić-Ristanović V. and Stevanović, I. 'The Method and the Sample', in V. Nikolić-Ristanović (ed.), *Women, Violence and War: Wartime Victimization of Refugees in the Balkans* (Budapest: Central European University Press, 2000), pp. 35–39.

Nollkaemper, A. 'Introduction', in H. van de Wilt, A. Nollkaemper et al. (eds.), *System Criminality in International Law* (Cambridge: Cambridge University Press, 2009), pp. 1–25.

Norrie, A. 'Pashukanis and the "Commodity Form" Theory', (1982) 10 Int'l J Soc L 419–437.

Crime, Reason, and History: A Critical Introduction to Criminal Law (2nd edn.) (Cambridge: Cambridge University Press, 2000).

Punishment, Responsibility, and Justice: A Relational Critique (Oxford: Oxford University Press, 2000).

Law and the Beautiful Soul (London: Glasshouse, 2005).

Nouwen, S. 'As You Set out for Ithaka: Practical, Epistemological, Ethical, and Existential Questions about Socio-Legal Empirical Research in Conflict', (2014) 27(1) LJIL 227–260.

O'Keefe, R. *International Criminal Law* (Oxford: Oxford University Press, 2015).

O'Reilly, M. *Gendered Agency in War and Peace: Gender Justice and Women's Activism in Post-Conflict Bosnia-Herzegovina* (London: Palgrave, 2018).

O'Rourke, C. *Women's Rights in Armed Conflict under International Law* (Cambridge: Cambridge University Press, 2020).

Oklopcic, R. 'Redeeming the Triple Struggle? The Yugoslav accounts of Non-Alignment', in L. Eslava, M. Fakhri et al. (eds.), *Bandung, Global History, and International Law* (Cambridge: Cambridge University Press, 2017), pp. 276–292.

Olujic, M. 'Embodiment of Terror: Gendered Violence in Peacetime and Wartime in Croatia and Bosnia–Herzegovina' (1998) 12(1) Medical Anthropology Quarterly 31–50.

Orentlicher, D. *Some Kind of Justice: The ICTY's Impact in Bosnia and Serbia* (New York: Oxford University Press, 2018).

Osiel, M. *Mass Atrocity, Collective Memory, and the Law* (Brunswick: Transaction, 2000).

Making Sense of Mass Atrocity (Cambridge: Cambridge University Press, 2009).

Pashukanis, E. *Law and Marxism: A General Theory* (London: Ink Links, 1978).

Selected Writings on Marxism and Law (London: Academic Press, 1980).

Pateman, C. 'Race, Sex, and Indifference', in C. Pateman and C. Mills (eds.), *Contract and Domination* (Cambridge and Malden: Polity, 2007), pp. 134–164.

Pavlović, O. 'The Participation of Women in Politics – Analysis of the 2000 Local and General Elections in Bosnia and Herzegovina', (2001) 4(3) South-East Europe Review 125–140.

Perović, L. 'The Surviving Victims of Violence as Subjects of Justice: Bottom up History', in S. Zajović and M. Urošević, (eds.), *Women's Court: About Event in Sarajevo and Continue the Process* (Belgrade: Women in Black, 2017), pp. 9–12.

Plaza, M. 'Our Damages and Their Compensation - Rape', (1981) 1(2) Feminist Issues 25–35.

Plesch, D., SáCouto, S. et al. 'The Relevance of the United Nations War Crimes Commission to the Prosecution of Sexual and Gender-Based Crimes Today' (2014) 25 (1–2) Crim L F 349–381.

Raitt, F. and Zeedyk, S. *The Implicit Relation of Psychology and the Law: Women and Syndrome Evidence* (London and New York: Routledge, 2000).

Ratner, S. 'The Schizophrenias of International Criminal Law' (1988) 33(2) Tex Int'l LJ 237–256.

Rawls, J. *A Theory of Justice* (Oxford: Oxford University Press, 1999).

Reid C., Tom, A. et al. 'Finding the "Action" in Feminist Participatory Action Research', (2006) 4(3) Action Research 315–331.

Reilly, N. (ed.) *Testimonies from The Global Tribunal on Violations of Women's Human Rights* (New York: Rutgers University Center for Women's Global Leadership, 1994).

Reinhard, K. 'Lacan and Monotheism: Psychoanalysis and the Traversal of Cultural Fantasy' (1999) 3(2) Jouvert 1–28.

Rimmer, S. 'Sexing the Subject of Transitional Justice', (2010) 32(1) AFLJ 123–147.

Roberts, P. and Zuckerman, A. *Criminal Evidence* (Oxford: Oxford University Press, 2010).

Robinson, W. 'Globalization and the Sociology of Immanuel Wallerstein', (2011) 26(6) International Sociology 723–745.

Röling, B. 'The Significance of the Laws of War', in A. Cassese (ed.), *Current Problems of International Law* (Milan: Dott A. Giuffre, 1975), pp. 133–155.

Rubin, G. *Deviations: A Gayle Rubin Reader* (Durham, NC: Duke University Press, 2011).

Rush, P. 'Jurisdictions of Sexual Assault: Reforming the Texts and Testimony of Rape in Australia', (2011) 19(1) FLS 47–73.

Rush, P. and Young, A. 'A Crime of Consequence and a Failure of Legal Imagination: The Sexual Offences of the Model Criminal Code', 1997 9(1) AFLJ 100–133.

Russell, R. and Van de Ven, N. (eds.), *Crimes against Women: Proceedings of the International Tribunal* (Berkeley: Russell Publications, 1990).

SàCouto, S., Sadat Nadya, L. et al. 'Collective Criminality and Sexual Violence: Fixing a Failed Approach', (2020) 33(1) LJIL 207–241.

Sassen, S. *Territory, Authority, Rights: From Medieval to Global Assemblages* (Princeton, NJ: Princeton University Press, 2008).

Sassoli, M. 'Taking Armed Groups Seriously: Ways to Improve Their Compliance with International Humanitarian Law' (2010) 1(1) IHLS 5–51.

Schabas, W. *The International Criminal Court: A Commentary on the Rome Statute* (Oxford, New York: Oxford University Press, 2010).

Scholte, J. *Globalization: A Critical Introduction* (2nd edn.) (Basingstoke: Palgrave Macmillan, 2005).

Schroeder, J. *The Four Lacanian Discourses* (Abingdon and New York: Birkbeck Law Press, 2008).

Schultz, V. 'Reconceptualizing Sexual Harassment', (1998) 107(6) Yale LJ 1683–1805.

Schwarzenberger, G. 'The Problem of an International Criminal Law', (1950) 3 CLP 263–296.

Sellers, P. Viseur. 'Individual('s) Liability for Collective Sexual Violence', in K. Knop (ed.), *Gender and Human Rights* (Oxford: Oxford University Press, 2004), pp. 153–194.

'Gender Strategy Is Not a Luxury for International Courts' (2009) 17(2) Am UJ Gender Soc Pol'y & L 301–323.

'(Re)Considering Gender Jurisprudence', in F. Ní Aoláin, N. Cahn, et al. (eds.), *The Oxford Handbook of Gender and Conflict* (Oxford: Oxford University Press, 2018), pp. 211–224.

'The Legal and Cultural Value of Sexual Violence', in K. Campbell, R. Mühlhäuser et al. (eds.), *In Plain Sight: Sexual Violence in Armed Conflict* (New Delhi: Zubaan, 2019), pp. 278–306.

Sellers, P. Viseur. and Nwoye, L. 'Conflict-Related Male Sexual Violence and the International Criminal Jurisprudence', in M. Zalewski, P. Drumond, et al. (eds), *Sexual Violence against Men in Global Politics* (New York: Routledge, 2018), pp. 211–235.

Senjak, M. 'The Women's Body as a Battlefield', in S. Zajović and M. Urošević, (eds.), *Women's Court: About Event in Sarajevo and About Continue the Process* (Belgrade: Women in Black, 2017), pp. 140–148.

Shapiro, B. *A Culture of Fact: England 1550–1720* (Ithaca: Cornell University Press, 2003).

Shaw, M. *International Law* (Cambridge: Cambridge University Press, 2003).

What Is Genocide? (Cambridge and Malden: Polity, 2007).

Silverman, K. *Male Subjectivity at the Margins* (London and New York: Routledge, 1992).

The Threshold of the Visible World (London and New York: Routledge, 1996).

Simpson, G. *Law, War, and Crime: War Crimes Trials and the Reinvention of International Law* (Cambridge and Malden: Polity, 2007).

Skjelsbaek, I. 'Sexual Violence and War: Mapping Out a Complex Relationship', (2001) 7(2) European Journal of International Relations 211–237.

Smart, C. *Feminism and the Power of the Law* (London and New York: Routledge, 1989).

Sobel, R. and Shiraev, E. (eds.), *International Public Opinion and the Bosnian Crisis* (Maryland: Lexington Books, 2003).

Spivak Chakravorty, G. *Outside in the Teaching Machine* (New York: Routledge, 2009).

Sriram, C. 'Justice as Peace? Liberal Peacebuilding and Strategies of Transitional Justice' (2007) 21(4) Global Society 579–591.

Stake, R., 'Case Studies', in N. Denzin and Y. Lincoln (eds.), *Strategies of Qualitative Inquiry* (Thousand Oaks, CA: Sage, 2003), pp. 134–164.

Sumner, C. 'Pashukanis and the "Jurisprudence of Terror"', (1981) 11(1) Insurgent Sociologist 99–106.

Suvin, D. *Splendour, Misery, and Possibilities: An X-Ray of Socialist Yugoslavia* (Brill, 2016).

Svedberg, B., Alodaat L., et al. *Women Organising for Change in Bosnia and Syria* (Geneva: Women's International League for Peace and Freedom, 2014).

Available at: https://wilpf.org/wp-content/uploads/2014/07/Women-Organising-for-Change-in-Bosnia-and-Syria.pdf

Swaine, A. *Conflict-Related Violence against Women: Transforming Transition* (Cambridge: Cambridge University Press, 2018).

Tapper, C. *Cross and Tapper on Evidence* (Oxford: Oxford University Press, 2010).

Teitel, R. *Transitional Justice* (Oxford: Oxford University Press, 2000).

Humanity's Law (Oxford: Oxford University Press, 2011).

Thurschwell, A. 'Specters of Nietzsche: Potential Futures for the Concept of the Political in Agamben and Derrida', (2003) 24(3) Cardozo L R 1193–1259.

Tilly, C. *From Mobilization to Revolution* (New York: Random House, 1978).

Coercion, Capital, and European States, AD 990-1992 (Oxford: Blackwell; 1992).

The Politics of Collective Violence (Cambridge: Cambridge University Press, 2003).

Twining, W. *Globalisation and Legal Theory* (London: Butterworths, 2000).

Valji, N. 'Gender Justice and Reconciliation', in K. Ambos, J. Large et al. (eds.), *Building a Future on Peace and Justice* (Berlin: Springer, 2009), pp. 217–236.

Valverde, M. 'The Rescaling of Feminist Analyses of Law and State Power: From (Domestic) Subjectivity to (Transnational) Governance Networks', (2014) 4 UC Irvine L Rev 325–352.

Vasiliev, S. 'The Crises and Critiques of International Criminal Justice', in K. Heller, F. Mégret et al. (eds.), *The Oxford Handbook of International Criminal Law* (Oxford: Oxford University Press, 2020), pp. 626–651.

Vaus de, D. *Research Design in Social Research* (London: Sage, 2001).

Verhaeghe, P. *Does the Woman Exist? From Freud's Hysteric to Lacan's Feminine* (London: Rebus, 1997).

'Lacan's Analytic Goal', in L. Thurston (ed.), *Re-Inventing the Symptom: Essays on the Final Lacan* (New York: Other Press, 2002), pp. 59–82.

Verrall, S. 'The Picture of Sexual Violence in the Former Yugoslavia Conflicts as Reflected in ICTY Judgements', in S. Brammertz and M. Jarvis (eds.), *Prosecuting Conflict-Related Sexual Violence at the ICTY* (Oxford: Oxford University Press, 2016), pp. 299–234.

Villegas Garcia, M. 'On Pierre Bourdieu's Legal Thought', (2004) 56–57 Droit et Société 57–71.

Wallerstein, I. *World-Systems Analysis: An Introduction* (Durham and London: Duke University Press, 2006).

'Robinson's Critical Appraisal Appraised', (2012) 27(4) International Sociology 524–528.

'Structural Transformations of the World Economy', (2016) 39(1) Review 171–194.

Werle, G. *Principles of International Criminal Law* (The Hague: TM Asser Press, 2005).

Whitford, M. *Luce Irigaray: Philosophy in the Feminine* (London: Routledge, 1991).

Williams, P. *The Alchemy of Race and Rights* (Cambridge: Harvard University Press, 1991).
Woodward, S. *Balkan Tragedy: Chaos and Dissolution after the Cold War* (Washington: The Brookings Institution, 1995).
   'Violence-Prone Area or International Transition? Adding the Role of the Outsiders in Balkan Violence', in V. Das, A. Kleinman, et al. (eds.) *Violence and Subjectivity* (Berkeley: University of California Press, 2000), pp. 19–45.
Young Marion, I. *Justice and the Politics of Difference* (Princeton: Princeton University Press, 1990).
   Responsibility for Justice (Oxford: Oxford University Press, 2010).
Yuval-Davis, N. 'Gender and Nation', (1993) 16(4) Ethnic and Racial Studies 621–632.
   Gender and Nation (London: Sage, 1997).
Zajović, S. 'The Women's Court – A Feminist Approach to Justice', in S. Zajović, (ed.), *Women's Court: About the Process* (Belgrade: Women in Black and Centre for Women's Studies, 2015), pp. 6–66.
Zajović, S. (ed.). *Women's Court: About the Process* (Belgrade: Women in Black and Centre for Women's Studies, 2015).
   'Witnesses at the Women's Court: Actors of Justice', in S. Zajović and M. Urošević, (eds.), *Women's Court: About Event in Sarajevo and About Continue the Process* (Belgrade: Women in Black, 2017), pp. 13–76.
Zajović, S. and M. Urošević, (eds.). *Women's Court: About Event in Sarajevo and About Continue the Process* (Belgrade: Women in Black, 2017).
Žarkov, D. 'Feminism and the Disintegration of Yugoslavia', (2003) 24(3) Social Development Issues 59–68.
   The Body of War: Media, Ethnicity, and Gender in the Break-up of Yugoslavia (Durham: Duke University Press, 2007).
   'Ontologies of International Humanitarian and Criminal Law', in D. Žarkov and M. Glasius (eds.), *Narratives of Justice In and Out of the Courtroom: Former Yugoslavia and Beyond* (New York: Springer, 2014), pp. 3–21.
   'Intersectionality – A Critical Intervention', in K. Campbell, R. Mühlhäuser et al. (eds.), *In Plain Sight: Sexual Violence in Armed Conflict* (New Delhi: Zubaan, 2019), pp. 223–229.
Zawati, H. *Fair Labelling and the Dilemma of Prosecuting Gender-Based Crimes at the International Criminal Tribunals* (Oxford: Oxford University Press, 2015).
Žižek, S. *The Sublime Object of Ideology* (London and New York: Verso, 1989).
   The Plague of Fantasies (London: Verso, 1997).
   The Fragile Absolute: or, Why Is the Christian Legacy Worth Fighting For? (London: Verso, 2000).
   'Against Human Rights', (2005) 34 New Left Review 115–131.
Žižek, S. (ed.), *Fredric Jameson, An American Utopia* (London and New York: Verso, 2016).

Cases

International Courts

International Court of Justice

Advisory Opinion, Reservations to the Convention on the Prevention and Punishment of the Crime of Genocide, 28 May 1951

Application of the Convention on the Prevention and Punishment of the Crime of Genocide (Bosnia and Herzegovina v. Serbia and Montenegro), 20 March 1993 (Merits)

Application of the Convention on the Prevention and Punishment of the Crime of Genocide (Bosnia and Herzegovina v. Serbia and Montenegro), 26 February 2007 (Judgment)

Ad Hoc Tribunals

Nuremberg Military Tribunal

France and ors v. Göring (Hermann) and ors, Judgment and Sentence (1946)

International Criminal Tribunal for the Former Yugoslavia

Prosecutor v. Aleksovski, ICTY-95-14/1
Prosecutor v. Banović, ICTY-02-65/1
Prosecutor v. Blagojević & Jokić, ICTY-02-60
Prosecutor v. Blaškić, ICTY-95-14
Prosecutor v. Bralo, ICTY-95-17
Prosecutor v. Brđanin, ICTY-99-36
Prosecutor v. Cešić, ICTY-95-10/1
Prosecutor v. Delalić et al., ICTY-96-21
Prosecutor v. Delić, ICTY-04-83
Prosecutor v. Dorđević, ICTY-05-87/1
Prosecutor v. Furundžija, ICTY-95-17/1
Prosecutor v. Gotovina, ICTY-06-90
Prosecutor v. Hadžihasanović, ICTY-01-47
Prosecutor v. Halilović, ICTY-01-48
Prosecutor v. Haradinaj et al., ICTY-04-84
Prosecutor v. Karadžić, ICTY-95-5/18
Prosecutor v. Kordić & Čerkez, ICTY-95-14/2
Prosecutor v. Krajišnik, ICTY-00-39
Prosecutor v. Krnojelac, ICTY-97-25
Prosecutor v. Krstić, ICTY-98-33

Prosecutor v. Kunarac et al., ICTY-96-23 & 23/1
Prosecutor v. Kupreškić et al., ICTY-95-16
Prosecutor v. Kvočka et al., ICTY-98-30/1
Prosecutor v. Limaj, ICTY-03-66
Prosecutor v. Lukić & Lukić, ICTY-98-32/1
Prosecutor v. Martić, ICTY-95-11
Prosecutor v. Milosević, ICTY-02-54
Prosecutor v. Milutinović et al., ICTY-05-87
Prosecutor v. Mladić, ICTY-09-92
Prosecutor v. Mrkšić et al., ICTY-95-13/1
Prosecutor v. Mucić et al., ICTY-96-21
Prosecutor v. Naletilić, ICTY-98-34
Prosecutor v. Nikolić, D., ICTY-94-2
Prosecutor v. Nikolić, M., ICTY-02-60/1
Prosecutor v. Plavšić, ICTY-00-39 & 40/1
Prosecutor v. Prlić et al., ICTY-04-74
Prosecutor v. Rajić, ICTY-95-12
Prosecutor v. Sainović et al., ICTY-05-87
Prosecutor v. Šešelj, ICTY-03-67
Prosecutor v. Sikirica et al., ICTY-95-8
Prosecutor v. Simić, B., ICTY-95-9
Prosecutor v. Simić, M., ICTY-95-9/2
Prosecutor v. Stakić, ICTY-97-24
Prosecutor v. Stanišić & Simatović, ICTY-03-69
Prosecutor v. Stanišić & Župljanin, ICTY-08-91
Prosecutor v. Tadić, ICTY-94-1
Prosecutor v. Todorović, ICTY-95-9/1
Prosecutor v. Zelenović, ICTY-96-23/2

International Criminal Tribunal for Rwanda

Prosecutor v. Akayesu, ICTR-96-4
Prosecutor v. Gacumbitsi, ICTR-01-64
Prosecutor v. Karemera & Ngirumpatse, ICTR-98-4
Prosecutor v. Muhimana, ICTR-95-1B
Prosecutor v. Ngirabatware, ICTR-99-54
Prosecutor v. Ngirumpatse, ICTR-98-44

Mechanism for International Criminal Tribunals

Prosecutor v. Karadžić, MICT-13-55
Prosecutor v. Mladić, MICT-13-56

Special/Hybrid Tribunals

Extraordinary Chambers in the Courts of Cambodia

Prosecutor v. *Nuon Chea and Khieu Samphan*, ECCC-002/02

Special Court of Sierra Leone

Prosecutor v. *Charles Ghankay Taylor*, SCSL-03-1

Legislation

International Instruments

Treaties, Conventions and Statutes

Charter of the International Military Tribunal, Annexed to the London Agreement for the Prosecution and Punishment of Major War Criminals of the European Axis, and Establishing the Charter of the International Military Tribunal, 8 August 1945, 82 UNTS 27

Control Council Law No. 10, Punishment of Persons Guilty of War Crimes, Crimes Against Peace and Against Humanity, 3 Official Gazette Control Council for Germany 50–55 (1946)

Convention on the Prevention and Punishment of the Crime of Genocide 1949, 78 UNTS 277

Convention on the Elimination of All Forms of Discrimination against Women, 18 December 1979, 1249 UNTS 13

General Recommendation No. 19 on Violence against Women, UN Doc A/47/38 (20–30 January 1992)

General Recommendation No. 35 on Gender-Based Violence against Women, CEDAW/C/GC/35 (14 July 2017)

Geneva Convention I for the Amelioration of the Condition of the Wounded and Sick in Armed Forces in the Field 1949, 75 UNTS 30

Geneva Convention II for the Amelioration of the Conditions of Wounded, Sick and Shipwrecked Members of Armed Forces at Sea 1949, 75 UNTS 84

Geneva Convention III Relative to the Treatment of Prisoners of War 1949, 75 UNTS 134

Geneva Convention IV Relative to the Protection of Civilian Persons in Time of War 1949, 75 UNTS 147

Rome Statute of the International Criminal Court 1998, 2187 UNTS 90

Statute of the International Criminal Tribunal for the former Yugoslavia (ICTY) 1993 (adopted 25 May 1993 by UNSC Res 827, (25 May 1993) UN Doc S/RES/827)

Statute of the International Court of Justice, 26 June 1945, 1 UNTS XVI 35

Secondary Legislation

ICC Elements of Crimes
ICC Rules of Procedure and Evidence
ICTY Rules of Procedure and Evidence

National Legislation

Socialist Federal Republic of Yugoslavia

Constitution of the Socialist Federal Republic of Yugoslavia, 21 February 1974
Criminal Code of the Socialist Federal Republic of Yugoslavia, 1 July 1977

INDEX

Abi-Saab, Justice Georges, 156
accountability, 312
Accused, 119
   Burden of proof, 98
   Rights of, 136, 142, 205
Affect, 140
Agamben, Giorgio, 15, 103, 166, 178, 188
   State of exception, 164–170
Agency, 229–231
Aggression, crime of, 297
Akayesu, Prosecutor v., 44–45
Anderson, Benedict, 172
Armed conflict, 41, 79, 82, 87
Arsenijević, Damir, 285
Asian Women's Human Rights Council (1991), 209
Atlija, Ivo, 128
Auschwitz, 165
Austin, J L, 176
Austro-Hungarian Empire, 185

Baig, Laurel, 49, 75, 89, 309
Bare life, 15, 165–169, 171–172, 178, 197, 239, 251–252
Bassiouni, Cherif, Mahmoud, 83, 93
Bauman, Zygmunt, 184
Biological weapons, 52
Boesten, Jelke, 215
Bosnia, 1–2, 24, 36, 89, 92, 124, 164, 186, 194, 201, 203, 206, 210, 221, 243, 248, 278, 285, 326–327
   EU accession, 246
Bosnian War Crimes Chamber, 24, 222
   Prosecutions, 186, 203

Bourdieu, Pierre, 151
Brammertz, Serge, 306
Brđanin, Prosecutor v., 99, 114–119, 123–128
Brown, Beverley, 108
Burden of proof, 102, 116
Burman, Michelle, 108
Buss, Doris, 14, 39, 91, 94, 125
Butler, Judith, 173, 272

Cahill, Ann, 58
Cain, Maureen, 30
Capitalism, 8, 179, 181, 188–189, 232, 236, 241, 256
   social relations and, 11
Cassese, Antonio, 52, 137
Centre for Women's Studies, Zagreb, 202
Charlesworth, Hilary, 323
Chemical weapons, 52
Chimni, Bupinder, 255
Chinkin, Christine, 13, 142
Cigelj, Jadranka, 192
Čirkić, Rašim, 118
Civilians, 51, 59, 62, 79, 81–82, 119, 250, 313
   Attacks upon, 294–297
   Protection of, 294
CNN, 187
Cockburn, Cynthia, 267
Coercion, 293
Collective criminality, 116, 297
   criminal responsibility and, 70–72
   Problem of, 75–77
   Role of state, 77
Collective responsibility, 68–69, 73–74, 79–80, 93–94, 137, 230–231

Collective violence, 18, 52, 54, 62–63, 72–73, 75–77, 79–80, 88, 117, 120, 122, 127–128, 140, 168, 176, 189, 224, 239, 249, 261–263, 265–267, 274, 278, 282, 292–294, 303
Collectivity
  Affected, 300, 305
  justice and, 257
  knowledge and, 128, 284
  loss and, 249
  sexual violence and, 76, 79
  truth and, 97
Collective experience, 217
Collective perpetration, 277–279
Collective politics, 229, 233–235, 237, 241, 253, 289
Collective testimonies, 282
Inclusion and exclusion, 172
Injury to, 260
Legal protection, 84
Social, 197, 248, 273, 279
Combatants, 82
Communism, 255
Community, 191
  witnessing and, 129, 285
Conflict-related sexual violence, 9, 150, 192
  feminist injustice model and, 271–275
  international criminal law and, 288
  justice and, 131, 274, 329
  social harm and, 292
  system violence and, 293–294
  As an international crime, 288
  As gendered harm, 246, 275, 292
  As individual criminal act, 75
  As system of commodity exchange, 189
  Criminalisation of, 29, 300
  Definition, 62
  Elements of offence, 289–294
  Gendered patterns of, 4
  Intersectional analysis, 93
  Victims of, 92
Confortini, Catia, 268
Convention on sexual violence as an international crime (proposed), 334–337

Convention on the Elimination of All Forms of Discrimination Against Women (CEDAW), 33, 49, 262
  General Recommendation No. 19, 34
Copelon, Rhonda, 13, 55, 61, 89, 162, 190
Cornell, Drucilla, 147, 159, 170
Corroboration, 107–108
Crime
  Accountability for, 243, 308
  Against women, 218
  As gendered injustice, 232, 259, 313
  Categories, 145
  Collective, 143
  Context of, 224
  Gender-based, 227
  Offences against the person, 291
Crimes against humanity, 1, 43, 47, 49–50, 54, 82, 88–89, 114, 293, 296, 298, 300, 336
  And sexual violence, 41, 53
  Persecution, 50, 62, 88
  Protected groups, 83
  Rape, 41, 88
Crimes against peace, 1, 297–300
Criminal intent, 300–301
Criminal law, 229, 245
  And Pashukanis, 13
  And social protection, 310
  Reform of, 252
Criminal liability, 303
Criminal responsibility, 78, 96, 278, 302
  And collective criminality, 70
Criminal trial, 205, 314
Criminalisation, 52, 55
Critical race feminism, 247
Croatia, 2, 36, 77, 92, 210, 220, 250, 278
Customary international law, 53
  And sexual violence, 44–47
  Rape as crime against humanity, 88

Dayton Peace Agreement, 186, 201, 239, 246, 325–329
Declaration on the Elimination of Violence against Women (1994), 34
Delalic, Prosecutor v., 55
Democracy, 183

INDEX

Derrida, Jacques, 144–145, 157
Dialectics, 182
Discourse
  feminist justice and, 232–236
  sexual violence and, 250
  Excluded term, 155
  Feminist, 148, 233
  Lacanian, 149
  Law as, 147–149, 176
Discrimination, 50, 296
Dolgopol, Ustinia, 327
Douzinas, Costas, 175
Drumbl, Mark, 77
Duhaček, Daša, 203, 214, 264

El Taller (NGO), 209
Engle, Karen, 14, 57, 86, 252
Epistemology and, 115, 125, 233, 237, 324
  evidence and, 116, 119
  feminism and, 283, 323
  justice and, 129
  legal trial and, 99
  Epistemic practices, 234
  Feminist standpoint, 217
Ethnic cleansing, 87, 191, 263, 295
  rape and, 36
Ethno-nationalism, 183, 247, 249, 275, 278, 296
European Union, 186, 246, 303
Evidence, 229, 231
  Gender analysis of, 320
Expert witness, 219, 227, 231, 239, 246, 290, 318
  Objective analysis, 206–223, 282

Fair trial principle, 318
Federici, Silvia, 188
Felman, Shoshana, 156, 285
Feminism, 186, 193, 237
  Activism against sexual violence, 1, 36, 92, 153, 190, 192, 194, 205, 209, 211, 218, 222, 240, 253
  accountability and, 308–313
  agency and, 229
  collective witnessing and, 320–323
  conflict-related sexual violence and, 271–275
  criminal responsibility and, 302–304
  discourse and, 148, 233
  epistemology and, 217, 233, 323
  feminist justice mandates and, 304–306
  feminist justice prosecutions and, 313–316
  gender justice and, 215
  global justice and, 238–241
  global social relations and, 188
  governance feminism and, 252
  injustice and, 263
  institutional legal justice and, 242–251
  international criminal law reform and, 253–255, 330–337
  judgement and, 283–285
  justice and, 216, 218, 222, 229, 233, 251, 337
  justice proceedings and, 279–287
  justice reform and, 304–325
  law and, 244
  legal relations and, 279–280
  legal subjectivity and, 280, 296
  peace-building and, 229–230
  politics and, 235, 284
  public witnessing and, 285–286
  relational legal justice and, 286–287, 325–330
  social injury and, 261–263
  symbolisation and, 235
  transformative justice and, 214–216, 231
  Enabling justice, 229–232
  Feminist justice judging, 306–308
  In Yugoslavia, 173, 184, 210, 216, 240
  International justice, 10–12, 238
  Justice for war crimes, 204
  On war and sexual violence, 190
  Trial norms, 316–325
Feminist epistemology, 233, 237, 283–285, 323–325
  Feminist standpoint, 217
Feminist justice proceedings, 279–287
Foča, 87, 152–153, 161
Formal legal justice, 203–206
Foucault, Michel, 181, 252, 266

Fraser, Nancy, 257
Freud, Sigmund, 134
Fricker, Miranda, 123
Furundžija, Prosecutor v., 29, 33, 45, 53–54, 69, 75, 99, 101–102, 109–112, 115, 125, 318

Gacumbitsi, Prosecutor v., 46
Galtung, Johan, 269
Gender, 188, 272, 308
  justice and, 231, 282
  Roles, 186
Gender analysis of crimes, 331
Gender justice, 197, 233, 286, 309
  Access to justice, 305
  Dayton and, 327
  Women's Court and, 215
  In transitional justice mechanisms, 207
  Practices, 307
  Relational review, 329
Gender-based crimes, 4, 89, 227, 330
Gender-based harms, 18, 217, 231, 260
  CRSV and, 271
Geneva Convention, 41, 43, 97
  sexual violence and, 42
Genocide, 1, 37–38, 50–51, 54, 82, 88, 90, 114, 224, 227, 278, 293, 296, 300, 336
  sexual violence and, 41, 91
  Gender-based crime, 90
  Intent, 89, 90
  Protected groups, 83
  Rape, 89
  Responsibility for, 297
  Sexual violence as, 53
Genocide Convention, 42, 83–84, 88
Germany, Nazi, 185
Global legal form, 239, 242, 258, 283, 288, 291, 337
  international criminal law and, 167, 251–260
  masculine subject and, 275
Global Tribunal on Violations of Women's Human Rights (1993), 209

Globalisation, 5, 12, 54, 56, 61, 122, 175–198, 240, 250, 287, 325
  Definition of, 12
Gopalan, P and Kravetz, D, 111, 127
Graeber, David, 270
Gramsci, Antonio, 173
Grewal, Kiran, 14, 86–87, 294, 318

Hagan, John, 23
Halley, Janet, 252
Haraway, Donna, 235
Harding, Sandra, 284
Hardt, M and Negri, A, 180, 182
Harm, 150, 222, 225, 233, 235, 243, 260, 282
  Aggregate social, 277
  gender and, 217, 225, 259–260, 321
  genocide and, 89
  international criminal law, 249
  As crime, 48, 261, 301
  Category of, 218
  Causation of, 301
  Compensation for, 243
  Ethnic-based, 91
  Gender-based, 64, 163, 250, 289, 295, 313
  Gendered, 227
  Identification of, 285
  Legal recognition of, 138, 254
  Means to address, 316
  Models of, 49
  Of war, 248
  Remedies, 328
  Sexual, 49, 57
  Social, 30
  To others, 221
  Women's experience of, 227
Hegemony, 13–16, 61, 112, 170, 173, 189, 233, 237, 273–275, 277–279
Helms, Elissa, 194
Hirst, Paul, 255
Hodžić, Refik, 311
Howe, Adrian, 30, 259, 262
Human rights, 32, 49, 81–83, 85, 88, 195, 227
Humanitarian law, 1, 40, 54, 82, 93
  sexual violence and, 38
  Rights of victims, 81

Humanity, 73, 84, 146, 156, 160, 174, 177, 233, 252
  As category of global social system, 168, 179, 286
  Crimes against, 54, 227
  Universal values, 54, 63, 74
Humphreys, Stephen, 166–167
Husanović, Jasmina, 15, 17, 182, 187, 194, 216, 240, 285

ICRC, 333
ICTR, 44–45, 50, 80, 195
ICTY, 2, 12, 29, 80, 83, 123, 186, 193, 222, 238, 240, 252, 308–309, 311, 315, 317
  92bis statements, 128
  Adversarial trial structure, 324
  collective criminality and, 71
  crime of aggression and, 297
  criminalization of conduct and, 52
  Dayton and, 325
  feminism and, 196
  gender justice and, 196
  global connections and, 187
  justice and, 137, 142, 157
  national law and, 53
  peace-building and, 138
  prosecution of female perpetrators and, 78
  prosecution of sexual violence and, 60, 62, 78, 80, 111, 119, 127, 149, 194–197
  reform of international criminal law and, 254
  responsibility for rape and, 71
  system criminality and, 78
  women and, 193
  Case study of, 6, 19–20, 22–24
  Closure, 3
  Completion Strategy, 113
  Defence, 104–106, 108, 111, 114, 118–119
  Definition of rape, 45
  Establishment of, 2–3, 31, 38, 56, 65, 69, 97, 132, 201, 204, 206
  Evidence, 118, 126
  Genocide, 90
  Institutional culture of, 194–197

Joint criminal enterprise, 70, 76
  Jurisdiction of, 40
  Leadership cases, 99, 113–114
  Legal form of, 22
  Models of evidence, 107
  Office of the Prosecutor, 196
  Procedural rules, 97, 100–101, 107, 112–113, 115, 132, 135, 142, 283, 318
  Prosecution, 102, 114, 116
  Protection of civilians, 83
  Rape, 154
  Rape as crime against humanity, 88
  Remedies, 143
  Sexual violence prosecutions, 195–197
  Staff of, 23
  Statute, 2, 97
  Testimony, 110
  Trial Chamber, 98, 106, 109, 115, 120, 124, 128, 142
  Victim and Witness Section, 100
  Witnesses, 99, 116, 123, 126
ICTY Completion Strategy, 314
ICTY Statute, 41, 88, 132
Identification, 234–235
Imaginary, 233
Injustice, 112, 144, 156–158, 162–163, 168, 208, 210, 217, 231, 236, 264
  gender and, 261, 274
  injustice and, 300
  As concrete harm, 260–263
  Experience of, 233
  Structural, 264
Institutional legal justice, 242–251
International Court of Justice, 38, 83, 297
International crime, 29–31, 294–302
  legal relations and, 84
  Category of, 52
  International elements of, 119
International Criminal Court, 42, 196, 293, 301, 304, 307, 320
  Elements of Crimes, 44, 334
  Victims' procedural rights, 81
International criminal justice, 130–132, 137
  As procedure, 135–137
  As punishment, 132–135

As recognition, 137–138
As reconciliation, 138–141
Existing models, 233
Institutions, 2
International criminal law, 2, 6, 51, 70, 96, 164, 168, 176, 181, 216, 227, 238–239, 242, 266
  crimes in Yugoslavian conflict and, 2
  criminal responsibility and, 74, 277
  ethnicised violence and, 161
  feminism and, 39, 86, 242
  feminist accountability and, 308–313
  feminist justice judging and, 306–308
  feminist justice mandates and, 304–306
  feminist justice prosecutions and, 313–316
  feminist reform and, 253–255, 304–325
  feminist social theory and, 13–19
  gender justice and, 197, 254, 312
  gender-based harms and, 260
  global legal form and, 175–198
  global social relations and, 179
  harm and, 150
  humanity and, 169
  ICTY and, 39
  identity critiques and, 276
  illegality and, 42
  individual rights and, 84–85
  institutional legal justice and, 242–251, 316
  international crime and, 302
  international crime categories and, 298
  international criminal norms and, 85
  justice and, 130–131, 141, 144, 157, 163, 325
  legal subject and, 94
  phantasy of justice and, 158–160
  proportionality and, 295
  protected interest and, 50
  sexual violence and, 42, 61–62, 64, 91, 143, 194, 249, 292, 302, 330–337
  social relations and, 176
  structural injustice and, 271
  subjects and, 146, 168, 174, 250
  system violence and, 271, 297, 302
  the imaginary and, 161

  the international criminal trial and, 96
  transitional justice and, 141
  trauma and, 162
  violence and, 51
  war crimes and, 250, 271
  Women's Court and, 227
  As a global legal form, 249
  As body of rules, 40
  As discourse, 146–147, 149–155, 163, 170
  As global legal form, 84, 232, 286–287
  As global social contract, 133
  As hybrid legal system, 324
  As law of exception, 167
  As legal system, 6
  As phantasy, 163
  As social bond, 177
  As socio-symbolic order, 15, 145–163
  Biosocial, 166
  Category of legal person, 65–67
  Concept of sexual violence, 76
  Convention on sexual violence as an international crime, 334–337
  Criminalisation of sexual violence, 37–39
  Definition of sexual violence, 57
  Emergence of, 178
  Ethno-fraternal contract, 192
  Feminist analysis, 61
  Feminist approach, 201, 259, 287, 328
  Feminist legal framework, 289–330
  Gender-neutrality, 57
  Global legal form, 174, 251–259
  Globalisation of, 40
  Humanitarian principles, 295
  In national courts, 249
  Individual guilt vs collective responsibility, 75
  Joint criminal enterprise, 71
  Legal categories, 147
  Legal category of international crime, 29–31
  Legal form, 40, 66–67, 145–146, 156, 166
  Legal relationships, 67

International criminal law (cont.)
  Legal social bond, 168
  Legal subject, 65, 67
  Liberal legal form, 270
  Limits of, 94, 144, 169, 251–259
  Perpetrators as legal subjects, 73
  Procedural reform, 317
  Prohibition of CRSV, 293
  Protected categories of persons, 82
  Protected group, 79, 93
  Protection of victims, 84
  Rape as crime against humanity, 88
  Recognition of victims, 138, 252, 313, 328
  Recognition of victims of sexual violence, 94
  Rights of sexual violence victims, 81
  Sexual violence and customary international law, 44–47
  Socio-symbolic order, 147
  Space of, 167
  Traumatic structure, 155, 169
  Victims, 81
International criminal trial, 7, 96–129
  subjects and, 146
  Evidence, 114
  Legal form, 122
  Phallogocentric, 112
  Prosecution, 80
  Witness support, 320
International law, 30
  global legal form and, 6, 258
  international justice and, 5
International legal subject
  Category of, 65–67
  Perpetrator as, 67–72
  Victim as, 80–85
International Women's Tribunal on Crimes Against Women (1976), 208
Irigaray, Luce, 171, 189, 237
Iveković, Rada, 9–10, 203, 205, 215–216, 232, 236, 249, 256, 270, 282

Jarvis, Michelle, 13, 49, 60, 62, 75–76, 89, 126, 306
Joint criminal enterprise, 70, 76, 298, 301
Judgement, 231
  And community of, 121
  And feminism, 283–285, 306–308
Judicial process, 98, 119, 136
Jurisprudence, 308
Justice, 1, 136, 158, 169, 178, 194, 201, 203, 214, 222, 229
  community and, 223
  conflict-related sexual violence and, 271–275, 289
  feminism and, 198, 204, 206, 213, 229, 232, 234, 237–241
  feminist justice prosecutions and, 313–316
  hermeneutics and, 123
  post-conflict reconstruction and, 246
  punishment and, 135, 310
  social change and, 215, 258
  victim-witnesses and, 212, 319
  Women's Court and, 214
  As social phenomena, 5
  As collective social good, 231
  As global justice, 251
  As human activity, 4
  As phantasy, 145–146, 158–163, 170
  As procedure, 135–137
  As punishment, 132–135
  As recognition, 137–138
  As reconciliation, 131, 138–141
  As social good, 216, 286
  At international level, 7
  Feminist approach, 6, 214, 247, 280
  Feminist justice proceedings, 279–287, 306
  Feminist legal relational, 325–330
  Feminist legal subject of, 280
  Feminist transformative, 214–216
  Formal legal justice, 203–206
  ICTY models, 132, 144, 157
  Limitations of, 206
  Models of, 4
  New forms, 249
  People's justice, 208–212
  Transitional, 207
  Victim-witnesses, 153

Witnesses demands for, 205
Women's Court and new models of, 212
Justice of humans, 4, 337

Karadžić, Prosecutor v., 89–91, 133, 139, 152, 164, 192, 278, 298, 319
Kašić, Biljana, 202
Kelsen, Hans, 51
Kesić, Vesna, 160
Kirk McDonald, Gabrielle, 193
Knox, Robert, 255
Korean 'comfort women', demands for justice, 35
Kosovo, 2, 185, 210, 220–221
Kotor Varoš, 115
Krstić, Prosecutor v., 91, 319
Kumar, Corinne, 202
Kunarac, Prosecutor v., 45–46, 56, 58, 86–87, 112, 149, 152–155, 161, 193, 235, 294
Kvočka, Prosecutor v., 59, 142

Labour, 190
 Sexual division of, 179
Lacan, Jacques, 74, 147, 153, 155, 158, 162, 178
Lacey, Nicola, 37, 48, 74
Law, 52, 56
 feminism and, 242, 244
 justice and, 145
 punishment and, 314
 subjectivity and, 147
 violence and, 51
 violence against women and, 253
 International justice form, 6
Leadership cases, 22, 75–76, 99, 113–114, 117, 195, 301
Legal categories, 7
Legal form, 80, 149, 163, 169, 176–177, 201, 214
 bare life and, 169
 globalisation and, 175–198
 signification and, 148
 symbolic operation and, 14
 As symbolic order, 147
 International criminal law, 145
 International criminal trial, 96
 Limits of, 163

Legal form theory, 8
Legal institution, 315
Legal responsibility, 231
Legal system
 Post-Westphalian, 74, 135, 239
 Western, 72, 82, 170, 172, 178
Lenin, Vladimir, 255
Levi, Ron, 23
Liability model of responsibility, 302
Longino, Helen, 324

Macedonia, 2
MacKinnon, Catherine, 13, 86
Malešević, Sinisa, 191
Manjoo, Rashida, 269
Marion Young, Iris, 247, 264, 269, 274
Marx, Karl, 189
Marxism, 255, 257, 299, 309
Masculinity, ideas of, 58, 109, 111–112, 126–127, 170, 173, 191–192, 272, 277
Medica Mondiale, 317
Medica Zenica, 224
Meger, Sara, 173, 189
Mégret, Frédéric, 174, 297, 300
Mens rea, 89, 301
Mertus, Julie, 13, 193
Methodology
 Feminist legal form, 21–26
 Socio-legal, 20–21
Mibenge, Chiseche, 14, 91
Mies, Maria, 10–11, 188, 194
Miéville, China, 7, 9, 51, 180–181, 254
Milošević, Slobodan, 204
Milutinović, Prosecutor v., 46
Mischkowski, Gabriela, 223, 285
Mladić, Prosecutor v., 89–91, 152, 278, 298, 319
Mlinarević, Gorana, 295–297
Model Legislative Provisions (CRSV), 317
Modernity, 165
Mucić, Prosecutor v., 74
Muhimana, Prosecutor v., 45
Mühlhäuser, Regina, 78
Mumba, Florence, 35, 193

Naffine, Ngaire, 49, 66
Naming, act of, 230

Nash, Kate, 179
Nation-state, 66, 77, 98, 165, 171, 193, 216, 230, 233, 236, 239, 245, 248, 252, 277, 299, 303
  globalisation and, 184
Nedelsky, Jennifer, 121, 253
Negri, Antonio, 197, 258
Neier, Aryeh, 143
Neoliberalism, 240
Neumann, Franz, 79
NGOs, 35, 187, 194, 203, 281, 319
Ní Aoláin, Fionnuala, 13, 254
Nijman, Janne, 84
Nikolić, Prosecutor v., 137
Nomination, 235
Norrie, Alan, 72, 175
Nullum crimen, nulla poena sine lege (No crime without law), 52
Nuremberg Charter, 298
Nuremberg Trials, 79, 228, 245, 265, 299
Nuremberg Tribunal, 68, 70

O'Reilly, Maria, 194, 202, 220, 222, 280
O'Rourke, Catherine, 254
Odio Benito, Elizabeth, 35, 193
Office of the High Representative (Bosnia), 246
Office of the Prosecution (ICTY), 197
Omarska, 149, 164–165, 191, 193
Oosterveld, Valerie, 13
Orientalism, 124
OSCE BiH, 24, 317
Osiel, Mark, 77
Other, the, 171, 191
Ottoman Empire, 185

Papić, Žarana, 202
Pashukanis, Evgeny, 11, 13, 16, 30, 66, 73, 81, 98, 175, 178
  global legal form and, 180–182
  law reform and, 254–256
  the legal subject and, 66
  Legal form theory, 7–9, 14
Pateman, Carole, 171

Patriarchy, 125, 190, 225, 229, 233, 236, 247, 249, 254, 257, 268, 274, 278, 281, 296
Peace, 230
  Crimes against, 227
Peace-building, 1, 212, 223, 244, 279
  justice and, 286, 329, 332
  women and, 329
  Difficulties of, 249
People's courts, 208
People's justice, 208–212
Perović, Latinka, 213, 226, 229, 238
Perpetrator
  Accountability, 243
  As legal subject, 67–74
  Punishment of, 140, 244
Perpetrators, 4, 67, 101, 113, 263, 265, 314
  harm and, 301
  legal responsibility and, 277–279
  As subjects, 74
  Collective responsibility, 71
  Gender analysis of, 323
  Identification of, 322
Phantasy, 158, 161, 169, 233
Plavšić, Biljana, 78
Plavšić, Prosecutor v., 78
Plaza, Monique, 274
Porobić Isaković, Nela, 295–297
Power, 257
Prevent Sexual Violence Initiative (UK), 196, 333
Prijedor, 164
Prisoners of war, 82
Proof, 29
Proportionality, 295
Prosecution of sexual violence, 315
PTSD, 102, 106, 108
Punishment, 29, 133
Punitur quia peccatur (the individual must be punished because he broke the law), 133

Rape, 116, 125, 127–128, 142, 154, 192, 321
  collective violence and, 88
  consent and, 300
  ethnic cleansing and, 36

gender and, 58
genocide and, 43, 88–94
stigmatisation and, 291
system violence and, 293–294
As a war crime, 35, 160, 245
As an international crime, 160, 204
As crime against humanity, 43, 62, 72, 166
As crime against women, 59, 225
As 'crime of circumstance', 290
As gender-based violence, 4, 58, 274
As violence, 264
Debates on genocidal rape, 92
Definition of, 31, 291–292
Elements of offence, 46, 48–49, 85–88, 289–294
Elements of offence - Consent, 85–88, 107
Elements of offence - Criminal intent, 300–302
Elements of offence - Corroboration, 108
Ethnicised construction, 92, 161
Furundžija, Prosecutor v., 69
ICTY definition, 45
In national law, 56, 87, 100, 112, 204, 245, 249
In war, 36, 61, 221, 225, 263
In war in former Yugoslavia, 4, 86, 92
Myths of, 318
Need for law reform, 252
Sexual penetration, 44
Ratner, Stephen, 62
REKOM (Regional truth commission for former Yugoslavia), 207, 211
Relation
  Juridical, 66, 182
  Legal, 66
  Social, 183
Relational legal justice, 286–287
Relations
  Gender, 186
  Legal, 30
Reparations, 143, 205–207, 222, 225, 244, 248–250, 259, 309, 316, 320, 327–328

Republika Srpska, 78
Responsibility, 29
  Collective, 283
  Command, 114
  Criminal, 115
  Of perpetrators, 228, 285
Retribution, 133
Rome Statute, 44, 298
Rubin, Gayle, 268
Rule of law, 98, 135–136, 165, 207, 246
Rush, Peter, 290

Sarajevo, 1, 3, 89, 201–202, 213, 218
  As site of Women's Court, 212
Sassen, Saskia, 183
Sassoli, Marco, 65
Schroeder, Jeanne, 152
Schwarzenberger, George, 40
Sellers Viseur, Patricia, 13, 22, 50, 89, 190, 192, 307
Senjak, Marijana, 206–224, 229, 244, 248, 285
Serbia, 77, 248, 278
Sex, biological, 59
Sexual assault, ICTY elements of offence, 46
Sexual autonomy, 87, 93
Sexual difference, 262, 272, 290
Sexual liberation, 253
Sexual penetration, 44
Sexual violence, 94, 110, 197, 263, 321
  Against men, 4, 36, 60, 80, 111, 127, 273, 306
  Against women, 80, 273
  accountability and, 249, 309
  armed conflict and, 62
  collective legal subject and, 88
  conflict and, 76, 128, 160, 189–190, 220, 224, 313
  consent and, 86, 294
  cultural value and, 192
  ethnic cleansing and, 114, 144
  justice and, 131
  law reform and, 254, 317
  policy and, 225
  stigmatisation and, 86
  As collective victimisation, 92

Sexual violence (cont.)
  As collective violence, 79, 225
  As crime against women, 267
  As crime under international law, 3, 42, 53–54, 94, 154, 249, 259, 293, 330–337
  As criminal violence, 61–62
  As gender-based crime, 59, 67, 91, 170
  As gender-based harm, 59, 85, 94, 162–163, 267, 320
  As gender-based violence, 274
  As harm to persons, 32–34, 93
  As international crime, 32, 40–64, 80
  As legal harm, 60
  As opportunistic crime, 76
  As persecution, 89
  As torture, 60
  Case study of, 20–21
  Category of acts, 289
  Coercive act, 62
  Conflict related, 191
  Conflict related, meaning of, 63
  Consent, 81, 85, 87
  Criminalisation, 63
  Definition of crime, 331
  Elements of offence, 22
  Evidencing, 99, 118, 125–128
  Feminist analysis, 55
  Feminist approach, 80, 330
  Gender-neutral, 46, 57–59
  Gendered, 126–127
  In former Yugoslavia, 37, 272
  International element, 42
  Policy framework, 333
  Problem of criminalisation, 55–57
  Prohibited acts, 43–44
  Prosecution of, 193, 336
  Rights of victims, 81
  Survivors of, 224, 247
  Systematic, 76
  Testimony of survivors, 221
Sexuality, 188, 190
Sexuation, 274, 290
Shaw, Martin, 278
Signifier, 150, 234
  legal discourse and, 150–153
  Law as, 151

Silverman, Kaja, 109
Simpson, Gerry, 75
Sinthome, 153
Sivac, Nusreta, 192
Skjelsbæk, Inger, 272
Slovenia, 2
Smart, Carol, 99
Social bond, 121, 148, 233, 246, 279, 287, 325
  feminism and, 288
  Fraternal, 170–179, 234, 237
  New, 249
Social contract, 171–172
  Ethnicised, 172
  Fraternal, 171, 191
Social injury, 30, 259, 261–263, 279, 292
Social order, 145
  Sexuated, 171
Social relations, 149, 166, 230–232, 237, 241, 247, 263–264, 283, 286, 337
  feminism and, 235, 251
  international criminal law and, 147
  justice and, 251
  violence and, 123, 216
  Capitalist, 184
  Feminist, 235
  On world-scale, 164, 179–180
Social subjectivity, 262
Social theory, 6
  feminism and, 10
  international law and, 13–19
Socialism, 216, 245, 256
Society, 304
Socio-symbolic order, 155, 169, 234, 309
  Limits, 169
  New, 235, 237
  Of international criminal law, 146–163
Sovereign, 80
Sovereignty, 175, 252
  Of states, 251
Srebrenica, 89–90
Stakić, Prosecutor v., 71, 76, 125
State
  Monopoly on violence, 245
  Responsibility, 37, 68, 143
State of exception, 164–170
Stereotypes, 174

Subject, 224, 233, 235, 262
  discourse and, 148
  feminist legal relations and, 279–280
  global legal relations and, 182
  identity and, 236, 273
  international law and, 66, 138, 146, 167
  justice and, 241
  legal form and, 66
  legal knowledge and, 283
  sexual violence and, 291
  social accountability and, 223
  symbolisation and, 234
  As feminist legal subject, 192, 275–280, 304
  As knowing subject, 281
  As legal person, 13, 65–69, 74–75, 80–95, 98, 145, 152, 165, 173
  As legal subject, 66, 152, 164, 172, 174, 218, 259
  As masculine legal subject, 171, 294
  As political subject, 230
  Collective legal subject, 83
  Construction of, 5, 67
  Female, 173
  International legal subject, 94, 146
  Masculine vs feminine, 110
  New, 233
  Of justice, 227, 229, 276, 279–280, 306, 316
  Perpetrator as legal subject, 67–74
  Position of, 236
  Right to bodily autonomy, 82
  Rights of, 49, 66
  Sexual identity, 60
  Sexuality, 60
  Universal subject, 170
  Victim as legal subject, 80–85
  Women as speaking, 236, 320
  Women as subjects of justice, 229–232
Subjects
  As epistemological, 237
Symbolic, 148, 233, 263
Symbolic violence, 269
System criminality, 77, 228
System violence, 263–271, 277, 286, 293
  gender analysis and, 322

Tadić, Prosecutor v., 71, 87, 112, 136, 149–152, 154, 156
Teitel, Ruti, 51
Testimony, 117, 229, 231, 270
  About violence, 264, 307
  collective responsibility and, 223
  community and, 121, 123
  epistemology and, 120
  procedure and, 281
  proof and, 107
  responsibility and, 222, 243
  sexual violence and, 115
  superstes and, 103, 116, 221
  testis and, 103–104, 116, 123
  As evidence, 106–107, 118–122, 219, 228, 239, 281
  As representation, 105, 116
  Before Women's Court, 212, 217, 262
  Challenges to, 106, 117–118
  Collective witnessing, 282–283, 316
  Falsification, 118
  Feminist modes, 280–281
  Gendered, 112
  Models of, 102
  Of victim-witness, 99, 101, 103–104, 110–111, 116, 118, 142, 164, 169, 210, 217–218, 220, 226–227, 229, 248, 280–281, 316, 319
  Oral, 113
  Procedural elements, 104–106, 218
  Realist model, 102
  Reliability, 109
Thurschwell, Adam, 165
Tilly, Charles, 265
Torture, 67
Transitional justice, 141, 206, 208, 215
  In Bosnia, 326
Trauma, 110, 140, 155, 160–161, 225, 233, 239, 248, 286
  Effects of, 105
  Of war-time experience, 221
Truth Commission
  Bosnia, 206

UN Charter, 38, 185
UN Commission of Experts, 38

UN Declaration on the Protection of Women and Children in Emergency and Armed Conflict, 33
UN Development Programme (Bosnia), 207
UN Security Council, 2, 37, 139
United Nations, 35, 225, 303, 311, 317
Universal justice, 141–142, 170
Universal values, 53
Universally Condemned Offences, 134, 136

Victim(s) 263, 278, 305
  coercive context of sexual violence and, 293
  Individual vs collective, 93
  As legal subject, 82, 84
  Duties, 81
  Participation in justice process, 332
  Protection, 138, 303
  Recognition of harm, 137–138, 214
  Rights, 81
  Rights at international law, 67
Victimisation, 276–277
Victim-witness, 236
  Rights of, 225, 310
Victim-witnesses, 126, 168
  And justice, 252
  As international legal subjects, 168
  Demands for justice, 243
  Evidence of, 290
  Feminist approach to testimony, 280–281
  Stigmatisation of, 205
  Testimony before ICTY, 100–101
  Testimony before Women's Court, 213, 263, 282
Vigneswaran, Kate, 62, 76, 127
Violence, 73, 125, 140–141, 143, 146, 156, 181, 192, 224, 231, 236, 253, 261, 263, 272, 283, 296
  Against international society, 63
  Against persons, 63
  Against women, 188, 239, 260
  gender and, 79, 267, 322
  As international crime, 54
  As system violence, 263–271
  Gender analysis of collective, 322
  Gender analysis of system, 322
  Illegal, 51
  Individual vs collective, 52, 64, 227, 298
  Political, 79
  Prohibited forms, 50
  Sexual, 57
  Sexualised, 188, 290
Vujadinovic, Dragica, 213

Wallerstein, Immanuel, 10–11, 179–180
War, 62, 141, 187, 216, 261, 264, 307
  And collective violence, 249
  As criminal act, 297
  As system violence, 265
  Effects of, 122, 224, 248, 268, 328
  Illegal conduct of, 38, 78, 250
  In former Yugoslavia, 4, 34, 38, 181, 183–188, 190, 201, 204, 212, 221, 224, 227, 239–240, 242, 249–250, 256, 263
  Rules of conduct, 294
  Sexual economy of, 191
  Women's experience of, 210
War crime(s), 1, 41, 43, 49, 50, 54, 82–83, 105, 114, 224, 227, 245, 250, 293, 298, 300
  Sexual violence as, 53
  Against women, 240
  And responsibility, 226
  And sexualised violence, 272
  In Bosnia, 89
  Srebrenica, 89
Wilding, Polly, 215
Williams, Patricia, 247
Witness A, 105–106, 108, 110
Witness BT-71, 117–118
Witness EK, 242
Witness KDZ080, 164
Witness MS, 249
Witnesses, 212, 280
  Assessment of, 106
  Before Women's Court, 202, 220, 226
  Credibility, 118
  Importance of testimony, 101, 212

Need for protection, 205, 248
Particular circumstances, 211
Protection of, 100
Rights of, 142
Statements, 116
Support for, 214, 244, 281, 319
Witnessing, 229
  context and, 238
  feminism and, 285–286, 317–323
  As collective act, 121, 127, 217, 222, 225–226, 231, 243, 282–283, 285, 312
  Effects of, 230
  Relational structure, 222
Women, 276
  injustice and, 233
  lived experience and, 217, 295, 321
  sexual violence and, 59
  As subjects of justice, 227, 229–232, 250, 313
  Bodies of, 58, 104, 189, 191, 227
  In post-war Yugoslavia, 249
  Journalists, 36
  Muslim, 91–92, 173, 262, 273
  Subordination of, 268, 305
  Supporting sexual violence survivors, 222
  Survivors of war, 229, 249
Women in Black, 202, 213
Women Organising for Change in Bosnia and Syria conference, 1
Women to Women (NGO), 202
Women's Court, 2, 12, 217, 226, 232, 234, 237, 242–243, 248, 259, 264, 267, 269, 271, 276, 280, 295, 309, 315, 317
  Alternative justice mechanism, 201
  crimes against peace and, 297–300
  feminism and, 11
  feminist justice judging and, 307
  gender-based crime and, 328
  institutional legal justice and, 242–245
  justice and, 325
  law and, 251, 255
  new justice paradigms and, 230

  transitional justice and, 256
  As non-state justice, 10
  Basic principles, 209
  Case study of, 6, 20, 24–26
  Establishment of, 2–4, 201–202, 204, 209–212, 240, 244
  Expert witnesses, 3, 213
  Feminist approach to justice, 241
  Hearings (2015), 213
  Inquisitorial proceedings, 324
  Judges, 283–285
  Judicial Council, 3, 25, 213, 219, 226, 282
  New forms of justice, 17–19
  Objectives of, 214
  On protection of civilians, 296
  Policy recommendations, 229, 246
  Preliminary Decision, 25, 213, 226–229, 250, 263, 265, 268, 277, 297
  Rationale, 2
  Reasons for, 211
  Role of expert witnesses, 213
  Rules, 213
  Rules of Procedure, 219–221, 224, 226–227, 244
  Victim-witnesses, 3
  Witness evidence, 318
  Women's Court - About Event in Sarajevo, 203
  Women's Court - About the Process, 204–207, 209, 213–214
Women's International League of Peace and Freedom, 1
Women's Tribunal, Tokyo, 35
World Conference on Women's Rights (1993), 35
World Court of Violence Against War (2001), 209
World War Two, 35, 40, 185, 204, 245, 299
World-system analysis, 5, 179

Young, Alison, 290
Yugoslavia, 141, 149, 184, 188, 221, 244

Yugoslavia (cont.)
  feminism and, 9, 32, 34–36, 92, 173,
    185–186, 192, 194, 202, 204,
    209–210, 240, 337
  women and, 230, 327, 337
  Existing legal order, 186, 208, 216,
    243, 245, 256
  Nazi occupation, 245, 299
  Need for accountability for war
    crimes, 205, 315, 327
  Peace-building, 311
  Post-war, 242, 245, 271, 325
  Post-war issues, 1, 92, 123, 139, 221,
    249, 313
  Post-war settlement, 239
  Responsibility for crimes of war, 228
  War in, 2

Yugoslavian conflicts (1990s), 123, 132,
    161, 183, 189
  sexual violence and, 39, 59, 111
  Gendered patterns of conflict, 78
  Media reporting, 35
  Sexual violence, 37
Yuval-Davis, Nira,
    172, 273

Zaharijević, Adriana, 213
Zajović, Staša, 202, 204, 207, 212–213,
    226, 235, 244
Žarkov, Dubravka, 14, 124, 178, 191,
    263
Zawati, Hilmi, 63
Žizek, Slavoj, 159, 169
Zvizdić, Memnuna, 202

For EU product safety concerns, contact us at Calle de José Abascal, 56–1°, 28003 Madrid, Spain or eugpsr@cambridge.org.

www.ingramcontent.com/pod-product-compliance
Ingram Content Group UK Ltd.
Pitfield, Milton Keynes, MK11 3LW, UK
UKHW020406060825
461487UK00009B/829